Lecture Notes in Computer Science 3154

Commenced Publication in 1973
Founding and Former Series Editors:
Gerhard Goos, Juris Hartmanis, and Jan van Leeuwen

T0211139

Robert L. Nord (Ed.)

Software
Product Lines

Third International Conference, SPLC 2004
Boston, MA, USA, August 30 - September 2, 2004
Proceedings

 Springer

Volume Editor

Robert L. Nord
Carnegie Mellon University, Software Engineering Institute
4500 Fifth Avenue, Pittsburgh, PA 15213 USA
E-mail: rn@sei.cmu.edu

Library of Congress Control Number: 2004110539

CR Subject Classification (1998): D.2, K.4.3, K.6

ISSN 0302-9743
ISBN 3-540-22918-3 Springer Berlin Heidelberg New York

Springer is a part of Springer Science+Business Media

springeronline.com

© Springer-Verlag Berlin Heidelberg 2004
Printed in Germany

Typesetting: Camera-ready by author, data conversion by PTP-Berlin, Protago-TeX-Production GmbH
Printed on acid-free paper   SPIN: 11315377   06/3142   5 4 3 2 1 0

Welcome to the Third Software Product Line Conference – SPLC 2004

Software product lines have emerged as an important new paradigm for software development. Product line engineering enables the coordinated production of whole families of related systems using the same underlying base of development assets. Organizations large and small and in all domains and sectors are achieving remarkable time-to-market gains and cost reductions as a result. In 1997, we at the Software Engineering Institute (SEI) launched a Product Line Practice Initiative to help develop, mature, and transition the important knowledge and expertise to help more organizations enjoy the benefits of product lines. Our vision is that product line development is a low-risk, high-return proposition for the entire software engineering community.

It was always one of our goals to help build a community of practitioners and researchers interested in learning about and applying the ideas behind software product lines. The Software Product Line conferences have been the realization of that goal. They have marked a growing and widespread interest in software product lines. More and more companies are launching product line efforts. Books on the topic are easy to find, and product lines and product families now appear in the topic list of many conferences besides the SPLC series. Due in no small part to this community of interest, the field is rapidly maturing, moving away from ad hoc approaches and towards repeatable strategies and recognized best practices.

SPLC 2004 marks the most successful conference to date. In addition to the high-quality papers found in this volume, we had the richest set of tutorials, workshops, panels, and tool demonstrations ever. We were gratified by the submissions from all parts of the globe, from industrial, academic, and government organizations. From these submissions, we assembled a wide-ranging program. For the first time, we were able to create specially themed tracks of interest in business and economic issues, quality assurance, and product line architectures. The very existence of these subareas of interest and the fact that we received enough material about each to fill the tracks are additional indicators that the field is maturing.

I would like to take this opportunity to thank the authors of all submitted papers and the members of the program committee who donated their time and energy to the review process that resulted in the high-quality papers you are about to read. I offer my special appreciation to David Weiss and Rob van Ommering, the program cochairs, who created such a superb program. I thank Robert Nord, the tireless editor of these proceedings, Pennie Walters, who assisted in the editing process, and Pat Place, who helped with word-processing matters. We hope you find the results of SPLC 2004 beneficial and enjoyable, and we look forward to seeing you at the next Software Product Line conference.

August 2004   Paul C. Clements

Program Chairs' Welcome

Welcome to the Third International Software Product Line conference — SPLC 2004. This year's program reflects the diversity and intensity of work in software product lines. It represents a healthy balance among research in universities, research in industrial laboratories, and industrial applications. The program is organized into three themes: business, architecture, and quality assurance. It covers topics ranging from how to start a software product line in a company that has not previously created one, to case studies of mature product lines and the technology used to create and maintain them, to test strategies for product lines, to strategies and notations for creating product line architectures, to the importance of binding times in creating product lines.

Our workshops and tutorials this year embody the same themes as the technical program and the same diversity among presenters and participants. They provide opportunities for learning and sharing by practitioners and researchers.

We also continue the tradition of concluding the conference with the Product Line Hall of Fame. Attendees are invited to come to this lively and fun session, propose an architecture for the Hall of Fame, and be prepared to defend their choices and cast their votes for architectures that deserve to be famous.

As with most conferences, the focus and quality of SPLC 2004 depends strongly on the work of the program committee members, who have the opportunity to help the field progress in needed directions and to showcase recent progress. They are the thought leaders who determine which ideas the attendees hear about in the technical presentations. We thank our program committee for the excellent job they have done in setting the direction for SPLC 2004 and the work that they have done to make this conference a success.

August 2004   David Weiss and Rob van Ommering

Organizing Committee

Conference Chair	Paul Clements (Software Engineering Institute, USA)
Program Co-chair	David Weiss (Avaya, USA) Rob van Ommering (Philips, The Netherlands)
Tutorial Chair	John D. McGregor (Clemson University, USA)
Workshop Chair	Klaus Schmid (Fraunhofer IESE, Germany)
Panel Chair	Charles Krueger (BigLever Software, USA)
Demonstration Chair	Dale Churchett (Salion, Inc., USA)
Proceedings Editor	Robert L. Nord (Software Engineering Institute, USA)

Program Committee

Table of Contents

Technical Papers

Keynote Abstract

Panel Overviews

Tutorial Overviews

Workshop Overviews

Governing Software Product Lines and Reorganizations*

Truman M. Jolley, David J. Kasik, and Tammy R. Ben

Boeing Commercial Airplanes
P.O. Box 3707
Seattle, WA 98124-3707 USA
truman.m.jolley@boeing.com
david.j.kasik@boeing.com
tammy.r.ben@boeing.com

Abstract. It's a fact of life that organizations love to reorganize. Reorganizations have a profound effect on the way product lines are governed. We introduce the concept of the Responsibility, Authority, and Accountability (RAA) network. An RAA network assists in the governance process of product lines for internal information systems, even in the face of massive reorganization. Armour ("Reorg Cycle" [1]) describes the pressures of reorganization to balance the "dimensions of organization" (e.g., geography, customers, product technology); we apply polarity management to balance the dimensions. Armour describes the difficulty of applying hierarchical organization charts—"single dimension management structures"—to the above "multidimensional environments"; we apply lean RAA networks to span organization charts and provide the multidimensional view needed for product lines. Armour observes that network organization approaches "do not have a good track record"; our experience is that lean, resilient RAA networks document the product line's governance architecture. These governance architecture patterns are applied repeatedly to the strata of products in the product line. We present the governance architect's RAA to define, monitor, and sustain governance health using these tools: polarity maps, polarity networks, RAA maps, and RAA networks.

1 Introduction

We describe an approach to reorganization pressures raised by Phillip Armour [1]. Our previous papers [2, 3] described the construction of extensible governance bodies for information system (IS) product lines internal to a company. In this paper, we address the pressures on "the organizational entity responsible for the architecture and other core assets of the product line" [2] as the company organization structures change.

Governance is the exercise of authority in an organization. Effective lines of authority and management are required to clearly define the roles and responsibilities needed to govern shared products, shared processes, and the shared architecture within an individual product line. Similar problems occur when a collection of

---

R.L. Nord (Ed.): SPLC 2004, LNCS 3154, pp. 1–17, 2004.
© Springer-Verlag Berlin Heidelberg 2004

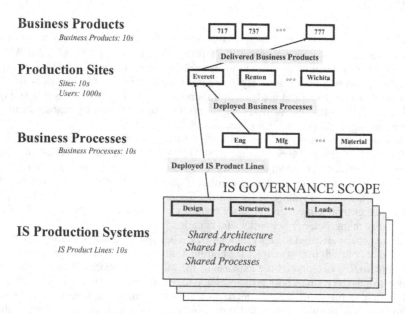

Fig. 1. Scope of paper is IS Governance. IS product lines, internal to the business, support business processes at production sites to build products like airplanes

product lines must be jointly delivered and sustained. Figure 1 limits the scope of this paper to the governance of a collection of IS product lines and its relationship to the internal customers.

As IS Production Systems span more products, product lines, and sites, support team members increasingly do not report directly and administratively to the responsible product line managers. The system straddles several administrative, software development, asset management, and funding cultures. It is critical to the effective governance of the product line to be clear about who are the formal, authorized decision makers for architecture, components, and processes shared across the product line. The clarity of responsibility, authority, and accountability (RAA) is critical in light of constantly changing organization structures.

We found polarity management [5] techniques useful for identifying and responding to the stresses of product line organizations requiring infrastructure governance. We prepare RAA networks to hold the organization polarities of the "dimensions." RAAs provide the authoritative governance clarity to address key organizational management key practice areas of the SEI *Framework for Software Product Line Practice* (Structuring the Organization, Customer Interface Management) [6]. Tuning the RAA networks provides flexibility to address reorganization pressures as polarities to be held.

2 Polarities

A polarity is defined as "two principles that are both true but conflict." For example, a polarity of meeting comportment is RUTHLESS WITH TIME ↔ GRACIOUS WITH PEOPLE. In other words, meeting-time stewardship can conflict with teaming efforts. Polarities provide a model to analyze organizational infrastructure in a way that is comparable to the structural analysis of an airplane. The analogy between structural analysis and infrastructure analysis highlights the value of polarity management in identifying significant organization structure risks.

Polarities are often mistaken as problems to be solved. However, polarities are *held*, not *solved*. Thus, "←→" is read as BOTH/AND, rather than EITHER/OR. The "←→"emphasizes that attempts to "solve a polarity" are fruitless and force us to honor the truth of the principles in conflict. Collins and Porras [7] summarize this phenomenon as the "Tyranny of Or and the Genius of And" as we work to hold polarities, rather than solve them. Polarity management needs techniques to *hold polarity*: polarity maps, polarity networks, and canaries.

Polarity maps are used to analyze polarities. The top of the map describes the positive benefits of each true principle; the bottom describes the negative consequences of overemphasizing one pole at the expense of the other. The polarity map presentation acknowledges the truth of both principles and the expectation that they will conflict.

The first step toward polarity management is to identify canaries for each pole. Borrowing from the historical practice of using canaries in coal mines to detect lethal levels of poisonous gases, a pole canary is the party most sensitive to overemphasis on the opposing pole. The canary helps hold a polarity to harvest the benefits of the principles without the negative consequence of overemphasizing one of the poles. For example, in 1787, James Madison was a canary for federal rights, and Thomas Jefferson was a canary for states rights [2]. Federal and state governments continue working to hold this part ←→ whole polarity today.

The polarity map in Figure 2 identifies the pole canaries holding the extended customer ←→ supplier [6, 3] polarity around the product line. For example, the product line project manager brokers the integration of committed schedules from all the project managers of the product line components. Similar canaries can be identified for each component of the product line.

The polarity network in Figure 3 depicts relationships between key polarities. The tri-pole in Figure 2 is viewed as a supplier by the system owner in Figure 3, who actually funds development of the product line, and the steering committee, who funds deployment.

The tension between customer and supplier is often palpable and tends to increase as reorganizations occur on either the customer or the supplier side.

Polarity Map System Mgt ⬅➡ Project Mgt Architecture Mgt		
CANARY: **System Mgr (SM)**	**Architecture Mgr (AM)**	**Project Mgr (PM)**
+: • broker system requirements and deployment with view of capability and affordability •Negotiate content, schedule and resources with AM & PM	• broker system design with view of performance and sustainability •Negotiate content, schedule and resources with SM & PM	• broker reliable, predictable construction of system with view of tractability •Negotiate content, schedule and resources with AM & SM **+:**
–: • scope creep	• ivory tower (architecture disconnected from real products) • bleeding edge technology	• "product out" • overly conservative commitments • inflexible overplanning **–:**

Fig. 2. Key tri-pole polarity map for software product line

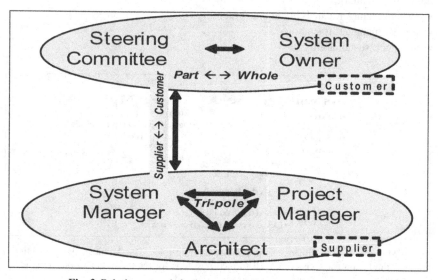

Fig. 3. Polarity network for key product line governance polarities

3 Armour Dimensions as Polarities

Armour describes important management dimensions of an organization as lines in a multidimensional coordinate system. The dimensions are customers, features, products, product technology, resources, skills, development technology, development tools, development processes, development dependencies, support, and geography. As a business changes, the pressure applied to each dimension changes. When the pressure becomes sufficiently onerous, people tend to reorganize to rebalance the pressure.

For example, Armour describes a supplier balancing the concerns of large and small customers. The designers of the U.S. Constitution held a similar polarity, small-state ←→ big-state, using the bicameral legislature and electoral college. Our decision-making integrated product teams (IPTs) must be designed to hold polarity between small and large customer concerns.

This paper introduces a key concept, the RAA network. The RAA network is useful in governing a product line in the face of organizational change. We apply polarity management to balance the Armour dimensional pressures for the three primary stakeholders in a product line: system manager, project manager, and architect. Each stakeholder 'feels' dimensional pressure as shown in Figure 4. The system sensitivities of these canaries are

- system manager: capability and affordability
- project manager: tractability
- architect: sustainability

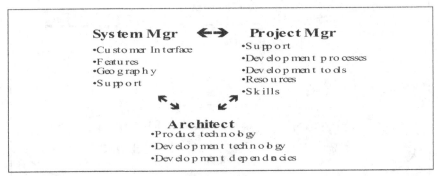

Fig. 4. Map the Armour dimensions to polarity-holding roles. The Architect IPT in Section 8 provides the forum for registering well-formed positions for the three dimensions assigned to the architect

An RAA network clearly defines the responsibility, accountability, and authority needed to govern a product line in a way that can be readily maintained and modified as organizational structures change.

4 Responsibility, Accountability, and Authority (RAA)

Organization governance identifies the authorized decision makers of that organization (e.g., the U.S. President, Congress, and Supreme Court for the federal government; governors, legislatures and supreme courts for states).

The RAA is helpful to describe the governance role of a team or person. The left part of Figure 5 defines responsibility (R), accountability (A), and authority (A). The example to the right bounds the architect's authority as definition, not implementation, and assigns a strong compliance monitoring role to balance the bound.

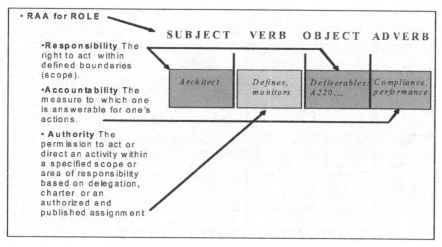

Fig. 5. RAA definition and sentence analogy

In addition, Figure 5 depicts a lean RAA, using a sentence analogy to anticipate the need to compare and integrate RAAs from several teams. Lean RAAs clarify team interfaces and spotlight gaps in governance coverage.

Translating existing RAAs to a neutral, lean RAA format is straightforward. Circle the key nouns, verbs, and measures in the RAA.

R: Responsibility defines "scope":
1. To produce the nouns, ask the question "responsible for what?" The objects of the preposition "for" are the nouns.
2. List the nouns under *Responsibility*.

A: Accountability defines what is "counted," both the object (thing) and the adverb (measure or standard). What is counted determines how much authority can be delegated.
1. To produce the adverbs, ask the question "accountable for what?" Adverbs yield measures describing the effectiveness or efficiency with which the object is delivered.
2. Governance effectiveness is assessed by the measures identified in *Accountability* (e.g., architecture compliance).

A: Authority defines the permission to decide within a scope (responsibility). Authority is derived from accountability and lists the scope and authority source, as shown in Figure 5.

1. To produce the verb phrase for Authority (e.g., approve architecture), the object of the verb is often a noun in *Responsibility*.

This abridged RAA becomes a single page that can be referenced or reviewed during team meetings. Similarly, the concise RAAs may be placed side by side in tables called RAA maps. RAA maps facilitate assessments of clarity, gaps, and overlaps. The RAA map in Figure 6 provides RAAs for the roles identified in Figure 3. The RAA map also presents the essential rationale for identifying the right number of team members.

	System Owner	Steering Committee	System Manager	Project Manager	Architect Manager
SCOPE	IS Product Line				
RESPONSIBILITY: The duty to supply a product or a service					
	❑ IS Product Line	❑ Funding ❑ Strategy ❑ Deployment	❑ Strategy ❑ Requirements ❑ Deployment	❑ Integrated content, resources, schedule	❑ Technical arch. ❑ Information arch. ❑ Data architecture
AUTHORITY: The power to act or the power to direct an activity based on budget control or direct reporting relationships, or the power given through an authorized and published assignment					
Authority Source:	Executive Sponsor	System Owner	System Owner	System Owner	System Owner
Escalate to:	Executive Sponsor	System Owner	System Owner	System Owner	System Owner
	❑ Approve funding ❑ Appoint System Manager ❑ Own IS Product Line ❑ Chair Steering Committee	❑ Approve funding ❑ Approve strategy ❑ Approve deployment	❑ Broker requirements and prioritize change requests ❑ Broker deployment ❑ Provide strategy ❑ Negotiate SoW and budget with Project Mgr and Arch. Mgr	❑ Construct product line ❑ Maintain product line ❑ Negotiate SoW and budget with System Mgr and Architecture Mgr	❑ Define technical, information and data architecture ❑ Monitor production system compliance with architecture ❑ Negotiate SoW and budget with Project Mgr and System Mgr
ACCOUNTABILITY: The responsibility to answer for a measured success of a product or a service					
	❑ IS Product Line fitness for use	❑ Compliance with business strategy, IS strategy, architecture ❑ Benefits	❑ System fitness for use ❑ Deployment penetration ❑ On-time SoW and budget definition	❑ System fitness for use ❑ On-time SoW and budget definition	❑ Architecture compliance ❑ Performance of production systems ❑ Reliability of production systems

Fig. 6. RAA map for product line RAA network

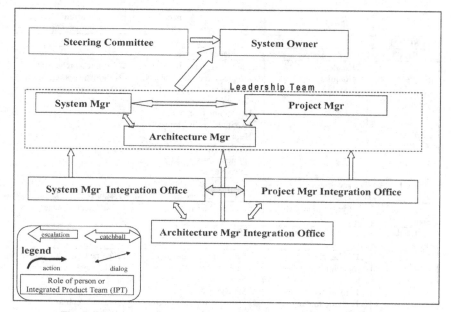

Fig. 7. RAA network depicts relationships between cross-functional roles

5 RAA Networks as Supplemental Organization Charts

The governance relationships of individuals and cross-functional IPTs can be usefully depicted as an RAA network (see Figure 7). This one-page diagram depicts relationships (escalation, catchball, dialog, actions) between individual and team roles. The catchball in Figure 7 denotes the negotiations among tri-pole stakeholders consistent with the RAAs in Figure 6.

The RAA network in Figure 7 addresses the polarities in Figure 3 and uses the RAA map in Figure 6. The supporting offices at the bottom of Figure 7 manage the processes used to prepare the deliverables identified as the responsibility of their counterpart role in the RAA map in Figure 8. When negotiations among supporting offices fail, the issue is escalated to the leadership team of which the tri-pole stakeholders are primary members.

While most people involved understand RAA maps quickly, the initial RAA networks of our current organization were difficult to interpret. Careful analysis has allowed us to define RAA network attributes that can be tuned to improve the quality and communication impact of the networks. The criteria we use to assess these attributes include

1. **All** decision makers have RAAs. RAAs may be accessed as reference links in the RAA network presentation. We routinely display RAA networks at the beginning of a meeting. Using the linked presentations, we observed several positive results:
   - less frequent IPT meetings

	System Manager Integration Office	Project Manager Integration Office	Architecture Manager Integration Office
SCOPE:	IS Product Line		
RESPONSIBILITY: The duty to supply a product or a service			
	❑ Strategy ❑ Requirements ❑ Deployment	❑ Integrated schedule, content , resources for projects, production systems, and common services ❑ Risk mitigation plan ❑ Architecture assessment ❑ Process assessment ❑ Project rules, tools, schools ❑ Project management center of excellence	❑ Technical architecture ❑ Information architecture ❑ Data architecture
AUTHORITY: The power to act or the power to direct an activity based on budget control or direct reporting relationships, or the power given through an authorized and published assignment			
Authority Source:	System Manager	Project Manager	Architect Manager
Escalate to:	System Manager	Project Manager	Architect Manager
	❑ Broker requirements and prioritize change requests ❑ Broker deployment ❑ Provide strategy ❑ Negotiate SoW and budget with Proj Mgr Office and Arch Office	❑ Plan and track integrated schedule, content, and resources ❑ Manage risk ❑ Plan and track architecture and process assessments ❑ Close projects ❑ Negotiate SoW and budget with Sys Mgr Office and Arch Office	❑ Define technical, information, and data architecture ❑ Monitor production system compliance with architecture ❑ Broker resolution of escalated architecture issues from production system archs, tech arch office, portfolio/app arch office, info/data arch office and common services arch office
ACCOUNTABILITY: The responsibility to answer for a measured success of a product or a service			
	❑ Deployment penetration ❑ On-time SoW and budget definition	❑ Performance to plan ❑ Project management process compliance ❑ On-time SoW and budget definition	❑ Architecture compliance ❑ Performance of production systems ❑ Reliability of production systems

Fig. 8. RAA map for additional offices in Figure 7. The offices insure that the counterpart role meets the commitments for deliverables of Responsibility

- improved virtual and face-to-face meeting participation
- improved membership transitions (a benefit essential in the face of reorganizations)

2. Individual decision-maker RAAs at lower strata/levels have clear decision escalation paths:
   - Each decision maker has a consistent scope.
   - Comparable RAA structures at multiple levels honor the lean RAA paradigm.
   - holding major product line organization polarities (e.g., appropriate decision voices for multiple sites, multiple business units, and multiple business processes)

The RAA map highlights scope inconsistencies and RAA overlaps. The polarity analysis of the RAA network emphasizes the logic of IPT membership and the expected representation roles of the IPT's members.

3. Decision-maker RAAs cover both products and processes. IPTs that use the processes own the processes. Those processes are implicitly nouns under Responsibility in the IPT RAA.

RAAs factor out much of the decision-making logic from processes, and the process deliverable handoffs between roles are highlighted as nouns under Responsibility in the supplier role RAA.

Thus, the RAA network is a supplemental, cross-functional organization chart that complements a standard hierarchical organization chart. The RAA network allows independent assessment of

• changes in the hierarchical organization
• special projects
• new components
• new products
• technology

The RAA network graphic is designed to show and manage the polarities among multiple stakeholders.

• decision making across multiple companies

6   Governance Architecture and RAA Network Patterns

Armour observes that "management is hierarchical; the world is a network." He remarks that "network management, while laudable ... in attempting to address the real issue," does not have a good track record. Supporting our growing track record, we introduce the governance architect role using polarity and RAA analysis to define and sustain a lean governance network structure. RAA networks can be leveled and balanced into multiple, cross-linked networks. These links are not constrained by hierarchical organizations, allowing more accurate depiction of team relationships. We suggest this interpretation of "governance architecture":

• Architecture partitions a system into parts, defines relationships, and then monitors the performance of the system and the relationships (define and monitor).
• Governance is the "exercise of authority in an organization."
• Governance architecture partitions a decision-making authority into parts, defines relationships, and monitors the performance of the decision-making authority and the relationships between the decision-making parts.
• The RAA for a governance architect is presented in Figure 9. The role levels and balances RAAs across three sources: (1) functional organization charts, (2) cross-functional teams and roles, and (3) cross-functional processes.

We are familiar with levels of political governance: city, county, state, and federal. Hierarchic, functional organization charts often follow this model because a single role can be played at multiple levels in the organization. Similarly, a cross-functional production effort may be stratified by component assemblies of the product. Team roles can apply to one or more levels (e.g., Project Management Integration Offices at multiple strata of product component aggregation).

Governance challenges occur both within and between the strata. The use of a consistent RAA network as a "context for a solution" across a product line allows a building block approach to governance and provides consistency across relationships. Proven RAA network patterns address the key governance tensions (e.g., customer←→supplier polarity) in the cross-functional organization. This significantly reduces the governance information that must be communicated and maintained. In addition, robust, proven patterns add reliability and confidence in the governance system.

	Governance Architect	
SCOPE:	Information System Product Line	
RESPONSIBILITY: The duty to supply a product or a service		
	❑ RAA (Responsibility, Authority, Accountability) integration across: ❑ RAAs for roles of functional organization charts ❑ RAAs for cross-functional teams and roles ❑ RAAs for roles of cross-functional process charts (swimlanes) ❑ Governance strata	
AUTHORITY: The power to act or the power to direct an activity based on budget control or direct reporting relationships, or the power given through an authorized and published assignment.		
Authority Source:	System Owner	
Escalate to:	System Owner	
	❑ Define governance strata and patterns (RAA networks) ❑ Define integrated RAAs for functional organization roles, cross-functional roles and processes (RAA networks and RAA maps) ❑ Monitor RAA health	
ACCOUNTABILITY: The responsibility to answer for a measured success of a product or a service		
	❑ Resilience of RAA networks and governance strata (withstand "Reorg Cycle"?) ❑ Hold governance polarities ❑ Communication via RAA network patterns, RAA maps, and lean RAAs	

Fig. 9. RAA for a governance architect

In summary, the lean RAA of each team role is a single page, and the RAA network of each governance stratum is a single page. This lean governance description approach factors out redundant information in team/role RAAs and demonstrates integration and completeness of decision coverage across teams/roles:

• Team/role RAAs can be reused at each stratum, changing only the scope of Authority and deliverables in Responsibility (e.g., component data architect vs. product line data architect). RAAs differ by the scope and granularity of deliverables.

• Proven RAA networks can be reused at each stratum, changing cross-functional teams to address key tensions in the production team (e.g., decision participants for component data architecture changes).

7 Information System Strata

To be useful, all the strategies discussed above must be applied to something to be effective. How one organizes IS product lines becomes most important in managing the customer ←→ supplier tension introduced in Figure 3.

From a customer perspective, the contents of IS product lines are essential to the conduct of all its business processes. Companies invest in understanding and improving their business processes to improve the manner in which they design, manufacture, and maintain their revenue-generating products. IS product lines are essential tools in process improvement.

Customers care about a consistent set of IS product line products—a set that can be easily understood, governed, and funded. Simultaneously, from a supplier's viewpoint, governance becomes more predictable when the set of IS products is stable, even when IS itself is reorganizing to react to a changing business climate. When governance teams, their RAA maps, and the RAA network are stable, significant amounts of time and effort are saved when hierarchic organizations change.

The challenge is determining what the organizing principle for IS product lines should be. There are a number of different alternatives:

- hardware platform. Each member of the product line contains IS products that run on a specific hardware base (e.g., Hewlett-Packard, IBM, Intel).
- operating system. Each member of the product line runs on a specific operating system (e.g., Windows, Linux, IBM MVS, Solaris).
- programming language. Cluster all IS products that use Java, Microsoft Development tools, C/C++, and so forth.
- support tools. Cluster all IS products that are based on Oracle, DB2, OpenGL, and so forth.
- customer products. Cluster all IS products used to build a specific airplane (e.g., 777, 747, 767, 737).
- customer business process. Cluster all IS products that affect primary business product sales, marketing, design, manufacture, maintenance, and so forth.
- customer information. Cluster all IS products around the data they generate to allow the business to operate. This view is different from the business process perspective because a substantial amount of business information is directly reusable across processes.

None of the organizing principles above are incorrect. However, we are striving to make the organization of IS product lines as invariant as possible to preserve decision-making governance bodies and maintain balanced membership. Our analysis has determined that the key attributes that vary at the slowest rate are

- customer-facing: Dramatically different user communities perform beta test.
- information focus: Fundamentally different information is authored and viewed.

We eliminated computer-centric organizing principles (hardware, operating system, language, tools) because they aren't critical to the business itself. Computer technology also changes rapidly, enough so that changing an internal system to a different computing environment may result in a significant cost savings.

Business processes also change reasonably quickly and must be directly supported by the *information* that IS product line components produce.

Production System	Dominant Information
as-designed information	1. Manufacturing BoM
as-engineered information	1. Engineering BoM 2. Geometry 3. Computerized test results 4. Manufacturing plans 5. Test of geometry
as-built information	1. Build 2. Quality assurance 3. As-built BoM
as-flying information	1. Maintenance information 2. As-is flying BoM
information access	1. External access control 2. Information protection 3. Supplier Management
business system information	1. Finance 2. People 3. Buildings 4. Contracts 5. customer relationship management (CRM)

Fig. 10. Identify six IS production systems based on information-focus and customer-facing attributes

The results of this analysis led to Figure 10, which identifies the dominant information and user community for the six Boeing Commercial Airplanes IS production systems.

From a governance perspective, using this organization results in

1. clear **alignment of production systems with business processes**. Figure 1 depicts production sites using IS production systems in Boeing Commercial Airplanes. The business process stakeholders are identified for each production system, and the system manager for each production system brokers requirements and deployment across the appropriate stakeholders.

2. **small numbers of categories within production systems** that address business information differences, but manage costs in computing infrastructure across airplane production sites in Figure 1. In Figure 10, six is a **minimum number of production systems** based on their dramatically different information.

3. a **stable, clear membership rationale** for cross-functional roles and teams making decisions about production systems. As a system grows to include more products, product lines, platforms, and sites, the team members increasingly do not report directly and administratively to the responsible product line managers. In addition, the system straddles several administrative, software development, asset management, and funding cultures. Therefore, it is critical to effective **governance** to be clear about who has a formal vote and who has a say, but not a vote, in directions for architecture, components, and processes shared across the constituent products. Stable production system definitions allow identification of **stable decision par-**

ticipants for schedule, content, and resources of the production systems. For example, cross-functional project management can provide a well-formed, integrated plan and schedule with the participation of a project manager from each production system, as well as project managers of components shared by multiple production systems.

4. a **stable, clear Bill of Materials** for production systems that is relatively invariant over time for cross-functional delivery teams

8 Example

We have established a conceptual framework for maintaining product line integrity and progress as organization change occurs. Boeing Commercial Airplanes Information Systems (BCA-IS) embarked on a large project to transform itself in 2003. The general goal of the IS Transformation project is to improve cost control. IS Transformation determined that the number of BCA applications in production use could be reduced by 75%. Importantly, IS Transformation addressed the root cause that allowed the proliferation of applications. As a result, cost control and technical architecture governance processes are being deployed to ensure that the total number of applications aligns with long-term business requirements.

We applied our conceptual framework to define the team structure needed for long-term governance. The team structure is designed to provide stability through numerous reorganizations. Describing all the activities affecting IS Transformation is beyond the scope of this paper.

In this section, we work through a specific example taken directly from our IS Transformation experience. We step through the polarity and RAA analysis to address the architect's dimensions shown in Figure 3. We show how we used the analysis and conceptual scaffolding to design the RAA and membership rationale for the Architecture Management Integration Office (AMIO).

Once we established the IS Transformation product line stratification for the production systems of Figure 10, we defined the polarities affecting AMIO decision making. The results of the analysis are shown in Figure 11.

The polarity analysis led us to develop the RAA network in Figure 12. Using this structure allows individual projects to insert their results into the production systems in the product line in a way that is consistent with current architecture definitions.

Figure 12 is the key picture for IS Transformation architecture governance. It clearly identifies that the architecture team must include

- lead architects from each production system (part) defined in Section 7
- lead architect(s) for the product line (whole)
- lead architects from four (whole) views: technical, application, information, and Core Infrastructure Products that are shared across the production systems. The lead architect for the Core Infrastructure Products is best considered as one of the canaries for the whole, not a component part. The Core Infrastructure Products—core assets of the product line—are delivery environment, development environment, test environment, and middleware environment. Essentially, they have been factored out to be developed and maintained by a separate Boeing business unit.

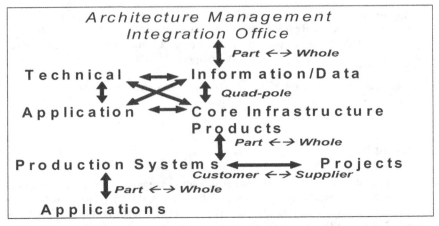

Fig. 11. Polarity network for the AMIO supporting the Architecture Integration Office

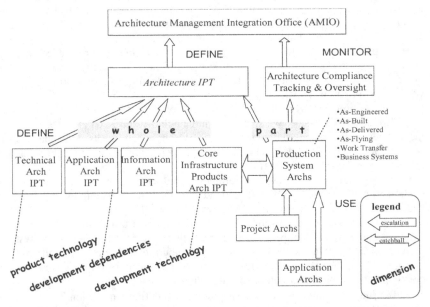

Fig. 12. AMIO IPTs broker the definition and monitoring of architecture deliverables. Armour's dimension tensions are addressed as well-formed positions and presented to the designated forums.

Each member has a well-defined constituency, maybe a supporting IPT, and is expected to bring a well-formed position to the decision-making IPT. A healthy forum exists where canaries can raise and jointly resolve issues (e.g., development dependency issues are assigned to the Application Architecture IPT, which may be quiescent, but healthy). Reorganizations within architecture are forestalled because polarity tensions are held, not "solved." Similar forums exist for the key polarity or dimension issues of the software product line.

The RAA map for the RAA network of Figure 12 is shown in Figure 13. The RAA for the AMIO identifies the oversight role to

- keep the Architecture IPT healthy
- perform periodic architecture assessments
- sustain an integrated set of architecture deliverables of stature
- monitor architect certifications for people in architecture roles
- negotiate joint commitments with the Project Management Integration Office and the System Management Integration Office

Contrast the Authority verbs: define, approve, and concur. The verbs are crafted to avoid overlap and provide careful delegation. The Responsibility nouns assign key deliverables to subordinate IPTs.

	Architect Manager	Architecture Mgt Integration Office	Architecture IPT
SCOPE:	ISPL	ISPL	ISPL
RESPONSIBILITY: The duty to supply a product or a service			
	❏ Tech & sys arch ❏ Info arch ❏ Data arch ❏ Core Infrastructure Products arch	❏ Tech & sys arch ❏ Info arch ❏ Data arch ❏ Core Infrastructure Products arch	❏ Tech & sys arch ❏ Info arch ❏ Data arch ❏ Core Infrastructure Products arch
AUTHORITY: The power to act or the power to direct an activity based on budget control or direct reporting relationships, or the power given through an authorized and published assignment			
Authority Source:	System Owner	Architect Manager	AMIO
Escalate to:	System Owner Boeing Arch	Architect Manager	AMIO
	❏ Concur tech, info and data arch ❏ Monitor prod system compliance with arch ❏ Broker resolution of escalated arch issues from AMIO ❏ Negotiate SoW, schedule, and budget with Proj Mgr and Sys Mgr	❏ Approve tech, info and data arch ❏ Monitor prod system compliance with arch ❏ Broker resolution of escalated arch issues from Arch IPT ❏ Negotiate SoW, schedule, and budget with PMIO and SMIO	❏ Define a technical, information and data architecture ❏ Monitor production system compliance with architecture ❏ Broker resolution of escalated arch issues from prod system archs, tech arch office, portfolio/app arch office, info/data arch office and core infrastructure product arch office
ACCOUNTABILITY: The responsibility to answer for a measured success of a product or a service			
	❏ Arch compliance ❏ Performance of prod systems ❏ Reliability of prod systems	❏ Architecture compliance ❏ Performance of prod systems ❏ Reliability of prod systems ❏ Certification of people in each arch role ❏ On-time SoW & budget defn	❏ Arch compliance ❏ Performance of prod systems ❏ Reliability of prod systems

Fig. 13. RAA map for architecture

9 Conclusions

Polarity language provides a useful view of the Armour's organization "dimensions." The neutral language of polarity maps and polarity networks helps address tensions and the overlap of dimensions. Functional organization charts with RAAs for each function are foundational.

RAA networks and RAA maps complement the foundational, hierarchical organization charts as cross-functional organization charts. The RAA networks hold polarity between Armour's dimensions; cross-functional decision-making teams can adapt membership and RAAs to the "fluid, event-driven interdependencies." Careful stratification of the software product line allows the recursive application of the RAA networks at each stratum by the proposed governance architect role.

Polarity maps, polarity networks, RAAs, RAA networks, and RAA maps provide scaffolding to construct lean and efficient governance architecture with clear and concise decision-making scope, escalation paths, and membership rationale for key cross-functional teams. Using these tools is essential to govern a product line efficiently and assure minimal disruption when hierarchical organizations change. This translates to a customer perception that product line releases continue to occur as planned, even when organizational chaos is reigning within the supplier organization.

Acknowledgements. We thank Fred Jarrett for RAA consultation. We thank Sharon Beatty for guiding us to RAAs to describe governance of products and processes. We honored the roles Fujitsu DMR's P+, extending them from project to product line scope.

References

1. Armour, P. *The Reorg Cycle*. CACM Feb.2003
2. Kasik, D., Kimball C., Felt, J., Frazier, K. *A Flexible Approach to Alliances of Complex Applications*. ICSE 99
3. Jolley, T, Kasik, D., Kimball C. *Governance Polarities of Internal Software Product Lines*. SPLC2 2002.
4. Bass, L., Clements, P., and Kazman, R. *Software Architecture in Practice*. Addison Wesley Longman, 1998.
5. Johnson, B. *Polarity Management*. HRD Press, 1996.
    http://www.polaritymanagement.com/
6. Clements, P., Northrop, L. *Software Product Lines: Practices and Patterns*. Addison Wesley Longman, 2002.
7. Collins, J.C., Porras, J.I. Built to Last: Successful Habits of Visionary Companies. HarperBusiness, 1994.

Software Product Line Support in Coremetrics OA2004

James Snyder, Harry Lai, Shirish Reddy, and Jimmy Wan

Coremetrics, Inc. 8940 Research Blvd. Suite 300, Austin, TX 78758
{jsnyder,hlai,sreddy,jwan}@coremetrics.com

Abstract. We present the transformation of the Coremetrics analytic application software engineering approaches from a traditional Java 2 Enterprise Edition (J2EE) environment to a software product line approach. Particular emphasis is placed on the motivation for a product line approach and the software engineering challenges faced particularly as an application service provider. We also discuss our definitions of product line variation and binding, and how we provide tool support using the open source Integrated Development Environment Eclipse. We also provide our observations about the software product line approach, how our work and findings relate to other work in this area, and lastly, how configuration management plays an integral and complementary role in our approach.

1 Introduction

Coremetrics Online Analytics 2004 (OA2004) is a hosted reporting and analysis solution that enables online marketers and e-commerce managers to attract and convert high-value visitors, optimize key site processes, improve product or service placement and pricing decisions, and increase customer lifetime value [1]. OA2004 is the industry's only platform that captures and stores all customer and visitor click-stream activity to build Lifetime 1 Individual Visitor Experience (LIVE) Profiles, which are stored in a data warehouse. In addition to our data collection services, we also provide a highly customizable analytic application platform—all delivered using the application service provider (ASP) software model.

1.1 A Brief History of Online Marketing Analytics

Over the course of a three-year period, the online marketing analytics space went through rapid changes.[1] Initially, most of the solutions were delivered using the Enterprise Software model in which there were large acquisition and installation costs. In addition, only simple Web-server log file analysis could be performed; essentially these systems counted Web-server events and produced simple reports. Given that it was not clear what to measure, this model was suitable for a period of time, even though it was not clear what business value was being gained. At this point in time, around late 2000, at least 70% of these first-generation solutions were delivered using the Enterprise Software model.

---

[1] This market space is also referred to as Web Analytics, but as the space has matured, so has the sophistication of the users. Much more than simple Web-server metrics can now be analyzed.

R.L. Nord (Ed.): SPLC 2004, LNCS 3154, pp. 18–33, 2004.

It was also during this period of time that the collapse of Enterprise Soft-ware was just starting to occur, and the ensuing years required the software providers to dramatically reduce costs while delivering demonstrable business value without significant customer investment or commitment. During the next two years, at least 70% of all the solutions offered in this space were provided using the ASP software model. In addition, the costs were dramatically reduced while the capabilities of the solutions became much more complex and focused on business value where clear and measurable results could be shown.

1.2   Market Challenges Driving Substantive Technology Changes

While the above transformation was taking place, the demand for both a wholly out-sourced, lower cost, increased capability, and individually tailored solutions became a primary requirement of customers in the Online Marketing Analytics space. In a traditional software engineering project, these requirements can create design problems that are difficult, if not impossible, to solve. As an ASP, we would ideally like to minimize complexity, while our customers are insisting on increasing complexity. Most companies now have to compete in rapidly changing markets; they, therefore, have unique reporting and analytic application requirements related to their organizational structures, product or service characteristics, enterprise data, and back-office activities that are not adequately served by a horizontal "one-size fits all" Web analytics solution.

On the other hand, large numbers of customers can be grouped together by industry segments (industry verticals in our terminology) because they share commonalities. For companies with unique reporting needs that go beyond Coremetrics' turnkey OA2004 solutions, we offer Coremetrics Online Analytics Custom Solutions that allow complete client customization by providing an outsourced platform that seamlessly integrates online behavioral information, custom online variables, and enterprise data. When taken as a whole, we can address the specific needs of our clients' business while maintaining the operational benefits of our clients being fully integrated into the hosted environment. In addition, they can continue to benefit from our continuous improvement of the offered products and product lines. Leveraging our platforms, analytics applications, and the LIVE Profile Data Warehouse (with over one billion distinct profiles), Coremetrics can scope, design, and implement a solution designed specifically to meet clients' analytical needs. Examples include personalized dashboards, unique product pricing/placement/promotion reports, contribution margin-based marketing reports, cross-channel views of customer behavior, and organizationally aligned analysis.

In the remainder of this paper, we discuss the software engineering challenges and solutions that reconciled the issues we faced during development to arrive at our current solution. Next, we present our approach to product line bind time and variation management. Additionally, we present the tools used to implement our variation binding and management approach. Lastly, we present some observations about the power of software product lines and some implications about using product lines as a software engineering technique.

2   The Software Engineering Challenges

Before we explain the solutions to our engineering challenges, it is important to point out that we were unaware of software product line approaches as we developed our solutions over time. We have been consulting the product line literature only recently.

Because the demand for customized and lower cost analytic solutions was becoming so great, it became clear to us that we needed to enlist the help of substantially different technology than we were using at the time. We initially believed that existing commercial reporting or business intelligence tools would provide a foundation on which we could build our analytic applications. After substantial research into the capabilities of these systems, we were quite surprised to find that we were unable to use them because they were rigid and would not support the types of client customization, variety, or complexity of the analytics we needed.

2.1   Basic Overview of the OA2004 Subsystems

A basic overview of the major subsystems in OA2004 is presented in Figure 1 below to help focus the discussion on where we are widely employing software product line techniques. The *Data Aggregation* subsystem collects real-time information from our clients' Web sites using third-generation Web analytics tagging technology. This information is then organized and added to our *Active Data Warehouse*; we use this term to indicate an important distinction from traditional data warehouses which are read-only in nature, whereas our systems are continually being updated. These two subsystems have not yet benefitted from the pervasive use of software product line approaches.

Our *Analytic Applications and Reporting* subsystem provides the client-access point to all the information collected and maintained on behalf of our clients. Specifically, this functional area is where our clients are needing the most amount of customization. Consequently, this area is where we have concentrated most of our research and development and is the focus of the remainder of this paper.

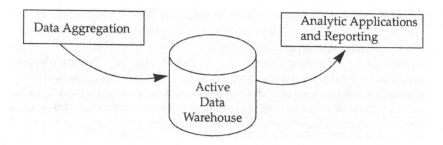

Fig. 1. Major software subsystems of OA2004

2.2   The Engineering Challenges of the ASP Model

Being an ASP allows us the potential to realize a substantial amortization of our hardware and software infrastructure without have client disruption or downtime. To attain such benefits, we needed to be able to reduce the overall number of hardware and, more importantly, software components. Using traditional software engineering approaches such as object-oriented application frameworks [2], we find that our ASP needs and support for customer-centric variation represent stark contrasts because we would most likely have to build different software systems. In the worst case scenario, we would build an analytic platform for each of our clients. It is important to note that we are not saying these software engineering techniques are not relevant; rather, we do not see them as sufficient on their own. If we do not account for the notion of variation explicitly, we believe these approaches will start to quickly suffer from the "architectural mismatch" problem stated by Garlan, Allen, and Ockerbloom [3].

   Another area we have the potential to benefit from is the grouping of clients into industry verticals where we can provide domain-specific enhancements while maximizing the use of the common aspects across verticals. As a complement to industry verticals, various application types can be built that span across verticals but have specific features independently from clients or verticals.

   Taken as a whole, all these challenges can essentially be viewed as aspects of variation within product lines. We believe that the ASP model is naturally complemented by product line approaches. However, we have found that the ASP model does not have much exposure in the product line literature. Most of the case studies we found (for example, in Clements and Northrop's book [4]) deal with software systems that resolve variation at system compile or build time such as embedded systems.

   We believe that the ASP model is better served if variation resolution is done as late as possible; ideally, we believe that the best type of solution is one where software systems do not have to be taken offline, and applications can be continually altered while they are being used by clients. As such, we believe our experiences with the product line approach are relatively unique.

2.3   Overall Analytic Platform Design Goals

After understanding the nature of the changes in the marketplace, the impact of the ASP model on our software systems, and the lack of commercially available solutions, we set out to research and develop a very different analytics platform than we had or could find commercially. As an overall design goal, we wanted to be able to create a wholesale replacement for the *Analytic Applications and Reporting* subsystem found in Figure 1. Additionally, we did not want or need to change the integration points to the *Active Data Warehouse*, that is, we wanted to use the identical database infrastructure. Our specific design goals are presented in the sections below.

Highly Customizable Analytic Applications. We needed to be able to support a large variety of customizations including the ability to integrate data and content from many sources about which we do not know. These customizations need to be scoped by many different variables including (1) client specific customization, (2) industry vertical customization, and (3) differing end-user interfaces.

These scopings require us to develop a solution that attempts to minimize the number of moving parts, while providing an efficient and cost-effective means of customization. It is important that our solutions have the right abstraction boundaries to effectively manage the tradeoffs between the granularity of customization and the ability to enable large-scale reuse. To help find a solution to this goal, we found it important to reflect on the diverse breadth and scope of software reuse techniques which are summarized nicely by Krueger [5].

Significantly Reduce Delivery Costs and Times. To meet the demands of the marketplace, we need the ability to reduce not only the overall customization delivery costs and times, but also the costs and times for any software platforms. Another major benefit we would like to exploit, to the largest extent possible, is the ability to decouple release cycles for the various aspects of our systems. Specifically, we would like to release any analytic platforms, analytic applications, industry verticals, or client customizations on a release cycle that is as independent as possible.

Change the Analytic Application Paradigm. We want to create software systems that are highly modifiable where customization is a continually occurring activity. However, we do not want customization to disrupt client access, that is, we want the ability to roll out a large variety of substantive and complex system changes without bringing our services down.

A complimentary need is to lower the skill set required to develop and roll out client customizations, applications, or industry verticals. While this goal will ultimately lower costs by decreasing the need for specialized skills, we see the need to allow people with industry domain experience to participate in the design or implementation of large aspects of new functionality. Without lowering the complexity barriers, it would be difficult for people without specialized software engineering skills to participate.

Lastly, we want to allow for the deployment of capabilities we did not anticipate with little or no platform modification, while maintaining as much backward compatibility as possible. We, therefore, need to provide an explicit path for evolutionary platform enhancement.

Minimize the Number of Hardware and Software Systems. As an ASP, we need to host multiple, different, and customizable application deployments on the same hardware and software platform deployments. Ideally, we would like to reduce the problem to simply deploying new hardware and platform software only to scale the degree of concurrent processing.

2.4 Software Architecture

It is important to point out that the recognition of the role software architecture plays in our solution is the cornerstone of our approach, that is, architecture is a critical aspect of our product line approach. We also believe that architecture is most likely an essential ingredient to other product line approaches and an interesting research topic that merits further work.

The essential approach to designing our software architecture was based on two observations. First, we recognized early on that we needed to build a robust content-generation and publishing software application platform. We essentially needed to properly characterize the fundamental nature of the problem we were trying to solve. Second, we also needed to structure the platform so we can decouple the product line variants from the rest of the platform and instantiate new variants into the platform while it services our clients. We call the variant parts of the design Customizable Resources (i.e., resources). Detailed definitions of resources are presented in later sections.

Invariant Aspects of Software Architecture. In Figure 2 below, we present the invariant part of our software architecture as a traditional n-tier view; we call this part of the software system the Rapid Report Deployment (RRD) platform. From right to left, the *Customizable Resources* are deployed into the *Active Data Warehouse* either at a particular scope where a scope consists of either an industry vertical/application pair or a client/application pair. Using the resources as processing instructions and inputs, the *Analytic Platform Services* tier produces the vast majority of the complex content (e.g., reporting, security filters, navigation abstraction, content structure, workflow logic, and so on) as Extensible Markup Language (XML) documents. The *Web Publishing* tier is responsible for receiving the content from the service tier while filtering, assembling, and transforming it into a form suitable for presentation (e.g., Hypertext Markup Language [HTML], print preview, csv, internationalization, skins, and so on). Once individual content is generated, it is processed by the *Aggregators* and presented to the requesting entity (e.g., a servlet that streams output to a browser, WAP phones, and so on).

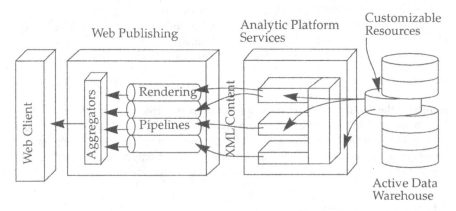

Fig. 2. Tiers of the RRD software architecture

Analytic Platform Services Tier. Because the service tier is intended to support generic and complex application capabilities, many of our services are session scoped, that is, they are aware of the session state and have efficient mechanisms to allow the infrastructure to cooperate with the more content-oriented services. We also provide platform services for security and authentication, session state management, data persistence, user preferences, globalization and localization services, and distributed model-view-controller state management. The abstractions for providing content as a set of structured views is an intrinsic part of the services tier.

While the high-level presentation of the services tier seems similar to other service tier implementations such as Java 2 Enterprise Edition (J2EE) Blue-Prints [6], we cannot stress enough that we could not realize our solution using any of the commercial or open source service tier application frameworks because they do not provide the appropriate service tier state management or allow for properly distributed model-view-controller implementations.[2] Along a similar vein, while we make use of J2EE technologies [7], our use of Enterprise JavaBean (EJB) abstractions is atypical precisely because of the design flaws and performance problems related to the EJB specifications, that is, we invested substantial effort in realizing efficient implementations of our designs in the EJB environment.[3]

As a complement to the infrastructure-oriented services, we also provide Resource Management Services including caching, retrieval, and resource execution and evaluation. The details of these services will be presented in later sections because they are difficult to explain without first explaining what resources are and the role they play in product line variation and variation management.

Web Publishing Tier. Because Web publishing has well-defined solutions, we can make use of the Cocoon2 open source Web publishing framework [8]. The rendering pipeline abstractions match our model-view-controller abstractions nicely, so we can use Cocoon as a rendering framework without modification.

Variant Aspects of the Software Architecture. As we stated previously, we explicitly model product line variants as Customizable Resource abstractions. It is important to point out that, depending on the resource type, a resource is either fully or partially defined when it is deployed; the importance of this definition will be explained in later sections. Table 1 describes the supported resource types.

---

[2] The justification for these claims is beyond the scope of this paper. However, we believe that most descriptions of the model-view-controller design pattern in a distributed or multi-tier environment do not solve the distributed state synchronization problem that is a natural outcropping of distributed computing. Specifically, we find the J2EE BluePrint definition of MVC+ to be lacking.

[3] Again, the scope of this paper precludes presenting the details of how we realized efficient implementations. For example, we do not use Entity Beans, and we employed techniques to not use the EJBHome RMI method invocation for calls that are not truly remote.

Table 1. RRD-supported Customizable Resources

Resource Type	Description	Deploy Complete
ClientDescriptor	Defines the basic description of the bootstrap client resource configurations including navigational rules and workflow executions	y
PageDescriptor	Page descriptors are a central, organizing concept in our architecture. They define the collection of resources used to generate content for a logical page. Page content can be dramatically variable depending on the other resources it enlists to generate content; for example, references to workflows, view layouts, resource bundles, page types, and so forth. Page Descriptors can optionally inherit definitions from Page Type Descriptors.	n
Navigation-Descriptor	Provides a tree-structured representation of logical application navigation points to a page descriptor	y
Resource Type	Description	Deploy Complete
WorkflowTemplate	Workflow Templates act much like functions in programming languages in that they can accept variable numbers of arguments and invoke other workflows or content generators.	y
ResourceBundle	The basic unit for supporting globalization and localization. Resource bundles automatically inherit attributes from parent resource bundles in less specific scopes.	n
ContentGenerator	Content Generators are very similar to Workflow Templates in nature with the key difference that the side effect of evaluation is the item of interest, that is, the output of the content generator is returned as the invocation result. We can use content generator to build any kind of content we need from Structured Query Language (SQL) Queries to complex XML documents.	y
RDLtemplate	Report Definition Language (RDL) Templates are specialized content generators that have compiler support for solving the data source and layout binding problem. We generate a content generator using our RDL compiler.	y
Schematron-Schema	To support complex user interface (UI) form inputs, we support form validation using Schematron.	y
ViewTree-Descriptor	A View Tree Descriptor allows us to recursively describe hierarchical, spatial layout containment relationships.	y
PageType-Descriptor	Page Type Descriptors allow us to create partially defined page descriptions that can be referenced by Page Descriptors.	y
ViewController-Template	View Controller Templates allow us to provide a specific layout resolution to composite view structures defined in our View Tree Descriptors.	y
SkinDescriptor	To support different styles of UI aesthetic schemes, we define all the substitutable parts for UI elements such as images and color schemes here.	y

3   Variation Scoping and Bind Times

There are two scopings for variations within the RRD platform namely by application and industry vertical or by application and client customization.[4] Additionally, the two binding times for resources are at deployment time and at platform runtime. The remainder of this section describes how the scoping and bind time interactions are supported in the RRD platform.

3.1   Files and Resource Deployment Bindings

Resource contents are defined by individual files that are version controlled (e.g., in CVS) largely independently from the RRD platform. The resource abstraction exists only in the Active Data Warehouse or in the runtime data structures of the RRD platform. We, therefore, support the notion of binding a Configuration Managed file to a resource declared at a particular scope. Deployment is the process of taking the contents of the bound file and writing it to the persistent representation of the declared resource in the Active Data Warehouse. Deployment bindings are a representation of the association between a resource and its content found in a particular file.

All resources are identified by a unique, system-assigned identifier. However, within a particular scope, resources can also be identified by name much like file systems manage the mapping between disk blocks and directory structures. Resource names are relevant to the discussions in later sections. It is also important to recall that, depending on the resource type, a resource is either fully or partially defined when it is deployed.

To illustrate these concepts, Figure 3 shows a three-dimensional block diagram where each dimension represents the *Application, Industry Vertical*, or *Client Customization* dimensions. In this model, the *Application* and *Industry Vertical* dimensions are one scope, while the *Application* and *Client Customization* dimensions are the other scope. Figure 3 also shows that files are logically bound to a particular cell in the three-dimensional space where a cell represents a collection of resources grouped together by scope. Specifically, we want to call out the ability for a single file to be mapped to multiple resources in different scopes. When we say a resource is deployed, we mean that the resource abstraction will be populated in the Active Data Warehouse with the file contents.

3.2   Runtime Inheritance Bindings

Most resources support the ability to reference and interact with other resources. For example, a Workflow can invoke a Content Generator or lookup a value in a Globalization Resource Bundle. The RRD platform also supports various forms of resource inheritance depending on whether a resource is fully or partially defined. For fully defined resources, we use the provided resource name to resolve references from the most specific to the least specific scope, that is, we first look in a client/application scope for a resource of that name, and if one is not found, we look in the vertical/application scope.

---

[4] As a simplifying assumption, we do not allow for clients to cross industry vertical boundaries. While potentially being interesting theoretically, we find in practice that this case is usually not interesting or valuable.

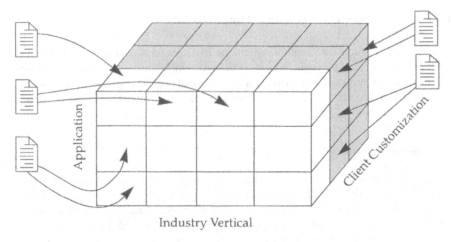

Fig. 3. Variation scoping using file to resource deployment bindings

For partially defined resources, the RRD platform provides additional inheritance resolution mechanisms that are invoked when a resource is instantiated at runtime. A simple but clear example is the Globalization Resource Bundle, which is a collection of key/value pairs to enable locale-sensitive information to be displayed; if a key is not found to exist in a more specific resource bundle, its logical parent is searched, that is, a resource bundle of the same name in a less specific scope is searched.

A visual depiction of these relationships is show in Figure 4 where each cell in the diagram represents a unique resource instance. Notice that the scoping structure is preserved between this model and the model from Figure 3. Also note that resource redefinition via inheritance causes two different kinds of variation.

This approach also allows us to defer binding until after the RRD platform has been started. We can also rebind resources as many times as we like while the platform is running without disrupting client utilization, that is, we can go through a bind, deploy, reinstantiate process much like a edit-compile-debug cycle in Java where you can hot-swap a class in an instantiated Java Virtual Machine.

3.3   Variations and Complexity

Within an industry vertical for our Web analytics application, we typically deploy about 600 resources where at least 50% of the resource contents are shared between verticals. We can achieve significant reuse between verticals and clients as we gain understanding about how to structure and modularize our resources. We have experimented with several approaches to modularization and are getting measurably better results over time.

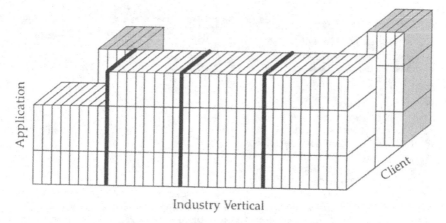

Fig. 4. Variation scoping using runtime resource inheritance

4   Tool Support for Variation Management

Because the complexity of our product line is high, we firmly believe that tool support is a mandatory aspect of product line variant management. We share a substantial number of the same views on this subject as described by Krueger [9].

4.1   The Deployer Plug-In and the Eclipse IDE

We provide tool support for managing product line variations using the open source Integrated Development Environment (IDE) Eclipse [10]. We chose this tool because of its native support for CVS, availability, quality, and ability to cost effectively extend the environment with specialized behavior using the IDE plug-in framework. We provide an Eclipse plug-in that manages the resource abstractions in our Active Data Warehouse as well as the resource bindings to the CVS managed files.

We present a screen shot of the Deployer Plug-In shown in Figure 5 below. There are several things to point that should help tie all the previously presented concepts into a concrete picture. First, the notion of scope is modeled in the Deployer Plug-In as a tree with the application being at the root, for example, *marketforce*, and the two industry verticals shown under the root are *Retail* and *Financial Services*.

In Figure 5, we also show how a resource is bound to a particular file at the leaf nodes of the tree where we have a resource name associated with a file name. In this example, we also show how the resource *Dialog/Calendar/Page* is defined by both the *Vertical Default* and the *test clientid* nodes. Most of the concepts presented in Section 3 are illustrated in this figure.

To invoke operations within the Deployer Plug-In, we follow the Eclipse convention of making the items in the context-sensitive, right-click menu aware of the state of the current selection. For example, if no file is bound to a resource, and you select that resource, you cannot invoke the Deploy operation. The operations we support are summarized in Table 2 below.

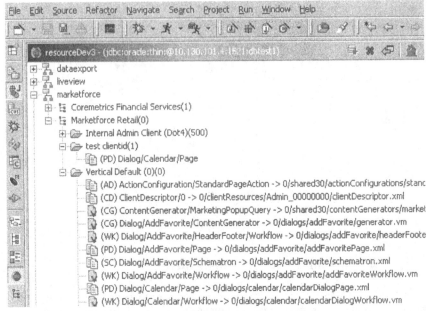

Fig. 5. A screen shot of the Deployer Plug-In

Table 2. Supported operations in the Deployer Plug-In

Operation	Description
Create DB Resource	Create a named resource at the selected scope in the Active Data Warehouse.
Delete DB Resource	Delete the selected, named resource including the file binding associated with it.
Bind Resource To File	Bind a configuration-managed file to the selected resource.
Deploy Resource	Create or update the selected, named resource with the contents defined by its bound file.
Audited Deploy Resource	Perform a deploy operation as above including an audit trail for later comparison and validation.

4.2   The Significance of Configuration Management and Product Lines

We have found that it is impossible to correctly manage product lines without having the means to synchronize Configuration Management and Variation Management. Specifically, we need to be able to understand what file versions *should* be part of particular scope versus what is *currently* being used. To support this kind of visibility we (1) require all files to make use of the CVS id tags so that we know what version of a file we are looking at, and (2) we can produce an audit trail of all the CVS versions of all the files in a particular scope upon deployment and compare that to what is expected. The deployment audit is itself then put under configuration management so we can move for-ward and backward in time and still validate what a scope should consist of.

4.3 The Deployer Plug-In and Manual Processes

In general, we have found it difficult to predict all the needed functionality of the Deployer Plug-In because it is not always clear what variation management problems will actually become significant in practice. While we provide tool support for managing variation, there are still some shortcomings that are worth noting.

File Sharing Variants. Because we allow a single file to be bound to multiple resources, we introduced a File Sharing Variant. Essentially, we have an *edit once—deploy many* problem where we currently have to find all the resources that are bound to a particular file. Keep in mind that the file may be bound to other industry verticals or applications.

File-sharing variants also occur when the same file is shared between multiple clients. For example, there are several custom Dialog resources that are shared customizations between clients. We have the same *edit once—deploy many* problem as found between verticals, but at the client level.

File Copy Variants and Replacement Resource Inheritance. Within the context of the RRD platform, we support the notion of client-level customization. Depending on the semantics of an individual resource type, a resource definition can be replaced in a wholesale fashion as previously stated. What may not be obvious is that if we copy the file associated with another scope and make modifications to it, we lose the information about where the original source came from; the resource replacement problem many times has a file variation angle to it as well.

File Copy Variants and Extension Resource Inheritance. In a similar vein, extension inheritance allows for more granular replacement semantics than full replacement. For example, a resource bundle will allow for new items to be added or existing items to be redefined. If an item is not found in at the client level, the parent resource is inspected. The problems that show up here are usually less intrusive because changes are at a more granular level. However, if we delete an entry from the vertical scope (i.e., parent), the child, by definition, will treat the previously redefined attribute as a new attribute; we may have wanted to actually remove support for the attribute but are not currently able to detect these cases without manual inspection.

4.4 Future Tool Support for Managing Product Variation

Given that we have pointed out some manually intensive operations, we outline several stages below that we need to progress through to help us manage our variation problem.

Understanding What Has Changed. We currently have no automated way of understanding what changes have been introduced into our resources, especially at the client level. The first step we need to take is to create a historical audit trail of the changes that have been introduced into the database tables. The most straightforward way for us to achieve this is to create a version history table and a set of triggers that will record the changes over time.

Second, we can annotate our tables with more diagnostic information that will allow us to quickly assess what has changed. Most, if not all, of these changes can be introduced into the Deployer Plug-In. Specifically, we need to know who deployed the resource at which time. We also would want to know any specific Configuration Management information (e.g., CVS tag).

Understanding the Impacts of a Change. As incremental changes are introduced into the OA2004 product line, we also need to be able to assess what the impact of change is. We will need to be able to identify and track all the variations outlined in Section 3. Again, the Deployer Plug-In is an appropriate vehicle for creating tools to assess the impact of a change. We will most likely need to extend the current deployment actions as well as create another Eclipse view that specifically allows for variation browsing.

Introducing Automation. The first two stages of this approach are basically tactical and short term. The longer term issues relate to the fact that we copy files and cut and paste bits of code manually. Essentially, we have to manually figure out what changes need to be made, and then we have to manually apply them.

To realize the full benefits of the software product line approach over time, we need to investigate effective ways to allow the application of most of these activities in an automated way. We propose that integrating existing Variant Management tools together, potentially with the Deployer Plug-In and the RRD platform, will allow us to maintain and even increase our ability to introduce rapid mass customization for our customers.

5   Observations

In this section, we make some observations about our experiences with the product line approach.

5.1   Similarities and Differences with Other Product Line Approaches

Our software product line approach fits nicely into the taxonomy scheme presented by Krueger [11]. Since our approach is so dynamic and intentionally late bound, we can be categorized as a runtime binding approach where our resources are the variation assets, the deployer file bindings are decision inputs, and the resource inheritance model is our approach to variation management at runtime. Note that while our platform remains active, we can redefine any aspect of these bindings at various levels of granularity and affect a compartmentalized change into as small or large a scope as we wish.

We are somewhat different in our product line approach as compared to other approaches because our platform software architecture provides an abstraction layer that intrinsically separates the variant and invariant parts of our system, allowing us to apply the product line technique to the variant parts. As a result, we can also continually extend and customize product lines while our systems are running. We have not yet seen this type of capability documented in the literature. We also believe that our approach presents some interesting research challenges that are unique when compared to the earlier binding time approaches.

5.2 Product Line Conversion Effort and Benefits

At the completion of our commercial role out of our systems using the product line approach, we were able to gather some historical metrics to do a coarse-grained cost benefit analysis. We were happily surprised to learn that the complete re-implementation of the analytics platform and reproduction of all the features was an order of magnitude smaller than the non-product-line solution. That solution was built using a pure J2EE/EJB software architecture, and,as such, we believe this result is relevant to the community at large. We also want to recall that our scope of work for product line adoption did not require all software subsystems to be rearchitected, so, at some level, we are both evolutionary and revolutionary in our approaches.

We also now find that our customization capabilities are a significant source of revenue, cost savings, and market leadership. We have also been able to substantially increase the speed by which we bring new functionality to market and provide highly tailored, cost-effective solutions for our customers. It is important to note that these benefits have been sustainable over multiple years; we do believe that the enhancements to deployment management outlined in Section 4 will become necessary to continue realizing these benefits at the same rate we have in the past. We have also found that the ability to introduce customization allows clients to engage in developing functionality that would otherwise be considered more speculative. We are also able to discover, develop, and incorporate generalized versions—both within and across industries—of client customizations into our standard offerings, thereby increasing the sustainability of the approach over time.

Lastly, communicating software product line approaches in industry has been relatively difficult right now because there are not many industry experiences readily available. However, we have found that industry efforts are making a difference (see Krueger's work [12]).

5.3 Proactive Versus Reactive

Given that the software product line approach is an intentional design activity, the question of how much up-front investment can or should be invested is a continuing question for us. These issues are articulated nicely by Clements and Krueger [13] who term the ends of the spectrum as *proactive* or *reactive*. Another way to think of these issues is from an investment perspective, that is, we need to determine how much up-front effort is required to make a solution work.

From our experiences and observations that software architecture plays a substantial role in the viability of a solution, we would tend to lean more towards the proactive end of the spectrum. However, we also believe that our deferred binding time is the major reason we have to be more proactive in our approach. From other evaluations of our software platforms, we suspect that the earlier the bind time, the less need there is for a globally proactive approach, and lower cost, reactive approaches can be more suitable. We believe that these questions are important research topics that deserve research effort.

6   Conclusions

We have found the software product line approach to system development has had a dramatic impact on our ability to produce competitive and high-quality software. We also believe that the ASP model and software product lines are naturally suited to each other, and we would also hope that more research would be done about this specific area as both of these forces will become increasingly important over time.

From our experiences and readings in the literature, we have concluded that software architecture must play an integral role in any product line approach or solution. Without recognizing this relationship early in our efforts, we would certainly not have had such dramatic success and would have mostly like had major failure.

Lastly, we also have found that product line support really requires soft-ware tools that must be complementary to configuration management. Specifically, we believe that any product line solution that ignores configuration management does so at its peril.

References

1. Coremetrics, Inc. http://www.coremetrics.com (2004).
2. Fayad, M. and D. Schmidt. "Object Oriented Application Frameworks" Communications of the ACM, Vol. 40, No. 10. (1997) pp. 85..87.
3. Garlan, D., Allen, R., and J. Ockerbloom. "Architectural Mismatch or Why It's Hard to Build Systems Out of Existing Parts" in Proceedings of the 17th Interna-tional conference on Software Engineering, April 24–28, 1995, Seattle, WA USA. pp. 179–185.
4. Clements, P. and L. Northrop. Software Product Lines: Practices and Patterns. Addison-Wesley, Longman, Reading, Mass (2001)
5. Krueger, C. "Software Reuse" ACM Computing Surveys. 24(2) (1992).
6. Sun Microsystems, Inc. J2EE BluePrints (2003).
7. Sun Microsystems, Inc. J2EE http://java.sun.com/j2ee (2004).
8. Apache, Inc. Cocoon2 Web Publishing Framework (http://www.apache.org/cocoon2) (2003).
9. Krueger, C. "Easing the Transition of Software Mass Customization" Proc. 4th Int'l Workshop Software Product Family Engineering, Springer Verlag, New York, (2001) pp. 282–293
10. Eclipse. http://www.eclipse.org (2004)
11. Krueger, C. Towards a Taxonomy for Software Product Lines Proceedings of the 5th International Workshop on Software Product-Family Engineering, PFE 2003, Siena, Italy, Nov 4–6, (2003).
12. Krueger, C. Introduction to Software Product Lines. http://www.softwareproduct-lines.com/introduction/introduction.html (2004).
13. Clements, P. and Krueger, C., Being Proactive Pays Off/Eliminating the Adoption Barrier. IEEE Software, Special Issue of Software Product Lines. July/August 2002, pages 28–31.

Introducing PLA at Bosch Gasoline Systems: Experiences and Practices

Mirjam Steger[1], Christian Tischer[1], Birgit Boss[1],
Andreas Müller[1], Oliver Pertler[1], Wolfgang Stolz[1], and Stefan Ferber[2]

[1] Robert Bosch GmbH, Gasoline Systems,
[2] Robert Bosch GmbH, Research and Advanced Engineering,
Postfach 30 02 20, 70442 Stuttgart, Germany
{Mirjam.Steger,Christian.Tischer,Birgit.Boss,Andreas.Mueller8,
Oliver.Pertler, Wolfgang.Stolz,Stefan.Ferber}@de.bosch.com

Abstract. Software engineering in the automotive domain faces outstanding challenges in terms of quality, cost, and functional complexity. To ensure process and product excellence, Bosch Gasoline Systems (GS) introduced a process improvement program based on Capability Maturity Model Integration (CMMI) and adopted the product line approach (PLA). Business strategies for software products, software sharing with customers, and common solutions for diesel and gasoline engine control software are inputs for the product line architecture. The steps towards the PLA started with an evaluation project followed by an evolutionary rollout. The lack of suitable mechanisms and tools for some crucial nonfunctional requirements is a major drawback for introducing the PLA. Nevertheless, GS considers it the only systematic approach to dealing with current and future challenges.

1 Introduction

Today's automotive software systems have to deal with a set of requirements that, when combined, are probably unique in the software community. Well-known requirements like cost-efficiency and variability are embodied in today's software solutions, but new challenges enter this domain such as standardization, software sharing, and growing system and organizational complexity. These changes require new approaches to find a tradeoff that satisfies the concurrent needs.

Figure 1 illustrates the increasing complexity of an engine control unit (ECU) in terms of ECU resources, system components, features, and software parameters that has to be handled in a state-of-the-art ECU for gasoline engines.

The approach of Bosch GS to offer "best in class" solutions in the past was based on a very powerful platform development including a broad range of functionality. With increasing product complexity and product variants, the strong focus on a platform-based development shows critical risks that result in less competitive project and product costs:

- high resource consumption
- complex software integration and calibration procedures

R.L. Nord (Ed.): SPLC 2004, LNCS 3154, pp. 34–50, 2004.

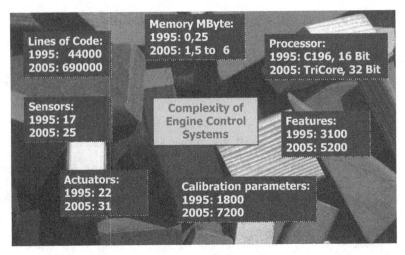

Fig. 1. Increasing complexity of gasoline engine control systems

The challenge of mastering increasing complexity at a low cost, with a high quality and shorter time to market was the main driver for starting improvement initiatives for process and product excellence. To improve the process maturity of the organization, GS started a process improvement program based on the Capability Maturity Model (CMM) in the year 2000, resulting in the achievement of CMM Level 3 in the year 2002. In parallel, with respect to product excellence, GS investigated the PLA in a technology project with the goal of evaluating the approach's applicability in the engine control domain.

With respect to our business context, the following characteristics had to be considered:

- Marketing to car manufacturers means having very competent and demanding customers in terms of functionality, quality, and cost in a highly competitive market.
- Due to the specific customer relation (no end users), software requirements have to be negotiated for every product. Our product line goal is to achieve an efficient implementation of the product requirements. Our ability to sell predefined solutions is limited, depending on the market segment, as the solutions are defined to a large degree by the customer.
- The need of our customers for differentiation from other manufacturers leads to a great amount of customer-specific software. Increasingly, customers require software sharing on object code level to protect their specific know-how.
- Innovation by adding or improving functionality faster than competitors is essential for car manufacturers. This leads to a continuous flow of change requests from our customers in all project phases.
- Engine control systems have to cover a tremendous range of variants. As a result, hundreds of program versions per year have to be handled.

The PLA offered a comprehensive, systematic concept for analyzing and improving business strategies and product development processes, as well as technical solutions within our products.

The product line practice areas provided helpful guidelines for a common under-standing of strategies throughout the organization, thus supporting the required cus-tomization of the PLA to the engine control domain. This will help us to achieve the demanding goals shown in Fig. 2, in line with our mid-term vision:

> *Software is built from a common architecture*
> *and set of components using a product line approach,*
> *so that high-quality individually tailored products*
> *can be built easily and predictably ,*
> *using as few hardware resources as possible,*
> *thereby reducing overall development costs.*

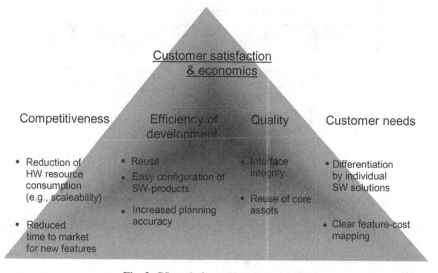

Fig. 2. GS goals for product line adoption

This paper summarizes some of the most important experiences in the adoption of product line methods:

Section 2 outlines the effects of the PLA on business strategy, work products, processes, and organization. As software architecture and process definitions are important basics for a successful product line, we discuss them in detail.

Section 3 addresses critical success factors like the important role of management and the interaction of the PLA and CMM(I).

The experiences presented here are, of course, specific to Bosch's GS division, but we confirm some essential general prerequisites for product line development such as strong leadership, high management commitment, and high process maturity.

2 Affected Areas

Introducing the PLA affects several practice areas of both management and engineering. The interdependencies of the practice areas require parallel change and improvement.

This section details our experiences concerning the influence of the PLA on the following aspects:

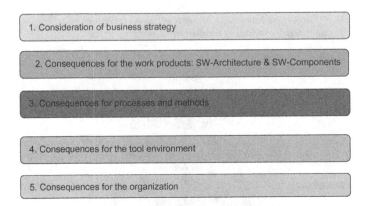

1. Consideration of business strategy

2. Consequences for the work products: SW-Architecture & SW-Components

3. Consequences for processes and methods

4. Consequences for the tool environment

5. Consequences for the organization

Fig. 3. Areas affected by the PLA

2.1 Consideration of the Business Strategy

Market requirements were analyzed in the context of strategic product portfolio planning, leading to the definition of different market segments [12]. Accordingly, the former strategy of "one platform for all" was changed in a strategic product line definition

- for basic engine control systems
- for standard systems and
- single-product development for high-feature systems

Each product line has clearly defined features and qualities (nonfunctional requirements, e.g., HW resource restrictions, software sharing). For the software that is standard in each product line, standard options and customer-specific software (SW) options were defined. Some features will be sold separately as SW product options. This definition has a strong influence on quotation and development activities.

Figure 4 shows, as an example, the mapping of markets, market segments, and product lines.

Other goals of the business strategy are common software for gasoline and diesel systems and software sharing with customers.

These aspects have a strong influence on the software architecture and process definition. They require exchange data formats (MSR [8, 10, 11]) and mechanisms (e.g., for know-how protection or interface management).

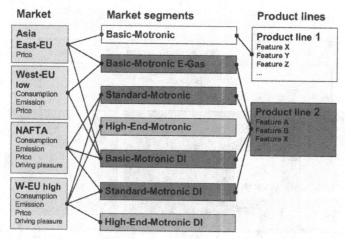

Fig. 4. Market segments and product line definition

2.2 Consequences for the Work Products

This section describes the development of an SW architecture and the design of SW components that fulfill the product line definition and the qualities, and address the business goals.

Figure 5 shows, in outline, the evolutionary path from the existing software to the new platform. The starting point for the activities is the analysis of market requirements and existing platform solutions. Driven by the product line definition and the prioritized qualities, there is an initial phase that includes both the design of an adequate SW architecture and a redesign of the SW components. The new architecture and the redesigned SW components provide the basis for product line maintenance.

Consequences for the SW Architecture. In the past, the engine control domain was driven mainly by functional requirements. As a consequence, nonfunctional requirements (qualities) were not considered explicitly in the SW architecture.

For the development of the new SW architecture for the EDC/ME(D)17-generation, the nonfunctional requirements were analyzed, prioritized, and considered as main drivers for the design [4]. One of the main results of the SW architecture design is the static view shown in Fig. 6.[1]

---

[1] Semantic: Boxes are graphical representations of software components. Interfaces and relations are described by Hammel and associates [4].

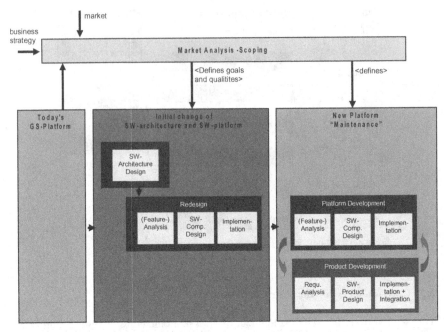

Fig. 5. The way to the new product line

Some of the most important qualities and the design decisions used to support them are listed below:

- Resource consumption (RAM, Flash, and runtime) is very critical in embedded systems due to its cost relevance. The main approach to achieving resource reduction is the redesign of software based on feature analysis using suitable variability mechanisms (Consequences for the SW Components, Section 2.2).
- Distributed development requires consequent interface management to achieve stable and lean interfaces.
- Software sharing with car manufacturers is supported by the adoption of layers in software architecture. Thus we achieve encapsulation. That means, for example, that a software component in the application layer is independent of how a sensor, actuator, or micro-controller works.
- The reuse goals are reflected in the architecture in several ways:
  - The "Application Software" can be used across different system generations.
  - The "Core" software is highly configurable and may be reused across projects without software changes, as only the configuration has to be changed.
  - The "Vehicle Functions" can be used in the gasoline engine domain as well as in the diesel engine domain.
  - The adoption of a layered software model with hardware encapsulation, device encapsulation, and an application layer supports reuse of software components.

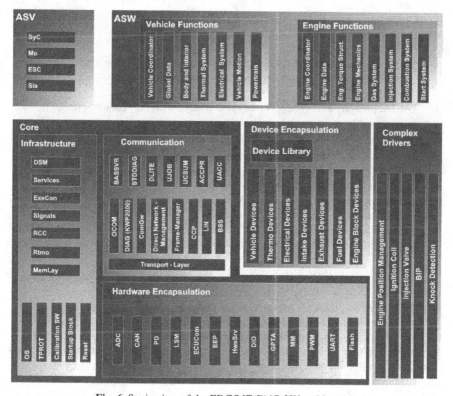

Fig. 6. Static view of the EDC/ME(D)17-SW architecture

- The standardization of architecture gains increasing importance. Structuring the application software according to the domain model and the adoption of appropriate layers qualify our architecture as a good basis for standardization efforts. We will introduce our experiences in developing a software architecture for an automotive domain into standardization initiatives like AUTOSAR [28].

To evaluate this new software architecture, the Architecture Tradeoff Analysis Method (ATAM) of the Software Engineering Institute (SEI) [13] was used to check the architecture against business goals and nonfunctional requirements, and to identify risks and non-risks.

Consequences for the SW Components. The principle qualities that affect the redesign of existing SW components are reuse, simplification of calibration, optimization of resource consumption, and stable interfaces.

We summarize the main activities in the redesign phase below (see Fig. 5).

Analysis of existing software (process step: Feature-Analysis [7]):
- Identify and document implemented features and variability (mandatory, optional, ...) in a feature-tree.

- Check on the necessity of these features in the product line definition (Section 2.1). Eliminate these features or make them configurable. Document these decisions in the feature-tree.
- Document feature interdependencies (required, exclude) in the feature-tree.

Concept development and design of SW components (process-step: SW Component Design):

- Use simpler physical concepts that sufficiently fulfill the requirements.
- Use a suitable variant mechanism to implement configurable features.
- Shift from function-driven to architecture-driven component structures.
- Document relations between features and implementations to support the ease of configuration and product derivation.
- Define interfaces (as stable as possible).
- Document the interfaces of the SW component as the basis for interface management and interface consistency checks.
- Provide "overview documentation" for the SW component and provide tailored documentation for the selected variant to give easy access to the functionality.

Baselines for Different Variants of SW Component (Process-Step: Reference Configuration)

- Document baselines for variants of the SW component. These baselines are helpful for product planning, product configuration, and integration.

After the initial development of these work products, it must be ensured that they are kept up to date and are used in the development process (e.g., interface management, product derivation, calibration).

2.3 Consequences for Processes and Methods

The improvement of processes and methods was motivated mainly by the cost and technology challenges. The PLA model [3] was used as a systematic approach, a framework, and a kind of "checklist" for existing and future product improvement activities. It was not intended to cover all PLA practice areas.

Although GS has had platform development for years, design and reuse was not systematic or driven by the business strategy. The organization had to become aware of the difference between our classic platform development and the product line idea.

In principle, we passed through three phases:
1. Phase 1: Investigate and customize PLA
2. Phase 2: Design and piloting of adequate processes and methods
3. Phase 3: Rollout and institutionalization in standard development process

Phase 1: Investigate and Customize PLA. The investigation and adoption of the PLA ideas were the main tasks in the first phase of the project.

GS applied the evaluation method Product Line Technical Probe (PLTP), provided by the SEI to identify the starting point in terms of organization readiness to adopt the PLA (strengths and challenges). The PLTP gave valuable feedback about the organizational status and a comprehensive analysis across roles and hierarchy levels, and provided helpful recommendations for the next steps. But we encountered reluctance to accept some of the results. Details of the analysis must often be known to judge the results, and, in contrast to CMM assessments, the participation of GS staff in the evaluation team was not intended.

Phase 2: Design and Piloting of Adequate Processes and Methods. Methods and processes to address the challenges were designed and piloted. One important step was to separate explicitly the tasks and work products for platform- and customer-specific development. The defined and implemented engineering process steps listed below are described briefly in Consequences for the SW Components, Section 2.2.

New engineering process steps:

- Feature-Analysis
- SW Architecture Design
- Interface Management
- Software Component Design
- Packaging/Reference Configurations

New technical management activities:

- Scoping (see Section 2.1)
- initial measurement for PLA goals

Phase 3: Rollout and Institutionalization in Standard Development Process. For the rollout and institutionalization phase, it was necessary to enable the organization to live the new process steps.

Key factors for success in this phase were strong management commitment and attention (Section 3.1). Other important enabling elements are shown in Figure 7.

	Roll out by redesign of existing platform	Series of PLA-process workshops with middle management	Embody new process steps in standard development process	Training program for PLA and architecture
purpose	Initial development of work products like interfaces, feature-trees, overview-functions, etc.	Understanding, Acceptance, and Management Support	Visibility of PLA Integration in process infrastructure	Understand PLA and internalize new methods
helpful	PLA Coaches	Management commitment	Management commitment, Existing process infrastructure	Use of domain-specific examples

Fig. 7. Elements of roll out and institutionalization

The rollout of the new processes and methods is strongly linked with the redesign of the existing platform software. For this technical redesign, we have a committed rollout plan, a steering committee, and measurement. However the risk is that developers and management focus on familiar technical aspects like resource consumption without paying enough attention to piloting and institutionalization of the new processes. To minimize this risk, we installed PLA coaches who provide initial support for the developers to implement the new processes in a consistent way.

It was important to embody the new process ideas and process steps in the standard development process. One initiative was a series of workshops with our middle management to discuss the new processes and gain their acceptance and support. The PLA must be visible in the standard process even if the new process steps are not binding for the whole organization. The PLA will be rolled out gradually and will become mandatory for all developers. A training initiative covering the software architecture and specific elements of the product line approach was also funded.

2.4 Consequences for the Tool Environment

To support the development and maintenance of the work products and to gain the benefit of the documented information in the development process, adequate tools and data formats are required. Here are some examples for required tool support:

- feature modeling
- architecture documentation
- interface documentation, interface checks, and interface management
- documenting the linkage between feature model and implementation
- feature-based product derivation

Due to the lack of commercial tool support for these tasks, we had to specify and develop tools of our own. The tool prototypes we used in the pilot phase were not very user-friendly and were not integrated in the tool chain. In most cases, they required more effort to use than they should save. As a result, it was very difficult to motivate the pilot users to use these tools. Based on the experiences with the prototype tools, requirements for the tool environment were specified. The lack of tools led to a delay of one to two years for the process institutionalization.

Another tool and data formats aspect concerns the need of software sharing with other business units and with customers. Standardization on the data format level is necessary. This standardization addresses not only the code level but also architecture definition and interface description. To address these aspects, we work in standardization initiatives like AUTOSAR [28] and MSR ([8, 10, 11]).

2.5 Consequences for the Organization

In addition to affecting processes and work products, the PLA has a strong influence on the organization. One main prerequisite for successful adoption of the PLA is the assignment of the necessary roles and responsibilities in the line and project organizations.

Consequently, adjustments of the organization, derived from the software architecture and the new technical development process, are in progress, including

- designation of specific groups for the subsystems Core and Complex Drivers (see Figure 6)
- establishing a group responsible for scoping and architecture design
- a clear separation of organizational units responsible for platform and product development, reflecting the process definition

3 Critical Success Factors

This section describes some critical success factors in terms of the management role and the process maturity of an organization for adopting the PLA.

3.1 Management Role

Changing large organizations is a major challenge for management. We summarize some of the main management success factors in the PLA-improvement initiative.

Building Up PLA Know-How at Bosch Research. In 1995, a Bosch research department manager adapted the software product line vision for Bosch's automotive software. Key success factors in his management role were

- building up PLA know-how
- hiring appropriate software engineers
- piloting small projects within corporate research

Setting Up a PLA Business Unit Project to Investigate and Customize PLA. A department manager for software serial development at Bosch GS learns about PLA technology in Bosch's research. Here, important management factors are

- setting up a project with the task of investigating and customizing the PLA
- assigning a project manager with acceptance and standing in the organization as well as high perseverance. Keeping the team motivated to deepen the PLA understanding, while dealing with resistance in the organization and steering the organization through a rapidly changing context was a difficult mission.
- stuffing the team with representatives from several development departments (domain experts, software developer, software integrator, and process and tool experts) and consultants from Bosch's corporate research
- having a powerful promoter in middle management, who ensured proper funding and continuously communicated the PLA vision to senior management and to the organization

Roll Out PLA into BU Organization. As the project team delivers relevant results, management decides to roll out the PLA in the organization, which necessitates increased management support. The vice president for system and software development supports the PLA:

- PLA aspects are embodied in the policy deployment of the software development departments.
- Capacity is planned and provided to redesign the software according to the requirements resulting from the PLA (Section 2).
- A steering committee for the project provides a communication link to other department managers.

At the same time, the project team communicates the ideas and approaches early and continuously to middle managers and key players on the developer's level. This is a major success factor because

- In our business culture, having a consensus and understanding new processes are very important for the involved stakeholders.
- Addressing key players on the developer's level ensures the applicability of methods.

A product line initiative potentially interfaces with every role in an organization. Therefore, proper and sustained management support is key in every software product line.

3.2 Product and Process Excellence – The PLA and CMMI

To establish an appropriate improvement strategy and focus the improvement effort, the following aspects have to be considered:

- market competitiveness
- product portfolio
- complexity of products
- complexity of organization
- process maturity

As described in Section 1, software for engine control units is developed for a highly competitive market in regard to innovation, quality, and price with additional requirements for SW sharing between the original equipment manufacturers (OEMs) and suppliers.

For an organization working in a highly competitive market with a medium or large product portfolio, a strong focus is required on product portfolio management. If the organization develops complex products within a complex (e.g., distributed) organization, a strong focus is required on process maturity.

In the case of Bosch GS, both statements apply. This leads to the demand for a high-maturity organization and the need to set up a clear product management that supports flexible reactions to changing market requirements.

Being aware of these needs, GS set up an improvement program consisting of two major steps:

1. CMM(I) ([1, 2]) to improve the organization's process maturity
2. PLA [3] to address SW architecture and product portfolio management

Comparing the two models on an abstract level, CMMI focuses on the process aspects, whereas the PLA model focuses on product and process. The improvement strategy can set its initial focus on either product or process excellence. As process excellence is the basis for successfully introducing a product line, CMMI was prioritized to be the major process improvement program. The PLA activities concentrated on the technical product definition and development issues. Nevertheless, it was necessary to coordinate overlapping improvement activities. In contrast to the CMMI program, it was not intended to cover all the PLA practice areas. The PLA was used as a framework and guideline but not as an assessment-relevant model. Figure 8 shows the time schedule and the main milestones of the two improvement activities.

The existing process infrastructure based on the CMM program was an important prerequisite to institutionalize the PLA. The most important elements were

1. the improvement team for the technical development process (Team Leader: senior manager of the software department and initiator of the PLA project)

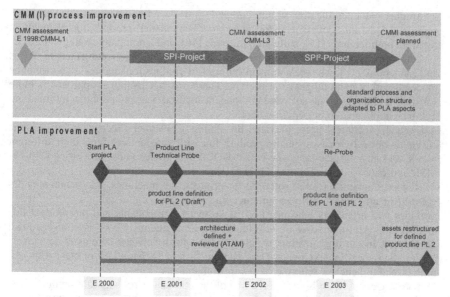

Fig. 8. Time schedule for the CMM(I) and PLA improvement activities

2. definition of process owners (department managers) and process representatives for the new process steps
3. documentation of the new process steps in the development handbook of the software and calibration departments, accessible via intranet
4. adaptation of existing role definitions and definition of new roles, where necessary
5. definition of control boards for product line and architecture issues

The experience with the two coexisting improvement initiatives over the past three year confirms the decision to put the initial emphasis on CMMI [6], because the PLA requires a stable, high-maturity process organization to be effective.

4   Related Work

There are several published software product line experience reports. The SEI offers a collection of technical reports on its Web site [13], and three in-depth case studies have been published [3]. The most comparable of these case studies is with Cummings Inc for a product line of engine software [3, Ch. 9; 14]. Though this case covers "our" domain, the company environment is quite different. Cummings had a very diverse and project-specific development environment. The company launched its product line effort in a bold way by stopping all ongoing projects. Bosch GS already had a strong reuse culture, many standard tools, and homogeneous processes across the organization even before the PLA initiative. The strategy was and still is evolutionary, cautious, and risk conscious.

Another car manufacturer supply company introduced software product line concepts but does not declare its effort as such: ZF published product line elements in software architectures [15], software processes [16], and a company strategy [17].

Comparing our experience with Lucent Telecommunication published in Weiss and Lai's book [18], we face a domain (physics of combustion engines) that cannot be modeled with a meta-language at present. Therefore, our technical approach is more software architecture and software component focused. Lucent's approach turned out not to be applicable in our environment.

From the technical point of view, the Philips Consumer Electronics [19] case is closer to ours. It focuses on the product line software architecture, their different views, and an interface language called KOLA that shares some properties with our MSR approach.

Hewlett Packard's (HP's) software for printers, fax machines, and scanners is developed in an "agile" software product line [20]. The organizational setting at HP provides two architects who monitor the software components and the product line architecture. All other software developers are simultaneously core asset and product developers. In our organization, we clearly distinguish between core asset developers and product-specific developers. Our experience showed that a lack of clear responsibilities lead to "unclear reusable" software components.

Today, Celsius Tech is considered one of the innovators for software product lines. In the published case study [21], the product line for a ship command-and-control system is described. Jan Bosch relates—like we do—product lines strongly to architecture in his case studies [22].

Introducing and adopting the PLA with respect to market, organization, business units, and the individual are covered in Bühne and associates' paper [23]—findings we can strongly confirm.

Bosch's Research early case studies were for a dashboard system [24] and for car periphery systems [25]. The goal of these studies was to evaluate appropriate processes, methods, and required artifacts for the Bosch automotive domain [26]. Another Bosch product line is part of a state-of-practice analysis [27].

More details about our work described here is available for the software architecture [4], the open software architecture mechanisms [5], and the variability analysis and management of requirements [7, 12].

Though we can observe several similarities in experience, methods, work products, and processes with other organizations, there was the need to select and tailor each specific asset for our own purpose or even to invent new ones. This is because PLA is driven strongly by our business and the technical domain.

5 Conclusion

In the last years, the approach of Bosch GS for developing software for engine control units was based on a very powerful platform development. To meet the market requirements regarding quality and costs, as well as to master the increasing product complexity, the PLA offers a good framework to further improve product and process excellence.

The main steps to adopting the PLA for us are scoping, architecture definition, and an evolutionary redesign of the existing assets. As a consequence, scoping has become a part of the product portfolio strategy and is used as a basic input for marketing, platform development, and product development. The SW architecture considers all important qualities of the engine control domain like encapsulation, software sharing, and reuse. This qualifies the architecture as a good basis for standardization. The product line definition and the architecture are essential inputs for the redesign of the existing SW components.

The process organization (set up in the CMM[I] program at Bosch GS), with clear responsibilities for the different process steps in the development process, supports the introduction of the new process elements and the systematic and effective development and maintenance of the software assets. The evaluation and adoption of the PLA were suitably supported by management in each phase. Additionally, early and continuous communication of the concepts was a major success factor for acceptance on the middle management and developer levels.

Standardizing SW architecture and supporting systematic SW sharing without jeopardizing other qualities will remain a challenge in the next years. The lack of (commercial) tools for many activities is a major risk for achieving the intended benefits and acceptance within the organization. Nevertheless, the PLA addresses product relevant issues that, in addition to CMM process improvement, are essential for our success in a highly competitive market.

6 Abbreviations

ATAM	Architecture Tradeoff Analysis Method
AUTOSAR	Automotive open system architecture
CMM	Capability Maturity Model
CMMI	Capability Maturity Model Integration
DI	Direct injection
ECU	Engine Control Unit
EDC	Electronic Diesel Control
GS	Gasoline Systems
HW	Hardware
ME(D)	Motronic with E-Gas and direct injection
MSR	Manufacturer Supplier Relationship
OEM	Original equipment manufacturer
PLA	Product line approach
PLTP	Product Line Technical Probe
SW	Software

References

1. M. Paulk, C. Weber, B. Curtis, M. Chrissis, *The Capability Maturity Model: Guidelines for Improving the Software Process*, Addison-Wesley, 1994
2. M. Chrissis, M. Konrad, S. Shrum, CMMI – Guidelines for Process Integration and Product Improvement, Addison-Wesley, 2003

3. P. Clements, L. Northrop. *Software Product Lines: Practices and Patterns*. SEI Series in Software Engineering. Addison-Wesley, Reading, MA, 2001
4. C. Hammel, H. Jessen, B. Boss, A. Traub, C. Tischer, H. Hönninger. *A Common Software Architecture for Diesel and Gasoline Engine Control Systems of the New Generation EDC/ME(D)17*, 2003 SAE World Congress, Detroit, Michigan, March 3-6, 2003
5. C. Tischer, C. Hammel, B. Weichel, S. Ferber. *Open Software Systems based on the EDC/ME(D)17 architecture*. 11. Internationaler Kongress Elektronik im Kraftfahrzeug (VDI), Baden-Baden, September 25-26, 2003.
6. M. Glaser, W. Grimm, A. Schneider, W.Stolz, H. Hönninger, H.-J. Kugler, P. Kirwan. *Success factors for software processes at Bosch Gasoline Systems GS*. 11. Internationaler Kongress Elektronik im Kraftfahrzeug (VDI), Baden-Baden, September 25-26, 2003.
7. Feature Interaction and Dependencies: *Modeling Features for Re-engineering a Legacy Product Line*. S. Ferber, J. Haag, J. Savolainen. 2nd Software Product Line Conference (SPLCII), San Diego, 2002
8. Internet MSR committee http://www.msr-wg.de/.
9. Internet Product Line Initiative. SEI. http://www.sei.cmu.edu/plp/plp_init.html
10. B. Weichel, *Strategies for implementing SGML/XML as a glue layer in engineering process*. SGML/XML Europe 1998. http://www.msr-wg.de/reports.html
11. B. Weichel, *A backbone in automotive software development based on XML and ASAM/MSR*. 2004 SAE World Congress, Detroit, Michigan, March 8-11, 2004
12. M. Küsell, B. Mencher, M. Steger, K.-J. Wald, *Requirements oriented system design for engine control systems*, 4th Symposium Powertrain Control Systems for Motor Vehicles, October 23-24. 2003. Berlin
13. Software Engineering Institute Internet Site http://www.sei.cmu.edu
14. James C. Dager: *Cummins' Experience in Developing a Software Product Line Architecture for Real-time Embedded Diesel Engine Controls,* in Patrick Donohoe (ed.) Proceedings of the First Software Product Line Conference, August, 2000, pp. 2345, Kluwer Academic Publishers
15. M. Wolff, U. Gillich, E. Bosch, W.-D. Gruhle, and J. Knoblach: *Softwareplattform und standardisierte Schnittstellen: Voraussetzungen für ReUse, Qualität und verteilte Systeme*, in 11. Internationaler Kongress Elektronik im Kraftfahrzeug, Baden-Baden, 25.-26. September 2003, VDI Berichte 1789, pp. 941-955, VDI Verlag, Düsseldorf, 2003
16. P. Feulner, M. Sieger, and F. König, *Workflow-Management in der Software-Entwicklung Effizienzsteigerung durch Wiederverwendung von Prozessen*, in 11. Internationaler Kongress Elektronik im Kraftfahrzeug, Baden-Baden, 25.-26. September 2003, VDI Berichte 1789, pp. 109-120, VDI Verlag, Düsseldorf, 2003
17. W. Runge, *Keynote*, 10. Internationaler Kongress Elektronik im Kraftfahrzeug, Baden-Baden, 27. September 2001, VDI-Gesellschaft Fahrzeug- und Verkehrstechnik (VDI FVT)
18. Weiss, D. and Lai, R.: *Software Product-Line Engineering - A Family-Based Software Development Process*, Addison-Wesley, 1999
19. Rob van Ommering and Jan Bosch: *Widening the Scope of Software Product Lines -- From Variation to Composition*, in Gary Chastek (ed.) Software Product Lines: Second International Conference SPLC2, San Diego, CA, August, 2000, Lecture Notes in Computer Science, vol LNCS 2379, pp.328-347
20. Peter Toft, Derek Coleman, and Joni Ohta: *A Cooperative Model for Cross-Divisional Product Development for a Software Product Line*, in Patrick Donohoe (ed.), Software Product Lines - Experience and Research Directions, pp. 111-132, Kluwer Academic Publishers, Boston, 2000
21. L. Brownsword, P. Clements: *A Case Study in Successful Product Line Development*, Software Engineering Institute, Carnegie Mellon University, Technical Report CMU/SEI-96-TR-016, 1996
22. Jan Bosch: *Design & Use of Software Architectures: Adopting and evolving a product-line approach*, Addison-Wesley, 2000

23. Stan Bühne, Gary Chastek, Timo Käkölä, Peter Knauber, Linda Northrop, Steffen Thiel: *Exploring the context of product line adoption in 5th International Product Family Engineering Workshop (PFE-5)*, Siena, Italy, November, 2003

24. Steffen Thiel and Fabio Peruzzi: *Starting a Product Line Approach for an Envisioned Market: Research and Experience in an Industrial Environment,* in Patrick Donohoe (ed.), Software Product Lines - Experience and Research Directions, pp. 495-512, Kluwer Academic Publishers, Boston, 2000

25. Steffen Thiel, Stefan Ferber, Thomas Fischer, Andreas Hein, Michael Schlick: *A Case Study in Applying a Product Line Approach for Car Periphery Supervision Systems,* In-Vehicle Software 2001, SAE 2001 World Congress, March 5-8, 2001, Cobo Center, Detroit, Michigan, vol SP-1587, 2001-01-0025, pp 43-55, Society of Automotive Engineers (SAE), Warrendale, PA, 2001

26. Steffen Thiel, Andreas Hein: *Modeling and Using Product Line Variability in Automotive Systems,* IEEE Software, 19(4), July/August, pp. 66-72, 2002

27. Andreas Birk, Gerald Heller, Isabel John, Klaus Schmid, Thomas von der Maßen and Klaus Müller: *Product Line Engineering: The state of the practice,* IEEE Software, 20(6), pp. 52-60, November/December 2003

28. Internet AUTOSAR http://www.autosar.org

Four Mechanisms for Adaptable Systems
A Meta-level Approach to Building a Software Product Line

Claudia Fritsch[1] and Burkhardt Renz[2]

[1] Robert Bosch GmbH, Corporate Research and Development,
P.O. Box 94 03 50, D-60461 Frankfurt, Germany
Claudia.Fritsch@de.bosch.com
[2] University of Applied Sciences Gießen-Friedberg, Department MNI,
Wiesenstr. 14, D-35390 Gießen, Germany
Burkhardt.Renz@mni.fh-giessen.de

Abstract. For more than ten years we have developed and maintained a software product line of legal expert systems. They share certain functionality, such as interaction with the user by means of a graphical interface, capturing data, storing information in a database, and printing documents. They differ mainly in two points: Domain descriptions and technical infrastructure.

When we designed the architecture for this software product line, we focused on two requirements in particular: Domain experts should be involved in development, but should not have to learn a general-purpose programming language. Changes in domain descriptions should leave technical code untouched – and vice versa.

Using a *meta-level architecture* we achieved a sound decoupling: Domain descriptions are kept in the meta level. Appropriate engines included in the base level act according to these descriptions.

We present the four meta-level *mechanisms* which we have developed for the design of this software product line. They separate domain descriptions from technical code in the following areas: data reference and access, input and output control, application and domain logic, and user command control.

Introduction

The software product line we are talking about is made by a German publishing house specialized in international civil law and law of civil status. The following is an account of the software developed at this company over a 10 year period. Today, the company continues successfully to develop this product line.

Chapter 1 introduces the product line, chapter 2 explains the architecture, chapters 3 – 6 contain the four mechanisms, and chapter 7 gives a résumé.

R.L. Nord (Ed.): SPLC 2004, LNCS 3154, pp. 51–72, 2004.
© Springer-Verlag Berlin Heidelberg 2004

1   A Product Line of Legal Expert Systems

The products in this software product line are made for registrars and similar offices. The product line covers the German and Austrian market. Variants reflect national and regional legislation and practice.

The software processes *legal events,* such as the registration of births or marriages. Inputs for each legal event are *personal data* which are processed according to complex legal rules. Output of each is a set of *documents.* Customers demand software guaranteed to be legally correct, i.e., observing the Law on Personal Status ([15]).

1.1   Scope

German and Austrian law of civil status have the same structure (as distinct from the Anglo-Saxon juridical system) but differ in many details. Austrian registrars additionally administer citizenship – an event which does not belong to the duty of German registrars. In Germany, Land law (state law) adds specific rules to federal law. This demands variants of the software. The government has assigned special tasks to some registry offices, requiring more variants. While these variations result from differences in the domain, other reasons for variability stem from technology.

The products have to support different technologies demanded by the customers. Registry offices are equipped with different hard- and software: Some have networks, others do not. Some use relational database management systems such as Oracle or MS SQL Server, others ask for a low-cost (or even no-cost) database. We call combinations of these technologies *platforms.* The use of these different platforms has consequences for the software. Nevertheless, the software has to offer the same, required functionality on each platform.

Some products in this product line have been on the market for more than ten years. Technology has been changing, accordingly the software has been subject to change. Customers follow the technology change. While some of them do it fast, the financial situation of others does not allow up-to-date technology. E.g., the switch to 32-Bit-Windows spread over more than 5 years. This is another reason why the product line has to support different platforms at the same time. The products' life cycles overlap.

Changes in the domain are initiated by changes of the law – or development of society reflected in law. They occur independently of changes in technology. Technical changes and domain-specific changes have to be made at the same time, but without interference.

1.2   Basic Product for German Registrars

To illustrate the characteristics of the domain we give an overview of the product for German registrars:

A German registry office is divided into 5 *departments.* The work in each department is divided into 4 – 12 *categories.* Examples of departments are births, deaths, and marriages. Examples of categories in the birth department are registration of a birth, legitimation of a child, and adoption. Altogether there are about 35 categories. In each category, *legal events* are processed. An example of a legal event is the registration of the birth of one child.

A legal event may come in many *varieties*, depending on the family background and number of people involved. The varieties of the events rank from simple standard to highly complex involving international law. So, even within the same category, the amount of data required for one legal event differs.

While many legal events are processed completely within an hour, others take weeks to be finalized. For example, the registrar may enter the data of a marriage up to 6 months in advance.

When a legal event has been processed, the output is a set of documents. *Forms*, required by law, must be filled out. Examples of documents are personal registration certificates, register entries, decrees, and notifications to other offices. The data are laid out on the documents in different combinations, even in different wording.

The output is strictly regulated by law ([14], [15]), but sometimes rules are incomplete or conflicting. These cases are left to the registrar's discretion. The software, although an expert system, must leave final decisions to the registrar.

1.3   Domain Characteristics

The following characteristics are the key results of domain analysis.

- The legal events have the following properties in common
  - a varying amount of data is required, depending on the background and number of people involved
  - the required data and the documents which have to be printed follow certain patterns, depending on circumstances such as nationality or marital status
  - a registrar may work at one legal event for a long time
  - data may be incomplete during processing
  - data may not be changed after registration
- The law of civil status
  - may change several times a year and time between proclamation and effective date is short
  - can be mapped to processing rules to a high degree, but these rules may not limit the registrar's authority
  - is incorporated in forms, certificates, and a flow of work; registrars fill out forms and domain experts "think" in forms, too
- The registrars and personnel in registry offices
  - may either be experts in the field or have basic knowledge
  - have different computer skills
  - work in about 6000 German registry offices equipped with various platforms

1.4 Requirements

From the domain characteristics we derive requirements our products have to fulfill. These requirements lead to the four mechanisms we are going to describe.

- Usability: The software should
  - capture domain expertise and map it to processing rules
  - adapt to working methods in the office (not vice versa)
  - reflect the registrars' way of thinking, the work process, and the division of labor in the offices
  - support many varieties of a legal event, depending on the current data
  - guarantee legal correctness
- Maintainability: The developers have to
  - adapt the software to changes of regulations several times a year
  - implement and test changes quickly
  - adapt the software to new technology without affecting the captured domain expertise and vice versa
- Platform independence: The software should
  - run on different operating systems
  - offer several databases
  - offer different user interfaces (GUIs)

2 Architecture

The products in our product line share a common architecture. We outline this architecture, focusing on the points which give reasons for the four mechanisms.

2.1 Architectural Decisions

1. Organize the processing of a legal event in a series of masks. Users and domain experts are used to work with *forms*. Forms guide through the processing of a legal event. The software should support this working method. Our basic decision was therefore to

- collect the data needed to process a legal event in a series of *masks* (data entry screens) that *act as a master form*
- use this data to print all documents (certificates, register entries, notifications, etc.)
- react on input immediately, guiding the user through the event.

This decision implies:

- The series of masks depends highly on the current data of the concrete event. The data affects the number and order of masks presented and the control of the input on the masks.
- The masks contain domain knowledge, both legal regulations and common practice.

With this, the domain logic and the presentation of the application (in the form of series of masks) would be coupled tightly if we implemented the masks in a general purpose language using the infrastructure of a specific GUI class library. Instead:

2. Describe masks in a domain-specific language. We designed a *domain-specific language* in which domain experts describe layout and behavior of masks, in particular

- input fields
- constraints on these fields
- control of input according to domain requirements

This language does not depend on any GUI class library, rather it yields a new level of abstraction. We regard this separating of the domain knowledge from the technical infrastructure as *decoupling by abstraction*. Masks are described without reference to a specific implementation, but are *translatable* into a representation for a certain GUI.

However, this second step in the development of the architecture has a drastic consequence: Naming data items and accessing their values have to be basic elements of the language.

3. Reference data by symbolic names. We abstract the actual storage of data to a data model where items are referenced by *symbolic names* (see mechanism #1). It turns out that this mechanism is the core of our architecture. The data items referenced by symbolic names form the *repository* that glues together

- the controlling of the masks
- the generation of documents and
- the control flow of the application

As a further result, data reference is database-independent.

These ideas lead to the following principles, which we will use over and over again:

A meta-level architecture separates domain descriptions from technical code. Prerequisite is to find the *properties* of the processing of a legal event, both the content and the workflow. These properties are not part of the code but allow us to describe the legal event at the meta level. The base level executes these domain descriptions by means of interpreters and data-controlled engines, written in general purpose languages (C, C++, Java). This permits us to move to another technology, e.g., a new database system or another operating system, without touching the expert knowledge.

Domain expertise is captured in executable descriptions. All expert knowledge is contained in *domain descriptions*, namely masks, documents, domain logic and the data model. The captured knowledge is highly complex and a most valuable core asset. Each description is in only one place. Domain descriptions are strictly separated from technical code. This allows us to embrace changes in the domain without touching code.

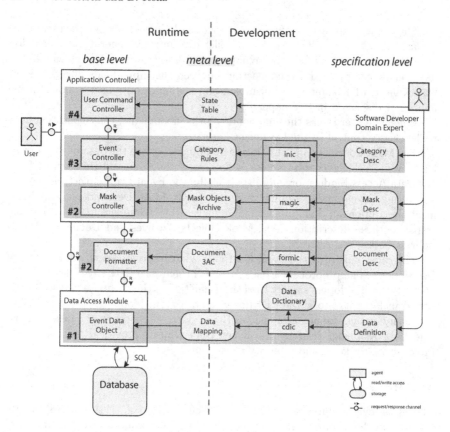

Fig. 1. Overview of the architecture (FMC notation).

2.2 Overview of the Architecture

Figure 1 shows the high level, compositional structure of our product line architecture. As notation we use Fundamental Modeling Concepts (FMC) developed by Siegfried Wendt and described in [10] and [9].

The components needed at runtime are shown on the left, development on the right. The behavior of the system is described on the *specification level*. These domain descriptions are transformed into the *meta-level* objects which control the components of the *base level* at runtime.

The Application Controller starts the application and passes control to the User Command Controller. The User Command Controller reacts to user commands invoked by the application menu according to the State Table which describes the dynamic behavior of the application. When the user chooses a category and opens a legal event for processing, the Event Controller reads from the Category Rules how to handle this legal event.

The Event Controller passes control to the Mask Controller when the user opens a mask to enter data. The Mask Controller dynamically generates presentation objects from the Mask Objects Archives and shows them on the screen. It uses data references to establish connection between the input fields and the Event Data Object. (The same mechanism is used for dialogs but neither shown in the figure nor discussed in this paper.)

When the user issues the command to print documents, the Application Controller passes control to the Document Formatter.

The Mask Controller and the Document Formatter need the data of the current legal event. Whenever data access is necessary, they demand this service from the Data Access Module, or, more specifically, the Event Data Object.

During development, domain experts specify Mask Descriptions and Document Descriptions in domain-specific languages. The compilers magic and formic translate these descriptions into Mask Objects Archives and Document Three-Address Codes, respectively.

The rules which tell the Event Controller what to do are specified in Category Descriptions. The preprocessor inic translates them into Category Rules.

Software developers specify the Data Definition of the database. The compiler cdic translates it into a Data Dictionary and a Data Mapping. Using the Data Dictionary, magic, formic, and inic verify the data references in the descriptions. The Data Mapping, read by the Event Data Object, provides information on tables, primary keys, and integrity constraints.

2.3   Remarks

The meta-level architectural pattern is discussed in, e.g., [11] and [18]. These descriptions focus on meta object-models which determine the creation and behavior of base-level objects at runtime by a reflection mechanism.

In our architecture we use four mechanisms to provide and use metadata:

- description of data based on a specific type of relational data model
- declarative and procedural domain-specific languages
- meta objects and rules given by logical expressions
- description of user command control by a specific type of statechart

Both the domain knowledge *and* its transformation into workflows should not be hard-wired into the code. We tried to find the most convenient way. The domain experts describe all layers of the application on the specification level – the data, the input and output, and the control – and these descriptions are transformed to control the base level. This solution is generic by means of mask and document generators. Their application, however, is very specific to the domain.

Interactive systems are often described by a *layer* architecture. Basically three conceptual layers are distinguished: the presentation, the domain logic, and the persistence layer, e.g., in [3].

Our architecture has layers in two dimensions, namely levels and responsibilities: in both the base level and the meta level we separate presentation, domain logic, and persistence. The most interesting aspects of the meta-level architecture with respect to layering are:

- The layers in the meta level are tightly coupled, supporting the required domain-specific dependencies. The construction of the meta level follows the way domain experts describe the processing of legal events. For this reason we avoid indirection wherever possible.
- The layers in the base level are extremely decoupled. Engines in each base-level layer interpret the meta-level descriptions at runtime. These engines do not hard-wire domain-specific logic but process the meta-level descriptions. The architecture provides access points to the layers; the engines do not depend on each other in any other way. Consequently the base-level engines can operate in different combinations in the various products of the product line.

3   Mechanism #1: Data Reference and Access by Symbolic Names

References to data items are needed in the meta level to specify data input, document contents, and workflow. We want to reference and access data items by names. We want to ignore where data is stored, and how:

3.1   Solution

Within an event, a symbolic name uniquely identifies a data item. The symbolic name determines the access path to the data in the database. At runtime, a dynamic data object serves as a container for this data and is responsible for its persistence.

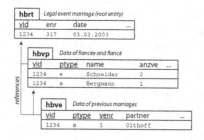

Fig. 2. A part of the data model illustrating the principle of relationships.

Data model. In order to define a naming convention for data items we need a convenient data model. In our application each legal event is assigned a unique *root entity* whose primary key is called **Event Identifier** (**vid**). We can then organize the event data in entities so that each entity has a 1:1 relationship or a cascading 1:n relationship to the root entity. Each entity type has a *compound primary key* whose first item references the **vid**.

Figure 2 shows the principle in an example: Root table **hbrt** contains one row for the marriage identified by **vid** 1234. In table **hbvp** there is one row for fiancé, Schneider and one row for fiancée

Bergmann, distinguished by ptype e and s, respectively. anzve holds the number of previous marriages. Mrs. Bergmann, now divorced, was previously married to Mr. Olthoff, while Mr. Schneider is unmarried. So table hbve has one entry. This row is linked to hbrt by the vid and to hbvp by the vid and ptype s.[1]

Data reference. A *symbolic name* consists of the *row identifier*, i.e., the name of the entity type and the key information, and the *field identifier*, i.e., the name of the attribute. A dot separates row identifier and field identifier. Using the example of figure 2, the symbolic name
hbve[s][1].partner
references Olthoff, name of the previous spouse of Mrs. Bergmann. It corresponds conceptually to the SQL statement
select partner from hbve where vid=? and ptype='s' and venr=1

Data access. The data of one legal event is encapsulated in an Event Data Object (edo). Assisted by the Data Mapping, edo translates the symbolic name into a data access path. To continue with our example, edo reads in the Data Mapping that the compound primary key of hbve is composed of the attributes vid, ptype, and venr. The vid is the identifying attribute of the edo. So edo has all necessary key information to access the data of hbve[s][1].partner.

The edo holds the data of an event in memory. It offers two strategies:

- Load all data rows identified by the same vid. This gives a full in-memory copy of the data belonging to this legal event.
- Load only those data rows requested by the application (lazy load). At each request edo checks if the requested data is already in memory, i.e., contained in the current edo.

Which strategy we choose depends on the infrastructure. It is even possible to mix both strategies, i.e., load the core data on creation of the edo, and load remaining data as requested by the application.

Concurrency control. The data values in the Event Data Object i.e., in memory, have to be synchronized to the database. The Event Data Object intercepts all database access and keeps a log of the state of the data in memory. Therefore, the Event Data Object has to perform long duration transactions [16].

As databases do not support long transactions, the Data Access Module uses a check-out/check-in mechanism. On creation of an edo the current user is recorded in the corresponding root entity, and access of other users is denied.[2]

3.2   Implementation

Figure 3 shows the implementation of edo: The class Event Data Object (edo) is a container of Row Data Objects (rdos). Each object of class edo is uniquely

---

[1] Please don't be troubled by cryptic abbreviations such as hbvp. They are reasonable abbreviations for Germans. Our domain experts love them.

[2] This is in no way a restriction. It meets the working procedure in the offices.

identified by the vid given on construction of the edo. edo's methods to retrieve and store the values in the database delegate this responsibility to the rdos, edo's components.

Each object of class Row Data Object stores one row of data. It has an attribute rdoName whose value is the row identifier. An rdoName is unique within the rdos contained in one edo.

Each rdo consists of a Row Data Buffer and a list of Field Descriptors. The Row Data Buffer stores the data. It is allocated dynamically at runtime. It is structured by the Field Descriptors. Each Field Descriptor contains the meta information of the corresponding database field: name, type, and length. This meta information is retrieved from the system catalog of the database at runtime. The Field Descriptor is used to make all necessary type conversions and to inform the application about the type of a data item in the database.

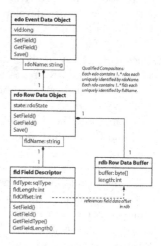

Fig. 3. Code structure of the Event Data Object (UML notation).

The rdo keeps track of its *state* with respect to the database in its attribute rdoState. The state of an rdo is characterized by the statechart in figure 4.

When created, the rdo is initialized from the database. If the corresponding row exists in the database, the data are loaded and the state of the object is PERSISTENT. Otherwise, it is TRANSIENT.

The methods of the rdo manipulate the data in the Row Data Buffer and change the state of the rdo accordingly. The methods SetField() and Save() change the state of the rdo to ensure the correspondence to the state of the data in the database.

The method Save() chooses the appropriate action on the database according to the state of the rdo. In

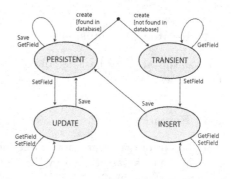

Fig. 4. Data Persistency and Synchronization (UML statechart notation).

state UPDATE Save() performs an update of the data row. In state INSERT it inserts a new row in the table. The primary key of the new row is given by the rdoName. In state PERSISTENT or TRANSIENT, nothing needs to be done.

3.3 Discussion

Data model and data reference are *simple:* The data model consists of 1:1 and 1:n relationships only. It is mapped directly to the data definition of relational databases. Software developers and domain experts can easily keep both the data model and data reference in mind.

Data reference is *database system independent* and *programming language independent:* The symbolic name is a character string. It introduces an indirection between the data reference and data access. Data reference assigns a meaning to a database field – it establishes the necessary coupling in the meta level. The symbolic name may be translated to any database access technique.

Changes in the data definition affect the users of the data (Mask Descriptions and Document Descriptions), while the data access mechanism remains unchanged.

Data access is *generic and dynamic:* edo provides a data access mechanism and a data container. But edo does not know which data to access. This information is contained only in the meta level: the symbolic names. edo resolves symbolic names at runtime.

Data access is *portable:* We had few problems with incompatibilities of SQL-databases, because we only use a small subset of SQL. We were even able to implement this SQL subset on a navigating database. A simple data model has led to database system independence.

The basic idea of the Event Data Object can easily be extended to a check-out/check-in mechanism with a more sophisticated data mapping and naming convention. An option is to use an XML data model and a subset of XPath as naming convention to identify individual data items or even groups of them.

3.4 Related Mechanisms

Mechanism #1 is the basis for the other three mechanisms. They use the symbolic names.

3.5 Remarks

The concept of the Event Data Object and the use of a statechart to control the state of the rdos was inspired by [12, Chap. 20].

The patterns in [3, Chap. 11 and 13] are closely related to our approach: the Unit of Work, Metadata Mapping, and Repository patterns share concepts with the Event Data Object. However, we use the Event Data Object to store and retrieve data values whose access paths are given *dynamically* – by symbolic names, in fact. So the Event Data Object is more restricted in terms of the data model, but within that more generic.

The disconnected data set of ADO.NET (see e.g. [17]) has many similarities to the Event Data Object. We already mentioned that an XPath-based naming convention could be used instead of ours.

4   Mechanism #2: Input and Output Control by Domain-Specific Descriptions

The data necessary to process a legal event is collected in a series of masks. The Mask Controller reacts on input immediately and guides the user through the event depending on the specific situation.

The data is then used to print all required documents. Usually, one event results in 5 – 20 documents, each comprising 1 – 4 pages.

4.1   Solution

For each event, platform-independent mask and document descriptions define which data is entered and how forms are filled out. They are written in domain-specific languages. At runtime, the compiled descriptions control the layout and behavior of masks and the content and formatting of documents.

Mask and document descriptions are written in languages which we designed according to the needs of the domain. Certain *functions* of the languages provide the domain-specific features, notably

- properties of fields on masks and documents
- processing of input
- formatting of output

We continue describing solution and implementation for masks and documents separately.

4.2   Masks

Concept. A Mask Description defines static structure and dynamic behavior:

- The layout of the mask is defined by placing labels and input fields according to a column raster[3]
- Each input field is assigned the symbolic name of the data item which stores the input
- Input is assisted in certain fields by domain-specific functions, such as date functions, auto-completion, and calculations
- Actions are triggered by user interaction events (enter or quit the mask, enter or quit a field, enter a certain character in a field). Actions are domain-specific and may depend on parameters, data in input fields, or data of the current event
  - (pre-)fill fields with data
  - disable/enable fields
  - check logical state of input

---

[3] A template defining the layout of the masks was developed by a UI designer.

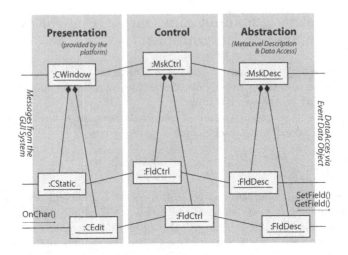

Fig. 5. The PAC architecture of the **Mask Controller**, exemplified with MFC (UML notation).

Implementation. The compiler **magic** translates the platform-independent **Mask Descriptions** into the platform-dependent **Mask Objects Archives**. E.g., for MS Windows these are serialized C++ objects. At runtime, the **Mask Controller** uses the **Mask Objects Archives** to control the mask.

The **Mask Controller** shown in figure 5 is designed according to the Presentation Abstraction Control (PAC) architecture ([11]). The Presentation manages the screen, intercepts arriving messages, and routes these to the Control. The Abstraction maintains the data via the **Event Data Object**. Moreover, the Abstraction keeps all meta-level information to provide the intelligence needed to handle user interactions which require executing functions, disabling fields, and so on. The Control – the mediator between Presentation and Abstraction – recognizes the input, asks the Abstraction what to do, executes the appropriate functions, passes the result back to the Presentation, and returns control to the operating system. This behavior is not hard-wired into the code but determined by the meta-level information contained in the Abstraction.

4.3   Documents

Concept. A Document Description defines layout and content:

- A set of fields defines the layout of the document. Each field is defined by a composition of rectangles, namely their positions on the document, length, and height.
- A set of formatting rules defines the properties of each field. A field may have several of about 20 properties, notably

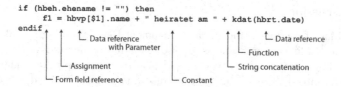

```
if (hbeh.ehename != "") then
    f1 = hbvp[$1].name + " heiratet am " + kdat(hbrt.date)
endif
```

Fig. 6. An example Document Description.

- generic properties, e.g., flush left/right
- domain-specific properties, e.g., the number of in-between lines
- Assignments define the content of each field.
    - A field may contain static text or data items or any composition of these.
    - The filling of fields may depend on parameters or on any data of the current event. The language provides if-then-else and switch-case for that.

For all this the language provides about 60 functions, implemented in the host language. Figure 6 gives an idea of the language.

Implementation. The compiler formic translates a Document Description into platform-independent Document Three-Address Code (see figure 1). One instruction consists of a destination, two operands, and an operator.

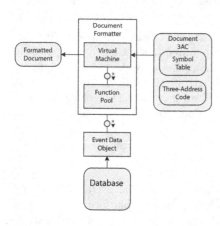

Fig. 7. Compositional structure of the Document Formatter.

At runtime, the Document Formatter composes a document from the Document Three-Address Code and the data provided by the Event Data Object (figure 7). First the Document Formatter loads the Three-Address Code and the Symbol Table into memory. With the help of the edo it replaces all data references in the Symbol Table with the current data values. Then the Virtual Machine processes the Three-Address Code. Using the Function Pool it computes the content of each field and stores it in its destination in the Symbol Table. After that, the Symbol Table contains all information necessary to produce the document, i.e., field contents and properties. Finally the Document Formatter traverses the Symbol Table and produces a virtual document in memory. The result is a completely processed, printable document.

4.4   Discussion

In each Mask Description and in each Document Description highly valuable domain expertise is captured and is readable, maintainable, and available for developers. Each description serves as specification, code, and documentation. It is also guaranteed to be up-to-date, because this domain knowledge is captured in no other place.

Mask Descriptions and Document Descriptions inherently expose a high degree of correctness, because the languages guarantee consistency and prevent programming errors. Testing is reduced to a black-box test of functionality.

Configuration management of masks and documents works ideally because each item is contained in one file, and the files have ASCII format.

"Coding" of masks and documents comes close to specifying because the languages are declarative. They are procedural only where necessary.

4.5   Related Mechanisms

Mechanism #1. Masks and documents rely on data reference and access provided by the Event Data Object (edo). Masks and documents only work properly if the data references they use correspond to database fields.

Masks and documents can be parameterized. For example, the same Mask Description can collect similar data for different people if a key attribute, such as ptype, is parameter. Likewise, the same Document Description is used for different people or different recipients.

Mechanism #3. Depending on the specific situation, the Event Controller determines which masks to present for input and which documents to offer as output.

Mechanism #4. The Mask Controller is part of a Chain of Responsibility ([4]): Messages resulting from user interaction are routed to the Control component of the Mask Controller. If the required reaction involves only the current input field, it is handled by the Field Controler (FldCtrl); if several fields are involved the Mask Controler (MskCtrl) is responsible; if another mask is involved the Event Controller comes into play. Finally the User Command Controller is the top level of this chain.

4.6   Remarks

We use the Presentation Abstraction Control architectural pattern [11] for the design of the user interface. The dependencies on the platform are encapsulated in the Presentation component. Abstraction and Control are platform-independent.

The concepts used for the design of the Document Three-Address Code and the implementation of formic come from [1] and [6].

Both compilers, magic and formic, are made with lex&yacc. Subroutines in formic are implemented with the m4 macro processor.

5   Mechanism #3: Application and Domain Logic by a Rule Engine

The handling of a legal event is organized as a workflow: it leads the user through a series of masks. It results – after a juridical check – in printing several documents. The order of the masks and the selection of the documents depends on the specific situation, i.e., on personal data.

While the structure of the workflow is common to all categories of legal events, the concrete series of masks and documents within a category is domain knowledge. As such, it would be inappropriate to program the workflow in technical code. Instead, we continue to keep the domain knowledge in the meta level.

5.1   Solution

The workflow is controlled by properties. The properties describe the series of masks and documents and the conditions on which masks should be presented and documents should be printed. These domain-specific properties are described in the meta level. At runtime, a rule engine controls the workflow using these descriptions.

Each mask or document has the following properties: A name, parameters which are substituted on invocation, and conditions which restrict its use depending on the current data of a legal event.

The complete workflow of a category of legal events consists of a list of all possible masks and documents and the conditions.[4]

The conditions – logical expressions – are the heart of the application and domain logic. All constraints are grouped in classes of conditions. Each class comprises all permissible states of interdependent data items. This is called a *logical class* and the *logical state* within a class. Each condition can be referenced by its logical class and logical state. To give an example: In processing a marriage, the logical class "marital status" permits the logical states "single" or "divorced, number of previous marriages > 0", whereas "married" is not allowed. The logical expressions for the fiancée are

```
hbvp[s].famstand=="ledig" && hbvp[s].anzve==0
hbvp[s].famstand=="geschieden" && hbvp[s].anzve>0 
```
[5]

---

[4] Some masks or documents are *repeated* several times. The number of repetitions depends on the current data, e.g., the number of children. Our descriptions allow to specify repetition, but we omit the details in this paper.

[5] famstand = marital status, ledig = single, anzve = number of previous marriages, geschieden = divorced

5.2 Implementation

A Category Description contains the properties of a category, i.e., the series of masks and documents and the conditions. Category Descriptions are files in ASCII format, structured by *sections* and *tags*.[6]

The preprocessor inic translates a Category Description into a Category Rules file. First, inic checks the syntax of data references against the Data Dictionary (see figure 1) to guarantee the correctness of all data references. Then inic transforms the conditions into Reverse-Polish Notation. This simplifies and speeds up evaluation of the expressions at runtime.

At runtime, the Event Controller starts the processing of a legal event by transforming the Category Rules into runtime objects. During input, the rule engine evaluates the conditions to control the behavior of the workflow.

5.3 Discussion

Using the concept of logical classes and states we initially intended to reach a more declarative way of describing the domain logic than we finally did. International civil law brings up a complexity which is hard to capture in a comprehensive set of logical expressions. Domain experts often prefer to design the processing of the legal event in terms of controlling the input on the masks. Many regulations of the domain are formulated in this manner ([14]).

5.4 Related Mechanisms

Mechanism #1. Category Descriptions reference data items by their symbolic name. The rule engine uses the edo to resolve these references and to access the values of the data items.

Mechanism #2. The Event Controller uses the rule engine to determine the series of masks and documents and gives control to the Mask Controller and the Document Formatter. In particular, it provides the parameters and the reference to the edo for the processing of masks and documents.

The Mask Descriptions refer to the Category Rules, which describe the integrity conditions of input values. At runtime the Mask Controller evaluates the conditions by means of the rule engine.

6 Mechanism #4: User Command Control by a Finite State Machine

So far we have described how data is entered on masks and is used to print documents. The controlling of the application is still missing. For example, before users can work at a legal event, they choose the category from the menu and open either an existing event or set up a new one. After entering the data, they issue a printing command.

---

[6] The style of Windows ini-files. Our product line started long before XML was invented.

6.1 Solution

> *Describe top level user commands as events which trigger actions and move the application from one state to another. At runtime, a finite state machine reacts to the events by executing the actions and transitions.*[7]

Our statechart consists of sets of states, events, actions, return codes, and two types of transitions. It is a variant of the statecharts introduced by Harel in [5].

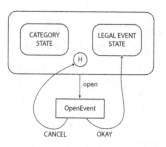

Fig. 8. Part of the user command control statechart.

In a *state* an *event* may occur. State plus event define the *action* to be executed. Each action issues a *return code*. Action plus return code define the follow-up state. Figure 8 gives an example. Both in **CATEGORY STATE** and in **LEGAL EVENT STATE** the user may **open** a legal event for processing. If the user confirms the **Open Event** dialog with **OKAY** he will arrive in **LEGAL EVENT STATE**. Otherwise he will return to the state where he came from, indicated by an **H**.

6.2 Implementation

The triggering of a menu command is routed to the **User Command Controller** whose finite state machine runs the statechart. The statechart is defined by a *state table*, a static data structure which contains the flattened statechart. At runtime, the **User Command Controller** uses this state table to control the behavior of the application. Events come from user interactions. Actions are methods of the **Application Controller**.

6.3 Discussion

Ergonomics. Modeling the control flow of a program with a statechart supports software ergonomy. The statechart maps the working procedure in the office to the control flow of the program. The result is a clear, transparent behavior of the program which users understand effortlessly. Our users have never asked questions such as "where am I?" or "how did I get here?".

It was possible to keep the statechart simple because all categories and events are processed according to the same pattern (see mechanisms #2 and #3). All of them are handled with the same actions.

Static data structure. We decided to implement the state table in a static data structure instead of a dynamic one, because statecharts rarely change in our products.

---

[7] Please do not confuse the events in the statechart with legal events.

Product Line. The description of the statechart in the meta level decouples application control from GUI infrastructure. E.g., on the MS Windows platform we redirect MFC's message map to the User Command Controller's state table.

The implementation of the finite state machine is reusable with other statecharts. E.g., the functionality of the software can be reduced by removing states and transitions from the statechart. Variant products can sometimes be obtained by providing a different state table.

6.4   Related Mechanisms

The User Command Controller is not directly connected to mechanisms #1, #2, or #3. The repository edo facilitates the use of the finite state machine: actions share data in the repository.

6.5   Remarks

There are several techniques to implement statecharts, see [13] and [7].

As shown in figure 8 our statechart is a bipartite graph where states are distinguished from actions. This notation visualizes behavior clearly and coherently. We used it long before UML came up. Nevertheless, this notation can easily be made UML conformant by using stereotypes to distinguish states from actions.

7   Conclusion

To conclude this paper, we discuss the contribution of the four mechanisms

- #1: Data Reference and Access by Symbolic Names
- #2: Input and Output Control by Domain Specific Descriptions
- #3: Application and Domain Logic by a Rule Engine
- #4: User Command Control by a Finite State Machine

to the realization of variability in the product line.

7.1   Realizing Variability of the Domain

Mechanism #1. The Event Data Object is a core asset used in all products. Each product gets a Data Definition of its own.

Mechanism #2. The domain-specific languages are core assets used for all products. They need extension for some products (e.g., Austrian registry offices need extra formatting which is not used in Germany).

Mask Controller and Document Formatter are core assets. They need adaptation if a certain function needs different implementations for a product.

Mask Descriptions and Document Descriptions are product-specific. Some descriptions can be used for more than one product.

Mechanism #3. Event Controller and inic are core assets used in all products, while Category Descriptions are product-specific.

Mechanism #4. The User Command Controller is a core asset used in all products, while the State Table is product-specific.

7.2   Realizing Variability of Technology

Mechanism #1. Different database technologies require different implementations of some parts of the Event Data Object and the Data Access Module, while data reference remains unchanged.

Mechanism #2. Changes due to technology do not affect Mask Descriptions and Document Descriptions at all.

Printing depends on printing technology, but the Document Formatter does not. (We do not go into the details here.)

The Mask Controller depends on GUI infrastructure to a high degree, so do the Mask Objects Archives and magic, which has to generate output appropriately. The mask description language depends to a certain degree on the possibilities which the platform provides. We kept both magic and the mask description language downward compatible.

Mechanism #3 is completely independent of technology.

Mechanism #4. The User Command Controller depends on the GUI. Events resulting from user interactions have to be redirected to the User Command Controller.

7.3   Applicability of these Mechanisms

Our mechanisms will suit if

- events have to be processed and follow certain patterns
- data can be modeled according to our principles
- many different masks and forms are needed
- several products are developed
- domain logic should be saved when technology changes and vice versa

7.4   Issues

If domain-specific languages are used to capture domain logic, the scope of these languages will define the capabilities of the products. This is both an advantage and a disadvantage.

The system has the advantage of being *uniform*. Both developers and users understand it easily. It's in the nature of this architecture that features of the same type behave in the same way. They appear in the meta level many times but their processing is implemented only once.

The disadvantage is that special cases, exceptions, or ad-hoc variations are impossible or only possible with more effort.

Developing this architecture and these mechanisms required not only a deep and thorough understanding of the domain but also the discovery of *patterns* in the *domain*. The mechanisms used in this architecture fit to these patterns. In particular, our data model matches the structure of the legal events. We took it as a basis to schematize the domain. "Problem analysis takes you from the level of identifying the problem to the level of making the descriptions needed to solve it" says Michael Jackson in [8].

We join domain expertise with software engineering. Domain experts directly contribute to software development: In the data references they have found a powerful, efficient means of expression. As the owners of **Mask Descriptions**, **Document Descriptions**, and **Category Descriptions** they have gained control over the domain-specific aspects of application development.

The analysis of the domain has led to languages which allow the description and specification of product behavior. Variant descriptions specify variants in the product line.

References

1. A. V. Aho, R. Sethi, and J. D. Ullman: *Compilers: Principles, Techniques, and Tools*, Addison-Wesley 1986
2. P. Clements, L. Northrop: *Software Product Lines*, Addison-Wesley 2002
3. M. Fowler: *Patterns of Enterprise Application Architecture*, Addison-Wesley 2003
4. E. Gamma, R. Helm, R. Johnson, J. Vlissides: *Design Patterns*, Addison-Wesley 1995
5. D. Harel: *Statecharts: a Visual Formalism for Complex Systems* in *Science of Computer Programming* No. 8, p. 231 – 274
6. A. I. Holub: *Compiler Design in C*, Prentice-Hall 1990
7. I. Horrocks: *Constructing the User Interface with Statecharts*, Addison-Wesley 1999
8. M. Jackson: *Problem Frames – Analyzing and structuring software development problems* Addison-Wesley 2001
9. F. Keller et al.: *Improving Knowledge Transfer at the Architectural Level: Concepts and Notations* in *Proceedings of the 2002 International Conference on Software Engineering Research and Practice* Las Vegas 2002
10. A. Knö'pfel: *FMC Quick Introduction*, Hasso Plattner Institute for Software Systems Engineering, Potsdam, Germany, 2003 <http://fmc.hpi.uni-potsdam.de>
11. F. Buschmann, R. Meunier, H. Rohnert, P. Sommerlad, M. Stal: *Pattern-Oriented Software Architecture*, John Wiley & Sons 1996
12. J. Rumbaugh, M. Blaha, W. Premerlani, F. Eddy, W. Lorensen: *Object-oriented Modeling and Design*, Prentice-Hall 1991
13. M. Samek: *Practical Statecharts in C/C++*, CMP Books 2002
14. H. Schmitz, H. Bornhofen (editors): *Dienstanweisung für die deutschen Standesbeamten und ihre Aufsichtsbehörden* 2. Auflage, Verlag für Standesamtswesen 2001
15. H. Schmitz, H. Bornhofen (editors): *Personenstandsgesetz* 10. Auflage, Verlag für Standesamtswesen 2003
16. A. Silberschatz, H. F. Korth, S. Sudarshan: *Database System Concepts* 4th edition, McGraw-Hill 2002

17. T. Thai, H. Q. Lam: *.NET Framework Essentials: Introducing the .NET Framework*, O'Reilly 2001
18. J. W. Yoder, R. Johnson: *The Adaptive Object-Model Architectural Style* in *Proceedings of the Working IEEE/IFIP Conference on Software Architecture* 2002 <http://www.joeyoder.com/papers/>

Automatic Generation of Program Families by Model Restrictions

Andrzej Wąsowski

Department of Innovation
IT University of Copenhagen
2300 Copenhagen S, Denmark
wasowski@itu.dk

Abstract. We study the generative development of control programs for families of embedded devices. A software family is described by a single common model and restriction specifications for each of the family members. The model and the specifications are used in the automatic generation of restricted programs. We describe an application of the process of modeling reactive systems with statecharts. A trace inclusion refinement relation is established for automatically generated family members, inducing a behavioral inheritance hierarchy over the generated programs.

1 Introduction

Manufacturers commonly face the problem of developing multiple versions of control programs for similar electronic devices. The programming languages employed in the development of such program families—typically assembly languages, C, and state-machine-based formalisms—poorly support code reuse and extension, while the object-oriented technology is hardly accepted in the development of resource-constrained systems, because of its size and speed overheads. As a consequence, maintaining even three versions of a simple product, such as home appliances or mobile devices, remains a troublesome task.

Generative programming [4] has been approaching the very same problem for some years now, but usually for bigger systems, focusing on highly customizable, component-based sophisticated products like cars and satellites (see an example in the work of Czarnecki and associates [3]). We shall discuss a class of program families, suitable for describing simple products and propose a suitable development strategy based on model restriction. The main assumption is that all family members can be generated from one model by means of simple transformations (restrictions). The process of restriction is driven by short terse specifications that, themselves, can be arranged in a behavioral hierarchy similar to a class hierarchy of object-oriented programming. The ultimate gain is that the production of many new family members and maintenance of the whole family become significantly cheaper than in the classical top-down approach.

The paper is structured as follows. Section 2 introduces the basic concepts. Section 3 describes the technical details of restrictions using the language of statecharts. Section 4 sketches the formal semantics, while Sections 5 and 6 introduce

R.L. Nord (Ed.): SPLC 2004, LNCS 3154, pp. 73–89, 2004.

restriction transformations and their correctness in a sense of behavioral refinement. An extension of the framework—namely support for more diverse program families—is discussed in section 7. Finally, Sections 8 and 9 discuss related work, conclusions, and future work.

2   Development by Restriction

Consider product families for which a total ordering can be introduced such that the simplest member of the family p_1 is the least element and the most advanced p_n is the greatest one:[1]

$$p_1 \preceq p_2 \preceq \ldots \preceq p_n$$

For each non-greatest element p_i, its successor p_{i+1} is a product that can be obtained solely by adding features to p_i, that is, by extension of p_i. No modifications of features already existing in p_i are allowed. The software for such a product family may be developed using incremental object-oriented programming. The simplest device p_1 is implemented first as the base class c_1. Then, additions are made, building an inheritance hierarchy with more advanced devices implemented by subclasses. Each class c_i adds new features to the implementation. The topology of the hierarchy strongly resembles the topology introduced on the product family. Since the ordering on classes in this example is total, the class hierarchy will actually be linear:

$$c_1 \leftarrow c_2 \leftarrow \ldots \leftarrow c_n.$$

This can be generalized easily to program families structured in lattices, where arbitrary hierarchies emerge.

Consider the dual of the extension relation—the reversed relation of *restriction*. One can view the ordering over the family in an alternative way: a predecessor p_{i-1} of each non-least element p_i would be obtained solely by *removal* of features from p_i. This yields a reversed implementation strategy: start with the development for the most advanced device p_n and obtain the rest by stripping parts away (see Fig. 1). This idea, although initially nonintuitive, exhibits a number of advantages attractive for the production of embedded software.

The main reason for adopting restriction as a program refinement operator is the possibility of automating the development process. The design of the greatest product and selection of restriction steps are the only necessarily manual steps. The production of restricted family members can be fully automated. This cannot possibly be achieved for program extension. An addition of a new family member in an object-oriented architecture demands at least an implementation of a new class. In the restriction approach, the generation of a new product can be done automatically, if the product is simpler than already implemented. If the

---

[1] We shall consequently use the words *least* and *greatest* only in the sense of ordering over the products and not in the sense of any physical properties.

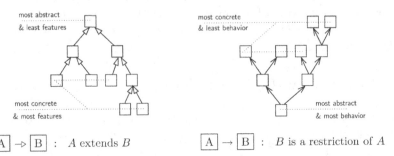

OO INHERITANCE HIERARCHY   RESTRICTION HIERARCHY

$\boxed{A} \dashrightarrow \boxed{B}$: A extends B $\boxed{A} \rightarrow \boxed{B}$: B is a restriction of A

Fig. 1. A comparison of extension and restriction hierarchies. Left: the hierarchy of classes in incremental programming. The simplest class is the root. The most able classes are leaves. Right: the hierarchy of programs in decremental programming. The most able program down with leaves being the simplified versions on top

product needs to incorporate genuinely new features, the addition is not much harder than in the object-oriented case. Automation makes prototyping new family members extremely cheap, which substantially aids business and technical decisions. A product manager can use a prototype of a new family member for the evaluation of its usability and merchantability. An engineer can use fast prototyping to select a set of features that most efficiently utilize resources of the hardware platform available for the specific version of the product.

The main arguments in favor of restrictions—efficiency and correctness—are also crucial in the development of resource-constrained embedded systems. Efficiency requirements (memory consumption mostly) still prevent the application of object-oriented programming and partial evaluation in this area. In contrast, restriction introduces neither runtime overheads nor any code growth and may be seen as an optimization pass before the code generation. Restriction addresses correctness issues, too, guaranteeing that behavioral refinement holds between related members of the family. If p_1 is a simpler derivative of p_2 ($p_1 \preceq p_2$), p_1 and p_2 behave in exactly the same way if run in the environment of p_1. Similar properties cannot be established easily for programming by extension.

We shall follow Parnas [16] in distinguishing a *product family* denoting a set of similar hardware devices and an isomorphic *program family* implementing control algorithms for these devices. In addition to that, a layer of *model families* is considered. Models are executable abstractions of programs that can be used for automatic synthesis. Members of the model family are generated from a single manually designed greatest model. The generation is driven by *restriction specifications*—a set of constraints imposed on the original model defining the expected configuration of features. Figure 2 illustrates the process for a simple example: a line of three compact disk (CD) players.

As we shall see later on, a restriction specification is a simple model (or type) of the environment in which the restricted software will be operating. It can

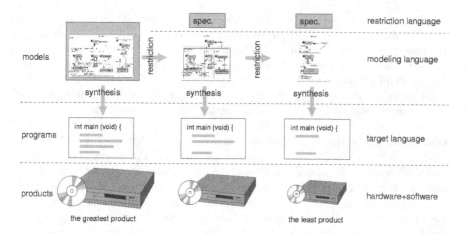

Fig. 2. Layers of development process for a simple family of three CD players. Gray shaded rectangles represent manually developed parts. Arrows represent automatically performed steps

include user behaviors, but, in most applications, it will describe the hardware in which the program will be embedded. The hardware will limit users' behaviors indirectly (i.e. the users cannot press a nonexistent button or observe an output of a nonexistent actuator).

In principle, there is no requirement that the hardware architecture is identical in all members of the product family. As long as a compiler is available for all the hardware platforms, it is still possible to support them within the same family. However, the gain is significantly higher for more homogeneous families, based on microcontrollers from the same family. In such cases, not only the control code but also the drivers for sensors and actuators can be reused. Homogeneous families are of our primary interest.

3   Restriction for the Development of Reactive Systems

Embedded appliances are often described as reactive synchronous systems [8], namely programs that continuously receive inputs and react by producing outputs. All outputs are emitted before the arrival of the subsequent input (so called *synchrony hypothesis* [1]). The inputs are environment events transmitted by sensors. The outputs are commands to influence the environment by means of connected actuators. A reactive system maintains an internal state during operation. Emission of the outputs and changes to the internal state depend solely on incoming events and the previous state of the system.

Reactive systems are conveniently described in highly imperative modeling languages with explicit control flow [6,1], usually exhibiting a close coupling of functional features and their implementations. Entities like inputs and outputs can be closely related to features they activate or perform. Let us consider a simple example of a CD player to illustrate this. The fundamental functionality of a CD player (see Fig. 3) is controlled by play and stop buttons. Additionally, the player has a built-in alarm clock that is related to the two buttons controlling the setup and the two actuators presenting the state of the alarm—a beeper and a small display indicator.

A set of inputs can be used to describe an implementation of a feature. The two events corresponding to the two buttons used to control the alarm clock define a part of the model (a *slice*) that implements the setup of the alarm clock. Removal of this slice leads to a simpler model that does not allow any control over the alarm clock. Similarly, the slice for the alarm state display and the beeper constitute the part of the model implementing the entire alarm clock feature. If the display's and the beeper's influence on the environment can be ignored, the alarm's entire implementation can be eliminated from the device without any loss. The slices defined by various inputs and outputs may overlap depending on the actual model. A sum of several slices may comprise the implementation of more sophisticated features.

3.1   Modeling Language

We shall study the implementation of restriction for the language of *statecharts* [6,15], the most popular language used in modeling discrete control. Several distinctive features of the language can be indicated on Fig. 3: nesting of states (hierarchy), explicit control-flow (transitions), and concurrency. Note that some inputs come from the environment (*Stop, Play, Next, StandBy*), and some come from the hardware itself (e.g., *EndOfTrack*). Despite this difference, all kinds of events are considered external inputs from the software's point of view.

The particular version of statecharts studied here [20,11] uses C as a host language.[2] It allows only simple integer and vector types for variables of the model, disallowing pointer arithmetic and aliasing. Transition guards follow a simple grammar:

$$guard \longrightarrow (\text{event (}"\vee"\text{ event)}^*) \; "\wedge" \text{ state (}"\wedge" \text{ state)}^*$$
$$("\wedge" \; "\neg" \text{state})^* \; ("\wedge" \; pure\text{-}C\text{-}cond)?$$

where event stands for an event identifier, state for a state identifier, and pure-C-cond for any side-effect-free arithmetic expression written in C. Transition actions are assumed to be relatively pure with respect to each other, which means that the order of transition firing is insignificant.

Statecharts incorporate model variables and external function calls. Both can be used to model communication with the external world. Unfortunately, both

---

[2] The choice of C as the host language is rather arbitrary. It has been enforced by the modeling tool IAR visualSTATE, which we use in the project. Other host languages could be used, including specification languages like Object Constraint Language (OCL). The host language does not have to be identical with the target language, but such a situation is obviously most convenient for tool developers.

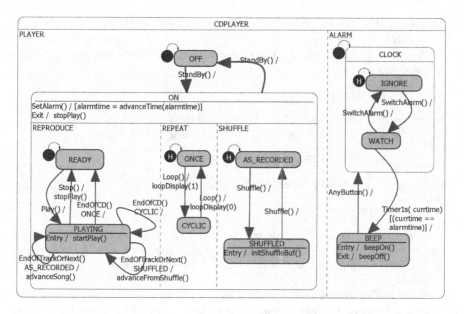

Fig. 3. A CD player modeled in IAR visualSTATE. Transitions are labeled by events, guards and outputs. Guards are optional and range over states and variables. Events *StandBy, SetAlarm, Stop, Play, Loop, Shuffle, SwitchAlarm, Next* correspond to buttons of the user interface. Events *EndOfCD, EndOfTrack* and *Timer1s* are internally produced by the hardware. *AnyButton* is in fact a disjunction of all button events. *EndOfTrackOrNext* is a disjunction of *Next* and *EndOfTrack*. Outputs are optional and preceded by slash. They correspond to driver calls: *advanceTime, stopPlay, startPlay, advanceSong, advanceFromShuffle, loopDisplay, initShuffleBuf, beepOn* and *beepOff*

can be used to model output and input as well. A variable may be bound to a hardware port representing a sensor or the command entry of an actuator. Similarly, a function call can be used to obtain values of sensors, or to control actuators. Furthermore, some variables and functions participate only in the internal computation of the model. Consequently, the syntactic categories can hardly be used to discover the meaning of a variable or a function. To remedy the confusion, we shall assume that events, variables, and functions are divided in three disjoint classes: (1) sensors (modeled by events, read-only variables, and pure functions), (2) actuators (modeled by write-only variables and non-pure functions), and (3) elements of internal logics of the model.

3.2 Restriction Language

We shall now consider restricted versions of the CD player and describe them in Restriction Language (RL), the language used to express restriction specifications. The fundamental concepts of RL are constraints on variables, functions, and events; hierarchical restrictions of interfaces; and the binding of interfaces to models in the family.

Assume that e is an event in the statechart model. Then, the meaning of an *impossibility constraint*

```
impossible e;
```

is that event e is not relevant for the restricted model and, thus, may be ignored. A version of the CD player without the shuffle feature can be specified by

```
impossible Shuffle;
```

A *purity constraint* may be written for a function f:

```
pure void f();
```

The meaning is that calls to f do not cause side effects (are not observable) and can be removed from the restricted model. The purity constraint is, thus, useful to eliminate outputs of the program in the absence of actuators connected to these outputs.

Groups of constraints are combined together in interface restrictions. A somewhat handicapped CD player with built-in alarm, but without any beeper can be described as follows:

```
restriction NoBeep {
        pure void beepOn();
        pure void beepOff();
};
```

New members of a model family are defined through the binding of model names to restrictions:

```
InterfaceName ModelName;
```

Figure 4 shows the restriction specification and the corresponding model of a CD player without any functionality related to the alarm clock.

Interface restrictions may be arranged in hierarchies by means of restriction inheritance. Any interface restriction can inherit declarations from one or more previously defined restrictions:

```
restriction Name restricts ancest₁, ..., ancestₙ
{ ... };
```

Figure 5 presents the very simplest player with no available alarm, shuffle, or looping features. Both the interface restriction and the model are obtained by further restricting the specification and the model of Figure 4. Transitions fired by Loop and Shuffle have been removed. Reachability analysis removes states CYCLIC and SHUFFLED, which allows the removal of more transitions in the REPRODUCE state. Finally, states ONCE and AS_RECORDED can be removed because they don't affect transitions or have any embedded side effects.

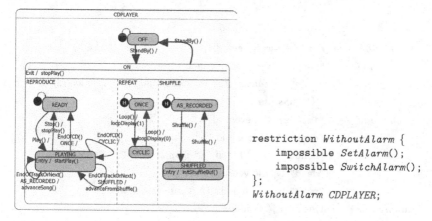

```
restriction WithoutAlarm {
    impossible SetAlarm();
    impossible SwitchAlarm();
};
WithoutAlarm CDPLAYER;
```

Fig. 4. CD player without the alarm clock: a restriction specification (right) and the corresponding model obtained by restriction (left)

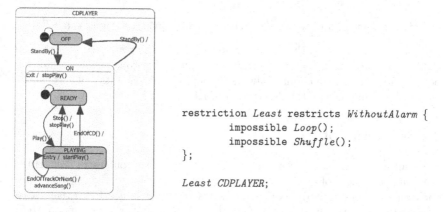

```
restriction Least restricts WithoutAlarm {
        impossible Loop();
        impossible Shuffle();
};

Least CDPLAYER;
```

Fig. 5. Simple CD player with neither the alarm clock nor the shuffle, and continuous play functions: a restriction specification and an automatically generated model

For any given variable v, one can consider a value constraint and a liveness constraint:

```
const int v = 1;   /* value constraint */
dead int v;        /* liveness constraint */
```

A value constraint substitutes a variable with a constant. A liveness constraint marks a variable as dead, which, in turn, means that assignments to that variable can be discarded. A useful application of a value constraint is to limit the value of a sensor. A liveness constraint may be used to indicate the absence of an actuator bound to the port represented by v. There is a similar value constraint for functions:

$$start \longrightarrow (restriction \mid binding)^*$$
$$binding \longrightarrow \text{restriction-id system-id ;}$$
$$restriction \longrightarrow \text{"restriction" restriction-id}$$
$$\text{("restricts" restriction-id ("," restriction-id}^*)?$$
$$\text{"\{" } constraint^* \text{ "\}" ";"}$$
$$constraint \longrightarrow \text{"impossible" event-id ";"}$$
$$\mid \text{"const" type-id var-id "=" value ";"}$$
$$\mid \text{"const" type-id fun-id "(" } param\text{-}types \text{ ")" "=" value ";"}$$
$$\mid \text{"dead" type-id var-id ";"}$$
$$\mid \text{"pure" type-id fun-id "(" } param\text{-}types \text{ ")" ";"}$$
$$param\text{-}types \longrightarrow \text{type-id ("," type-id}^*$$

Fig. 6. Grammar of RL specifications

```
const int f(int) = 4; /* value constraint for function */
```

This specification states that f always returns 4 in the restricted model. Note that it implicitly says that f is a pure function. Value constraints should only be used for sensors, which must always be pure by the semantics of statecharts.

Figure 6 summarizes the description of RL, giving its grammar.

4   Semantics of RL

We shall model the semantics of statecharts using execution traces [10]. Traces are finite sequences of events. If $e_1, \ldots, e_n$ denote events, $\langle e_1, \ldots, e_n \rangle$ is a trace consisting of their occurrences. If t is a trace and A is a set of events, $t \upharpoonright A$ denotes t after restricting it to members of A (all nonmember events are omitted). Concatenation on traces is written $s \hat{\ } t$. Finally, the inclusion of traces is defined to be

$$s \text{ in } t \equiv (\exists p, q. \ t = p \hat{\ } s \hat{\ } q)$$

Let us assume that the semantics of model m is given by a set of all its execution traces over an alphabet αm:

$$traces(m) \subseteq (\alpha m)^*$$

The alphabet includes all the input events (discrete events and readings of sensors) and all the output events (control commands for actuators) of m. Discrete events of m are represented directly as members of αm. All reads from and all writes to a variable v are visible in the trace, written $v.l$, where l is the value read or written. Calls to a function f are members of αm, too. A call to f that returns a value l is written $f.l$. Finally, all the events belonging to internal logics of the model—changes in local variables, triggering local signals, and calls to local computations—are excluded (concealed) from αm.

Our models are reactive, so they never generate actions autonomously. Formally, it means that all traces start with an input event. Each input event is followed by a possibly empty subsequence of output events.

Knowing that, we can give the semantics of restriction. First, the restriction hierarchy shall be flattened. An interface restriction A that further restricts B is equivalent to all constraints of B being included in A. The flattening is applied transitively to all interface restrictions defined in the specification. Simple consistency checks are carried out simultaneously to flattening:

i. The types of events, variables, and functions must be identical in all constraints of a given element (invariance).
ii. If there are multiple value constraints for the same variable or function, all constraint values must be identical (no contradiction).

The semantics of a flattened interface restriction r is defined with respect to a model m, which is syntactically consistent with r (m defines all the elements referred to in r with the same types as in r). We shall only give the semantics for restrictions over events and over variables and functions that describe sensors and actuators. The semantics is given as a function on sets of execution traces:

$$RL[\![\cdot]\!]_m \ : \ \mathcal{P}(traces(m)) \longrightarrow \mathcal{P}(traces(m))$$

Impossibility constraints only allow execution traces without impossible events:

$$RL[\![\text{ impossible e; }]\!]_m \ = \ \lambda S. \ \{ \ t \mid t \in S \ \wedge \ \neg(\langle e \rangle \text{ in } t) \ \}$$

The two types of constraints over sensors only allow traces with sensor reads returning the actual value of a constraint:

$$RL[\![\text{ const T v = k; }]\!]_m \ = \ \lambda S. \ \{ \ t \mid t \in S \ \wedge \ \forall \langle v.l \rangle \text{ in } t. \ l = k \ \}$$
$$RL[\![\text{ const T f() = k; }]\!]_m \ = \ \lambda S. \ \{ \ t \mid t \in S \ \wedge \ \forall \langle f.l \rangle \text{ in } t. \ l = k \ \}$$

Constraints over actuators do not remove entire traces. They remove single calls to actuators instead:

$$RL[\![\text{ dead T v; }]\!]_m \ = \ \lambda S. \ \{ \ t \upharpoonright (\alpha m \setminus \{v.l \mid \forall l \in values(T)\}) \mid t \in S \ \}$$
$$RL[\![\text{ pure T f(); }]\!]_m \ = \ \lambda S. \ \{ \ t \upharpoonright (\alpha m \setminus \{f.l \mid \forall l \in values(T)\}) \mid t \in S \ \}$$

Finally, several constraints may be combined using function composition:

$$RL[\![\ c_1 \ c_2 \ ]\!]_m \ = \ RL[\![\ c_2 \ ]\!]_m \cdot RL[\![\ c_1 \ ]\!]_m$$

The composition of constraints is commutative, since we have allowed value constraints only for sensors, and purity and liveness constraints only for actuators.

As an example, consider three extreme restriction specifications. *Universal* is an empty specification. It does not modify the original model at all:

$$\forall m. \ RL[\![\ \textit{Universal} \ ]\!]_m traces(m) = traces(m)$$

Inactive models an environment, which never generates any inputs (all inputs are **impossible**). It can be easily observed that

$$\forall m. \ RL[\![\ \textit{Inactive} \ ]\!]_m \, traces(m) = \emptyset$$

Finally, *Blind* models an environment that does not care about any outputs of the system (all outputs are **pure**):

$$\forall m. \ RL[\![\ \textit{Blind} \ ]\!]_m \, traces(m) = traces(m) \restriction (\alpha m \setminus Out_m),$$

where Out_m denotes all possible output actions of m. Note that both *Inactive* and *Blind* allow an empty model as a result of restriction over any statechart.

The semantics of RL has been given only for nonparameterized events and outputs. The parameterized events and outputs are not a problematic extension. They have been avoided in RL only for clarity of the presentation.

5   Model Transformations

Model restriction can be implemented as part of the framework for model-based development. A code generator can be divided into two parts: (1) the specializer of models and (2) the synthesizer of programs. The technique is being developed as part of the SCOPE [17] tool, which also incorporates a full C-code generator for statecharts [19].

In principle, any model transformation that preserves the semantics under conditions of restriction specification can be used as a restriction function. However, for the purpose of the current investigation, we limit ourselves to functions that indeed decrease the model in a syntactical sense (i.e., the only transformations they perform are the elimination of model elements and substitutions of variables and function calls by constants). We relax this requirement by allowing an optimization pass to be performed over the resulting restricted model:

$$\omega : Model \longrightarrow Model$$

The type of the optimizations used depends on the application domain. If the reaction time is the main concern, speed optimizations should be applied. Size optimizations should be used for embedded systems with limited memory. We focus on the latter case here, which limits the range of possible optimizations to the static evaluation of subexpressions, constant propagation, and dead-code elimination.

Assume that m_2 is the original model, and m_1 is a restricted version of m_2 (so $m_1 \preceq m_2$). The specialization step is considered correct if it does not affect the execution of the model—the semantics of m_2 is exactly the same as those of m_2 executed under conditions expressed in restriction specification. If restriction is based solely on dead-code elimination, the correctness condition is even simpler: the restriction is correct if it never removes any code that is live under specification conditions.

Consider a simple specialization step. Transitions fired by impossible events are removed. Read references (rvalues) of a constrained variable are substituted by the variable's value. Assignments to dead variables are removed (preserving the right-hand side or side effects). Read accesses to dead variables can be substituted by any value. Constrained function calls are replaced with their value.

The optimization step is somewhat more complicated and leaves more choices. We propose the iteration of basic optimization steps until a fixpoint is reached:

i.   Statically evaluate all parts of expressions that can be evaluated (constant propagation).
ii.   Remove pure expressions whose value is never used.
iii. Remove transitions whose guards are proven to be false.
iv.   Remove pure state machines that do not produce any outputs and are not referred from other machines.
v.   Remove the triggering of internal events that do not fire any transitions.
vi.   Remove sibling-less basic states that contain no actions.
vii. Remove nonreachable components (nonreachable states and the transitions targeting them).

All the optimizations but the last one are fairly simple. The quality of reachability analysis [13,14] depends strongly on the level of abstraction it takes. Unfortunately the exact computation of reachable state space is not feasible for arbitrarily big systems. Actually even over-approximations applied in the verification of safety properties are too expensive to apply in a code generation tool. A radical over-approximation can be achieved by the reduction of reachability analysis to the easily solvable reachability problem in a hierarchical directed graph without labels on the edges. This approximation is not so weak as it may seem: the control flow in statecharts is explicit, and simple restrictions like **impossible e** easily break it into nonreachable pieces.

6   Refinement

The inheritance hierarchy of interface restrictions is accompanied by an isomorphic hierarchy of restricted models. In this section, we shall study the meaning of the hierarchical relation between models.

Definition 1 (Trace Inclusion). *Consider two statechart models m_1 and m_2. We say that m_1 refines m_2 with respect to the alphabet α, written $m_1 \lesssim_\alpha m_2$, iff*

$$\forall t_1 \in traces(m_1). \ \exists t_2 \in traces(m_2). \ t_1 = t_2 \upharpoonright \alpha \ .$$

Intuitively, m_1 refines m_2 with respect to αm_1 if it can be executed with the same trace, modulo some m_2-specific events. Let m_1 be the least CD player of Figure 5. One of its execution traces might be

$$t \ = \ \langle StandBy, \ Play, \ startPlay(), \ Stop \rangle$$

This trace is included in the following trace of the greatest CD player of Figure 3:

$$t' = \langle StandBy,\ SwitchAlarm,\ SwitchAlarm,\ Play,\ startPlay(),\ Stop \rangle$$

Since each execution trace of m_1 can be included in some trace of m_2, we can say that m_1 will emulate m_2 if run under the conditions assumed in the restriction for m_1 (so only events from αm_1 can occur). This can be formalized for all models obtained by automatic restriction:

Theorem 2 (Soundness of Restriction). *If m_2 is a statechart model of a reactive system and m_1 has been obtained from m_2 by restriction with respect to the RL specification S, then m_1 refines m_2 with respect to αm_1. More precisely*

$$m_1 \preceq_S m_2 \Rightarrow m_1 \precsim_{\alpha m_1} m_2.$$

Theorem 3 (Completeness). *If m_2 is a statechart model and m_1 has been obtained from m_2 by restriction with respect to the RL specification S, then*

$$\forall t_2 \in RL[\![\ S\ ]\!]_{m_2} traces(m_2).\ \exists t_1 \in traces(m_1).\ t1 = t2$$

or briefly $m_1 \preceq_S m_2 \Rightarrow m_2 \precsim_{\alpha m_1} m_1$.

These results follow directly from the conservative construction of specialization transformations, based solely on dead-code elimination.

Note that if the restrictions on internal logics (nonsensors and nonactuators) were allowed, the above results would not hold. Conservative dead-code elimination would not be a viable specialization algorithm any more. One could modify the behavior of the model arbitrarily by forcing some internal variables to behave like constants, where they are not constants indeed. Restrictions over sensors and actuators avoid this: sensors are never changed inside the model, and actuators are never read inside the model.

7   Mutually Exclusive Features

The greatest member of a model family can be understood as a description of the domain, from which all family members are selected by restriction. It seems, that since model elements can only be removed, the approach does not support selection from sets of mutually exclusive features. We propose the use of *compile-time sensors* to deal with this problem.

Compile-time sensors are input variables that should be fixed to constants in restriction specifications. More precisely, we relax the condition that the greatest model must describe a working product. Conflicting behaviors should be determinized (guarded) by a compile-time sensor. Entire replaceable system components could be defined in this fashion by guarding their conditions with proper sensor values.

Figure 7 presents a more general CD player model. This model contains two possible reactions to an alarm timeout event. One CD player will presumably turn on the music; when the alarm time outs, the other should just start beeping.

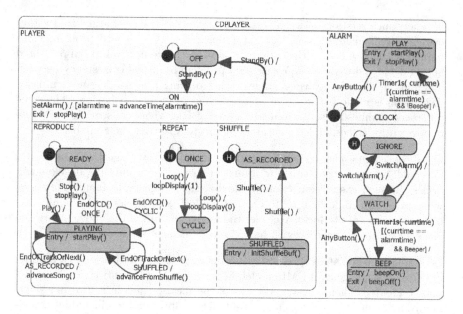

Fig. 7. A CD player model containing conflicting modes of waking up: a beeper and an automatic start-up of a CD. Note the determinizing use of a compile-time sensor *Beeper* on the two transitions leaving the *WATCH* state

Actual models describing physical devices can be created from generalized models by restricting enough until all compile-time sensors are specialized out. In fact, nothing prevents the introduction of several levels of restriction before the model becomes executable. We can speak of a hierarchy part that is closer to the root as of abstract models—models that describe narrower, less customizable families than the greatest model, but still cannot be instantiated into concrete running programs. Only models sufficiently deep in the restriction hierarchy can be used successfully for program synthesis. Abstract models correspond to abstract classes, while concrete deterministic models correspond to concrete classes. However, the notion of being abstract or concrete relates to behaviors, not to the structure of entities as assumed in object-oriented programming.

As a side effect, compile-time sensors can also be propagated forward to the C preprocessor to allow the control of driver code in the traditional fashion conditional compilation.

8   Related Work

The notion of refinement between two statecharts has been studied for Unified Modeling Language (UML) models, however, mostly in the context of consistency verification rather than in the context of transformation. A recent account of such work is given by Harel and Kupferman [7], proposing a formal notion of inheritance relation between statecharts. Noteworthy they argue that establishing a refinement relation for a top-down design is a hard problem. This refinement is obtained by the construction in the bottom-up approach presented here. Engels and associates [5] discuss a problem of formal consistency between diagrams produced at various stages of a modeling process. As an example, a distinction is made between the *invocable* and *observable* behaviors. The same difference manifests itself in our semantics of RL, where constraints on inputs remove entire traces while constraints on outputs restrict the alphabet.

A consistency checker similar to that described by Engels and associates [5] could be used to extend our framework to support multiple development cycles. In such cases, restriction would be used to generate family members, while extension could be used to create the most-general model of a family of a new generation of products. We refer the reader to both of the above mentioned texts for extensive references on behavioral refinement for statecharts.

Ziadi and associates [21] describe a framework for the derivation of a product line from a single general UML model. First, a model of the entire variability domain is created. Then, a systematic way of specification and derivation of a single family member is proposed. Their approach is appealing for including consistency constraints into the model, restricting legal configurations. Unfortunately, they do not explain how the consistency is validated. Our contribution and the work of Ziadi and associates [21] are complimentary. They are concerned solely with structural modeling (class diagrams), while we only consider behavioral modeling (statecharts). In particular, [21] does not seem to consider program derivation, only model derivation for family members. It remains a question how the two problems should be solved generatively in a single framework.

The methodology presented here is an example of generative programming [4]. The ideas have been inspired strongly by program slicing [18] and partial evaluation [9,12]. Indeed, the restriction mechanism performs well-known tasks in both techniques. Restricting by inputs (forward restriction) resembles partial evaluation, while restricting by outputs (backward restriction) is similar to the removal of program slices. While partial evaluation and slicing are applied typically to programs, we have proposed using them on the model level, which has an advantage of access to explicit control-flow information. This information is lost in the generated code, where a model is encoded typically in big integer arrays, with packed fields, interpreted in a noncompositional way. Such programs are very hard, if not infeasible, for analysis with general-purpose specializers.

In program slicing, one usually computes slices because they are of interest. Here we compute slices to remove them (the complementary slice is of interest). Partial evaluation, especially polyvariant partial evaluation [2], usually replicates pieces of code for several values of a variable to uncover the control hidden in data structures. Consequently, a partial evaluation is likely to produce bigger but faster programs. My tool only decreases the models. The discovery of control in data is not crucial in a language with an explicit control flow like statecharts.

9   Conclusion and Future Work

We have presented a software development methodology for product families based on the automatic generation of restricted programs from the model of the most complex one. The methodology has been demonstrated for the language of statecharts using a combination of intuitions from program slicing and partial evaluation. Provided the restriction algorithm is sound, a behavioral refinement relation is established between members of the family. Finally, a way of handling mutually exclusive features has been discussed.

Development with restrictions is not a silver bullet. The idea of removing features to generate new members might be not very useful for big and diverse families. The development of the single greatest model may not be feasible for them. We claim, though, that restriction can significantly simplify the development process of well-defined, relatively small program families met in the production of simple home appliances, ranging from kitchen equipment through Hi-Fi systems to mobile phones.

The class of restriction specification chosen here seems to match very well the industry needs. We have undertaken projects with two partners from the embedded systems industry in Denmark, aiming at the practical evaluation of our approach. We shall report on the experiences as soon as the case studies are over. So far, our partners are very positive about the proposed extensions to the modeling language. Nevertheless, we believe that extending the restriction language even more, giving it the behavioral power of true models of environments, will multiply the benefits of the approach. We are currently working on providing a theoretic framework for this.

Acknowledgments. The author would like to thank Peter Sestoft, Kåre Kristoffersen, Kasper Østerbye, Henrik Hulgaard, and Krzysztof Kaczmarski for discussions on the above material. The visualSTATE division of IAR Systems and the cooling division of Danfoss A/S provided practical evidence on shortcomings in the present development process. Last, but not least we would like to thank all three anonymous reviewers for suggesting some important improvements.

References

1. Gérard Berry. The foundations of Esterel. In Gordon Plotkin, Colin Stirling, and Mads Tofte, editors, *Proof, Language and Interaction. Essays in Honour of Robin Milner*, Foundations of Computing Series, pages 425–454. The MIT Press, Cambridge, Massachusetts, 2000.

2. Mikhail A. Bulyonkov. Polyvariant Mixed Computation for Analyzer Programs. *Acta Informatica*, 21(5):473–484, December 1984.

3. Krzysztof Czarnecki, Thomas Bednasch, Peter Unger, and Ulrich Eisenecker. Generative programming for embedded software: An industrial experience report. In Don Batory, C. Consel, and Walid Taha, editors, *Generative Programming and Component Engineering (GPCE)*, volume 2487 of *Lecture Notes in Computer Science*, pages 156–172, Pittsburgh, PA, USA, October 2002. Springer-Verlag.

4. Krzysztof Czarnecki and Ulrich W. Eisenecker. *Generative Programming: Methods, Tools, and Applications*. Addison-Wesley, 2000.
5. Gregor Engels, Reiko Heckel, and Jochen Malte Küster. Rule-based specification of behavioral consistency based on the UML meta-model. In Martin Gogolla and Cris Kobryn, editors, *4th International UML Conference – The Unified Modeling Language, Modeling Languages, Concepts, and Tools*, volume 2185 of *Lecture Notes in Computer Science*, pages 272–286, Toronto, Canada, October 2001. Springer-Verlag.
6. David Harel. Statecharts: A visual formalism for complex systems. *Science of Computer Programming*, 8:231–274, 1987.
7. David Harel and Orna Kupferman. On object systems and behavioral inheritance. *IEEE Transactions on Software Engineering*, 28(9):889–903, September 2002.
8. David Harel and Amir Pnueli. On the development of reactive systems. In Krzysztof R. Apt, editor, *Logic and Model of Concurrent Systems*, volume 13 of *NATO ASI*, pages 477–498. Springer-Verlag, October 1985.
9. John Hatcliff, Torben Æ. Mogensen, and Peter Thiemann, editors. *Partial Evaluation: Practice and Theory. DIKU 1998 International Summer School*, volume 1706 of *Lecture Notes in Computer Science*. Springer-Verlag, Copenhagen, Denmark, 1999.
10. C.A.R. Hoare. *Communicating Sequential Processes*. International Series in Computer Science. Prentice Hall, 1985.
11. IAR Inc. IAR visualSTATE®. http://www.iar.com/Products/VS/.
12. Neil D. Jones, Carsten K. Gomard, and Peter Sestoft. *Partial Evaluation and Automatic Program Generation*. International Series in Computer Science. Prentice Hall, 1993. http://www.dina.kvl.dk/ sestoft/pebook.
13. J.R. Burch, E.M. Clarke, K.L. McMillan, D.L. Dill, and L.J. Hwang. Symbolic Model Checking: 10^{20} States and Beyond. In *Fifth Annual IEEE Symposium on Logic in Computer Science*, pages 1–33, Washington, D.C., 1990. IEEE Computer Society Press.
14. Jørn Bo Lind Nielsen. *Verification of Large/State Event Systems*. PhD thesis, Technical University of Denmark, April 2000.
15. Object Management Group. OMG Unified Modelling Language specification, 1999. http://www.omg.org.
16. David L. Parnas. On the design and development of program families. *IEEE Transactions on Software Engineering*, Vol. SE-2(No. 1):1–9, March 1976.
17. SCOPE: A statechart compiler, 2003. http://www.mini.pw.edu.pl/ wasowski/scope.
18. Frank Tip. A survey of program slicing techniques. *Journal of Programming Languages*, 3(3):121–189, September 1995.
19. Andrzej Wąsowski. On Efficient Program Synthesis from Statecharts. In *ACM SIGPLAN Languages, Compilers, and Tools for Embedded Systems (LCTES)*, San Diego, USA, June 2003. ACM Press.
20. Andrzej Wąsowski and Peter Sestoft. On the formal semantics of visualSTATE statecharts. Technical Report TR-2002-19, IT University of Copenhagen, September 2002.
21. Tewfik Ziadi, Jean-Marc Jézéquel, and Frédéric Fondement. Product line derivation with UML. In *Software Variability Management Workshop*, University of Groningen Departement of Mathematics and Computing Science, February 2003.

Dynamic Configuration of Software Product Lines in ArchJava

Sebastian Pavel[1], Jacques Noyé[1,2], and Jean-Claude Royer[1]

[1] OBASCO Group, Ecole des Mines de Nantes - INRIA
4, rue Alfred Kastler, Nantes, France
[2] INRIA, Campus Universitaire de Beaulieu
Rennes, France
{Sebastian.Pavel,Jacques.Noye,Jean-Claude.Royer}@emn.fr

Abstract. This paper considers the use of a state-of-the-art, general-purpose, component-programming language, specifically ArchJava, to implement software product lines. Component-programming languages provide a more straightforward mapping between components as assets and components as implementation artifacts. However, guaranteeing that the implementation conforms to the architecture raises new issues with respect to dynamic configuration. We show how this can be solved in ArchJava by making the components auto-configurable, which corresponds to replacing components by component generators. Such a scheme can be implemented in various ways, in particular with a two-stage generator. This solution goes beyond the initial technical ArchJava issue and complements the standard static generative approach to software product line implementation.

1 Introduction

The *software product line* approach [9,11] is one of the three use cases of *software architectures* [6,15,26,27]. When applicable, it represents one of the most promising approaches to increased reuse of software, increased quality, and decreased time to market and maintenance costs. The software product line approach is an intra-organizational software reuse approach that has proven successful and achieved substantial adoption by the software industry. The key to software reuse is to move the focus from engineering single systems to engineering families of systems. Software product lines take advantage of the commonalities and variabilities that define the software architecture of these families in order to delay design decisions. A basic strategy is to divide the process of creating product line applications into two major activities: (1) *domain engineering* and (2) *application engineering* [11]. Domain engineering is the activity of creating reusable assets. Application engineering is responsible for creating specific products according to customer needs by reusing and specializing the assets created during domain engineering.

Software components [16,28] are the building blocks of modern software architectures. In the software product line approach, Component-based software

R.L. Nord (Ed.): SPLC 2004, LNCS 3154, pp. 90–109, 2004.
© Springer-Verlag Berlin Heidelberg 2004

engineering (CBSE) is at the root of domain engineering. In fact, most of the reusable assets created during this activity are components targeted to be reused in specific products.

On the one hand, architecture description languages (ADLs) have been defined to describe, model, check, and implement software architectures [23]. Most of the ADLs help specify and analyze high-level designs. On the other hand, so-called *component programming languages* (e.g., Fractal [10], ArchJava [3], Koala [30]) integrate different ideas from ADLs into practical programming languages. As a result, component-programming languages are interesting target implementation languages for software product lines. They potentially provide a more straightforward mapping between components at the design level and the implementation. This holds the promise of facilitating the traceability between the design and the implementation level, and of improving the quality of the software products.

As a way to better understand the level of support provided by current state-of-the-art component-programming languages, we considered a standard example of a software product line that was described well in the literature: the bank account example [11]. We first implemented this case study using Java as a basis for our experiment and then considered its implementation in ArchJava. ArchJava is a component-programming language that extends Java with architectural features that enforce *communication integrity* [21,24]. The ArchJava architectural specifications (which include an explicit hierarchical architecture, components, communication interfaces called *ports*, bindings, and connectors) are similar to those of Darwin [22]. Darwin is an ADL designed to support dynamically changing distributed architectures, and ArchJava inherits some of its dynamic capabilities like dynamic component creation and definition of communication patterns between components. Another good point of ArchJava is that, compared to other component-language prototypes, its implementation is fairly robust. In spite of these qualities, the implementation of our case study turned out not to be so easy. A major issue was the constraints imposed by communication integrity on dynamic configuration, making it impossible to configure a component from the outside.

This paper reports on this experiment. It describes how the above-mentioned problem can be solved by making the components auto-configurable, which corresponds to replacing components with component generators. This is presented as a general pattern. From an ad hoc implementation, two other implementations are derived: (1) an interpretive one based on *connectors* and (2) a compiled one based on a second generator. This leads to a two-stage configuration scheme whereby a static generator, resulting from domain engineering, produces a dynamic generator responsible for dynamic configuration. This solution goes beyond the initial technical ArchJava issue and complements the standard static generative approach to software product line implementation.

The remainder of this paper is structured as follows: Section 2 presents our case study and discusses its object-oriented implementation in Java. Section 3 summarizes the main features of ArchJava. Section 4 describes the issue raised by communication integrity and presents our dynamic configuration pattern and its implementation. Related work is pointed out in Section 5. The paper ends with a conclusion and some ideas about future work.

2   Case Study and Object-Oriented Implementation

We start from a case study that is described well in the literature. First, we provide a classical object-oriented implementation in Java, and then, we discuss its applicability in software product line development. We chose to base our work on the study of the bank account example as described by Czarnecki and Eisenecker [11]. The reason for doing this is that the domain of banking applications is very well suited to illustrating the difficulties that appear when trying to apply a certain technology in a business domain. It is also a well-described case study including both domain and application engineering with an implementation in C++.

In Figure 1, we present an excerpt of the *feature model* representing the concept of "personal account" as detailed in [11]. The main advantage of such a feature model is that it makes it possible to represent variability in an implementation-independent way. For instance, Unified Modeling Language (UML) diagrams force the designer to choose implementation mechanisms like inheritance, composition, or template classes when modeling variation points.

The diagram shows some of the possible variation points: **owner**, **payment**, **currency**, and **number of transactions**. All but **payment** are features with several *alternative* subfeatures (symbolized by empty arcs of a circle). The subfeatures of payment are *or*-features (symbolized by filled-in arcs of a circle), that is, we can select any nonempty subset of them. For the sake of simplicity and because the presented features are sufficient to exemplify the difficulties encountered, we do not include other details (see [11] for a complete analysis).

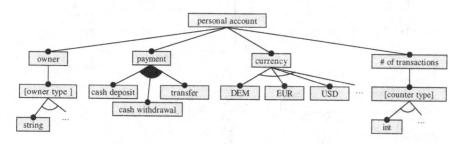

Fig. 1. Feature model of "personal account"

The next subsection presents a classical implementation approach of the case study in the Java object-oriented language.

2.1   Object-Oriented Implementation

There are various object-oriented design techniques for implementing variability in a software product line. Anastasopoulos and Gacek [5] analyze the use of aggregation, inheritance, overloading, and so forth. A short survey about this work is provided in Section 5.

For the sake of illustration, let us consider a solution based on inheritance. From an object-oriented point of view, it is natural to express commonalities as abstract classes (or interfaces), while variabilities are implemented in concrete subclasses.

Using these ideas, we can implement the *personal account* concept as a Java class called `Account` (see Figure 2) that offers three *services/methods* to clients: `deposit`, `transfer`, and `withdraw`. The aggregated entities of `Account` (`owner:String, nbTransactions:String, Currency`, and `PaymentFacilities`) represent the variation points in the architecture. The UML class diagram follows the *AbstractFactory* pattern ([14]) closely to express the `Account` configuration. Jézéquel presents and discusses the benefits and applicability of a very similar approach [20].

The `AccountFactory` class defines abstract methods to configure `Account` object instances. These methods are implemented in different ways depending on the subclasses of `AccountFactory`. The only concrete method is `makeAccount`, which creates a non-configured `Account` instance. This instance is responsible for calling back the configuration methods (`generateCurrency`, `generatePaymentFac`) on `AccountFactory` when needed.

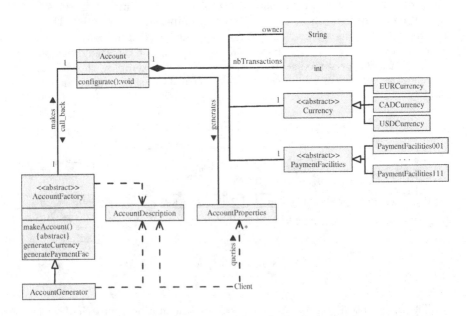

Fig. 2. Class diagram modeling the bank application

The PaymentFacilities class encapsulates the specification for a bank account that provides no payment facilities (the methods for deposit, transfer, and withdraw are abstract), while the classes PaymentFacilities001 to PaymentFacilities111 provide the different combinations of the three possible services. Each digit in the class name suffix indicates whether the services deposit, transfer, and withdraw, respectively, are present (1) or absent (0).

Considering the concrete factory AccountGenerator, a client creates an AccountDescription object first, and then passes it to the AccountGenerator and finally calls the business methods on the newly instantiated Account object.

When trying to perform the operations provided by Account, the client calls the corresponding method on the object instance. Because the actual subclass that incorporates the payment facilities is PaymentFacilities, all the requests are forwarded to it. Before actually performing an operation, this object queries the different subcomponents of Account to check the validity of the request and the availability of the Account instance.

If the client wants the properties of an account at a given moment, it can request an AccountProperties object representing both the internal structure and the financial status of the account.

2.2 Discussion

When speaking about software product lines, some items like configurability, reuse, and evolution must be taken into account. The following paragraphs discuss each of these items.

For the presented model, the configurability mechanism is fixed in the framework. The newly created Account instance calls back the AccountFactory instance, which, based on the information stored by AccountDescription, sets up the variation points in Account.

The framework can be reused only to create instances sharing the same internal structure. In other words, there is no mechanism for creating Account instances that have different instance structures.

When speaking about evolution, the framework could be evolved by adding either new variants at the existing variation points (Currency, PaymentFacilities) or new variation points.

In our implementation (as in any other implementation based on a classical object-oriented language), "software component" is actually represented by an ordinary class. A component instance is therefore an object. In much more complicated examples, we expect the relation between component and class to be 1 to N, making the task of understanding and evolving "component-based" applications more difficult.

Using component-programming languages makes software architectures easier to understand, implement, and evolve. Components in architectures have a corresponding component instance in implementations, and the connections between implementation components are more explicit. Evolving an application means changing components and connections, which is much easier than evolving a set of related classes (playing the role of components) and their relations with other sets of classes.

In the next section, we present ArchJava, a component-programming language, and, in the following sections, we present our proposals based on this language.

3   ArchJava

ArchJava [2,1,3] is a small, backwards-compatible extension to Java that integrates software architecture specifications into Java implementation code. It extends a practical implementation language to incorporate architectural features and enforce *communication integrity* [21,24]. *The benefits of this approach include better program understanding, reliable architectural reasoning about code, keeping architecture and code consistent as they evolve, and encouraging more developers to take advantage of software architecture* [3]. In ArchJava, a *component* is a special kind of object capable of communicating with other components in a structured way. The communication is performed using logical communication channels called *ports*. Each port is allowed to declare methods qualified by the keywords **requires** and **provides**. Only the provided methods have to be implemented in a component.

The hierarchical software architecture is expressed with *composite components* made of connected subcomponents. To connect two or more ports in an architecture, the **connect** primitive is employed. This primitive binds each required method in a port to a provided method with the same signature in other ports.

It is possible to create pass-through connections to subcomponents or other ports using the **glue** primitive. That primitive differs from the connect primitive in that it glues the inside of a port to another port instead of connecting the outside of that port.

ArchJava supports component inheritance and architectural design with abstract components and ports. This allows an architect to specify and type-check an ArchJava architecture before beginning program implementation.

ArchJava also supports the design of dynamically changing distributed architectures. It allows the creation and connection of a dynamically determined number of components. Components can be dynamically created using the same **new** syntax used to instantiate objects in Java. At creation time, each component records the component instance that created it as its *parent component*.

Dynamically created components can be connected together at runtime using *connect expressions*. Each connect expression must match a *connect pattern* declared in the enclosing component. A connect pattern describes a set of possible connections. A connect expression matches a connection pattern if the connected ports in the expression are identical with those in the pattern and if each connected component instance is an instance of the type specified in the pattern.

Often, a single component participates in several connections using the same conceptual protocol. In ArchJava, a *port interface* describes a port that can be instantiated several times to communicate through different connections. Each port interface defines a type that includes the set of the required methods in the port. A port interface type combines a port required interface with an instance expression that indicates the component instance to which the port belongs. Port interfaces are instantiated by connect expressions that return objects representing the corresponding connections.

The connector abstraction supported by ArchJava [4] cleanly separates reusable connection code from application logic, making the semantics of connections more explicit and allowing the easy change of the connection mechanism used in a program. In ArchJava, each connector is defined modularly in its own class, and the components interact with the connectors in a clean way using Java method call syntax. The connector used to bind two components together is specified in a higher level component. In this way, the communicating components are not aware of and do not depend on the specific connector used. This makes it easy to change connectors in a system without having to modify the communicating entities.

Developers can describe both the runtime and type-checking semantics of a connector by using the `archjava.reflect` library, which reifies connections and required method invocations.

Connectors get instantiated whenever a connect expression that specifies a user-defined connector is executed at runtime. *The principal benefit of using connectors in ArchJava is that the same connector can be reused to support the same interaction semantics across many different interfaces, while still providing a strong, static guarantee of type safety to clients* [4]. The main drawback is that they are defined using a reflective mechanism implying runtime overhead associated with dynamically reifying method calls.

Communication integrity [21,24] is a key property in ArchJava. It ensures that the implementation does not communicate in ways that could violate reasoning about control flow in the architecture. *Intuitively, communication integrity in ArchJava means that a component instance A may not call the methods of another component instance B unless B is A's subcomponent, or A and B are sibling subcomponents of a common component instance that declares a connection or connection pattern between them* [2]. ArchJava enforces communication integrity in the cases of direct method calls and method calls through ports using both static (compile-time) and dynamic (runtime) checks. It also places restrictions on the ways in which the components are used. In particular, subcomponents are not allowed to escape the scope of their parent component.

4   Proposals/Experiments

Let us now see how to implement the example in Section 2 using ArchJava. Our proposals are oriented towards facilitating the use of ArchJava components in dynamic architectures. More specifically, we want components to be created and (re)configured at runtime. In the case of our banking application, the architecture is far from being static. The accounts are created, configured, and connected dynamically at any time after the application is started and running. It is also necessary to allow the reconfiguration of these account components at runtime without having to instantiate new components to meet the new requirements. For example, we can imagine an account component that allows `deposit` and `transfer` as its services. At runtime, we could also add the `redraw` service. This change has to be done without recreating a new account (providing the three services) but rather by seamlessly modifying the existing one.

Based on Java, ArchJava supports only a limited number of the mechanisms presented in [5] that could be used to code variability. We chose to use inheritance as for the Java implementation of the bank account example. The commonalities are represented by abstract component classes, while the variabilities are represented by concrete ones.

Due to the fact that the ArchJava model focuses on keeping the communication integrity property, components cannot be passed as arguments through ports. This makes impossible the creation of components outside a component and their assignment as subcomponents of that component. So, there is no mechanism for configuring a component when the configuration details are located outside the component. The only solution is to encapsulate in the composite component all the information about the possible configurations of its subcomponents. At runtime, the component instance takes some external description and uses it to specialize the component's direct subcomponents. This mechanism is heavy and not extendible. Each time we add a new component class or extend an existing one, each component including the configuration information has to be updated and then reinstantiated in all the applications that use it.

A more natural way of performing the internal configuration of a component is to keep the needed information outside the component and to use specific ports to perform the configuration. The diversity interfaces in the Koala model [29, 30] provide such a mechanism but only for static configuration. In many cases, a static approach is sufficient. However, in the case of a product line that requires the dynamic creation and configuration of components in an architecture, ArchJava does not provide a direct mechanism to implement variability.

In the case of static architectures where the component are created, configured, and connected at compile time, the general components could be specialized for a specific application using generators. Using ArchJava, a generator takes all the specifications for the specific application and all the general components and specializes these components to match the specifications. The result is a specific architecture made of specific components. After the instantiation of the components, nothing can be modified. The architecture remains the same along the life of the application.

Adopting a dynamic approach, all our proposals are based on the same pattern. To facilitate the internal configuration of a component we use what we call a component configurator (see `ComponentConfigurator` in Figure 3). This special component plays the role of a dynamic generator. At runtime, it takes an external description containing implementation details for an account. Using this description, it generates its specific component (`Component` in Figure 3) as a subcomponent, declares the same external ports, and glues these ports to the ports published by Component. A client (the Application using its *internal port*) sees and interacts only with the component configurator instance as it provides the same ports as the actual one (the generated one).

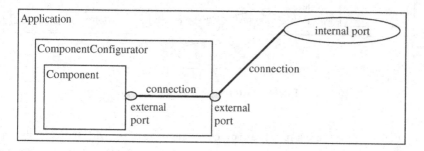

Fig. 3. The Component configurator pattern

While all three proposals are based on the same pattern, they differ in how component configurators are created or components are connected and communicate.

In the first proposal, all the component configurators (there is one for each composite component type) are created manually by the software engineer. Trying to overcome this drawback, the second proposal addresses the issue of using static software generators (created during domain engineering). We see these generators as software entities used to automatically generate (usually during application engineering) all the component configurators in an application, starting from a set of input descriptions. In the third proposal, we use custom connectors instead of simple connections between components to specialize communication at runtime and avoid the generation of multiple component configurators.

In the following, we present the details of each proposal focusing on the issues raised by the implementation of the bank account example.

4.1   Ad Hoc Implementation

The first proposal is the direct implementation of the ideas presented above.

Principles. Figure 4 presents a configuration based on the pattern in Figure 3. This configuration involves two account instances (AccountX and AccountY) and two corresponding component configurators (ConfigAccountX and ConfigAccountY). The two component configurators are connected to two internal ports (properties and payment) of BankApplication, which plays the role of the banking application.

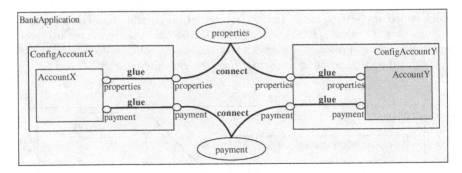

Fig. 4. Pattern-based configuration

In general, the `BankApplication` component instance will dynamically create `ConfigAccount` subcomponents as needed. A `ConfigAccount` is responsible for instantiating and configuring its `Account` subcomponent. The ports and associated methods declared by `Account` are the same as those declared by `ConfigAccount`. The ports are connected using the glue primitive. All the outside requests to a port of `ConfigAccount` are delegated to the glued port in the `Account` component. Methods in the ports declared by `ConfigAccount` do not need to be implemented; they are just declared identically as those in the ports of `Account`.

The two accounts are represented by `ConfigAccountX` and `ConfigAccountY`, respectively. Each of them declares two ports:

- `properties`, to give access to the properties of the account instance
- `payment`, to give access to the payment services

To allow the dynamic connection of `ConfigAccount` instances, we use the dynamic connection facilities of ArchJava. We declare, just once, a connect pattern for each port:

```
connect pattern payment, ConfigAccount.payment;
connect pattern properties, ConfigAccount.properties;
```

representing the pattern of connections between the *internal* ports of `BankApplication` (`properties` and `payment`) and each port of the `ConfigAccount` component class. After creating a `ConfigAccount` instance, we use connect expressions to actually connect the ports; for example, `connect(payment, account.payment)`.

The implementation details of an `Account` component are presented in Figure 5. All the subcomponents representing variation points in `Account` (`Currency`, `PaymentFacilities`) are connected to only one internal port in `Account`: the `properties` port within `AccountX`. `Currency` publishes a port named `type`, containing its specific methods. `PaymentFacilities` declares two ports: `payment` and `interncommunication`. The first one represents the services

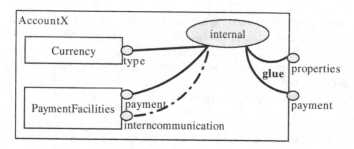

Fig. 5. Account details

(deposit, transfer, withdraw) provided by PaymentFacilities. The second one is only used to communicate with the other subcomponents of Account (Currency in our particular case). This communication is needed for checking the necessary internal properties before answering payment service requests. The purpose of connecting all these ports to the same internal port (properties in AccountX) in their parent component is to centralize all the possible method calls coming from either the outside or the inside. This need becomes more evident when multiple subcomponents need to communicate together in order to reply to a client. For example, PaymentFacilities needs to call methods in the Currency port before validating client requests. Instead of declaring all the possible connections among the subcomponents, we chose to declare a kind of proxy port: the internal port. The properties and payment ports are glued to the same internal port.

Implementation. The configurability of components at runtime is the purpose of this design, and using a component configurator is the key to realizing it in ArchJava. The component configurator plays the role of a dynamic generator. To create a specific Account instance at runtime, a client simply passes some input description data to the ConfigAccount instance. This data includes the name of the account component and parameters defining its variation points. A parent component can only access public methods in its direct subcomponents. In this case, Currency and PaymentFacilities are not visible from ConfigAccount. To allow the configuration of a specific Account component (containing specific Currency and PaymentFacilities subcomponents), ConfigAccount generates the corresponding source code, compiles it, and then instantiates it.

The actual mechanism used for specializing the Account component is inheritance. Firstly, we declare a general Account component class. Secondly, we generate the source code for a specific Account component–say AccountX–that extends the Account class. The effort of generating a specific account is reduced due to the fact that we will generate only the needed functionality according to input requirements. These requirements are transmitted to the constructor of ConfigAccount. When creating a new ConfigAccount instance with these requirements, the constructor also creates the required Account instance.

It is also possible to reconfigure an existing `Account` component at runtime. We simply pass the new configuration parameters to the corresponding `ConfigAcount`. While it remains unchanged when regarded from the outside, `ConfigAccount` reinstantiates the required `Account` subcomponent. Notice that the connections between `ConfigAccount` and its possible clients remain unchanged; only inside glue connections need to be reestablished.

Discussions. The ideas presented in the example above can be fully applied to any other application that requires the creation, specialization, and dynamic connection of ArchJava components at runtime. This is an important requirement for product line applications requiring the specialization of composite components at runtime.

The example presented above considers only one configuration component (`ConfigAccount`) because we have only one composite component in the application. In a product line approach, however, there are usually a large number of possible composite components. Applying this proposal requires manually defining a generic component class and a specific configuration component class for each composite component.

The effort of building the assets (component and component configurator classes) for this proposal in the phase of domain engineering for a product line is usually huge. Since the components are defined manually, the code can easily become error prone. When trying to evolve a component in a product line application, we also need to modify the corresponding component configurator, for instance, by inheriting from the older one. When adding new components, new configuration components have to be created too. Doing all this work manually is not an easy task. The next proposals try to address this shortcoming.

4.2   Using Component Configurator Generators

The second proposal aims to reduce the effort of building the components by using generators.

Principles. The idea is to automatically generate all the component configurators. Instead of manually implementing a component configurator (e.g., `ConfigAccount` in Figure 4) for each composite component in the application, a generator is made responsible for automatically creating the configurators. The generator takes a description of all the composite components in the application and generates the corresponding component configurators. The generator is made as general as possible. It encapsulates all the knowledge for generating the different component configurators needed in different product lines.

The generator represents an additional tool that comes with the product line software. It is created during the domain engineering phase and could be reused each time component configurators are required (either at domain or application engineering time).

To properly generate component configurators, the generator needs a detailed description of the corresponding components. Another idea is to make the generator as general as possible to allow the generation of as many different component configurator structures as possible.

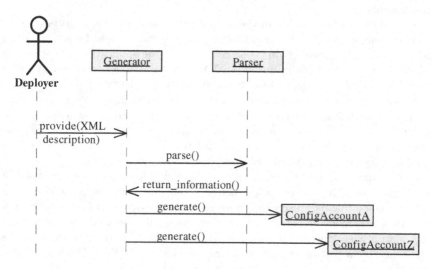

Fig. 6. Generator scenario sequence diagram

Implementation. While generators are usually very complex tools, in our case, the generator is a simple Java program. We used it to test the creation of component configurators for the bank account example. It takes a description of our general components and generates the corresponding component configurators. This description includes the names of the general (abstract) components serving as a base for the creation of new specific generated components. In addition, for each general component, there is a list of ports and the corresponding requires/provides methods that the specific component will contain. This information is also used to create the ports (glued to the actual specific component) in the component configurator.

To simplify the component descriptions as much as possible, we chose to use XML and additional technologies [32]. The generator takes a .xml file containing a structured description of components, uses a parser to extract the information, and then generates the component class files (see Figure 6).

At the implementation level, the XML file conforms to a predefined XSL schema. This schema describes how the .xml documents are structured. To facilitate the use of XML files in Java applications, we rely on Java XML Binding (JAXB) technology [19].

Discussion. The generator generates components starting from a general (common) architecture and by adding functionality. In our case, this common architecture is related to the fact that all the generated configuration components deal with the same kind of account. In other applications, the structure of the configured component dictates the common architecture of all the configuration components.

Based on the first proposal, the second proposal is more appropriate to the product line approach. The generator is very general; it could be reused across many product line applications. The effort during the application deployment is reduced to the simple definition of an XML file, containing the descriptions of the components, to be passed as an argument to the generator.

Another benefit of using generators is that the resulting code is more reliable than handmade code. In particular, code complexity and performance can be controlled using generators. A generator encapsulates the logic for creating and optimizing the code. Once developed and tested, a generator guarantees the quality of the resulting generated applications.

At runtime, the application remains as configurable as in the first proposal. A component is configured using another corresponding component configurator.

The asset that is reused the most in this approach is the generator. The fact that it is made as general as possible, encapsulating the logic for creating any kind of component and its corresponding configuration component, makes the generator a first-order asset in a product line application. The generator is reused for each component type necessary in an application.

The evolution of existing components, seen as assets of the product line, is a simple step. We just change the descriptions of the desired components, and the generator creates the corresponding component types. After this step, the resulting assets (component and component configurators types) can be reused in any kind of product line application that requires their presence.

4.3   Using Custom Connectors

The third proposal is based on connectors, as described by Aldrich and associates [4].

Principles. Instead of manually building or automatically generating all the configuration components as in the first and second proposals, why not have only one component configurator that is as general as possible (see Figure 7)?

A component has its ports connected to a single port of the ConfigComponent. Instead of a classical connection, we chose to employ a custom connector. The role of the connector is to intercept all the invocations coming from either inside the component instance or outside the ConfigComponent. Once intercepted, the requests are transformed to match the signature of the target method in the specified port. A component instance in a product line could have a number of ports not known when building the configuration component. Moreover, the number of components in the architecture is not constant during

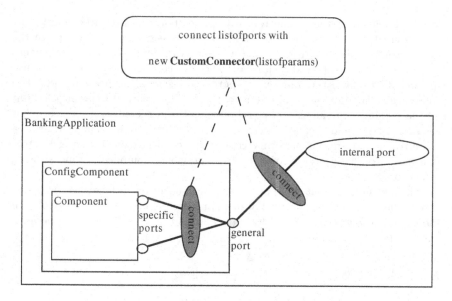

Fig. 7. The connector pattern

the life cycle of the product line application. In this context, it is important to define a generic port that can potentially be connected to any other port. Allowing such flexibility involves two major difficulties:

- the definition of the port (the general port in Figure 7) in the `ConfigComponent` component
- the definition of the custom connector that codes/decodes the requests between the ports

When intercepting calls from methods in component ports, the connector first encodes all the information about the request: required method signature and calling parameters. Then, it calls the methods in the `ConfigComponent` port with this information. From there, the information is decoded by another custom connector instance and transmitted to the final port. The connector represents a communication channel that is invisible to the ports at its edges. It has no knowledge of the specific ports it connects. Its job is just to code/decode and forward the requests.

Implementation. Unfortunately, the actual version of the prototype compiler of ArchJava is not fully operational with respect to the connector specifications. For this reason, we could not test whether the ideas presented above could be applied successfully to create a specific custom connector.

Discussion. The use of custom connectors in ArchJava simplifies the previous proposals. When assembling a product line configuration, we simply plug in a well-defined custom connector between the ports we need to connect. The step of creating the configuration components for each component type in the application is omitted. A general custom connector is created during domain engineering. Then, it is reused each time we need to connect a component instance to its configurator or the configurator port to the general application ports. The code encapsulated in the general connector is very complex. It takes into account all the possible communication possibilities between the edges it connects. For the same reason and because, in ArchJava, connectors are implemented using a reflective mechanism, the performance of such a connector component is limited. It is a kind of "interpreted" version of the previous "compiled" proposal using generators.

The advantage is that the connector, as the generator in the second proposal, is reusable across all the specific products in the product line. We simply plug in the connector between two components. The connector will eventually perform exactly the same in all cases.

5   Related Work

5.1   Implementing Product Line Variabilities with Components

Anastasopoulos and Gacek survey a number of techniques making it possible to produce code for generic product line assets [5]. This includes a wide range of techniques going from conditional compilation to aspect-oriented programming, but component-oriented programming is not considered. However, component-oriented programming has some very interesting properties with respect to the list of qualities that Anastasopoulos and Gacek consider for assessing the implementation techniques: scalability, traceability, and separation of concerns. Indeed, scalability is one of the main objectives of component-oriented programming, which is designed to program in the large. Traceability is improved by keeping the architecture explicit in the implementation. Actually, this goes beyond traceability as conformance of the implementation to the architecture of the product line is provided. Finally, component-oriented programming facilitates the separation of architectural concerns and global reasoning from behavioral concerns and local reasoning.

5.2   Koala

In the middle of the 90s, Philips had some in-depth experience in developing a large range of televisions worldwide. The hardware was reasonably modular, but the software parts were developed using a classic approach. To handle diversity, the approach mainly used compiler switches, runtime options, and code duplication with changes. But the new coming products needed more and more functionalities and combinations of these functionalities. The company had to integrate different pieces of software coming from different areas and developed at different times. Since, at this time, the existing component technology was not suited to the existing constraints, the Koala language was designed [30].

Koala was inspired by the Darwin language [22] dedicated to distributed system architectures. Koala is a component-programming language that provides interfaces (provided, required), first-class components, and configurations and that is targeted to the C language. Most of the connections are known at configuration time, but the language also defines switches or code to dynamically bind components. It offers an easy-to-use graphical notation and an elegant parameterization mechanism. Interface diversity is a specific kind of interface for managing configuration from outside of the component, providing better independence from context. Partial evaluation is used to optimize static configuration. A compiler has been developed in addition to a user interface and component Web-based repositories. Koala was designed for resource-constrained systems; it makes it possible to apply the component technology at a small grain with no significant overhead.

The main criticism about Koala is that it deals exclusively with static architectures. Once created, a configuration already deployed cannot be modified in the final product (in C code). Any modification requires changing the configuration and possibly the definitions of components and interfaces and then recompiling all of the application. This perfectly fits the domain of consumer electronics where the architecture of internal components, once deployed, will not change. However, some applications require a dynamic architecture–an architecture that makes it possible to create new components and connections or to change existing ones during the lifetime of the product. In its actual form, Koala is not usable to describe and implement such a dynamic architecture.

On the other hand, ArchJava, inspired from the same Darwin [22] language as Koala, was especially designed to support dynamically changing architectures. Even if Koala proved its benefits in developing software product lines in the domain of consumer electronics, ArchJava seems to be more suited to implementing software products with a dynamic structure.

5.3   Components and Generators

The idea that generators are an effective way of automating component customization and assembly in the context of program families is not new (see for instance [8,18,13,12]). However, generators are usually presented as operating at compile time only. From a description of the configuration of the product to be built, they customize and assemble prefabricated generic components in one stage. Our case study has hopefully made clear that, although this approach remains valid when dynamic configuration must be taken into account, it has to be generalized to a two-stage approach. This means that, apart from dealing with static customization and assembly, the (static) generator has also to prepare dynamic generation. This can be done in two different ways: (1) in an interpretive way, relying on connectors or (2) in a more specific and efficient way, using a (dynamic) generator.

6   Conclusion

To assess the benefits of using a component language to implement software product lines, we have experimented with different implementations in ArchJava of a well-known example from the literature. When implementing component-based applications, software architectures in ArchJava are much more explicit than architectures in a standard object-oriented language like Java. Using components makes the architecture application architecture easier to understand, implement, and evolve. However, trying to implement a software product line application in ArchJava is not an easy task. Even if the language is well suited to dealing with architectural concepts, communication integrity turns out to be a constraint. This important consistency property in ArchJava guarantees that the *implementation components only communicate directly with the components they are connected to in the architecture* [3]. The drawback is that, due to this property, a component instance cannot be passed as an argument through ports, an important requirement for a composite component that has to be specialized (or configured) at runtime.

There is no direct relation between the software product line approach (which is the organization of some activities to achieve reusable software architectures) and communication integrity (which is an architecture implementation property). Despite this remark, the modality of integrating this property into the ArchJava language does not allow the easy creation of software product lines with dynamic architectures.

Our main contribution was to design and develop a pattern allowing the implementation of software components in ArchJava that can be dynamically specialized at runtime. In addition to this advantage, the pattern also keeps the communication integrity property as proposed by ArchJava.

All our implementation proposals are based on this pattern. The basic proposal uses what we call a *component configurator*. This is actually a dynamic generator used to create/configure component instances at runtime. The second proposal automates the ad hoc building of component configurators using static generators. These generators are used to automatically generate all the component configurators. The third proposal replaces the generation of component configurators by the use of a unique custom connector. While the first proposal was fully implemented in ArchJava, the second one was only partially implemented in order to solve our specific case study. The implementation of the third proposal is still waiting for the ArchJava prototype compiler to come to maturity.

While initially developed to solve the problem of specializing component instances at runtime for our case study, the pattern could be used successfully to solve any problem requiring the dynamic creation, specialization, and connection of composite component instances at runtime. While the first proposal involves a great development effort, the connector-based proposal raises some efficiency problems. Based on two-stage generators, the second proposal is the most interesting in terms of generality and efficiency.

The question then is whether such a pattern could be better supported within a general-purpose component-programming language. We have seen that static configuration is well covered in Koala through the combination of diversity interfaces (used to define configuration information) and partial evaluation (used to do the actual configuration) without the explicit manipulation of generators. This should be extended to dynamic configuration. As far as ArchJava is concerned, one could imagine introducing a notion of *diversity port* that would be less restrictive than regular ports. A more general direction would be to provide linguistic and tool support for the two-stage generator approach. Another important issue that we have not addressed here is to explicitly support the specification of various forms of variabilities.

Acknowledgements. This work was supported in part by the *ACI Sécurité Informatique*, in the context of the DISPO project.

References

1. J. Aldrich, C. Chambers, and D. Notkin.
   ArchJava web site. http://www.archjava.org/.
2. J. Aldrich, C. Chambers, and D. Notkin. Architectural reasoning in ArchJava. In B. Magnusson, editor, *ECOOP 2002 - Object-Oriented Programming, 16th European Conference*, number 2374 in Lecture Notes in Computer Science, pages 334–367, Malaga, Spain, June 2002. Springer-Verlag.
3. J. Aldrich, C. Chambers, and D. Notkin. ArchJava: Connecting software architecture to implementation. In ICSE2002 [17], pages 187–197.
4. J. Aldrich, V. Sazawal, C. Chambers, and D. Notkin. Language support for connector abstractions. In L. Cardelli, editor, *ECOOP 2003 - Object-Oriented Programming, 17th European Conference*, number 2743 in Lecture Notes in Computer Science, pages 74–102, Darmstadt, Germany, July 2003. Springer-Verlag.
5. M. Anastasopoulos and C. Gacek. Implementing product line variabilities. In Bassett [7], pages 109–117.
6. L. Bass, P. Clements, and R. Kazman. *Software Architecture in Practice*. Series in Software Engineering. Addison Wesley, Reading, MA, USA, 1998.
7. P.G. Bassett, editor. *Proceedings of SSR'01 - 2001 Symposium on Software Reusability*, Toronto, Canada, May 2001. ACM Press.
8. D. Batory and S. O'Malley. The design and implementation of hierarchical software systems with reusable components. *ACM Transactions on Programming Languages and Systems*, 1(4):355–398, October 1992.
9. J. Bosch. *Design and Use of Software Architectures - Adopting and Evolving a Product Line Approach*. Addison-Wesley, 2000.
10. T. Coupaye, E. Bruneton, and J.-B. Stefani. The Fractal composition framework. Specification, The ObjectWeb Consortium, February 2004. Draft, Version 2.0-3.
11. K. Czarnecki and U. W. Eisenecker. *Generative Programming: Methods, Tools, and Applications*. Addison-Wesley, 2000.
12. K. Czarnecki and U.W. Eisenecker. Components and generative programming. In Nierstasz and Lemoine [25], pages 2–19.

13. S. Eckstein, P. Ahlbrecht, and K. Neumann. Techniques and language constructs for developing generic informations systems: A case study. In Bassett [7], pages 145–154.
14. E. Gamma, R. Helm, R. Johnson, and J. Vlissides. *Design Patterns: Elements of Reusable Object-Oriented Software*. Addison Wesley, 1994.
15. D. Garlan and M. Shaw. An introduction to software architecture. Technical Report CS-94-166, Carnegie Mellon University, School of Computer Science, 1994.
16. G.T. Heineman and W.T. Councill, editors. *Component-Based Software Engineering – Putting the Pieces Together*. Addison-Wesley, 2001.
17. *Proceedings of the 24th International Conference on Software Engineering*, Orlando, FL, USA, May 2002. ACM Press.
18. S. Jarzabek and P. Knauber. Synergy between component-based and generative approaches. In Nierstasz and Lemoine [25], pages 429–455.
19. Java web site. http://www.sun.java.com/.
20. J.-M. Jézéquel. Reifying variants in configuration management. *ACM Transactions on Software Engineering and Methodology*, 8(3):284–295, July 1999.
21. D.C. Luckham and J. Vera. An event-based architecture definition language. *IEEE Transactions on Software Engineering*, 21(9):717–734, 1995.
22. J. Magee and J. Kramer. Dynamic structure in software architectures. In *Proceedings of the Fourth ACM SIGSOFT Symposium on the Foundations of Software Engineering*, pages 3–14, San Francisco, CA, USA, October 1996. ACM Press.
23. N. Medvidovic and R.N. Taylor. A classification and comparison framework for software architecture description languages. *IEEE Transactions on Software Engineering*, 26(1):70–93, January 2000.
24. M. Moriconi, X. Qian, and R. A. Riemenschneider. Correct architecture refinement. *IEEE Transactions on Software Engineering*, 21(4):356–372, 1995.
25. O. Nierstasz and M. Lemoine, editors. *Software Engineering – ESEC/FSE'99: 7th European Software Engineering Conference*, volume 1687 of *Lecture Notes in Computer Science*, Toulouse, France, 1999. Springer-Verlag.
26. D. E. Perry and A. L. Wolf. Foundations for the study of software architecture. *ACM SIGSOFT Software Engineering Notes*, 17(4):40–52, October 1992.
27. M. Shaw and D. Garlan. *Software Architecture. Perspectives on an Emerging Discipline*. Prentice-Hall, 1996.
28. C. Szyperski, D. Gruntz, and S. Murer. *Component Software: Beyond Object-Oriented Programming*. ACM Press and Addison-Wesley, 2nd edition, 2002.
29. R. van Ommering. Building product populations with software components. In ICSE2002 [17], pages 255–265.
30. R. van Ommering, F. van der Linden, J. Kramer, and J. Magee. The Koala component model for consumer electronics software. *Computer*, 33(3):78–85, 2000.
31. J. Withey. Investment analysis of software assets for product lines. Technical Report CMU/SEI-96-TR-010, Software Engineering Institute, Carnegie Mellon University, 1996.
32. XML - Extensible Markup Language - web site. http://www.w3.org/xml.

Software Product Family Evaluation

Frank van der Linden,[1] Jan Bosch,[2] Erik Kamsties,[3]
Kari Känsälä,[4] and Henk Obbink[5]

[1]Philips Medical Systems,
frank.van.der.linden@philips.com
[2]University of Groningen,
Jan.Bosch@cs.rug.nl
[3]University of Duisburg-Essen,
kamsties@sse.uni-essen.de
[4]Nokia Research Center,
Kari.Kansala@nokia.com
[5]Philips Research Laboratories
henk.obbink@philips.com

Abstract. This paper proposes a four-dimensional evaluation framework for software product family engineering. The four dimensions relate to the software engineering concerns of business, architecture, organisation, and process. The evaluation framework is intended for use within software developing organisations to determine the status of their own software product family engineering and the priorities for improving. The results of the evaluation can be used for benchmarking, roadmapping, and developing improvement plans. An initial evaluation of a real industrial case is presented to show the validity of the framework.

1 Introduction

The main arguments for introducing software product family engineering are to increase productivity, improve predictability, decrease the time to market, and increase quality (dependability). To improve the overall system family engineering capability in Europe, a series of Information Technology for European Advancement (ITEA) projects on this topic is being executed, namely if99005 ESAPS (1999-2001), if00004 CAFÉ (2001-2003), and if02009 FAMILIES (2003-2005) 7. We are involved in all or some of these projects. The initial evaluation framework for software product family engineering was prepared during the ITEA project called From Concepts to Application in System-Family Engineering (CAFÉ) 9. In this paper, we provide an improved framework as well as a more extensive explanation of the different development concerns in relation to software family engineering. Within the recently started FAMILIES project, an improved and refined version will be produced and tested. The framework has been developed based on experiences with a wide variety of software product families and is illustrated in this paper using a case within Philips Medical Systems.

The focus of this paper is on embedded systems. Software product family engineering originated from embedded systems development, where product families

R.L. Nord (Ed.): SPLC 2004, LNCS 3154, pp. 110–129, 2004.
© Springer-Verlag Berlin Heidelberg 2004

already existed. Software in embedded systems was introduced originally to improve the flexibility and later for the introduction of more functionality. When the amount of software was growing, the family engineering approach had to be applied on software as well. As software behaves differently than other product assets, it was initially not clear how to deal with it. In this paper, we look at all the concerns around *software* product family engineering. Below, we often denote products built by software product family engineering. We refer then to embedded systems that have software inside produced in a family-wise way. Our approach works, however, also for pure software systems, but we have not seen many examples of such systems.

The remainder of the paper is organised a follows. In the next section, the Business, Architecture, Process, Organisation (BAPO) model is introduced. BAPO is used as the basis of the evaluation framework. Subsequently, the four evaluation dimensions are discussed. Then, we give a validation example, discuss related work, and finally, provide our conclusions.

2 The Business, Architecture, Process, Organisation (BAPO) Model

Within the ITEA project called Engineering Software Architectures, Processes, and Platforms for system family Engineering (ESAPS), we identified four interdependent software development concerns, BAPO 1:

1. **Business**, how to make profit from your products
2. **Architecture**, technical means to build the software
3. **Process**, roles, responsibilities, and relationships within software development
4. **Organisation**, actual mapping of roles and responsibilities to organisational structures

Figure 1 gives an overview of the BAPO concerns. Links denote the interrelationships between the concerns that exist between all pairs. In principle, applying changes in one concern is though, because it induces changes in the others. Arrows denote a natural order to traverse the concerns, giving an order to the acronym as well. The Business is the most influential factor: it has to be set up right in the first place. The architecture reflects the business concerns in software structure and rules. The process is set up to be able to build the products determined by the architecture. Finally, the organisation should host the process.

Through the clarification of these dimensions, the ESAPS, CAFÉ, and FAMILIES projects consider all the concerns in the context of software product family engineering. In fact, although architecture is an important topic for family engineering, the process had a much larger emphasis in these projects, since it was often neglected in earlier approaches. Due to the realisation that is it crucial for software family engineering to address the business and organisation well, effort was also directed to these dimensions, resulting in a more complete view of what is necessary for software product family engineering.

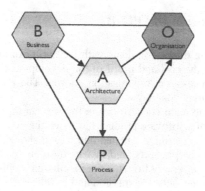

Fig. 1. The BAPO concerns

We will use this separation of concerns to provide four dimensions of the family evaluation framework. An organisation will have a separate evaluation level for each BAPO concern. The interdependence between those concerns becomes obvious as soon as one studies the effects of changes. Changes in one dimension virtually always have consequences for the other dimensions as well. In fact, actions to improve the evaluation result for one concern may give rise to a lower evaluation result for some of the others. Therefore, improvement actions have to consider all BAPO concerns.

Through BAPO, our evaluation framework collects and structures characteristics of a software production unit, division, or company that are proven by experience to be effective. It is based on the experience of the companies involved in the aforementioned ITEA projects, and, as such, it consolidates a large body of knowledge. The purpose of the model is to

1. serve as a benchmark for effective software product family engineering
2. support the assessments of software product family engineering for capability evaluations of software production units, divisions, or companies
3. support the improvement of software product family engineering, which involves producing assessments and improvements plans

The result of the evaluation (i.e., an evaluation profile) is the representation of a software product family engineering evaluation for an organisation, represented in four separate evaluation scales for Business, Architecture, Process, and Organisation evaluation.

Setting the target evaluation profiles for improving software product family engineering has to include the consideration of possible dependencies and tradeoffs between the evaluation dimensions.

In the next several sections, we describe the different evaluation levels for each BAPO concern. Subsequently, we describe the relationships and influences between these concerns. Finally, the evaluation framework is validated and illustrated using a case.

3 Business Dimension (BAPO-B)

The business evaluation dimension deals with the ability of an organisation to manage, predict, and steer the cost and profit of the development. The cost is dependent on the architecture process and organisation chosen. The profit relates to customer satisfaction and the market position.

For our purposes, the main concern lies in the way an organisation can determine the costs and payoffs of a software product family engineering approach. The organisation should be able to determine whether and how it should invest in software family engineering, for which products, and in which order. It should be able to understand and quantify the necessary investments in software family engineering. A well-organised organisation has only one mission and a well-defined set of objectives. The software family engineering should fit in them.

When a software family engineering approach is chosen, the business goals should be in alignment with the software family engineering goals in order to improve the competitiveness. One of the questions addressed by the business aspect is *scoping* 12, which deals with the question of what products should be subject to software family engineering and why, based on market and technology expectations.

In the evaluation framework, four main aspects are used in the evaluation of the business dimension. The selection of these aspects is a first guess, but they are related with important aspects recognised in business literature. These aspects are partially dependent of each other; often, a higher level for one aspect corresponds to higher levels for the others as well.

1. **Identity**: How well has the organisation formulated an identity relating to software family engineering? Low levels for this aspect correspond to software product family engineering that is not visible in the identity. At higher levels for this aspect, there has to be a strong relationship between the development of the products and the identity. For instance, the similarity between the products is visible at the marketing level and used in the communication of the management to the employees and customers.

2. **Vision**: How well does the organisation aim for a future where software product family engineering fits? At lower levels for this aspect, the software product family engineering is not present in the vision. At higher levels for this aspect, the presence of software family engineering is available in the determination of the future goals and communicated to the customers.

3. **Objectives**: How well does the organisation determine its future goals, aimed at marketing and selling what the software family engineering produces? At lower levels, no specific marketing for similar products based on reusable platforms is available. At higher levels, products in the family will be marketed as such, aiming to sell family members instead of one-of-a-kind systems.

4. **Strategic planning**: How well does the organisation plan the family business and development? At lower levels, no specific planning is available for the software family engineering. At higher levels, roadmaps of what will be developed are available and used.

Below, we present a five-level structure that is more refined than the one presented by van der Linden and associates 9. The levels are

1. **Reactive** - The business does not actively influence the software family engineering. Instead, it *reacts* to the situation.

2. **Awareness** - The business is *aware* of the software family engineering. However, it does not know the right instruments to influence and use it for the business's sake.
3. **Extrapolate** - The business is *extrapolating* on the results of the software family engineering. It influences software family engineering for obtaining business goals.
4. **Proactive** - The business is *proactively* planning and managing the software family engineering and the business goals to obtain the best business results out of it.
5. **Strategic** - The software family engineering is *a strategic* asset for reaching the business goals.

Below, we discuss each level in more detail

3.1 Level 1: Reactive

The business does not actively influence the software family engineering. Instead, it *reacts* to the situation.
1. **Identity**: implicit
2. **Vision**: short term (just cash flow)
3. **Objectives**: missing
4. **Strategic planning**: missing

This is the basic level for the business dimension. The identity of the organisation is derived from the activities it happens to perform. If there is software family engineering, it is not visual at the business level. There is no software family engineering vision. The objectives and business-planning process do not support software family engineering. The reuse of assets in product development is mainly for opportunistic reasons. Decisions about whether to make or buy assets, or obtain them differently, are taken only for opportunistic reasons. There is no strategy to align marketing to software family engineering. Products from the family are marketed just as any other product.

3.2 Level 2: Awareness

The business is *aware* of the software family engineering. However, it does not know the right instruments to influence and use it for the business's sake.
1. **Identity**: available
2. **Vision**: short to medium term
3. **Objectives**: partially, and qualitative
4. **Strategic planning**: ad hoc process

At this level, there is an awareness of the software product family engineering at the business level. The business sees the benefits of software family engineering for the short or medium term, but is unable to connect it to all the relevant objectives of the organisation. There is no strategic plan in relationship to software family engineering.

3.3   Level 3: Extrapolate

The business is *extrapolating* on the results of the software family engineering. It influences software family engineering for obtaining business goals.

1. **Identity**: identified
2. **Vision**: medium term
3. **Objectives**: qualitative
4. **Strategic planning**: ad hoc process

At this level, planning for the software product family engineering is available. Scoping is performed to determine the borders of the product range, and roadmaps are used to plan the software product family engineering and to decide on making assets or obtaining them differently. Often, the roadmaps are based on business and technological scenarios. On a regular basis, the roadmaps and scopes are updated.

There is an ad hoc strategy to align marketing to software family engineering. Products produced are predominantly marketed as any other product. However, the long-term vision of the marketing department is taken into account in scoping and family planning.

3.4   Level 4: Proactive

The business is *proactively* planning and managing the software family engineering and the business goals to obtain the best business results out of it.

1. **Identity**: communicated
2. **Vision**: medium/long term
3. **Objectives**: partially quantitative
4. **Strategic planning**: defined process

At this level, decisions are based on partial cost models. Scoping is based on expectations of the parameters of the software family engineering effort. Roadmaps are based on intra-company agreements, time-to-market estimations, and profit expectations. Scope definitions and roadmaps are maintained locally and communicated with other departments of the company. Expectations on resources, as well as key and core technologies for the company, influence decisions about whether to develop family assets, or to buy, mine, or commission assets.

There is a process available to align marketing to software family engineering. The marketing long-term vision is adapted according to the family planning.

3.5   Level 5: Strategic

The software family engineering is *a strategic* asset for reaching the business goals.

1. **Identity**: managed
2. **Vision**: long term
3. **Objectives**: quantitative
4. **Strategic planning**: institutionalised process

Once the business dimension has the highest maturity, decisions are based on quantitative cost models. Scoping is based on quantitative predictions of the return on investment of the software family engineering effort. Roadmaps are defined based on intra-company agreements, time-to-market estimations, and profit expectations. Scope definitions and roadmaps are aligned between the different units within a single company. Resource availability, key and core technology for the company, time-to-market expectations, and profit and cost models influence decisions about whether to develop family assets, or to buy, mine, or commission them.

Marketing aligns with software family engineering. The family is marketed as a whole, and the position of the product in the family is part of the marketing strategy. New products requiring little development effort are actively promoted. Products that involve expensive developments (e.g., due to architectural mismatches) are avoided.

4 Architecture Dimension (BAPO-A)

The architecture of software product families differs significantly from architecture in single-product development. It is essential to detect, design, and model the variable and common parts of the software family engineering (i.e., software variability is a key concern). Variability management needs to start during requirements engineering. Common parts will useably be implemented as a reusable platform, where the variable parts fit in at explicit variation points.

The development of software product families is aimed at a dynamic set of resulting products. Platform technologies typically evolve very rapidly. Because of this, systems in production cannot be re-implemented for each change in technology. In parallel, the quality of products within the family needs to be improved, and product variants have to be delivered in less time. This results in a need for software architectures that will enable us to move to new emerging platforms against a minimal investment.

The technological approach taken to the development of software products varies substantially between different organisations. From our experience, these approaches can be categorised in five levels 3, where the first level exhibits no sharing of software artefacts and the highest level requires no product-specific software development. The preferred approach for an organisation depends on the business goals that the organisation aims to achieve with the software family engineering, as well as the application domain of the software products and the maturity of the organisation in the process and organisation dimensions.

In our experience, one can identify four aspects that define the five approaches to the technology of the software product family engineering. As with the business dimension, the aspects are partially dependent on each other. A higher level for one aspect often goes together with higher levels for the others as well. Below, these aspects are discussed in more detail:

1. **Software product family architecture**: The software product family architecture can exist at several levels. The level determines what is and is not shared among the produced products. At higher levels, the influence of the architecture on the development increases. Higher levels of software product family architecture do not mean larger amounts of shared software between the products. At low levels, the software product family architecture may only make a distinction between infrastructure and product-specific components. At higher levels, the software architecture is enforced.

2. **Product quality**: The quality of the set of products as a whole is, at lower levels, typically accidental as all the attention is towards providing the right functionality. With increasing levels, quality is managed more and more explicitly within the architecture.
3. **Reuse levels**: The reuse level indicates the amount of relative effort spent on producing shared, reusable assets, when compared to application or product engineering.
4. **Software variability management**: At lower levels, the management of the software variability is focusing mainly on supporting compile-time and link-time binding. At higher levels, the complete software life cycle is taken into account, determining when to introduce and bind which variability, and which mechanism should be used.

We have defined the following level structure. Below, we discuss the levels in more detail:

1. **Independent product development** – There is no software family engineering. Instead, *products are developed independently.*
2. **Standardised infrastructure** – The family architecture focuses itself on the *standardisation of the infrastructure.*
3. **Software platform** – The family architecture defines a *software platform* to be used as the basis of product development.
4. **Variant products** – The family architecture determines the construction of *variant products.*
5. **Self-configurable products** – The family architecture defines pervasive rules that enable the automatic selection of assets to *configure products.*

4.1 Level 1: Independent Product Development

There is no software family engineering. Instead, *products are developed independently.*
1. **Software product family architecture**: not established
2. **Product quality**: ignored or managed in an ad hoc fashion
3. **Reuse level**: Although ad hoc reuse may occur, there is no institutionalised reuse.
4. **Software variability management**: absent

An organisation developing products independently has no sharing of external or internal software artefacts. The commonality between products is not exploited.

4.2 Level 2: Standardised Infrastructure

The family architecture focuses itself on the *standardisation of the infrastructure.*
1. **Software product family architecture**: specified external components
2. **Product quality**: The infrastructure supports certain qualities; for the remaining qualities, an overengineering approach is used.
3. **Reuse level**: only external components
4. **Software variability management**: limited variation points from the infrastructure components

The first step that an organisation typically takes when evolving towards exploiting commonality in its products is to standardise the infrastructure on which product development is based. This infrastructure typically consists of the operating system and the usual commodity components on top of it, such as a database management system and a graphical user interface. In addition, the organisation may acquire some domain-specific components from external sources. Typically, these components are integrated through some proprietary glue code.

4.3 Level 3: Software Platform

The family architecture defines a *software platform* to be used as basis for the development of the products.
1. **Software product family architecture**: Only the features common to all products are captured.
2. **Product quality**: inherited from the platform
3. **Reuse level**: reuse of internal platform components
4. **Software variability management**: managed at the platform level

As a first step in achieving the intra-organisational reuse of software artefacts, the organisation may develop, maintain, and evolve a platform on which the creation of the products or applications is based. A platform typically includes a standardised infrastructure as a basis (as discussed in the previous section) that typically contains generic functionality. On top of that, the platform captures domain functionality that is common to all products or applications. The common functionality that is not provided by the infrastructure is implemented by the organisation itself, but typically, the application development treats the platform as if it were an externally bought infrastructure.

4.4 Level 4: Variant Products

The family architecture determines the construction of *variant products*.
1. **Software product family architecture**: fully specified
2. **Product quality**: a key priority for development
3. **Reuse level**: managed
4. **Software variability management**: many variation points and dependencies between them

Once the benefits of exploiting the commonalities between the products become more accepted within the organisation, a consequent development may be to increase the amount of functionality in the platform to the level where functionality common to several but not all of the products becomes part of the shared artefacts. Now we have reached the stage of variant products. Variation is managed strictly, and functionality specific to one or a few products is still developed as part of the product derivation. Functionality shared by a sufficient number of products is part of the shared artefacts, with the consequence that individual products may sacrifice resource efficiency for development effort offered by the software family engineering. In addition, all products are developed based on the defined family architecture. In particular, it specifies how and when to configure variants.

4.5 Level 5: Self-Configurable Products

The family architecture defines pervasive rules that enable the automatic selection of assets to *configure products*.
1. **Software product family architecture**: enforced
2. **Product quality**: Quality attributes are implemented as variation points in the architecture and components.
3. **Reuse level**: automatic generation of software family engineering members
4. **Software variability management**: The automated selection and verification of variants at variation points have been optimised.

Especially if the organisation develops products in relatively stable domains and derives many product instances, there is a tendency to further develop the support for systematic product derivation. The consequence is that the architecture is enforced for all the products, and derivation is performed through the application of the defined rules. Large parts of the product derivation can be automated and/or performed at the customer's site.

5 Process Dimension (BAPO-P)

The process dimension emphasizes the process, roles, work products, and corresponding responsibilities and relationships within software development. The Capability Maturity Model for Software (SW-CMM) and its current successor Capability Maturity Model Integration (CMMI) 5, 6 (both developed by the Software Engineering Institute [SEI]) are the de facto standards in assessing and evaluating software processes. For that reason, CMMI is the most natural choice to be the basis of the evaluation approach for software product family engineering in the BAPO-P dimension. Of course, the practices for software family engineering are more extensive and more special, which is a basis for further refinement. Many of the ITEA project's best practices 8 and the work of the SEI on software product line engineering 4 have to be considered as input. The levels of the CMMI (Staged Representation) are introduced briefly using the original text from the SEI's technical report 6 in the following by using the following aspects to depict their differences:
1. **Predictability**: How predictable is software development at each level?
2. **Repeatability**: How repeatable is the development process at each level?
3. **Quantifiability**: How quantifiable is software development?

The staged representation of the CMMI 6 offers its maturity levels to be used also in the software product family engineering context. We do not go into details here, because we just follow the CMMI terminology. For software family engineering, the different stages will have different focus areas and/or basic practices.
1. **Initial** – There is no managed and stable process available. Development proceeds in an ad hoc way.
2. **Managed** – There are planned processes available.
3. **Defined** – Processes adhere to standards.
4. **Quantitatively managed** – Processes are quantitatively tracked, and improved.
5. **Optimising** – Processes are continuously improved based on quantitative data.

5.1 Level 1: Initial

There is no managed and stable process available. Development proceeds in an ad hoc way.
1. **Predictability**: unpredictable
2. **Repeatability**: not repeatable at all (i.e., there is no related learning in the organisation)
3. **Quantifiability**: No data is available about past projects.

5.2 Level 2: Managed

There are planned processes available.
1. **Predictability**: tolerably
2. **Repeatability**: Good practices can be applied, and bad practices can be avoided.
3. **Quantifiability**: Data is available on past projects.
Planned processes are available guiding the work of the development. Their execution is measured to determine problems in time. No explicit tracking and learning are available. For most CMMI-identified practices at this level, there will be specific consequences for software product family engineering. Many of them stem from the interconnection of different processes and the distinction between common and variable software.

5.3 Level 3: Defined

Processes adhere to standards.
1. **Predictability**: satisfactorily
2. **Repeatability**: The process is tailored from the organisational software process.
3. **Quantifiability**: Data on past projects is available and analysed to be more effectively used by future projects.
Processes adhere to standards that are improved over time. Process measurements are used for process improvement. For most CMMI-identified practices at this level, there will be specific consequences for software product family engineering. Many of them stem from the interconnection and the continuity of different processes and the use of common software over project boundaries.

5.4 Level 4: Quantitatively Managed

Processes are quantitatively tracked and improved.
1. **Predictability**: very predictable
2. **Repeatability**: The process is tailored from the organisational software process with corresponding quantifiable data.
3. **Quantifiability**: Software development data from past projects have been packaged into quantified models to be used to estimate and predict future projects.
Processes are quantitatively tracked and improved. The organisation adheres to these processes. It is not clear whether software product family engineering has much im-

pact at this level. It may well be that just doing software product family engineering eases the execution of this level.

5.5 Level 5: Optimising

Processes are continuously improved based on quantitative data.
1. **Predictability**: extremely predictable
2. **Repeatability**: fully repeatable given the commonality and variability between past and new projects
3. **Quantifiability**: The process of new projects can be optimised based on the data and corresponding analysis of past projects.

Processes are improved continuously based on a quantitative understanding of the common causes of variation inherent in processes. Just as for level 4, it is not clear whether software product family engineering has much impact at this level. It may well be that just doing software product family engineering eases the execution of this level.

6 Organisational Dimension (BAPO-O)

The organisational dimension deals with the way the organisation is able to deal with complex relationships and many responsibilities. This dimension is refined with respect to the work of van der Linden and associates 9 and combined with the taxonomy presented by Bosch 2.

Software family engineering results in a separation of activities, often over organisational borders. In addition to software assets, other artefacts such as development plans and roadmaps are shared over these borders. This means that the organisation should have individuals or teams that are responsible for the interaction of the shared artefacts between the different parties involved in the development.

Despite the emergence of a variety of technological solutions aimed at reducing the effects of geographical location, the physical location of the staff involved in the software product family engineering still plays a role. It is simply more difficult to maintain effective and efficient communication channels between teams in disparate locations and, perhaps even, time zones, than it is between collocated teams. Therefore, units that need to exchange much information should preferably be located closer to each other than units that can cooperate with less information. The following aspects can be identified that influence the evaluation in the organisational dimension:
1. **Geographic distribution**: How complex is the geographic distribution of the software family engineering organisation: local projects, and departments, companywide or even over company borders.
2. **Culture**: What are the shared values related to the software family engineering: internally or cooperatively focused, individual or central valued, conservative vs. innovative, product vs. process focused
3. **Roles & Responsibilities**: How well does the organisation manage the distinct responsibilities and relationships occurring in the software family engineering: undifferentiated vs. specialised roles for software family engineering

4. **Product life cycle**: An important factor influencing the optimal organisational model is the type of systems that are produced, in relationship to the characteristics of the product life cycle. Factors that play a role are the length of the life cycle, the pace of the generations, and the kind of maintenance that is provided.

We have defined the following level structure. Below, we discuss the levels in more detail:

1. **Unit oriented** – The software family engineering takes place within single, small development *units*.
2. **Business lines oriented** – The software family engineering takes place within several units of a *business line* responsible for a single range of products.
3. **Business group/division** – The software family engineering takes place over business line borders within a single *business group* or product *division*, responsible for many business related products.
4. **Inter-division/companies** – The software family engineering takes place between several *divisions* and *companies*, with mutual trust, each with their own commercial responsibility, which may be conflicting.
5. **Open business** – The software family engineering is not restricted to a collection of companies that trust each other. The open business involves everybody who sees the advantage.

6.1 Level 1: Unit Oriented

The software family engineering takes place within single, small development *units*.
1. **Geographic distribution**: local projects
2. **Culture**: internally focused
3. **Roles & Responsibilities**: software family engineering undifferentiated
4. **Product life cycle**: medium term

This level is referred to as the "development department" by Bosch 2. In this model, software development is concentrated in a single development department. No organisational specialisation exists with either the software product family engineering assets or the systems in the family. The model is especially suitable for smaller organisations. The primary advantages are that it is simple and communication between staff members is easy, whereas a disadvantage is that it does not scale to larger organisations.

The internally focused culture supports the trust and respect that people have for each other, leading to ease in the distribution of work and taking over work from each other. The products have a medium or long life span, with no large maintenance commitments, resulting in only a low-maintenance burden on the developers.

6.2 Level 2: Business Lines Oriented

The software family engineering takes place within several units of a *business line* responsible for a single range of products.
1. **Geographic distribution**: multiple application engineering units
2. **Culture**: cooperative within the business line
3. **Roles & Responsibilities**: software family engineering roles and asset roles
4. **Product life cycle**: medium to long term

In Bosch's work 2, this level is called "Business units." The software family engineering takes place in a single business line involving several development units. An advantage of the model is that it allows for the effective sharing of assets between a set of organisational units. A disadvantage is that business units easily focus on the concrete systems rather than on the reusable assets.

Often, each development unit is assigned the additional responsibility of evolving a subset of the domain assets that are to be reused by the other application units. People are relatively close to each other, but the number of developers within the family is large. Therefore, specialisation is necessary. In particular, the roles for software family engineering and application development are recognised and distributed. People are assigned to be responsible for the maintenance of certain family assets, such as components, or the architecture. In this situation, specific departments in the units, allowing longer life cycles of the products, can conduct product maintenance.

6.3   Level 3: Business Group/Division

The software family engineering takes place over business line borders within a single *business group* or product *division* responsible for many business-related products.
1. **Geographic distribution**: multiple units within one company
2. **Culture**: cooperative across business lines
3. **Roles & Responsibilities**: coordinated roles across business lines
4. **Product life cycle**: short to long term
This level is referred to as the "Domain engineering unit" by Bosch 2. At this level, the software family engineering takes place over different business lines within a single business group or division. A domain engineering unit is responsible for the design, development, and evolution of the reusable assets. Product engineering units are responsible for developing and evolving the products built based on the software family engineering assets. The model is widely scalable, from the boundaries where the business unit model reduces effectiveness up to hundreds of software engineers. Another advantage of this model is that it reduces communication from n-to-n in the business unit model to one-to-n between the domain engineering unit and the system engineering units. Finally, the domain engineering unit focuses on developing general, reusable assets, which addresses one of the problems with the aforementioned model—too little focus on the reusable assets.

6.4   Level 4: Inter-division/companies

The software family engineering takes place between several *divisions* and *companies*, with mutual trust, each with their own commercial responsibility, which may be conflicting.
1. **Geographic distribution**: consortium-based cooperation over company borders
2. **Culture**: externally focused
3. **Roles & Responsibilities**: liaison roles (between companies)
4. **Product life cycle**: short to long term
This level is called "Hierarchical domain engineering units" by Bosch 2. However, it generalises too many kinds of engineering structures. At this level, the development is

spread over several cooperating companies. Some of them will act as the subcontractor of others. In particular, this applies when different companies serve different parts of the domain. The structure is necessary to distribute the workload of the domain engineering. This model is applicable especially in large or very large organisations with a large variety of long-lived systems. The advantage of this model is that it provides an organisational model for effectively organizing large numbers of software engineers.

6.5 Level 5: Open Business

The software family engineering is not restricted to a collection of companies that trust each other. The open business involves everybody who sees the advantage.
1. **Geographic distribution**: industry-wide cooperation
2. **Culture**: extremely cooperative, competitive
3. **Roles & Responsibilities**: lobbying, marketing, standardization bodies
4. **Product life cycle**: very short to very long term
At this level, there is an open standard for the structured software family engineering. Several companies improve parts of the family through additions adhering to the standard. Often, but not necessarily (see open source), a single company is strong enough to set the standard.

7 Illustrative Example

In this section, we take the development described by Jaring, Krikhaar, and Bosch 7 to provide an example for evaluation and validation purposes. Although our evaluation framework is clearly not finished, it may already be useful to get initial ideas about its merits. The example development is about a family of magnetic resonance imaging (MRI) scanners. MRI is based on the principles that the nuclear magnetic relaxation times of different tissues differ, which opted magnetic resonance for scanning the inside of the human body.

A warning is in place here. We did not do a formal assessment of the development described here. The evaluation of the example below is done in a very global way, since, for most of the dimensions, a set of precise criteria is not yet available. These still have to be determined. We are aiming for this result for next year. However, the result gives an *indication* of what the evaluated level of the development will be, and where the focus on improvements will be.

7.1 Business Dimension

1. **Identity** – This is very clear: the business is to provide high-quality MRI scanners to the hospitals. The scanners are organised in families at the business level.
2. **Vision** – It is recognised that a software family engineering approach will improve the products' quality and time to market, resulting in a medium-term vision.

3. **Objectives** – The objectives for doing software family engineering within the business are mainly qualitative.
4. **Strategic planning** – The business has a process in place for planning the family.
Based on these findings, we come to a level 3 at the business dimension.

7.2 Architecture Dimension

1. **Software product family architecture** – This is enforced within the organisation.
2. **Product quality** – Quality is tracked from stakeholders to assets and tests.
3. **Reuse levels** – The reuse is managed through many architectural guidelines, rules, and frameworks.
4. **Software variability management** – There are many variation points that are managed through the architecture.
Based on these findings, we come to a level 4 at the architecture dimension.

7.3 Process Dimension

The organisation is assessed to be at CMM level 3. Of course, this does not mean that the process level would be 3 for the family-specific point of view, but presumably, it is close to this level.

7.4 Organisation Dimension

1. **Geographic distribution** – The development as discussed here is part of a development within several units within one company.
2. **Culture** – cooperation over business lines
3. **Roles & Responsibilities** – coordination across business lines
4. **Product life cycle** – very long life cycle. Separate departments for maintenance, distributed development within company borders, and the development are parts of a structured software family engineering.
Based on these findings, we come to a level 3 at the organisation dimension.

Concluding, we arrive with total assessment results in a profile of B3 A4 P3 O3 (i.e., intermediate in all dimensions). This may be very satisfactory for this business, as all dimensions are taken into account. This result implies that none of the dimensions is stressing too far with respect to the others. If the products are serving a mature product domain where the group itself can be seen as a shaper of the business itself, more effort may be put into the business dimension, moving towards level 4. If this grows, the process and organisation can grow to level 4 as well. The precise choice for improvement actions is, however, also dependent on the wishes and goals of the development organisation itself. Please note that *this assessment result does not reflect the actual maturity of the business group. It is intended for illustrative purposes only.* However, the maturity model for software product family engineering offers a highly useful technique for evaluating software-developing organisations that employ product families.

8 Looking Back: Related Work

Since the late 80s, a number of capability evaluation models have been developed for various fields of assessment including systems engineering, software engineering, software acquisition, workforce management and development, and integrated product and process development. The overall idea is to compare a process carried out by an organisation to an ideal that is presented by a capability evaluation model. Process improvement is the elimination of differences between the current and the ideal process. This approach can be characterised as normative and top down. The assumption behind this approach is that improved processes lead themselves to improved products.

The most prominent process improvement framework is the CMM, which was developed by the Software Engineering Institute (SEI) and published in 1993 5, 11. The "non-U.S." counterpart to the CMM is the International Organisation for Standardization/International Electrotechnical Commission (ISO/IEC) 15504 Standard for Software Process Assessment (commonly called SPICE). For systems engineering, the CMM for Software Engineering (SE-CMM) and the Electronic Industries Alliance Interim Standard EIA/IS 731 were developed. CMMI 6 has been created recently by the SEI to integrate the SEI's SW-CMM, EIA/IS 731, and the Integrated Product Development CMM (IPD-CMM) into a single coherent process improvement framework 5 6. Some of the developments resulting in the CMMI are shown in Figure 2.

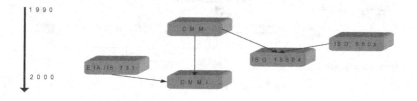

Fig. 2. History of process improvement frameworks

The SEI's Product Line Technical Probe (PLTP) allows the examination of an organisation's readiness to adopt or its ability to succeed with a software product family engineering approach. The PLTP is based on the SEI's Framework for Software Product Line Practice[SM] (version 4.0 was published in Clements and Northrop's book 4) as a reference model in the collection and in analysis of data about an organisation. The results of applying the PLTP include a set of findings that characterize an organisation's strengths and challenges relative to its product line effort and a set of recommendations.

The Framework for Software Product Line Practice distinguishes 29 practice areas that are divided loosely into three categories 10. Software engineering practice areas are necessary to apply the appropriate technology to create and evolve both core assets and products. Technical management practice areas are those management practices necessary to engineer the creation and evolution of the core assets and the products. Organisational management practice areas are necessary for the synchronization of all the activities for software product family engineering.

Our model is an improvement with respect to the Framework for Software Product Line Practice in the fact that it clearly separates the distinct BAPO development concerns. The focus of the SEI framework is mainly on what we call process concerns because the practice areas of that framework roughly cover the different issues addressed by CMMI, engineering, support, process, and project management. We have identified architecture, business, and organisation aspects as important as the process, which will be pursued to get a better understanding of them. Another important difference between the SEI framework and our model is their structure. The SEI framework does not comprise any levels, implying a direction of improvement, while our model offers levels and is thus also suitable for benchmarking and roadmapping.

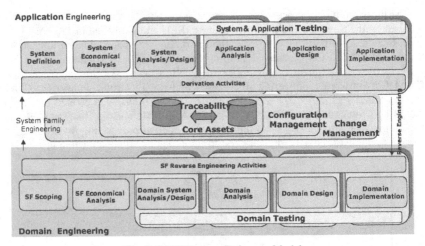

Fig. 3. CAFE Process Reference Model

The ITEA's CAFÉ project has developed a reference framework for software family engineering practices (CAFÉ-RF) 7. The CAFÉ-RF takes into account the different BAPO aspects and consists of several models: a reference information technology (IT) life cycle for system families (which identifies the major phases in an IT organisation when carrying out a system family effort), a process reference model (CAFÉ-PRM, which represents major engineering activities operating on the core assets), and an asset reference model (CAFÉ-ARM, which represents the major assets of interest). The reference process model shown in Figure 3 shows only the most important activities on software family engineering, grouped according to domain engineering (development for reuse) at the bottom, application engineering (development with reuse, for customers) at the top, and supporting processes for asset management in the middle. No explicit flows between activities are depicted since they can change over and within organisations. Application engineering processes are put at the top, since they are the most important business concerns. Domain engineering and asset management are supporting and only necessary for an efficient software family engineering process.

9 Conclusion and Future Work

This paper improves the evaluation frameworks for software family engineering presented in the work of van der Linden and associates 9 and Bosch 3. The framework serves for benchmarking the organisation against others, enables assessments for single organisations, and provides directions for improvement. As there are four groups of development concerns (BAPO), we have defined four distinct evaluation scales. Evaluation of an organisation will lead to a profile with separate values for each of the four scales. Depending on the organisation context, there will be an optimum profile for that organisation (i.e., top marks for each dimension may not be optimal from a business and economic perspective). The organisation may use the framework to determine whether it has the optimum profile. In case it does not have the right profile, it helps to select those actions that should be done to reach the optimum. Care should be taken that improvement actions for one of the profile scales may lead to reduced values for the other scales.

We plan to improve the present evaluation framework by providing more details and clear descriptions, taking into account the practices in present industrial software product family engineering. This improvement will be performed mainly in the ITEA FAMILIES project.

Acknowledgments. We thank Lech Krzanik for the discussions during the Dagstuhl Seminar 03151 on Product Family Development, April 6 – 11, 2003, Schloss Dagstuhl, Wadern, Germany. These discussions were the basis of the first paper 9 on the framework to which all have contributed. Moreover, we thank Klaus Pohl, Peter Knauber, Linda Northrop, and Günter Böckle who were co-organizers (with Frank van der Linden) of this Dagstuhl seminar, facilitating the discussions. Finally, we thank all those involved in the ITEA projects ESAPS, CAFÉ and FAMILIES presenting and discussing best practices in family engineering in many workshops and other meetings. There are too many people involved in these projects to name them all.

References

1. Pierre America, Henk Obbink, Rob van Ommering, Frank van der Linden, CoPAM: A Component-Oriented Platform Architecting Method Family for Product family Engineering, Proceedings SPLC-1 pp. 167-180
2. Jan Bosch, Software Product Lines: Organisational Alternatives, Proceedings of the 23rd International Conference on Software Engineering (ICSE 2001), pp. 91-100, May 2001.
3. Jan Bosch, Maturity and Evolution in Software Product lines: Approaches, Artefacts and Organisation, Proceedings of the Second International Conference on Software Product Lines (SPLC 2), Springer LNCS 2379 pp. 257-271, August 2002.
4. Clements, Paul; Northrop, Linda; Software Product Lines – Practices and Patterns, Addison Wesley, 2001.
5. CMMI for Systems Engineering/Software Engineering/Integrated Product and Process Development/Supplier Sourcing, Version 1.1, Continuous Representation (CMMI-SE/SW/IPPD/SS, V1.1, Continuous), Technical Report CMU/SEI-2002-TR-011, Carnegie Mellon University, Pittsburgh, 2002

6. CMMI for Systems Engineering/Software Engineering/Integrated Product and Process Development/Supplier Sourcing, Version 1.1, Staged Representation (CMMI-SE/SW/IPPD/SS, V1.1, Staged), Technical Report CMU/SEI-2002-TR-012, Carnegie Mellon University, Pittsburgh, 2002
7. Michel Jaring, René L. Krikhaar and Jan Bosch, Visualizing and Classifying Software Variability in a Family of Magnetic Resonance Imaging Scanners, Software Practice and Experience, June 2003.
8. Frank van der Linden, Software Product families in Europe: The Esaps and Café Projects, IEEE Software, July/August 2002, pp. 41-49
9. Frank van der Linden, Jan Bosch, Erik Kamsties, Kari Känsälä, Lech Krzanik, Henk Obbink, Software Product Family Evaluation, Proceedings PFE 2003, 5th workshop on product-family engineering, November 2003, Springer LNCS 3014, pp. 376-394.
10. Northrop, et al. A Framework for Software Product Line Practice Version 4.1, http://www.sei.cmu.edu/plp/framework.html
11. M. Paulk, et. al., Capability Maturity Model of Software, Version 1.1. Tech Report CMU/SEI-93-TR24, Carnegie Mellon University, Pittsburgh, 1993
12. Klaus Schmid, Scoping Product lines, Software Product lines - Proceedings of the First Software Product Line Conference (SPLC1), Kluwer, August 2000, pp. 513-532

Practical Evaluation of Software Product Family Architectures*

Eila Niemelä, Mari Matinlassi, and Anne Taulavuori

VTT Technical Research Centre of Finland
P.O. Box 1100, FIN-90571 Oulu, Finland
{Eila.Niemela,Mari.Matinlassi,Anne.Taulavuori}@vtt.fi

Abstract. Faster time to market and decreased development and maintenance costs are goals most companies are trying to reach. Product family engineering (PFE) provides a means of achieving these goals. Product family architecture (PFA) is the key issue in family engineering. However, companies have to decide how to adopt PFE and how to develop their software PFA. This paper introduces the basic issues essential to PFA development, explores three different approaches to applying PFAs in industrial settings, and, finally, presents the evaluation results through an evaluation model of software product families.

1 Introduction

During the last decade, industrial companies have been applying product family engineering (PFE) intensively to shorten the time to market, decrease the development costs, and increase the quality of software products. The core idea in software PFE is to use the same software assets (i.e. requirements, architecture, components, test cases, and so on) as much as possible in all family members. The adoption of the PFE approach involves, however, not only remarkable investments, but also changes in work organization and in the use of special development methods and techniques. Thus, a company intending to apply PFE in software production should first investigate the benefits, preconditions, and constraints entailed in the application of PFE and what can be learned from the experience of companies that have already applied the approach in practice.

Several attempts have been made to explain what the preconditions are for a successful adoption of PFE regarding business, architecture, organization, and process. The context of product family adoption has been explored from the points of view of market, organization, business unit, and individual person [1]. The economics of product line adoption have also been considered [2], as well as the development and evolution of product family architectures (PFAs) [3, 4]. Furthermore, a model for software product family evaluation has been proposed suggesting four dimensions that relate to common software engineering concerns: (1) business, (2) architecture, (3) process, and (4) organization (BAPO) [5]. The model is designed to be used for the benchmarking and assessment of software product family development, thus also

---

* This work was carried out in the Eureka Σ! 2023 Programme, ITEA project ip02009, FAMILIES. We wish to thank the interviewed companies for their contribution.

R.L. Nord (Ed.): SPLC 2004, LNCS 3154, pp. 130–145, 2004.

providing support for justifying why and how to develop a product family and how to improve product family development. However, none of these approaches explicitly define how to evaluate PFAs.

In this paper, we attempt to investigate the concerns related to the evaluation of PFAs. Although the focus is on architecture, we have already discovered that architecture is not a concern isolated from the other dimensions of PFE. Therefore, we also considered how architecture development is related to business, process, and organization. The work presented in this paper is based partly on a number of our earlier findings concerning software PFE [6] and on the experiences of the development of software PFAs in industrial settings [7, 8]. We also introduce an evaluation method that uses empirical information collected from industry by structural interviews along with reviews of PFA artifacts. The evaluation results are presented using the evaluation model of software product families based on the work of van der Linden and associates [5]. We also examine how well the evaluation model matches the findings made by the authors in the industry and propose some refinements for the improvement of the evaluation model.

The main contribution of this paper is to introduce how software PFAs can be evaluated and presented through a standard evaluation model. The other contribution of this paper is to leverage information about how small- and medium-sized companies apply PFE in their product development: specifically, which kinds of approaches are applied, why they are chosen, and how they work in practice when applied.

This paper is structured as follows. Section 2 presents the three evaluation approaches: (1) evaluation criteria for product families [6], (2) the BAPO reasoning framework [9], and (3) an overview of the Family Evaluation Framework (FEF) [5]. Section 3 introduces the family architecture evaluation (FAE) method, and Section 4 illustrates how to apply the method in practice. Section 5 discusses the lessons learned. The paper closes with conclusion remarks and future directions for this research in Section 6.

2 Background

The evaluation criteria for product families, as defined by Niemelä and Ihme [6], represent the categorized elements to be investigated when adopting PFE practices. These elements cover various issues of reuse infrastructure that comprises three parts: (1) organization culture and processes, (2) PFA, and (3) assets management. The first part consists of business drivers that identify the most important characteristics concerning product assortment and business manners. The second part concentrates on defining domains by preconditions and goals for PFE. The third part covers organization, process, architecture, and management issues related to the development and evolution of core assets. The evaluation criteria were defined based on the knowledge gained from industrial companies through a set of interviews and from the development of several component-based software architectures for industrial embedded systems.

The BAPO reasoning framework [9] places architecture in company-wide component-based software engineering and identifies logical relations between business and architecture, and architecture and process. Architecture is further divided into five views: (1) customer, (2) application, (3) functional, (4) conceptual, and (5) realization

(CAFCR) [10]. The customer and application views explain the rationale behind the architecture. The functional view sets functional requirements for products. The conceptual view defines the architectural concepts used in family engineering, and the realization view defines which kinds of technologies are used to build systems. Thus, the customer/application (CA) part defines the link to business and application domain(s), and the realization view links architecture to the development process. The functional/conceptual (FC) part considers pure architectural issues. CAFCR views have been applied also to the analysis of evolving variation points in PFAs, extended by experts' knowledge and an automatic analysis tool [11].

FEF [5] supports all four dimensions of BAPO and suggests five levels for architecture (FEF-A), process, and organization, and three levels for business. The business levels are reactive, extrapolate, and proactive. On the reactive level, architecture is based on the best guess because business vision is short term, and objectives are missing. On the extrapolate level, business is based on a medium-term vision and qualitative objectives; therefore, the architecture should be able to reflect them and provide feedback to strategic planning. On the proactive level, business gives the direction for architecture planning.

The architecture dimension (FEF-A) is categorized to five levels [4]. On the first level (independent product development), there is no sharing of artifacts. On the second level (standardized infrastructure), only external components are specified and used. On the third level (software platform), the architecture defines common features for all products, using internal platform components. On the fourth level (software product family), the architecture and variation points are fully specified and managed. On the fifth level, the PFA is enforced, and product members are generated automatically. On this level, the complete organization has to support the PFA because it has to remain stable and adaptive for a considerable period of time. FEF is explained in more detail by van der Linden and associates [5].

3   Family Architecture Evaluation Method

This section describes the FAE method developed for use by companies and product family architects wishing to benchmark their PFA. The FAE method defines how to use the above mentioned frameworks in family architecture evaluation. Although the applicability of the method was validated through three industrial case studies in small- and medium-sized companies, the method is likely to be useful in a wide variety of applications in analyzing PFAs.

The FAE method includes four steps, which give an overview of the method:

1. Evaluation Framework for Interviews. Three companies that applied the product family approach in different contexts were selected for the interviews. The questions were defined based on the evaluation criteria framework [6]. The number of questions was limited by setting a maximum time of three hours for the interviews. However, in the first interview, we discovered that a reasonable duration for an interview was more likely to be two than three hours. Thus, the questions were reformulated to fit that limit. The evaluation criteria were used because the framework supports a classification of questions into three categories: (1) business, (2) domain, and (3) technology related to the development and maintenance of PFA. Depending on the size of a company, these categorized issues are covered by different stakeholders:

business managers, research and development managers operating in specific domains, and product family architects. Thus, the categorized issues support carrying out the interview in several parts.

Although business and domain analysis have similar topics (e.g. context and variability), the topics are considered from different points of view. While business analysis includes the parts of architecture that are visible outside the company, domain analysis concentrates on the specific characteristics of a domain. The core asset analysis, again, concentrates on the methods, techniques, and technologies used in the design, implementation, testing, and maintenance of the PFA. The analysis also considers the assets shared among family members and the reasons behind their selection.

2. Review/Inspection of Architectural Artifacts. The aim of review is to gain an understanding of the kind of product family approach a company is applying in PFE. If the architecture is documented and the documentation is up-to-date, architectural descriptions provide the best source for architecture evaluation. In two cases, the architectural documentation was up-to-date and available for review. The purpose of the review was not only to gain insight into the PFA, but also to propose improvements if needs were identified. Depending on the size of architecture, the review/inspection took one to two weeks.

Architecture descriptions did not have a key role in the third company because of its small number of employees, the common platforms used, and the maturity of the product family. Essentially, the architecture was captured inside platforms, configuration mechanisms, and a specific application-programming language. Consequently, getting acquainted with all of these would have taken too much time and provided only a negligible contribution to our main goal.

3. Analyzing Results. In the analysis phase, the results from interviews were collected and reformulated to a comparison framework. That framework was created by reorganizing the questions of the interview framework in such a way that they would match the aspects of the FEF-A. Relevant questions connected with the relations between business and architecture, and architecture and process. Architecture and organization were also classified. This reorganization resulted in 44 questions that were rated relevant to PFAs. Most of the removed questions were purely related to business. Although these questions did not make any direct contribution to the architecture evaluation, they provided valuable insight into the business context where the PFA was used. They also provided justification for the architectural decisions made and the information used to identify the company properties that were meaningful for the organization of the evaluation results.

4. Evaluation Framework for Benchmarking. Based on the comparison framework and the levels and aspects defined in the architecture dimension of the family evaluation framework (FEF-A), an evaluation framework was constructed (Table 1). FEF defines four aspects that are used to identify the maturity level of the PFA: (1) product family architecture, (2) product quality, (3) reuse level, and (4) domain. Furthermore, software variability management, driving forces, and relations to the organization, processes, and business have to be considered. The aspects from level 1 to level 5 vary in the following way [5]:

- **Aspect 1:** Product family architecture :=
  < not established | specified external components | common features captured |
  fully pecified | enforced >

Table 1. Evaluation framework for PFAs

Relation/PFA	Aspect	Item
Business to PFA	Domain	• Driving force: technology, application, both • Main functional properties • Quality requirements • Change frequency in a domain • Life-cycle or customer-specific features • Trend in customer needs
	Openness	• Number of third-party components • Number of subcontractors/component providers
	Variability	• Number of members in a product family • Different parts; %/features; number of functional subsystems/components, %/total software • Reasons for differentiation • Assembling is based on existing components, (re)used/modified and new components • Variable quality requirements • Variability management • Customized third-party components
PFA	Context	• Identified domains • Reasons for their importance • Visibility of domains in the PFA
	Domain knowledge	• Common architecture for family members • Platforms • Shared components
	Variability	• Common properties • Binding time
	Core assets	• What are they? • Architectural styles and patterns • Design patterns • Component model • Appropriateness of the component model • Separation of hardware-related variability
PFA to process		• Methods in architecting • Modeling languages • Validation practices • Selection of third-party components • Stakeholders of the PFA • Guidelines • Guidelines in practice
PFA to organization		• Number of domain analysts • Applied standards • Open standards • Constraints set by other authorities • PFE familiarity • Model-driven architecture (MDA) familiarity • Effort used for sharing domain/design knowledge • Importance of documentation in knowledge sharing

- **Aspect 2:** Product quality :=
  < ignored or ad hoc | through infrastructure, overengineering | inherited from plat-
  form | a key priority | implemented as variation points >
- **Aspect 3:** Reuse level :=
  < ad hoc | external components | internal platform components | managed | auto-
  matic generation of family members >
- **Aspect 4:** Domain :=
  < emerging | late emerging phase or early maturing phase | mature | late maturing
  phase or established | established >

Additional characteristics on each level are:

- *Variability management* :=
  < absent | limited variation points in infrastructure | managed in platform | manage
  variation points and dependencies between them | automatic selection and opti-
  mized verification of variants in variation points >
- *Forces* :=
  < business case based | knowledge sharing between units through infrastructure |
  core software | freedom restricted by PFA | stable and adaptive PFA >
- *Relation to organization, process, and business* :=
  < responsibilities assigned to business units; no separation of business and process |
  infrastructure and its harmonized evolution; process and business interest unrelated
  | larger part of organization involved; process separates platform and product de-
  velopment; business defines the profit of the platform development | organizational
  commitment; process considers the stakeholders; business determines variations in
  the PFA | complete organizational support for PFA; interdependent processes and
  businesses >

4   Results of the Family Architecture Evaluation

This section presents the evaluation results of product families in three companies by
applying the FEF-A dimension of FEF. First, the companies are characterized by a set
of business related properties.

4.1   Business of the Interviewed Companies

To give insight into the interviewed companies (A, B, C), we briefly introduce their
business contexts by a set of properties (Table 2). The presentation of companies is
age order based; the age of the product family varies from 1 to 10 years. Each company represents a different application field: information systems, measurements
systems, and analyzer and simulation software. Thus, the last one is a pure software
company, whereas the others produce embedded systems. The company size varies
from a couple of persons to over 100 software developers. Company C has three sites,
while the others are operating in one place.

Whereas software development costs are a dominating factor in software and
measurement systems, this is not the case in the development of networked information systems (company A). The use ratio of one's own proprietary software is high:
from 80% to 100%. Thus, software is developed in relatively closed development

environments. Companies A and B produce customized products, whereas company C delivers only releases. The customization degree is normally 10 to 25%/software, but it can be as high as 50%/software. Unlike the other two companies, company B also customizes hardware annually.

Table 2. Business context

Property	A	B	C
Age of product family (PF)	1 year	8 years	10 years
Size of PF	2 family members 2 products outside PF	12 family members	2 families (5 and 2 members)
Size of products	System/networked system/part of a networked system	Networked system	PC applications
Application field	Information system	Measurement systems	Analyzer and simulation software
Number of software developers	20	2-5	110
Software (SW) cost %/ total cost	50% (delivers differ): SW-cost is maintenance based; hardware (HW)-cost is delivery based.	60%	80%
Own/third-party software	80%/20%	100%/0%	95%/5%
Customized deliveries	9/10	Each product	2-5/releases/year
Scope of customization	10-20%/sometimes 50%	15-25% customized 5-15%/new features	0%
Customized products/year	5-10	Customized SW: 5-10/year Customized HW: 2-3/year	0

4.2 Preconditions for Product Family Architecture

To analyze the preconditions for the development of a PFA, three issues were considered: (1) the characteristics of the domain(s) where a company is operating, (2) the dependence on third-party components, and (3) the scope, reasons, and management of the various product features.

Considering the stability of the domains included in a PFA, the following commonalities and differences were identified:

- Most products included several domains and their PFAs were both application driven and technology driven. This was obvious in the two embedded systems cases. In the software product family, application-driven software and technology-driven software were separated into product families of their own. In system families, the domains were also separated to different parts of the architecture if the product family was mature enough.

- Companies focused on the one or two domains in which they showed a high degree of competence. Thus, the precondition of high domain knowledge was present in all cases.
- Hardware technologies drove all the product families. In the case of company B, the driving force was measurement technology. Although company C was a pure software company, it turned out to observe the trends of hardware manufacturers and used this information for predicting customers' needs.
- The main functionality was allocated to different subsystems or different families. System families used subsystems for separation, whereas software product families allocated main functionality to separate families.
- Quality drivers proved to be dependent on core competence or a business role. In the case of company B, quality drivers were set by measurement technologies. Because company A was acting as an integrator, maintainability had the first priority; however, several execution qualities were also important. The software provider considered qualities visible to the software users to be of top priority.
- Changes within domains and those in hardware technologies were intertwined. Normally, domain changes were seen as forces of new hardware technologies. However, company B, which provided two to three customized hardware to the market per year, did not see this as a change of domain. This means that the product family of company B included both hardware and software, whereas the other two companies considered their product families to contain only software.
- Changes in customers' needs did not prevent the adoption of PFE practices. In most cases, coming changes were known in advance thanks to observation and domain-specific knowledge. If changes occurred, they could be handled by normal business practices.

The use of third-party components was quite low; two companies (A and C) used five to six components delivered by the same number of providers. The original software component manufacturer (OCM) component was considered as the company's own component (i.e., no special practices). Thus, companies A and C could be considered integrators: A was a system integrator and C a software integrator. Company B used only one third-party component.

Considering variability, the aim was to study how variability was seen from a business point of view: why it was needed, where it was to be found, and how this information was used. The observations can be summarized as follows (Table 3):

- Commonalities were included in the product families. The differences between products were analyzed before including them in a product family. For example, only 50% of company A's products were family members.
- Differences were managed in different ways. For example, integrators mapped differences to PFAs, whereas the software provider managed them through features.
- The reuse level of components was high: 70 to 100%. The variation can be explained by different business manners. While company C produced only release-based deliveries, the others turned out customized products. This means that in company C, domain engineering produces components, and product engineering assembles products from those components.

- Variable qualities were execution qualities. This was obvious in all cases. The other observation was that whenever a product family included wired and wireless product variants, there were also variabilities in qualities.
- Variability was used for pricing and configuration. System integrators used variability for pricing, while the software provider employed it as a configuration code.
- Integrators could benefit from customized third-party components. While this may be too strong a generalization based on only three cases, our earlier experience shows that system integrators more often need customized components and software providers merely use COTS components (if using third-party components at all).

Table 3. Variability management

Item	A	B	C
Similar products	50 %	all	all
Differences	In three parts mainly (positioning, travel card, security)	around 30% (application part)	20%/features
Why different	Environment Customer needs	Market segments Customer needs	Technologies
Assembling	90% reused (10% third party) 10% modified	70% reused 30% modified or new	100% from existing components
Differences in quality	HW: cold, robustness SW: security, performance	Performance	Reliability: correctness and accuracy
Variability management	Basic/extra price	The manager makes decisions; visible in price	Logistics: special product codes
Customized third party	2	0	0

4.3 Product Family Architecture

Considering the relations of the PFA to its context, domain knowledge, variability, and core assets, the following observations were made:
Context:
- Companies had two or four domains. The domains of the software provider were more focused than system integrator domains that defined a domain, for example, as an information or measurement system.
- Domains were important because of three possible reasons: (1) the company was a market leader in Finland, (2) the domain provided a promising market globally, or (3) the domain knowledge provided an advantage on the national and international level.
- All domains were visible in the PFA; as a family, platform, subsystem, layer, or even as components or an application layer. Thus, the PFA was used for managing business, organization, and domain knowledge.

Domain knowledge and variability:
- All companies had a PFA.
- Company B had two platforms: a technology platform and an application platform. Company C had also two platforms: one for each product family. Company A did not have a platform, but the reason may be found in the short age and small size of the family.
- Software components were shared as (1) a core functionality, (2) subsystems, and (3) platforms. Components were binary, dynamic link libraries, source code, or design components.
- Binding times showed remarkable differences. Company A used all levels: architecture, compilation, assembling, installation, and runtime. Some parts were fixed on the architecture level, but, in most cases, each part of the system had four types of features: those bound up with (1) compile time, (2) assembling, (3) installation, or (4) runtime. Company B used compile-time and runtime bindings for variation. Company C used assembling and runtime bindings. Within the context of the FEF, late binding is considered a sign of the PFA's maturity. The short age of the family architecture in case A was an obvious reason for the use of all kinds of variation bindings. However, there can also be other reasons. For example, different domains are likely to require different kinds of bindings (company A had more domains in its product family than the others). Openness may also require several variation-binding techniques (company A used customized third-party components, and its family was also the most custom-specific one vis-à-vis the other product families).

Core assets:
- The scope of core assets varied remarkably; company B considered designs, source code, and test cases as core assets. Besides the former, company C also regarded configuration rules and product delivery process guidelines as core assets. The delivery process was valued as a very important asset. Furthermore, company A named requirements, product family architecting, and product derivation methods as core assets.
- It proved to be difficult to figure out the use of architectural styles and patterns without architectural descriptions. The reason is that usually companies do not use styles or patterns intentionally, but rather due to the fact that they are present in their architectural descriptions. This was the case, for example, with company C that was using architectural styles and patterns along with design patterns, although staff members were convinced in the interview that they did not use them. In summary, two companies were in fact using architectural styles and patterns. The third one reported not using them, and no architectural descriptions were available for checking the situation. The most often used architectural styles were client-server, layered, and independent-component styles. The most often used design patterns were proxy and bridge; other patterns used included visitor, abstract factory, factory method, active object, singleton, composite, and observer. Thus, the architectures were defined exactly enough, and they were mature enough to be considered a PFA.
- The CORBA and COM component models were used. Company B did not use any component model, but its architecture supported components on the subsystem level, and fine-grained modularization was handled as functions and procedures,

configured through the company's own application-programming language. Technically, all the component models were suitable for use in their respective contexts. In one case, however, the use of a common component model was considered too expensive.

- The separation of hardware-caused variability from other types of software variation was appropriate in all cases except for one subsystem in company A's product family.

4.4 Linking Architecture to Processes and Organization

Regarding process and organizational matters, only the issues related to PFAs were examined. The identified differences and similarities in **architecture-process-related issues** are summarized in the following:

- Two methods were used for architecture: a proprietary method and QADA[SM]. Company B did not use any particular method. The Unified Modeling Language (UML) was used in two cases. Company B used only the structural text possibly because the company was very small and its product family was heavily based on platforms and its own application-programming language. Company B's product family was also the only one in which an assembly language was used to some degree.

- Unit testing and integration testing were employed in all cases. Company A made integration testing also for third-party components. The companies that had more than five developers also used inspection. Company C revealed that it would be using test automation in the near future. Company A was the only one also to test its products in real environments; the tests were carried out by end users.

- The selection of third-party components was supported only in one company that had been applying guidelines for component acquisition for 14 years. That company also used trials before making decisions.

- PFE was supported by several guidelines. Company A followed the ISO 9001 quality standard and had process models and guidelines for UML usage, coding, change management, and product data management. Company B did not have any documented guidelines. Neither did it seem to need any; the company had only two to five employees, so design practices were communicated in an informal way. Company C had guidelines for domain engineering, component specification, component acquisition, variability management, and version management. However, only variability and version management guidelines were in company-wide use.

There were also some important **organizational aspects** related to PFAs:

- The number of domain analysts depended on the size of the company and the size of the domain. Company B, the smallest one, had only one domain analyst. Company C had 50 domain experts in the technology-driven domain and only some in the application-driven domain. This means that about 50%/personnel were considered to have obtained domain expertise. In company A, 90% of the developers

---

[SM] QADA (Quality-driven Architecture Design and quality Analysis) is a service mark of VTT Technical Research Centre of Finland.

were also domain experts. The only reason identified was that the number of domains in that company was twice the number of domains in company C.

- Open standards were used in companies A (one standard) and C (four standards). Company B used hardware standards and some application-specific standards, depending on the customer. Hardware and application-specific standards were used in companies A and C as well. Company C also used telecom and protocol standards (domain specific). Standard component models and interface standards (software specific) were used in companies A and C.

- It was obvious that each domain had its own authorities setting constraints to the PFA. Domain-specific authorities (such as cities, towns, provinces, ministries of transportation and communication, bankers' associations, and so on) limited the scope of PFA and, in many cases, caused considerable variation. However, the companies were trying to manage the situation by using some widely used standard (e.g., ISO or country-related standards).

- Although the skills of software developers were rated very high regarding domain knowledge, their familiarity with PFE was astonishingly low. Companies B and C, which had been applying PFE for over eight years, affirmed that only a few of their employees were familiar with PFE. The reasoning is that although staff members were applying PFE in their practices, they were not familiar with the latest publications on it. Thus, despite the fact that there was some knowledge of PFE, it was not regarded as familiarity with PFE. This justification is also based partly on the results from company A; although its product family was the youngest, all software developers were familiar with PFE. Companies B and C, which had been operating in the field for a considerable period of time, did not consider their knowledge of PFE remarkable. PFE was just their everyday life, whereas the company that had just entered into PFE had used considerable effort to learn what PFE was. However, the common thing for all the companies was the unfamiliarity with MDA.

- Domain knowledge sharing was managed mainly in an informal way—through pair-work and conversions (about one hour/day). However, organizational change had modified the situation in one case, requiring more effort in knowledge sharing. That may be why this company estimated that documentation played a key role in its knowledge sharing (rating it four on a scale of one to five). The importance of documentation was rated medium in company A and marginal in company B, which is natural for a small company.

5 Discussion

5.1 Mapping the Cases to the FEF

The main identifiable reasons for the differences in the application of PFE in the interviewed companies were *the size of the company, business forces, business roles, and the types of products.* In the following, a brief summary is given of all the cases mapped to FEF-A.

Company A is the market leader in a niche market in Finland and has a high market share in Europe. Its PFA was defined, but it did not have a common platform. The reason was to be found in the relatively high degree of customization, even 50% in some cases. Company A's business role could be seen as that of an integrator; it used third-party components and application-specific standards, but only one open standard. The company used a standard component model, architectural styles and patterns, design patterns, and modeling languages. In summary, it aimed at using standard software technology as much as possible and managing variation through application standards and variation points. In summary

- PFA was explicitly specified and implemented (level 5).
- Quality was considered the key priority in software development, and some evolution qualities were implemented as variation points (level 4 or 5).
- Reuse level was managed (level 4).
- Domain was in the late maturing phase (level 4).
- Variation points and the dependencies between them were managed (level 4).

An automatic generation of family members was not possible because of customer-specific systems (i.e., automatic generation did not match the business idea). *Thus, company A matches level 4 in the FEF relatively well.*

Company B is operating in a niche market in Finland and Scandinavian and is just entering the market in Europe and Asia. Although the hardware technology was changed two to three times per year, this was regarded merely as changes in customers' needs. The company was using two platforms: a technology platform for managing hardware changes and an application platform for handling the variation in applications. The company was also using its own application language for customization and configuration, but no PFA was defined explicitly. Therefore, the company's

- PFA was on level 3
- quality level was 4
- reuse level was 4 or 5
- domain was established (level 5)
- variability management was on level 4 or 5

Although no PFA was specified, it was implemented by configurable application and technology platforms. However, only part (70%) of the software of a family member could be generated through their configuration. *Thus, the FEF levels do not match this case very well.*

Company C is operating in the global marketplace.

- The PFA of the simulator family was enforced (level 5); the other was on level 3.
- Product quality was the key priority, but was not implemented as variation points in the architecture or components (level 4).
- The reuse level was based on assembling (not automatic generation) of product family members (level 4 or 5).
- Domain was maturing or established (level 4).
- Software variability management was not based on automated selection, and the verification of variants at variation points had not been optimized yet.

The maturity of PFA differed widely between product families. Although company C's product families show a lot of variation, on the average, they represent FEF level 4.

5.2 Potential for Improvements

Table 4 summarizes some key items that seem to have a remarkable influence on the selected approach to applying PFE.

Company A, which is on level 4, is a system integrator. The company includes two products in the family, while the others remain outside. The focus is on customization, and the reuse degree is high. However, the scope of changes is sometimes very high. Problems may be the result of the company not using any platforms and including too many domains in its product family. Some of the domains are technology driven, and others are application driven. Improvements may be achieved by

- a separation of technology-driven and application-driven software into two different product families
- developing two platforms for the components that change relatively rarely: a technology platform and an application platform—both including the necessary mechanisms for managing quality attributes, variation points, and variability dependencies
- totally removing frequently changing software from the product families

Table 4. Identified variable key items in analyzed cases

Case	PFA maturity level	Business role	Forces	Re-use%	Scope of changes
A	Software Product Family	Integrator	Technology + Application	90	10-25 (up to 50)
B	Software Platform/ Configurable Product Base	System provider	Technology + Application	70	5-25
C	Configurable Product Base	Software provider	Technology/ application	100	0

Company B does not directly match any of the FEF levels. It is a system provider using a software product family as a means of customizing its high-level domain knowledge in a particular domain. Although (1) company B has separated technology-driven and application-driven parts to different platforms, (2) its software reuse degree is high, and (3) customization is perfectly limited, the company's software development costs were estimated as high as 60%/total costs. However, the share of software costs turned out to vary significantly between the different products, and the system requirements specification was also included in the software development costs because most new features were implemented by software. In the future, company B may have to regenerate its product family by applying new software technologies. In that case, it will be possible to integrate new mechanisms for handling quality attributes, variation points, and variation dependencies as part of the platforms already in use.

Company C, which is considered to be on level 4, is a pure software provider with two product families: one driven by technology, the other by application. The reuse degree of company C is 100%, meaning that all developed components are used in more than one release. Company C's products are release-based, and no customization is needed. Only the management of quality attributes and variation seems to require further improvements. This is also necessary because the company is aiming at introducing automatic testing.

Although the age of company C's product family is the highest, its evolution has been managed well, nearly achieving the top-level maturity ranking. Company B's product family is also top level, but its evolution seems to need some reshaping. Despite company A's product family being just at the beginning of its life cycle, there is already evidence that the company's actions were accurate and well timed. So far, two of three interviewed companies have already started to carry out the proposed improvements, and the third has planned to work on them in the near future.

The purpose of this paper was to introduce the FAE method and how it can be applied to improve PFAs. Although the set of questions included in the evaluation may change as we gain more experience in its applicability, we maintain that this kind of lightweight evaluation is necessary for every company applying PFE.

5.3   Enhancements to Family Evaluation Framework

Two of the companies were small; the third one was medium sized. The size of a company had proved to have a remarkable influence on how the relations from architecture to business, process, and organization were managed. The conclusion is that the FEF should categorize the relations between architecture and other FEF dimensions according to company size (e.g., to small, medium, enterprise, multisite, and multi-organizational levels). At present, the FEF supports the enterprise and multisite levels.

It was also obvious that it would be difficult, or even impossible, to give an overall ranking for a PFA because a company may show different maturity levels regarding the various aspects of PFA. Sometimes, it is not even appropriate to try to achieve the same level for the various aspects. For example, a company producing customized products can not achieve a fully automatic generation of product family members, which is why the definition of reuse level (aspect 3) needs to be enhanced on level 5.

The product quality aspect also seems to need improvement. At the moment, that aspect only considers evolution qualities that can be implemented as variation points (equals to level 5 in aspect 2), while failing to cover the execution qualities. Execution qualities do not allow mapping directly to variation points. Instead, they influence different architectural elements, which is why those qualities should be mapped to architectural components and connectors.

The FEF considers variability management as an additional characteristic at each level. In addition, variability management may show different levels in different parts of a PFA. For example, platforms can be rated level 5 and applications level 4. Therefore, variability management should be considered as an additional characteristic of different architectural elements/subsystems.

6   Conclusions

In this paper, a practical evaluation method for PFAs was presented. Any company intending to benchmark or improve its PFE approach will be able to benefit by applying this method. The application of the method was demonstrated by applying it in three cases representing three different kinds of business roles—integrator, system provider, and software provider—in three different business fields.

Although the FEF was defined originally for software product families, it appears to be applicable to systems families as well. However, the relations between architecture and other framework dimensions need to be enhanced for small- and medium-sized companies and also for multi-organizational software development. This applies to service-oriented software development, in particular.

The goal of benchmarking is to find out how to improve a particular product family. In all cases, one or more improvements could be proposed. Although this indicates that the method is applicable as such, future research will focus on applying the developed method to different kinds of PFAs and making it more systematic and accurate.

References

1. Buhne, S., Chastek, G., Käkölä, T., Knauber, P., Northrop, L., Thiel, S.: Exploring the Context of Product Line Adoption. Proceedings of PFE 2003, Lecture Notes in Computer Science, Vol. 3014. Springer-Verlag. (2004)
2. Schmidt, K., Verlage, M.: The Economic Impact of Product Line Adoption and Evolution. IEEE Software, 19 (4), (2002), 50-57.
3. Clements, P., Northrop, L.: Software Product Lines: Practices and Patterns. Boston, MA, USA: Addison-Wesley. (2002)
4. Bosch, J.: Design and use of software architectures: adopting and evolving a product-line approach. Harlow: Addison-Wesley. (2000)
5. van der Linden, F., Bosch, J., Kamsties, E., Känsälä, K., Krzanik, L., Obbink, H.: Software Product Family Evaluation. Proceedings of PFE 2003, Lecture Notes in Computer Science, Vol. 3014. Springer-Verlag. (2004), 376-394.
6. Niemelä, E., Ihme, T.: Product Line Software Engineering of Embedded Systems, ACM SIGSOFT Software Engineering Notes, 26 (3), (2001), 118-125.
7. Purhonen, A., Niemelä, E., Matinlassi, M.: Viewpoints of DSP Software and Service Architectures. Journal of Systems and Software, 69 (1-2), (2004), 57-73.
8. Matinlassi, M., Niemelä, E.: The Impact of Maintainability on Component-based Software Systems. The 29th Euromicro conference, Component-based software engineering. (2003), 25-32.
9. Obbink, H., America, P., van Ommering, R., Muller, J., van der Sterren, W., Wijnstra, J. G.: COPA: A Component-Oriented Platform Architecting Method for Families of Software-Intensive Electronic Products. SPLC1, (2000)
10. America, P., Rommes, E., Obbink, H.: Multi-View Variation Modeling for Scenario Analysis. Proceedings of PFE 2003, Lecture Notes of Computer Science, Vol. 3014. Springer-Verlag. (2004)
11. Wijnstra, J.G.: Evolving a Product Family in a Changing Context. Proceedings of PFE 2003, Lecture Notes of Computer Science, Vol. 3014. Springer-Verlag. (2004).

On the Development of Software Product-Family Components

Jan Bosch

University of Groningen, Department of Computing Science,
PO Box 800, 9700 AV Groningen, The Netherlands.
Jan.Bosch@cs.rug.nl, http://segroup.cs.rug.nl

Abstract. Several approaches to the development of shared artefacts in software product families exist. Each has advantages and disadvantages, but there is no clear framework for selecting among these alternatives. As a consequence, mismatches between the optimal approach and the one currently used by an organization may lead to several problems, such as a high degree of erosion, mismatches between product needs and shared components, organizational "noise" and inefficient knowledge management. This paper (1) presents the problems resulting from the aforementioned mismatch, (2) presents the relevant decision dimensions that define the space of alternatives, (3) discusses the advantages and disadvantages of each alternative and (4) presents a framework for selecting the best alternative for each decision dimension based on a three-stage adoption model.

1 Introduction

Software product families have achieved a broad recognition in the software industry. Many organizations either have adopted or are considering to adopt the technology. One of the key items in software product families is the development, evolution and use of shared components. Being able to develop a component once and use it in several products or systems is, obviously, one of the main benefits to be achieved.

The sharing of components among multiple systems is a great concept in theory and has been quite successful in the context of interorganizational reuse. Modern operating systems, database management systems, graphical user interfaces, component infrastructures, Web servers, Web browsers, and so forth offer a rich infrastructure based on which products can be quickly and easily developed. Intra-organizational reuse of components (i.e., software product families) on the other hand, has experienced considerably more problems in achieving a high degree of component sharing. In many organizations, achieving effective and efficient reuse of product-family components proves, in many cases, to be not trivial at all.

In the literature (e.g., books by Weiss and Lai [1] and Clements and Northrop [2]) as well as in our own publications (e.g., Bosch's book [3]), reasoning around the scoping of a shared software artefact in a product family is typically organized around the amount of sharing of features by the customers of the component team developing the shared component. However, although this provides an overview of the scoping of product-family components, it leaves many details to be implemented by the organization adopting software product families.

R.L. Nord (Ed.): SPLC 2004, LNCS 3154, pp. 146–164, 2004.

In our experience from several industrial cases, several decisions need to be made about the scoping of product-family artefacts, the way to organize for the development and evolution of these artefacts, the funding model used to finance the development of shared components, the features that are selected for implementation in shared components, as well as the amount of architecture harmonisation required. However, these decisions are often made implicitly rather than explicitly based on clearly stated objectives. The consequence is that the organization may experience a mismatch between the employed and the optimal approach. This may result in several problems, such as a high degree of erosion, mismatches between product needs and shared components, organizational "noise," and inefficient knowledge management.

The contribution of this paper is that we present a framework for deciding the optimal model for organizing the development of shared components. In particular, we present the dimensions that define the space of approaches and discuss the advantages and disadvantages. Subsequently, we present a framework for selecting the best alternative for each decision based on a three-stage adoption model. Although the paper is based on extensive industrial experience, we are unable to present any case studies due to confidentiality and the lack of time for obtaining approval for publication.

The remainder of the paper is organized as follows. In the next section, we present the problems that an organization may experience when a mismatch between the chosen and optimal approach to the development of shared artefacts is chosen. Subsequently, in Section 3, we discuss the dimensions for which the organization needs to make decisions when developing shared software artefacts. Section 4 presents the three stages of product-family adoption and the decision framework for the development of shared components associated with each stage. Section 5 discusses related work, and the paper is concluded in Section 6.

2 Problem Statement

The key benefit of software product families results from the ability to share the implementation of components over multiple products, resulting in overall lower development and maintenance costs. Achieving these benefits in practice, however, proves to be quite a challenge. Our claim in this paper is that this difficulty is caused in part by the mismatch between the approach used for the development of shared artefacts and the optimal approach. If such a mismatch is present, an organization may experience several problems. From the cases that we have been involved in, a common denominator for all mismatches is a shared perception among the research and development (R&D) staff that "it doesn't feel right." This feeling is due to the staff experiencing too many mismatches between different roles in the organization in the process of product-family-centric software engineering. Below, we discuss the problems that, in our experience, are the most predominant.

- **Mismatch between shared components and product needs:** The first problem that an R&D organization may encounter is that the staff experiences a mismatch between the product requirements and the behaviour provided by the shared component. This mismatch may be of an architectural nature, due to differences in assumptions about the architectural context in which the component operates. The mismatch may be concerned with interfaces provided and required by the shared component. A third reason may be concerned with the quality attributes provided by the shared component. Finally, the mismatch may be in time, that is, between the roadmap and the release schedule of the shared components and the product.

- **Design erosion of shared components:** Due to schedule or other pressures on the shared components, initial development or evolution of the shared component may be performed without sufficiently considering all aspects of the design, resulting in a high degree of design erosion. The design may be extended with too-product-specific functionality, additions are not sufficiently integrated in the original design, or variability requirements need to be integrated that have a crosscutting effect. The high level of design erosion increases maintenance costs, complicates component integration in products, and causes early retirement of the component.

- **Complex interface:** Delivering a component that is to be extended with product-specific code, which is one approach to developing shared components, requires the availability of some kind of interface to the internals of the component. Although ideally this interface is clean and reveals minimal details of the internals of the component, in practice, this is very difficult to achieve in the case where the component is extended with product-specific features. This is due in part to the fact that features tend to be crosscutting in nature with respect to the basic elements of software development.

- **High degree of "organizational noise":** During an adoption process, many staff members are affected in their roles and responsibilities. The organization has to learn to operate in the new role, but this is generally not achieved without problems. These problems lead to a certain amount of "organizational noise" (i.e., complaints and discussions) especially in the informal organization. A limited amount of organizational noise over a limited amount of time during the early phases of adoption is normal, but if there is much "noise" over an extended period, this is a clear indicator that the approach towards the development and evolution of shared components does not fulfil the organization's needs. This may result in problems associated with the productivity and predictability of the schedule, but also affects softer factors, such as motivation, team spirit, and the momentum for the product-family initiative.

- **Inefficient knowledge management:** In the case where a shared component is delivered to several products and most product teams need to extend that component with features specific to their product, this means that, in addition to the staff in the component team, at least one person in each product team needs to maintain a sufficient, typically high, level of understanding with respect to the internals of the component. The cost of maintaining this level of expertise is an often underestimated factor and detriments the benefits of the product-family approach.

- **Evolution causes ripple effects through the R&D organization:** Like all software, the shared component will typically evolve with a certain heartbeat. Whereas it often is feasible to maintain the existing provided interface, experience shows that it often is more difficult to maintain the extension interface. This means that for most new releases, all product engineering units that extend the component need to reevaluate and evolve their extensions to work with the new interface. Depending on the complexity of the changes, this may be quite effort-consuming. In addition, the amount of effort required is often difficult to predict before the component is available, creating difficulty in the planning of software development in the unit.

- **Component value not linear:** An assumption rather widespread in the software industry is that a shared component that fulfils X% of the features required from it in a product context also represents X% of the value of a product-specific component. Based on our experience, we conclude that this relation is not linear, but rather exponential. Due to the problems discussed above, the value of a shared component increases exponentially with its support of product-specific requirements. This increase is illustrated graphically in the figure below. The figure also shows that a component that satisfies substantially more than the product requires is less valuable, due to higher resource demands and more complex interfaces.

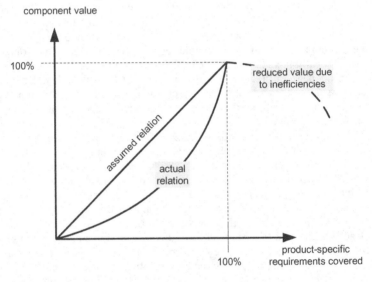

Fig. 1. Relation between component value and support for product-specific requirements

3   Decision Dimensions for Shared Component Development

Organizations adopting or employing software product families need to decide which shared components to develop, how to organize their development, and in what order they should be developed. As we discussed earlier in this paper, these decisions are often made in an implicit manner, as the organization has, at the point in time when these decisions need to be made, little experience in the domain during adoption. The consequence, however, is that the development approach adopted may be different from the approach that would be optimal for the organization, resulting in mismatches and associated problems as discussed in the previous section.

In this section, we present five decision dimensions that we, based on our industrial experiences, consider to represent the most important decisions that an organization should make. These dimensions are feature selection, architecture harmonisation, R&D organization, funding model, and shared component scoping. Each dimension presents a number of alternatives and discusses the advantages and disadvantages of each one. The dimensions are not fully orthogonal and cannot, as discussed in the rest of the section, be combined arbitrarily. In the next section, we discuss the three stages of product-family adoption and the typical approach associated with each stage.

Finally, we use the term "component team" to identify a group that is responsible for the development of a shared (or product-family) component. However, a component team is not necessarily an organizational unit. A component team may be part of a product unit or a virtual team consisting of members located at different product units. The term "unit" does refer to an organizational entity.

3.1 Feature Selection

An important decision that must be made early in the adoption of a software product-family approach is which features and functionality to first move from the product-specific to the product-family realm. As discussed by Geppert and Weiss [4], especially the first components typically require a careful balance between the greatest perceived benefit and the highest chance of success. One can identify three approaches to selecting the first product-family components:

1. oldest, most generic, lowest components
2. existing, but evolving components
3. new, but common features

Oldest, most generic, lowest components. The first approach is to start from the easiest components, maximizing the chance of success. These are typically the oldest, most generic components, often located in the lower layers of the product software architectures. The product teams often consider these components necessary, but not relevant from a competitive perspective. Consequently, there is typically little resistance to moving to a model where these components become shared among the products.

Advantages. As mentioned, there is typically little resistance to sharing these components. Also, the variability required from the shared component is well understood. In the case of multiple, evolving infrastructures that need to be supported, there can be a real benefit from having to evolve only one shared version of the component rather than multiple product-specific ones.

Disadvantages. The product-specific component versions typically have existed for a long time and are often rather eroded. Consequently, the investment required for integrating the product-specific versions into one shared version may be substantial, whereas the benefit, in terms of reduced development effort, often is limited. Finally, commercial off-the-shelf (COTS) components may already or soon be available, removing the need for an internal component version.

Existing, but evolving, components. As a second starting point for the selection of components, one can focus on the product-specific components that have a relatively high change rate. Typically, these components implement features that are part of the products' competitive advantage, but due to the quick evolution, substantial maintenance costs are associated with these components.

Advantages. Assuming the changes are orthogonal to the product portfolio, a substantial reduction in maintenance costs can be achieved by merging the product-specific components into one shared version. In addition, the required behaviour, although it is evolving, is understood reasonably well, simplifying the effort required.

Disadvantages. The main disadvantage is that initially several product-specific versions of a component were developed and, after a relatively short time, merged into a shared component, with the associated effort requirements. In addition, when the evolution of the component is rather product specific, the effort required for maintaining the shared component implementing the superset of features may be easily underestimated.

New, but common features. Finally, one may aim to develop shared components that implement currently unavailable functionality that is present on all or most product roadmaps. Rather than being reactive, the product-family effort is proactive, developing shared components before the products need them.

Advantages. The main advantage over the first two alternatives is that no product-specific versions of the component are developed, so none have to be replaced. This reduces the development as well as the maintenance effort required for the new features.

Disadvantages. The concern one may have is that the product-family R&D staff has to predict future requirements that the products themselves, being close to their markets, have not yet started to implement. There is, consequently, a high degree of uncertainty that may cause certain investments to be invalidated, due to changing requirements.

3.2 Architecture Harmonisation

The second dimension that we discuss is the level of software architecture harmonisation between the products for which the organization strives. In the case where a customer may use multiple products from the portfolio, harmonization of user interfaces as well as integration of product functionality (e.g., access to data stored in one product from the other product) is of considerable market value. In addition, the integration of shared components is considerably easier if the architectures are similar. On the other hand, products that, up to now, have evolved independently may require substantial effort to achieve architectural harmonization, and the benefits of such products may be limited.

Component-centric. The first model that the organization may decide to use is to forego all architecture harmonisation and to only develop shared components. As the integration of these components in the products will be more effort-consuming, the organization needs to find a balance between the responsibilities of the component team versus the product teams with respect to facilitating and achieving component integration.

Advantages. The obvious advantage is that no effort has to be invested in architecture harmonisation. Secondly, the product teams maintain their relative freedom and are not required to achieve consensus over architectural issues.

Disadvantages. The component integration cost per product is often relatively high, reducing the benefits of a software product-family approach. This may lead to organizational tension between the component team and the product teams. The product teams may demand that the component team better prepare its component for integration in the products. The component team is concerned with the effort associated with preparing the component for inclusion in each product and generally not inclined to give in to the demands of the product unit.

Iterative product architecture harmonisation. For most organizations that adopt software product-family engineering, there is a benefit associated with harmonisation of the product architectures. However, the cost of achieving this harmonisation is so high that it cannot be achieved in one release cycle. Instead, a roadmap is defined and architecture harmonisation is pursued in an iterative fashion, taking the process one step forward with every release cycle. A prerequisite for this approach is a reference product-family architecture that is used as a (long-term) goal. This reference architecture needs to be designed jointly by the product and component teams.

Advantages. The main benefit of this approach is that, by starting with the architecture harmonisation of the product around the location of the shared components, the component integration cost can be reduced.

Disadvantages. There are some drawbacks with this approach as well. First, there is a need for product teams to invest in product architecture harmonisation, which has no immediate return on investment. Second, the product teams must agree on a reference architecture, which is often a lengthy and effort-consuming process.

Revolutionary architecture adoption. In earlier work, we have described the revolutionary adoption model. In this case, a product-family architecture and set of shared components is developed. Products that aim to use these shared components need to perform all the architecture harmonisation at once without the ability to spread it out over multiple release cycles. On the other hand, once the harmonisation is achieved, integrating shared components is trivial.

Advantages. The main advantage is the ease of integrating shared components, once the architecture harmonisation has been achieved. Also, integrating multiple products at customer sites and user interface harmonisation is greatly simplified.

Disadvantages. The effort associated with performing all architecture harmonisation in one release cycle typically leaves little effort for adding new features, potentially reducing the competitive advantage that the products have in the marketplace.

3.3   R&D Organization

The third decision dimension is concerned with the organization of the R&D staff involved in the development of shared components. Again, we have three alternative models that we discuss:
1. mixed responsibility for product teams
2. virtual component team
3. component unit

Mixed responsibility for product teams. The first model, not requiring any changes to the formal R&D organization, is where product teams assume responsibility for developing one or more shared components in addition to evolving the product or products in their portfolio. There are two alternative approaches. A product team may evolve a shared component with functionality needed for one of its products, releasing a new version of the shared component that can, at a later stage, be extended with other functionality by another product team. Alternatively, a product team may have permanent responsibility for a shared component and extend it with new functionality in response to requests from other product teams.

Advantages. Simplicity is one of the key advantages; no organizational changes, which often require support from management, are required. In addition, there is no risk of shared components being extended with functionality that has no immediate market benefit.

Disadvantages. An important disadvantage is that, in this model, shared components often suffer from a high degree of design erosion. Product teams often have a tendency to add too-product-specific functionality to a shared component. In the case of permanent component responsibility, a product team has to balance requests from other product teams against its own release schedule demands.

Virtual component team. Especially in the case of replacing existing, product-specific components with one shared component, the organization uses a virtual component team. The members of this team originate from the involved product groups and remain formally part of the product groups. However, as part of the virtual component team, the members develop the shared version of the component.

Advantages. The members of the virtual team have, due to their experience in the product teams, a good understanding of the product requirements on the component. Also, this approach requires no changes to the formal R&D organization.

Disadvantages. The members of the team often feel split in loyalty between the product and the component team to which they belong.

Component unit. When a first release of a shared component, or a set of components, is available, it frequently becomes necessary to create an explicit component unit that has responsibility for the component(s). In the case of a virtual component team, the team may even be converted into a unit.

Advantages. The responsibilities in the organization are clearly delineated, and the places where tradeoffs need to be made align with the boundaries in the R&D organization.

Disadvantages. The main disadvantage is that a component team has a clear risk of focussing more on its own goals than on the goals of the product teams, especially in the time dimension. There is a tendency in component teams to build a "perfect" component, rather than satisfying the immediate needs of the product teams.

3.4 Funding

In all commercial organizations, the final metric is "the bottom line," that is, the financial consequences of decisions. Adopting product families is no different in this respect. As the profit and loss responsibility in many organizations exists even at the product-team level, the development and evolution of shared components require a suitable funding model. Below, we discuss three models for funding product-family initiatives that are used in the software industry:
1. "barter"
2. taxation
3. licensing/royalty

"Barter." In organizations that use this model, the effort that is invested is not quantified in terms of effort or value. Instead, different product teams agree to develop shared components and to provide the components to the other product teams. Negotiations are based on a form of equal sharing of the development and evolution effort and on trust concerning the ability and willingness of the other teams to deliver their contributions in time and according to specifications.

Advantages. The main advantages are that this model requires no changes to the budget or the organization, lacks any bureaucratic overhead, and can be initiated easily by a few enthusiastic people at the right places in the R&D organization.

Disadvantages. The handshake deals that are associated with this model require a high level of trust in the organization. One product team may run into delays in an ongoing project, causing delays in the delivery of shared components. Unforeseen events may easily put pressure on the agreements, causing the initiative to fail.

Taxation. In this model, product teams agree on a form of taxation where each product team, based on its size, profit, and expected use of the shared components, agrees to contribute development effort or financial support. The taxation may be implemented through the initiation of a separate component team or by the product team itself committing to the development of some shared component. This model is basically an investment model and is more formal than the "barter" model; that is, the investment is quantified and delivery schedules agreed are upon.

Advantages. The model provides a more formal agreement, increasing the level of trust towards the initiative. Also, it becomes feasible to develop explicit roadmaps and release plans based on the available investments.

Disadvantages. The investment in product-family engineering becomes explicit in the budget and, in the case of a component team, in the organizational structure. Also, especially in the case where a taxation-based component team exists for a number of years, there is often a tendency to develop "perfect" components rather than helping product teams address their immediate concerns due to the lack of market pressures.

Licensing/royalty. Once a usable version of a shared component is available, it becomes feasible to move to a royalty or licensing model. In this case, the component team is not funded through taxation but rather through the royalties it receives based on product sales of the products that contain the shared component. The component team may be in direct competition with other component teams in the organization or with external COTS components and consequently under substantial market pressure. Also, in the case of too-high royalties, product teams may decide to develop the component themselves.

Advantages. This model provides the market pressures for the component team that are necessary to keep it focused on satisfying customers and on innovating and evolving its components. Also, once the team is unable to fund itself based on its royalties because lower priced COTS components have become available, this method provides a natural way to dissolve the component team and to assign its members to other tasks.

Disadvantages. The model should not be applied until the shared component has achieved a level of maturity that allows the component team to have a realistic budget for component evolution and innovation. If the organization decides that the shared component represents core competencies that should be maintained, this model is not appropriate as the market pressure is lacking.

3.5 Shared Component Scoping

The final decision dimension that we discuss in this paper is the scoping of the shared component. Of the features required by the products that use the shared component, the component can implement only the most common ones, the subset used by some or more products, or all features, including those required by only one product.

Only common features. The starting point for most shared components is to implement only those features that are common for all products. The product teams have to extend the component with the features their product needs.

Advantages. Assuming the common features represent a substantial subset of the features, this approach provides an efficient way to achieve early successes in the product-family adoption.

Disadvantages. One concern with this approach is the often complex interface between the shared component and the product-specific functionality that has to be developed on top of it. In addition, all product teams have to maintain staff with knowledge of this interface and often the component internals, resulting in inefficient knowledge management.

Complete component with plug-in capability. Over time, a shared component evolves by incorporating more and more features until only those features required by one or two products need to be added to the component. For this need, the component provides a plug-in interface.

Advantages. This model resolves, to a large extent, the issues identified for the previous model concerning the complex interface and the inefficient knowledge management.

Disadvantages. The main concern often is the integration of the component into the product. Depending on the complexity of the interaction between the component and the remaining product, that integration may be a substantial challenge.

Encompassing component. In this model, the component team aims to incorporate all product needs for the component in the component itself. In addition, the component team may take responsibility for (part of) integrating the component into the products of the team's customers.

Advantages. Especially in the case where the component has a complex (e.g., real-time) interface with the rest of the product, this model is the most efficient as the component team has a better understanding of the behavioural characteristics of the component.

Disadvantages. The component team will typically need to be larger than in the earlier models, due to the service that it provides to the product teams. This need may easily be viewed as inefficient by the organization.

3.6 Summary

As we discussed in the introduction to this section, organizations adopting or employing software product families need to decide what shared component to develop, how to organize their development, and in what order they should be developed. Due to the implicit manner in which these decisions typically are made, organizations often experience problems due to mismatches between the optimal model and the one actually used.

We have presented five decision dimensions that, based on our industrial experiences, we consider to represent the most important decisions that an organization should make. These dimensions are feature selection, architecture harmonisation, R&D organization, funding model, and shared component scoping. In the figure below, these dimensions and their alternatives are presented graphically.

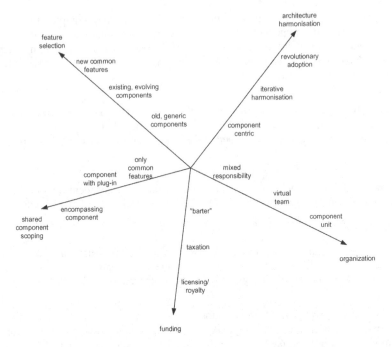

Fig. 2. Five decision dimensions and associated alternatives

4 Decision Framework

When implemented successfully, software product families provide substantial benefits to the organization in terms of development effort, time to market of new features and products, and the level of integration of the product portfolio. However, to achieve these benefits, the organization first has to adopt the product-family approach, which is a major change process in the organization, primarily affecting the R&D organization, but also product management, marketing, and other groups in the organization.

The adoption of a product-family approach is primarily a business, organization and process challenge, and the technical challenges, although present, are not of predominant importance. Because of the breadth of the challenge, it is important, especially early in the adoption, to select the starting point that provides maximal benefit to the organization, but also has a high likelihood of success. Based on this, one can identify three stages that product-family adoption typically evolves through: (1) the early success phase, (2) the expanding scope phase, and (3) the increasing "maturity" phase. Once the last stage is reached, product-family engineering has been embedded as the normal way of working in the organization. The business strategy of the organization then influences the evolution of the product family.

In the sections below, we discuss, for each of the decision dimensions, the typically preferred alternatives. Specific organizations may deviate from these alternatives for legitimate reasons.

4.1 Initial Adoption – Early Successes

The first stage that organizations adopting software product families go through is the initial adoption. During this stage, the first steps are made away from independent product teams. Although the R&D organization may have a positive attitude towards the overall initiative, the complete adoption process will initiate many changes and, especially, increase the dependencies between different R&D teams. Because of this, it is important to minimize the impact of the required changes, to maximize the chance of success, and to maximize the benefits from the success. The principles that should guide the initial adoption are

- Assign a champion or adoption team that champions the approach.
- Avoid organizational changes.
- Minimize the product-family-specific processes to a bare-bones set.
- Select features that create maximal visibility and benefit.
- Failure is not an option: if, in this stage, the initiative fails to deliver, its termination is guaranteed.

The initial adoption phase ends with the successful integration of one or more shared components in at least two products. At this point, the product-family initiative has, hopefully, achieved its first successes, and there is hard evidence that the benefits of product-family engineering can be achieved in the context of the organization.

In the sections below, we discuss, for each decision dimension, the preferred alternative as well as the situations in which an organization should deviate from it.

Feature selection: new, but common features. The preferred alternatives for the features to be implemented as a product family are those that have not yet been implemented by the existing products, but are needed by at least one or two products in the next release.

Sometimes the products service fundamentally different markets, leading to a lack of common new features. In this case, existing product-specific components with a high change rate where the changes are preferably crosscutting the product portfolio are suitable alternatives.

Architecture harmonisation: component-centric. R&D organizations are typically hesitant to invest in changes that have no obvious, short-term return on investment. Although harmonisation of the product architectures is of importance in the long term, due to the reduced integration effort, it is also an effort-consuming activity with no immediate pay-back. Consequently, at this stage in the adoption process, effort should be directed towards creating product-family components.

Organization: mixed responsibility for product teams. It is difficult to present a general preference for this dimension as it is preferable to have a component team developing the first product-family components. However, obtaining the management support for creating a component team is typically difficult, due to the scarceness of R&D resources. The main risk of the recommended alternative is, obviously, the prioritization by the product teams. The aim should be to assign the responsibility for component development to product teams that have an immediate need for incorporating the product-family components in their product.

Funding: "barter." Similar to the decision dimensions already discussed, the main challenge is to achieve the early successes with minimal changes. In the case where different product teams decide to share responsibility for the development of shared components, it is preferable to initially achieve agreement based on estimations that can be made part of the normal product development budgets. If substantial organizational support is available, a taxation model can be considered.

Shared component scoping: only common features. Assuming product teams have shared responsibility for components and products, the least intrusive approach is to have product teams implement the features needed by their own product, leaving extension points for likely future extensions. The next product team that requires use of the product can extend the first version of the shared component with its requirements. The main challenge in this model is one of discipline, that is, each product team is responsible for maintaining the general applicability of the shared component.

4.2 Expanding Scope

Once the first product-family components have been successfully integrated in two or more products and the R&D organization is experiencing the benefits of product-family engineering, the product-family initiative evolves to the second phase. That phase is concerned with expanding the scope of the product family in terms of the functionality in the product-family domain. R&D teams have grown accustomed to the additional dependencies and learned to trust other teams to an extent. The situation is becoming more complicated in that product-family artefacts developed in the first phase need maintenance, and an organizational model for this has to be established. In short, after the initial rather ad hoc, but efficient, adoption phase, more structure is needed to institutionalize the product-family approach. The principles that guide the second phase are addressing this need:

- Preferably, each product team should contain a product-family champion.
- Some organizational change is necessary to embed product-family engineering in the R&D organization.
- Introduce product-family processes that safeguard the reliability of the shared components as well as their predictable evolution.

The second adoption phase ends at the point when no obvious extensions to the shared components can be identified by the R&D organization. At that point, the challenge shifts to increasing the "maturity" [5] of the product-family artefacts as a means of decreasing the product derivation cost.

In the sections below, we discuss, for each decision dimension, the preferred alternative as well as the situations in which an organization should deviate from it.

Feature selection: existing, but evolving, components. Assuming the product-family components for new, common features have already been developed in the first phase, the next step is to address the components that currently have product-specific implementations, but share common features. In particular, the components that experience a high chance rate in response to new requirements, that preferably are orthogonal to the product portfolio, are of interest. Frequently, these components are considered to be problematic within product teams, creating momentum for moving to a shared implementation. The second phase marks, in this sense, a shift from reducing development effort to reducing maintenance effort.

Obviously, any existing opportunities for the development of shared components for new, common features should be pursued as well.

Architecture harmonisation: iterative product architecture harmonisation. With the increasing number of shared components, the cost of integrating them into the product architecture often becomes a concern. This calls for the design of a product-family architecture that captures the commonality and variability of the products in the product-family scope. The product teams use this architecture as a reference and aim to iteratively harmonize the product architecture with the product-family architecture.

Organization: virtual component team. The shared components developed in the first phase need to be maintained. In addition, the shared components created in this phase are mined based the product-specific implementations of these components. This requires, on the one hand, a team of people that is permanently assigned to a set of components. On the other hand, the team needs detailed knowledge of the product-specific requirements. A virtual team, consisting of staff formally located at the product teams, provides an optimal balance between these concerns.

Funding: taxation. The effort required for the product-family initiative as well as the importance of the continuity of the members of the virtual component demand a strong commitment from the R&D organization. Informal agreements about development need to be replaced with a more formalized model that guarantees more continuity. The taxation model requires all units and teams, during the budget rounds, to reserve part of their resources for the product-family initiative.

Shared component scoping: complete components with plug-in capability. The shared components replacing their product-specific counterparts should, preferably, be as easy to integrate as the original components. Consequently, it is necessary for these components to cover most of the features required by the products, only requiring plug-ins for the features that are used by only one product.

4.3 Increasing "Maturity"

Once the obvious product-family components have been developed and the second phase of product-family adoption has ended, the main challenge becomes increasing the "maturity" of the product-family artefacts. In the paper titled "Maturity and Evolution in Software Product Lines: Approaches, Artefacts, and Organization" [5], we present five maturity levels for product families:

- **Independent products:** Initially, the organization develops multiple products as several independent entities. These products do not share software artefacts in any planned way, only by coincidence.
- **Standardized infrastructure:** The first step towards sharing takes place when the organization decides to standardize the infrastructure on which a set of products is built.
- **Platform:** A subsequent development is to extend the standardized infrastructure with internally developed software artefacts (i.e., a platform) that provide functionality common to all products in the scope. Each product is developed on top of the platform.
- **Software product family:** The fourth level of maturity is when the organization employs a software product family in the traditional sense of the term [3]. The shared artefacts in the product family contain functionality that is shared by all or a subset of the products. Products may sacrifice efficiency or other requirements for the benefits of being members of the product family.
- **Configurable product base:** The final level is the situation where the differences between the products are so well understood they can be mapped to variation points that can be bound at installation or runtime. As a consequence, individual products are derived by configuring the shared software artefacts appropriately.

The challenge in this phase is to lift the product family from the platform level where it typically is after the second adoption phase to the product family and, if feasible, the configurable product base level.

In the sections below, we discuss, for each decision dimension, the preferred alternative as well as the situations in which an organization should deviate from it.

Feature selection: all components. With the ambition to bring all products in a configurable product base, the scope for feature selection is now extended to all components, including the old, common and low-level components. Of course, for all components considered for inclusion in the product family, a positive cost benefit evaluation should be available. The ultimate goals remain to reduce development and maintenance effort, improve time to market, and increase integration between different products in the portfolio.

Architecture harmonisation: revolutionary architecture adoption. At this stage in the product-family adoption, the products that were part of the initial adoption have evolved through several iterations of architecture harmonisation. However, new products interested in joining the product-family initiative need to go through a revolutionary architecture adoption process. Reusing the product-family components will require the new products to make substantial changes to their architecture.

Organization: component unit. Even if up to now, no component units were created, the product family is, at this point, so embedded in the R&D organization that it is no longer feasible to proceed without component units. However, as discussed below, after initial taxation-based funding, these component units should be funded through licensing or royalty fees. The aim is to make sure that component units are exposed to market pressures from within and outside the organization.

Funding: licensing/royalty. As the R&D organization instantiates component units, it is important for these units to be exposed to market pressures. A taxation-based model easily leads to component units that are more concerned with creating a "perfect" component than with the needs of their customers.

Shared component scoping: encompassing component. A logical consequence of the customer focus of component units is the attention towards minimizing the integration problems of the component in specific products. In this stage, one can typically identify a shift from shared components extended by product teams to shared components prepared by component units for easy integration (i.e., the encompassing component model).

5 Related Work

Several authors have discussed the different aspects concerning the adoption and institutionalisation of software product families. Weiss and Lai [1] present an approach to product-family engineering that aims to achieve generation of products from the product-family artefacts. Although we agree with the authors that automated generation is the long-term goal for most product families, the focus of this paper is on the early phases of adoption.

Clements and Northrop [2] present 29 practice areas that can or should be addressed for software product-family engineering. Launching and institutionalizing is discussed as one practice area, and some of the issues discussed in this paper are also addressed. Different from these authors, we present the five decision dimensions and present a three-stage adoption process.

Böckle and others discuss the importance of adopting and institutionalizing a product-family culture [6]. Some aspects discussed, such as the adoption approach, have relations to this paper, but are presented much more briefly. Also, Wijnstra discusses the importance of the "weight" of introduction and supports our approach of limiting up-front investments and iteratively extending scope and maturity [7].

Table 1. Stages of Product-Family Adoption

	Early successes	Increasing scope	Increasing maturity
Feature selection	New, but common features	Existing, but evolving, components	All components
Architecture harmonisation	Component-centric	Iterative product architecture harmonisation	Revolutionary architecture adoption
R&D organization	Mixed responsibility for product teams	Virtual component teams	Component units
Funding	"Barter"	Taxation	Licensing
Shared component scoping	Only common features	Complete components with plug-ins	Encompassing component

Kang and others discuss the use of marketing and product plans to select and drive the development of product-family components [8]. The work discussed in that paper provides valuable input to the feature selection during product-family adoption. Others discussing the process of scoping and roadmapping include Van Ommering [9], Schmid [10], and Kishi, Noda, and Katayama [11].

6 Conclusion

Once adopted successfully, software product families provide a considerable benefit for software R&D organizations. However, achieving successful adoption proves, in many organizations, to be nontrivial. Our claim is that this is due to the mismatch between the optimal and applied approach to the development, evolution, and use of shared product-family artefacts. The mismatch may lead to several problems, such as the mismatch between shared components and product needs; a high level of design erosion and complex interfaces of shared components; a high degree of "organizational noise," inefficient knowledge management; ripple effects through the R&D organization due to component evolution; and incorrect assumptions about the value of shared components.

To address these problems, we have presented five decision dimensions that are of relevance to the development of shared components: feature selection, architecture harmonisation, R&D organization, funding model, and shared component scoping. For each dimension, we have presented three alternatives.

These dimensions are used in a decision framework that describes the preferred alternative for each stage in the adoption of software product families. We recognize three main stages in product-family adoption: early successes, increasing scope, and increasing maturity. In the table below, the stages and the preferred alternatives are presented.

The contribution of this paper is that we present a framework for deciding the optimal model for organising the development of shared components. In future work, we intend to add more detail to the model in terms of advantages, disadvantages, and risks. In addition, we hope to add a number of industrial cases to the presentation of the decision framework to further illustrate and validate the decision framework.

References

1. Weiss, D. M., Lai, C. T. R.: Software Product-Line Engineering: A Family Based Software Development Process, Addison-Wesley, ISBN 0-201-694387 (1999)
2. Clements, P., Northrop, L.: Software Product Lines: Practices and Patterns, SEI Series in Software Engineering, Addison-Wesley, ISBN: 0-201-70332-7 (2001)
3. Bosch, J.: Design and Use of Software Architectures: Adopting and Evolving a Product Line Approach, Pearson Education (Addison-Wesley & ACM Press), ISBN 0-201-67494-7 (2000)
4. Geppert, B., Weiss, D.: Goal-Oriented Assessment of Product-Line Domains, 9th International Software Metrics Colloquium, Sydney, Australia (2003)

5. Bosch, J.: Maturity and Evolution in Software Product Lines: Approaches, Artefacts and Organization, Proceedings of the Second Conference Software Product Line Conference (SPLC2) (August 2002) 257-271
6. Böckle, G., Bermejo Muñoz, J., Knauber, P., Krueger, C.W., Sampaio do Prado Leite, J.C., van der Linden, F., Northrop, L., Start, M., Weiss, D.M.: Adopting and Institutionalizing a Product Line Culture, Proceedings SPLC2, LNCS 2379 (2002) 49-59
7. Wijnstra, J.G.: "Critical Factors for a Successful Platform-Based Product Family Approach," Proceedings SPLC2, LNCS 2379 (2002) 68-89
8. Kang, K.C., Donohoe, P., Koh, E., Lee, J., Lee, K.: "Using a Marketing and Product Plan as a Key Driver for Product Line Asset Development," Proceedings SPLC2, LNCS 2379 (2002) 366-383
9. van Ommering, R.: "Roadmapping a Product Population Architecture," Proceedings of the 4th International Workshop (PFE 2001), LNCS 2290 (2001) 51-63
10. Schmid, K.: "A Comprehensive Product Line Scoping Approach and Its Validation," Proceedings of the 24th International Conference on Software Engineering (ICSE 2002) (2002) 593-603
11. Kishi, T., Noda, N., Katayama, T.: "A Method for Product Line Scoping Based on a Decision-Making Framework," Proceedings SPLC2, LNCS 2379 (2002) 348-365
12. van Gurp, Jilles, Bosch, Jan: "Design Erosion: Problems & Causes," Journal of Systems and Software, 61(2) (March 2002) 105-119, Elsevier
13. Jansen, Anton, van Gurp, Jilles, Bosch, Jan: "The Recovery of Architectural Design Decisions," submitted (2004)

Experiences in Software Product Families:
Problems and Issues During Product Derivation

Sybren Deelstra, Marco Sinnema, and Jan Bosch

University of Groningen, PO Box 800, 9700 AV Groningen, The Netherlands,
{s.deelstra,m.sinnema,j.bosch}@cs.rug.nl,
http://segroup.cs.rug.nl

Abstract. A fundamental reason for investing in product families is to minimize the application engineering costs. Several organizations that employ product families, however, are becoming increasingly aware of the fact that, despite the efforts in domain engineering, deriving individual products from their shared software assets is a time- and effort-consuming activity. In this paper, we present a collection of product derivation problems that we identified during a case study at two large and mature industrial organizations. These problems are attributed to the lack of methodological support for application engineering, and to underlying causes of complexity and implicit properties. For each problem, we provide a description and an example, while for each cause we present a description, consequences, solutions, and research issues. The discussions in this paper are relevant outside the context of the two companies, as the challenges they face arise in, for example, comparable or less mature organizations.

1 Introduction

Software product families have received substantial attention from the software engineering community since the 1990s [5, 10, 24]. The basic philosophy of software product families is intra-organizational reuse through the explicitly planned exploitation of commonalities of related products. This philosophy has been adopted by a wide variety of organizations and has proved to substantially decrease costs and time to market, and to increase the quality of their software products.

The ability to derive different products from the product family is referred to as variability. Variability in software systems is realized through variation points that identify locations at which variation will occur [13]. Managing the ability to handle the differences between products at the various phases of the life cycle (i.e., variability management) is a key success factor in software product families [7].

Product development in software product families is organized into two stages: domain engineering and application engineering [19]. Domain engineering refers to the activities that involve, among other things, identifying commonalities and differences between product family members, and implementing a set of shared software artifacts (e.g., components or classes). The shared software artifacts are constructed in such a way that the commonalities can be exploited economically, while preserving the variability. The second stage, application engineering, refers to the activities that involve,

R.L. Nord (Ed.): SPLC 2004, LNCS 3154, pp. 165–182, 2004.
© Springer-Verlag Berlin Heidelberg 2004

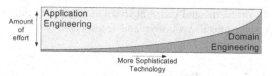

Fig. 1. This figure presents the fundamental reason for researching and investing in more sophisticated technology such as product families, that is, decreasing the proportion of application engineering costs

among other things, product derivation, that is, constructing individual products using a subset of the shared software artifacts.

The idea behind this approach to product engineering is that the investments required to develop the reusable artifacts during domain engineering, are outweighed by the benefits of deriving the individual products during application engineering. A fundamental reason for researching and investing in sophisticated technologies for product families is to obtain the maximum benefit out of this up-front investment, in other words, to minimize the proportion of application engineering costs (see Figure 1).

Over the past few years, domain engineering has received substantial attention from the software engineering community. Most of those research efforts are focused on methodological support for designing and implementing shared software artifacts in such a way that application engineers should be able to derive applications more easily. Most of the approaches, however, fail to provide substantial supportive evidence. The result is a lack of methodological support for application engineering, and, consequently, organizations fail to exploit the full benefits of software product families.

Rather than adopting the same top-down approach where solutions focused on methodological support for domain engineering imply benefits during application engineering, we adopt a bottom-up approach in our research. By studying product derivation issues, we believe we will be better able to provide and validate industrially practicable solutions for application engineering. This paper is a first step in the bottom-up approach: it provides an overview of the problems and issues we identified at two industrial case studies: Robert Bosch GmbH and Thales Nederland B.V.

The case studies were part of the first phase of Configuration in Industrial Product Families (ConIPF), a research project sponsored by the IST-programme [11]. Robert Bosch GmbH and Thales Nederland B.V. are industrial partners in this project. Both companies are large and relatively mature organizations that develop complex software systems. They face challenges during product derivation that arise in other, comparable or less mature organizations. The identified issues are therefore relevant outside the context of the respective companies.

The main contribution of this paper is that we show that, although software product families have been applied successfully in industry, there is room for improvement in the current practice. Solving product derivation problems will help organizations exploit the full benefits of software product families.

The remainder of this paper is organized as follows. The next section provides a description of a generic product derivation process. This description is the basis of our discussion in subsequent parts of the paper. In Section 3, we briefly describe the research method of the case study. We discuss the case study organizations in Section 4 and the identified problems and cause analysis in Section 5. Finally, we present related work and conclusions in Sections 6 and 7, respectively.

2 Product Derivation Process

In earlier work [12], we generalized the derivation processes we encountered in practice to a generic process. In this section, we discuss the aspects of this process that are relevant for discussions in subsequent parts of this paper. For a more elaborate description, we refer to the paper titled "A Product Derivation Framework for Software Product Families" [12].

The generic product derivation process consists of two phases: the initial phase and the iteration phase. In the initial phase, a first configuration is created from the product family assets. In the iteration phase, the initial configuration is modified in a number of subsequent iterations until the product sufficiently implements the imposed requirements.

In addition to the phased selection activities described above, typically, some code development is required during product derivation. This adaptation aspect can occur in both the iteration phase and the initial phase. Below, we provide a more detailed description of both phases, as well as a separate description of the adaptation aspect.

2.1 Initial Phase

The input to the initial phase is a (sub)set of the requirements managed throughout the entire process of product derivation (see also Figure 2). These requirements originate from, among other things, the customers, legislation, the hardware, and the product family organization. In the initial phase, two different approaches towards deriving the initial product configuration exist: assembly and configuration selection (see Figure 2). Both approaches conclude with the initial validation step.

Assembly. The first approach to initial derivation involves the assembly of a subset of the shared product family assets to the initial software product configuration. Although three types of assembly approaches exist (construction, generation, and composition—a hybrid of the first two) [12], the construction type is primarily relevant to this paper.

Construction. In the construction approach, the initial configuration is constructed from the product family architecture and shared components. The first step in the construction process is to derive the product architecture from the product family architecture. The next step is, for each architectural component, to select the closest matching component implementation from the collection of shared components. Finally, the parameters for each component are set.

Configuration Selection. The second approach to initial derivation involves selecting a closest matching existing configuration. An existing configuration is a consistent set of components, namely an arrangement of components that, with the right options and settings, can function together. Two types of configuration selection are relevant for this paper:

- An *old configuration* is a product implementation resulting from a previous project.
- A *reference configuration* is an old configuration (or a subset of it) explicitly designated as the basis for developing new products.

Where necessary, the selected configurations are modified by re-deriving the product architecture; adding, reselecting, and deselecting components; and setting/resetting parameters.

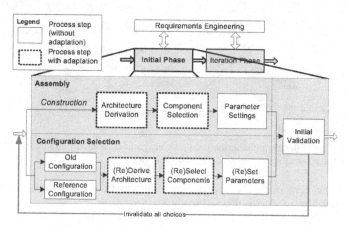

Fig. 2. During the initial phase, a first product configuration is derived by assembly or configuration selection

Initial Validation. The initial validation step is part of both the assembly and configuration selection approaches. It is the first step concerned with determining to what extent the initial configuration adheres to the requirements. In the rare case that the initially assembled or selected configuration does not provide a sufficient basis for further development, all choices are invalidated and the process goes back to start all over again. If the initial configuration sufficiently adheres to the requirements, the product is finished. Otherwise, the product derivation process enters the iteration phase.

2.2 Iteration Phase

The initial validation step marks the entrance of the iteration phase (see Figure 3). In some cases, an initial configuration sufficiently implements the desired product. In most cases, however, one or more cycles through the iteration phase are required for a number of reasons.

First, the requirements set may change or expand during product derivation; for example, if the organization uses a subset of the collected requirements to derive the initial configuration, or if the customer has new wishes for the product. Second, the configuration may not completely provide the required functionality, or some of the selected components simply may not work together at all. This reason particularly applies to embedded systems. In such systems, the initial configuration is often a first approximation mainly because the exact physics of the controlled mechanics are not always fully known at the start of the project, and because the software performs differently on different hardware (e.g., due to production tolerances and approximated polynomial relationships). Finally, the product family assets used to derive the configuration may have changed during product derivation; for example, due to bug fixes.

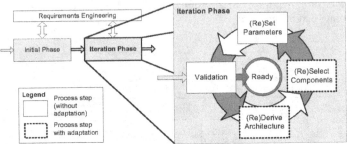

Fig. 3. During the iteration phase, the product configuration is modified in a number of iterations, until the product is deemed ready by the validation step

During the iteration phase, the product configuration is therefore modified and validated until the product is deemed ready.

Modification. A configuration can be modified on three levels of abstraction: architecture, component, and parameter. Modification is accomplished by selecting different architectural component variants, selecting different component implementation variants, or changing the parameter settings, respectively.

Validation. The validation step in this phase concerns validating the system with respect to adherence to requirements and checking the consistency and correctness of the component configuration.

2.3 Adaptation

Requirements that are not accounted for in the shared product family artifacts can be accommodated only by adaptation (denoted by the dashed boxes in Figure 2 and Figure 3). Adaptation involves adapting the product (family) architecture and adapting or creating component implementations. We identify three levels of artifact adaptation: product specific adaptation, reactive evolution, and proactive evolution.

Product-Specific Adaptation. The first level of evolution is where, during product derivation, new functionality is implemented in product-specific artifacts (e.g., product architecture and product-specific component implementations). To this purpose, application engineers can use the shared artifacts as the basis for further development, or develop new artifacts from scratch. As functionality implemented through product-specific adaptation is not incorporated in the shared artifacts, it cannot be reused in subsequent products unless an old configuration is selected for those products.

Reactive Evolution. Reactive evolution involves adapting shared artifacts in such a way that they can handle the requirements that emerge during product derivation and can also be shared with other product family members. As reactively evolving shared artifacts have consequences with respect to the other family members, those effects have to be analyzed prior to making any changes.

Proactive Evolution. The third level, proactive evolution, is actually not a product derivation activity, but rather a domain engineering activity. It involves adapting the shared artifacts in such a way that the product family is capable of accommodating the needs of the various family members in the future, as opposed to evolution as a reaction to requirements that emerge during product derivation. Proactive evolution requires both analysis of the effects with respect to current product family members, as well as analysis of the predicted future of the domain and the product family scope. Domain and scope prediction is accomplished in combination with technology roadmapping [16].

Product-specific adaptations can be fed back in the product family reuse infrastructure. This approach is often applied when the implications of changes are not well understood (e.g., in the case of supporting new technology). Integrating product-specific changes at a later stage, however, does require analyzing the impact on the other product family assets, and often implies retesting and additional development effort.

We have now established a framework of concepts regarding product derivation that consists of three main aspects: the initial phase, the iteration phase, and adaptation. We use this framework as the basis for understanding our discussion on the case study organizations in Section 4 and the identified product derivation problems in Section 5.

3   Research Methodology

The case study was part of the first phase of Configuration in Industrial Product Families (ConIPF), a research project sponsored by the IST-programme [11]. Robert Bosch GmbH and Thales Nederland B.V. are industrial partners in this project. Both companies are large and mature industrial organizations that mark two ends of a product derivation spectrum; Robert Bosch produces thousands of medium-sized products per year, while Thales Nederland produces a small number of very large products.

The main goals of the case study were to gain an understanding of product derivation processes at large organizations that employ software product families and to determine the underlying problems and causes of challenges faced during this process. We achieved these goals through a number of interview sessions with key personnel involved in product derivation: system architects, software engineers, and requirement engineers, among others.

Although questionnaires guided the interviews, there was enough room for open, unstructured questions and discussions. We recorded the interviews for further analysis afterwards and used documentation provided by the companies to complement the interviews.

4 Case Study Organizations

In this section, we present the business units of the organizations examined as part of the case study. We provide a description of product derivation at these business units in terms of the product derivation process presented in Section 2.

4.1 Case 1: Thales Nederland B.V., The Netherlands

Thales Nederland B.V., a subsidiary of Thales S.A. in France, operates in the Ground Based, Naval, and Services areas of defense technologies. Thales Naval Netherlands (TNNL), the Dutch division of the business group Naval, is organized in four business units: (1) Radars & Sensors, (2) Combat Systems, (3) Integration & Logistic Support, and (4) Operations. Our case study focused on software parts of the SEnsor WeApon Control – Fully Distributed (SEWACO-FD) naval combat systems family produced by the Combat Systems business unit.

A TACTical Information and COmmand System (Tacticos) Combat Management System is the prime subsystem of SEWACO-FD Naval Combat Systems. Its main purpose is to integrate all weapons and sensors on naval vessels that range from fast patrol boats to frigates.

Derivation Process at the Combat Systems Business Unit

Initial Phase. Combat Systems uses configuration selection to derive the initial product configurations. To this purpose, the collected requirements are mapped onto an old configuration, whose characteristics best resemble the requirements at hand. When all components and parameters are selected, adapted, and set in subsequent steps, the system is packaged and installed in a complete environment for the initial validation. If the configuration does not pass the initial validation, the derivation process enters the iteration phase.

Iteration Phase. The initial configuration is modified in a number of iterations by reselecting and deselecting components, adapting components, and changing existing parameter settings, until the product sufficiently adheres to the requirements.

Adaptation. Combat Systems applies both reactive evolution and product-specific changes when components need to be adapted (see Section 2.2.3). Components are also adapted through proactive evolution during domain engineering. Whether requirements are handled by reactive evolution or product-specific adaptation is determined by several Change Control Boards, that is, groups of experts (such as architects) that synchronize change requests within and between different projects.

4.2 Case 2: Robert Bosch GmbH, Germany

Robert Bosch GmbH is a worldwide operating company active in the Automotive, Industrial, Consumer Electronics, and Building Technology areas. Our case study focused on two business units, which, for reasons of confidentiality, we refer to as business units A and B. The systems produced by these business units consist of both hardware (e.g., the sensors and actuators) and software.

Derivation Process at Business Unit A

Initial Phase. Starting from requirements engineering, business unit A uses two approaches to derive an initial configuration of the product: one for lead products and one for secondary products. For lead products, the initial configuration is derived by construction, namely by deriving the architecture, selecting the appropriate components, and setting the component parameters. For secondary products (i.e., when a similar product has been built before), reference configurations are used to derive an initial configuration. When necessary, components from the reference configuration are replaced with ones that are more appropriate.

Iteration Phase. In the iteration phase, the initial configuration is modified in a number of iterations by reselecting components, adapting components, or changing parameters.

Adaptation. If the inconsistencies or new requirements cannot be solved by selecting a different component implementation, a new component implementation is developed through reactive evolution, by copying and adapting an existing implementation, or developing one from scratch.

Derivation Process at Business Unit B

Initial Phase. Each time a product needs to be derived from the product family of business unit B, a project team is formed. This team derives the product by construction. It copies the latest version of the architecture and the shared components, and selects the appropriate components from this copy. Finally, all parameters of the components are set to their initial values.

Iteration Phase. When the set of requirements changes, or when inconsistencies arise during the validation process, components and parameters are reselected and changed until the product is deemed finished.

Adaptation. When, during the initial and iteration phases, the requirements for a product configuration cannot be handled by the existing product family assets, copies of the selected components are adapted by product-specific adaptation.

5   Case Analysis

In the previous section, we presented the derivation processes of business units at Robert Bosch GmbH and Thales Nederland B.V. Based on the case study described in Section 3, we identified a number of problems relevant outside the context of these organizations. We discuss these problems in this section.

The outline of our discussion is illustrated in Figure 4. We begin by describing the high-level challenges that served as motivation for investigating product derivation problems. In the observed problems section, we discuss the main problems that were identified during the case study and that underpin those challenges. The core issues are the common aspects of these problems. On the one hand, product derivation problems can be alleviated by process guidance and methodological support that finds a suitable way to deal with these issues. On the other hand, product derivation problems can be alleviated by addressing the underlying causes of the core issues. The core issues and related methodological support issues are discussed in Section 5.3. The underlying causes of the core issues are addressed in Sections 5.4 and 5.5.

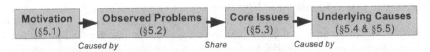

Fig. 4. The outline of the discussion in Section 5

5.1 Motivation

Two main observations prompted the need to investigate product derivation: time, effort, and costs; and expert dependency.

Time, effort and costs. The first observation involved the classic software engineering problems such as the high costs associated with deriving individual products, the time and effort consumption due to difficulties in individual product derivation steps, and the large number of cycles through the iteration phase.

Expert Dependency. The second observation involved the fact that the product derivation process depends very much on expert involvement. This not only resulted in a very high workload on experts, and as such in the lack of accessibility of these experts, but also made the organizations very vulnerable to the loss of important derivation knowledge.

5.2 Observed Problems

During the data collection phase of the case study, we identified several underlying problems for the observations discussed in the previous section. In the remainder of this section, we provide a description for each underlying problem, followed by an example.

False Positives of Compatibility Check During Component Selection
Description. During product derivation, components are selected to add to or replace components in the (partial) configuration at hand. Whether a component fits in the configuration depends on whether the component interacts correctly with the other components in the configuration, and whether any dependencies or constraints are violated. The interaction of a component with its environment is specified contractually through the provided and required component interface. Thus, the consistency of the cooperation with the other components can be validated by checking the correct-

ness of the use of the provided interfaces, the satisfaction of the required interfaces, the constraints, and the dependencies of the selected component. The problem we identified occurs when the (manual or automated) consistency check finds no violations, but testing shows that some components are incompatible. As a result, extra iterations and expert involvement are necessary to correct the inconsistent configuration.

Example. Part of the compatibility check between components during component selection is performed by tooling at business unit A. This automated check is based on the syntactical interface specification, that is, function calls with their parameter types. One cause of multiple iterations is that, in some cases, although the interface check indicates a positive match for components in the configuration during the earlier phases, some components turn out to be incompatible during validation on the test bench.

Large Number of Human Errors

Description. Due to the large amount of variation points (ranging up to the tens of thousands), and the possibly even larger number of (implicit) dependencies between these variation points, product derivation at both organizations has become an error-prone task. As a result, a substantial amount of effort in the derivation process of the interviewed business units is associated with correcting these human errors in the iteration phase.

Example. Parameter settings at TNNL Combat Systems account for approximately 50 percent of product derivation costs. The engineers indicated that most of the effort for this activity results from correcting unintended side effects introduced by previous parameter setting steps.

Consequences of Variant Selection Unclear

Description. Software engineers often do not know all the consequences of the choices they make in the derivation process. Sometimes, in later phases of product derivation, variants selected earlier proved to complicate development because the earlier choice had negative consequences.

Example. In addition to automated checks, the interviewed business units check component compatibility and appropriateness by manually inspecting the component documentation. The software engineers indicated that despite the fact that the component documentation for individual products comprises up to thousands of pages, during testing, selected components often implement requirements insufficiently or turn out to be incompatible.

Repetition of Development

Description. The organizations identified that, despite their reuse efforts, development effort is spent on implementing functionality that highly resembles the functionality already implemented in reusable assets or in previous projects.

Example. The asset repository of business unit A contains several thousand component variants and several tens of thousands of older versions of these component variants. Product derivation at this business unit comprises selecting several hundreds of components from these component variants and setting several thousand parameters. Occasionally during component selection, this leads to a situation where the component variants implementing certain requirements are not found, though they are present.

Different Provided and Required Interfaces Complicate Component Selection

Description. Variants of variation points communicate with other parts of the system through the provided and required interfaces. The problem we address here involves the situation where several variants of a particular variation point have different provided and required interfaces. This complicates component selection because, in some cases, multiple versions of the same variant provide the same required functionality, but differ in their provided or required interfaces. Another case is that two variants of different variation points cannot both be selected because they provide incompatible interfaces. As a result, selecting a required variant can invalidate the selection of variants or require adaptation.

Example. This problem was identified primarily at business unit A. Complications in component selection occur frequently as a result of different provided and required interfaces.

5.3   Core Issues

Upon closer inspection, the problems listed above share the combination of two core issues as a common aspect: complexity and implicit properties.

Complexity. The first core issue identified is the complexity of the product family in terms of the number of variation points and variants. This complexity makes the process of setting and selecting variants almost unmanageable by individuals.

Implicit Properties. The second core issue involves the large number of implicit properties (e.g., dependencies) of variation points and variants, that is, properties that are undocumented and either unknown or known only by experts.

Coping with Complexity and Implicit Properties. In themselves, complexity and implicit properties are not problematic. Problems arise when they aren't dealt with effectively. Product derivation problems can therefore be alleviated by process guidance and methodological support that provides a suitable way to deal with these issues; for example, hierarchical organization; first-class and formal representation of variation points and dependencies; and reactive documentation of properties.

Hierarchical Organization. The large number of variation points and variants is a problem, in part, because none of the product families in the case study organized variation points explicitly in a hierarchical fashion (e.g., in feature diagrams [23]). As a consequence, during product derivation, software engineers are required to deal with many variation points that are either not at all relevant for the product that is currently being derived, or that refer to the selection of the same higher level variant.

First-Class and Formal Representation of Variation Points and Dependencies. The lack of first-class representation of variation points and dependencies makes it hard to assess the impact of selections during product derivation and of changes during evolution, as it is unclear how variations in requirements are realized in the implementation

[7]. If formalized, these representations enable tool support that may significantly reduce costs and increase the efficiency of product derivation and evolution.

Reactive Documentation of Properties. The problems caused by implicit dependencies are associated not with just a one-time occurrence, but also with the recurrence of mistakes in several projects. This is due to neglecting to document the implicit properties that frequently result in mistakes. One approach to dealing with implicit properties is therefore through a reactive documentation process that ensures the documentation of important implicit dependencies.

Rather than focusing on dealing with the issues, product derivation problems can be alleviated by addressing the source of the core issues. During cause analysis, we identified that both core issues have a number of underlying causes. We discuss those causes in the next two sections. For each cause, we provide a description and consequences, as well as solutions and topics that need to be addressed by further research.

5.4 Underlying Causes of Complexity

Complexity in product families is due to both the inherent complexity of the problem domain (e.g., complex system properties, number of product family members) and the design decisions regarding variability that are made during the evolution of the shared software assets. In the following cause analysis, we focus on increases in complexity that result from the evolution of variability. The causes we identified relate to scoping during product derivation, obsolete variation points, and the nonoptimal realization of variability.

Scoping During Product Derivation: Product-Specific Adaptation Versus Reactive Evolution

Description. As briefly discussed in Section 2.3, changes that are required during product derivation (e.g., new features), can be handled through product-specific adaptation or reactive evolution. An important aspect here is scoping, that is, determining whether to handle a change with product-specific adaptation or reactive evolution.

Such a scoping decision is optimal if the benefits of handling the change through reactive evolution (possible reuse) outweigh the benefits of product-specific adaptation (no unnecessary variation points and variants). At Bosch, we identified two extremes in the balance between product-specific adaptation and reactive evolution. In the one extreme, all required changes for the products were handled through product-specific adaptation (business unit B), while in the other extreme, all changes were handled through reactive evolution (business unit A). In other words, no explicit asset scoping activity existed that continuously interacted with product derivation.

Consequences. The drawback of not scoping each feature individually during product derivation is that, for possibly a considerable amount of functionality, a nonoptimal scoping decision is made, namely a decision resulting in either the repetition of development in different projects or in more variation points and variants than are actually needed. The lack of scoping during product derivation is thus the first underlying cause of complexity.

Solutions and research issues. Product derivation processes should include continuous interactions with the scoping activities during domain engineering. In that respect, the way Change Control Boards are employed in TNNL Combat Systems (see Section 4) provides a good example for large product families. For smaller product families, this continuous interaction is the responsibility of the product family architect(s). Currently, however, there is a lack of variability assessment techniques that consider both the benefits and the drawbacks of scoping decisions. We consider these techniques to be crucial in assisting the system engineers and architects during evolution.

Proactive Evolution: Obsolete Variation Points

Description. The problem we address here is twofold. First, a typical trend in software systems is that functionality specific to some products becomes part of the core functionality of all product family members (e.g., due to market dominance). The need to support different alternatives—and therefore variation points and variants for this functionality—may disappear. Second, variation points introduced during proactive evolution are often not evaluated with respect to actual use.

Both phenomena lead to the existence of obsolete variation points, that is, variation points for which (in each derived product) the same variant is chosen, or, in the case of optional variants, is not used anymore. At both organizations, these obsolete variation points were often left intact rather than being removed from the assets.

Consequences. Removing obsolete variation points increases the predictability of the software's behavior [7], decreases the cognitive complexity of the software assets, and improves the traceability of suitable variants in the asset repository. We also note that if variability provided by artifacts is not used for a long time and is removed from the documentation, engineers may start to forget that some facilities are there. For example, the interviewees indicated the existence of parameters whose purpose is unknown and consequently, no one knows what their optimal values are. In addition to handling all changes through reactive evolution, we therefore identify the existence of obsolete variation points and the lack of removing them as the second underlying cause of complexity.

Solutions and research issues. The solution to this issue is not as simple as just removing the variation point. Besides the fact that it may prove to be hard to pinpoint the exact moment at which a variation point becomes obsolete ("but it might be used again next month!"), removing obsolete variation points requires effort in many areas. All variation points related to the previously variable functionality have to be removed, which may require redesign and reimplementation of the variable functionality. There may be dependencies and constraints that have to be taken care of. Also, changing a component may invalidate existing tests and thus require retesting.

To reduce complexity, we identify the need for methodologies regarding roadmapping and variability assessment that consider the necessity and feasibility of including new functionality in the shared software assets and regularly consider the removal of unused functionality (and thus variation points and variants).

Nonoptimal Realization of Variability

Description: Over the past few years, several variability realization techniques have been identified [13, 23]. Mechanisms for those techniques typically have a large impact on the performance and flexibility of a software system. Therefore, the following decisions should be made carefully: selecting a mechanism (based on aspects such as the size of the involved software entities) and deciding when the variation should be introduced, when it should be possible to add new variants, and when it needs to be bound to a particular variant. In practice, however, the number of different variability realization techniques used is often very limited and inappropriate for the problem at hand because

- As some variation mechanisms require extra computational resources (such as memory or CPU cycles), organizations—especially those that produce embedded systems—often choose mechanisms that minimize the overhead.
- The number of variability mechanisms used is further limited by the technology used. The programming language C, for example, does not allow for techniques such as inheritance.
- Software architects typically aren't aware of the advantages and disadvantages of certain mechanisms and often map only variation to the mechanisms they know [7].
- Customer requirements may demand the use of a certain mechanism that is not recommended from a technology point of view. An example of such a situation is when runtime binding is prohibited, as shipment of the code is restricted to one customer only.
- Reactive evolution is concerned mainly with incorporating the requirements specific to a product in relation to existing product family requirements, rather than analyzing how they relate to requirements in future products. In addition, reactive evolution suffers from the time-to-market and budget pressures of individual projects. With this focus, implementing variation points and variants for a specific product is prioritized over reusability in other products.

Consequences. Although choosing only a few mechanisms simplifies design and implementation, the drawbacks of disregarding the other mechanisms are not always understood [7]. In the interviewed business units, most variation is mapped to variant component implementations and parameterization. The drawback of this approach for business unit A, for example, is that even small changes to the interfaces needed to be implemented through new component implementations. This contributed to the fact that the asset repository of business unit A now contains several thousand component variants and tens of thousands of older versions of these component variants. Realization of variability is therefore identified as a third underlying cause of complexity.

Solutions and research issues. We identify the need for detailed comparative studies of realization techniques to understand the qualities and drawbacks of selecting certain mechanisms. Adequate training of software architects with respect to design for variability helps to create awareness of different variability mechanisms.

5.5 Underlying Causes of Implicit Properties

The second core issue, implicit properties, is related to the creation and maintenance of documentation. In the following cause analysis, we identify three underlying causes: the erosion of documentation, insufficient and overexplicit documentation, and the lack of specifying semantics and behavior.

Erosion of Documentation

Description. Documentation has to be actively maintained to keep it useful. During the original development of software artifacts, the specification can be correct, or at least intended to be correct. If, in a later stage, an artifact is changed, the specification should also be changed accordingly. Quite often however, investigating all the consequences of changes and updating the documentation accordingly is not a priority.

Consequences. The severity of situations in which documentation shows signs of erosion range from minor inconsistencies that result in errors, and thus iterations, up to the stage were it is outdated and rendered almost useless. For example, eroded documentation further contributes to the need for several years of training for personnel at TNNL Combat Systems.

Solution and Research Topics. The issue discussed here confirms the documentation problem regarding reuse discussed in earlier work [4]. Solutions and research issues suggested in that article, such as investigating novel approaches to documentation and not allowing engineers to proceed without updating the documentation, gaining a higher status, and obtaining a larger amount of support from management, therefore also apply here. A technique that specifically addressed erosion is literate programming [17], where source code and documentation live in one document. Literate programming is state of the practice through, for example, Javadoc [14] and may provide a large and easy step forward for many C-oriented systems.

Insufficient, Irrelevant, and Voluminous Documentation

Description: Software engineers often find it hard to determine what knowledge is relevant and therefore should be documented. Although problems with documentation are usually associated with the lack of it, the large amount and irrelevance of documentation were identified as problems as well.

Consequences: In addition to the automated check, component compatibility at the interviewed business units is performed manually by inspecting the component documentation. The software engineers indicated that the component documentation for individual products often comprise thousands of pages. On the one hand, the volume and irrelevancy of the information contained in the documents made it hard to find the aspects (e.g., dependencies) relevant for a particular configuration. On the other hand, the software engineers also indicate that, at times, even large amounts of relevant documentation seem insufficient to determine the provided functionality or compatibility.

Solution and research topics: Besides good structuring, documentation requires an acceptable quality-to-quantity ratio to be effective. Relevant research issues have been discussed in the research issues for erosion of documentation.

Lack of Semantics and Behavior

Description: Component interface specifications often consist of a set of provided and required operations in terms of argument and return types. Such specifications do not specify the semantics and behavior of the interface.

Consequences: One of the reasons for the false positive problem discussed in Section 5.2 is that syntactically equal operations can have different meanings (e.g., a temperature 'delta' parameter may indicate a positive or negative delta) or not be accessible at all times (e.g., in case of slow producers and fast consumers).

A second drawback of the lack of semantics is that dependencies and constraints often specify merely that components are incompatible, rather than why. From the point of view of an engineer who has to consider selecting a closely matching component, however, it is also very important to know why certain components exclude or depend on other components, or whether certain constraints are weak or strong, in addition to knowing that certain components cannot be selected as is.

Solution and research topics: Relevant research issues, such as novel approaches to documentation, and literal programming have been discussed in earlier work [4] and the research issues on the erosion of documentation.

6 Related Work

The notion of software product families has received substantial attention in the research community. The adoption of software product families has resulted in a number of books (those by Bosch [5], Clements and Northrop [10], and Weiss and Lai [24]), workshops (PFE 1-4), conferences (SPLC 1 and 2), and several large European research projects (e.g., PRAISE, ESAPS, and CAFÉ [19]).

The notion of a variation point was introduced by Jacobson, Griss, and Jonsson [13]. Those three authors also identified several variability realization techniques [13], as did Svahnberg, van Gurp, and Bosch [23]. The notion of variability has also been discussed in the earlier work of our research group and other groups by discussing variability issues that are related to problems presented in Section 5 [7] and presenting a taxonomy of variability realization mechanisms [23]. The contribution of this paper is that we have identified a number of issues that are related specifically to the evolution of variability.

In the context of evolution, Bayer and associates [2] and Clements and Northrop [10] propose periodic scoping during domain engineering as a solution for dealing with the continuous evolution of a product family. In this paper, we have proposed using a feature scoping activity that continuously interacts with product derivation, to prevent nonoptimal scoping decisions. Product family scoping is further discussed by Kishi, Noda, and Katayama [15] and Schmid [21].

Well-known process models that resemble the ideas of the phased product derivation model we presented in Section 3 are the Rational Unified Process [18] and Boehm's spiral model [3]. More related work and an elaborate description of the generic process are provided by Deelstra, Sinnema, and Bosch [12].

The problems with implicit properties confirm problems regarding documentation in the context of software reuse discussed in earlier work [4]. Nonaka and Takeuchi discuss the process of externalization, which is converting tacit knowledge into documented or formalized knowledge [20]. Literate programming was introduced by Knuth [17] and addresses the erosion of documentation problem discussed in Section 5.5.

Several industrial case studies have been performed inside our group; for example, on product instantiation [6] and evolution in software product families [22]. In addition, several case studies have been presented outside our group over the years [1, 8, 9]. The contribution of this paper is that it specifically identifies and analyses product derivation problems, whereas earlier case studies focused primarily on domain engineering.

7 Conclusions

In this paper, we have presented the results of a case study on product derivation that involved two industrial organizations: Robert Bosch GmbH and Thales Nederland B.V. The case study results include a number of identified problems and causes.

The discussions in this paper focused on two core issues. The first issue is complexity. Although the assumption that variability improves the ability to select alternative functionality and thus increases the ease of deriving different product family members, the results of our case study suggest otherwise. At a certain point, each additional variation point leads to an increase in the cognitive complexity of the product family and possibly complicates the derivation process. On the one hand, product derivation problems can be alleviated by product derivation methodologies that deal effectively with complexity (e.g., through hierarchical organization and first-class representation of variation points and dependencies). On the other hand, problems can be alleviated by addressing the main source behind the complexity—the evolution of variability. We have identified research issues related to that evolution, such as variability assessment techniques that help software engineers determine the optimal scoping decision during product derivation, as well as assessment techniques for determining the feasibility of removing obsolete variation points, and selecting a particular variability realization mechanism during domain engineering.

The second important issue is the large number of implicit properties (such as dependencies) of software assets. An approach to coping with this issue is to reactively document implicit properties that frequently result in mistakes. Problems can further be alleviated by addressing the sources of implicit properties, such as the erosion of documentation, insufficient and overexplicit documentation, and the lack of semantics and behavior in specifications. Parts of these causes confirm the problems related to documentation and reuse discussed in earlier work [4]. Research issues related to this topic can therefore also be found in that work.

Concluding, software product families have been applied successfully in industry. By studying and identifying product derivation problems, we have shown that there is room for improvement in the current practice. Solving the identified problems will help organizations exploit the full benefits of software product families. Therefore, the future work of the ConIPF project (see Section 3) aims to define and validate methodologies that are practicable in industrial application and that address the product derivation problems discussed in this paper.

Acknowledgments. This work was sponsored by the CONIPF project, under contract no. IST-2001-34438. We would like to thank the participants of the case study for their valuable input.

References

1.   Ardis, M., Daley, N., Hoffman, D., Siy, H., Weiss, D., 2000. Software Product Lines: A Case Study, Software – Practice and Experience, Vol. 30, No. 7, pp. 825–847

2. Bayer, J., Flege, O., Knauber, P., Laqua, R., Muthig, D., Schmid, K., Widen, T., DeBaud, J.-M., 1999. PuLSE™: A Methodology to Develop Software Product Lines, Proceedings of the Fifth ACM SIGSOFT Symposium on Software Reusability (SSR'99), pp. 122-131.
3. Boehm, B. W., 1988. A spiral model of software development and enhancement, IEEE Computer, Vol. 21, No. 5, pp. 61–72
4. Bosch, J., 1999. Product-line architectures in industry: a case study, Proceedings of the 21st International Conference on Software Engineering, pp. 544-554
5. Bosch, J., 2000. Design and Use of Software Architectures: Adopting and Evolving a Product Line Approach, Pearson Education (Addison-Wesley & ACM Press), ISBN 0-201-67494-7
6. Bosch, J., Högström, M., 2000. Product Instantiation in Software Product Lines: A Case Study, Second International Symposium on Generative and Component-Based Software Engineering, pp. 147-162
7. Bosch, J., Florijn, G., Greefhorst, D., Kuusela, J., Obbink, H., Pohl, K., 2001. Variability Issues in Software Product Lines, Proceedings of the Fourth International Workshop on Product Family Engineering (PFE-4), pp. 11–19
8. Brownsword, L., Clements, P., 1996. A Case Study in Successful Product Line Development, Technical Report CMU/SEI-96-TR-016, Software Engineering Institute, Carnegie Mellon University
9. Clements, P., Cohen, S., Donohoe, P., Northrop, L., 2001. Control Channel Toolkit: A Software Product Line Case Study, Technical Report CMU/SEI-2001-TR-030, Software Engineering Institute, Carnegie Mellon University
10. Clements, P., Northrop, L., 2001. Software Product Lines: Practices and Patterns, SEI Series in Software Engineering, Addison-Wesley, ISBN: 0-201-70332-7
11. ConIPF project (Configuration of Industrial Product Families), http://segroup.cs.rug.nl/conipf
12. Deelstra, S., Sinnema, M., Bosch, J., 2003. A Product Derivation Framework for Software Product Families, accepted for the 5th Workshop on Product Family Engineering (PFE-5), November 2003
13. Jacobson, I., Griss, M., Jonsson, P., 1997. Software Reuse. Architecture, Process and Organization for Business Success. Addison-Wesley, ISBN: 0-201-92476-5
14. Javadoc, 2003. http://java.sun.com/j2se/javadoc/
15. Kishi, T., Noda, T., Katayama, T., 2002. A Method for Product Line Scoping Based on Decision-Making Framework, Proceedings of the Second Software Product Line Conference, pp. 348–365
16. Kostoff, R. N., Schaller, R. R., 2001. Science and Technology Roadmaps, IEEE Transactions on Engineering Management, Vol. 48, no. 2, pp. 132-143
17. Knuth, D.E., 1984. Literate programming, Computer Journal Vol. 27, pp. 97-111
18. Kruchten, P., 2000. The Rational Unified Process: An Introduction (2nd Edition), ISBN 0-201-707101
19. Linden, F. v.d., 2002. Software Product Families in Europe: The Esaps & Café Projects, IEEE Software, Vol. 19, No. 4, pp. 41-49
20. Nonaka, I., Takeuchi, H., 1995. The Knowledge-Creating Company: How Japanese companies create the dynasties of innovation, NewYork: Oxford University Press
21. Schmid, K., 2000. Scoping Software Product Lines - An Analysis of an Emerging Technology, Proceedings of the First Software Product Line Conference, pp. 513–532
22. Svahnberg, M., Bosch, J., 1999. Evolution in Software Product Lines: Two Cases, Journal of Software Maintenance, Vol. 11, No. 6, pp. 391-422
23. Svahnberg, M., van Gurp, J., Bosch, J., 2002. A Taxonomy of Variability Realization Techniques, ISSN: 1103-1581, Blekinge Institute of Technology, Sweden.
24. Weiss D. M., Lai, C. T. R., 1999. Software Product-Line Engineering: A Family Based Software Development Process, Addison-Wesley, ISBN 0-201-694387

A Feature-Based Approach
to Product Line Production Planning

Jaejoon Lee,[1] Kyo C. Kang,[1] and Sajoong Kim[2]

[1] Department of Computer Science and Engineering,
Pohang University of Science and Technology (POSTECH), PIRL,
31 San, Hyoja-Dong, Nam-Gu, Pohang, Kyoung-buk, Republic of Korea
{gibman, kck}@postech.ac.kr
http://selab.postech.ac.kr
[2] Korea Software Institute (KSI), Korea IT Industry Promotion Agency (KIPA),
KIPA Bldg., 79-2, Garakbon-dong, Songpa-gu, Seoul, Republic of Korea
sjkim@software.or.kr

Abstract. A production plan, which describes how core assets are used to develop products, has an important role in product line engineering as a communications medium between core asset developers and product developers. Recently, there have been efforts to address issues related to production planning, most of which focus on the process and business/management aspects of production planning; not much emphasis is given to technical issues such as deciding which features will be made as core assets and what their granularity will be.

In this paper, we introduce a feature-based approach to product line production planning and illustrate how our approach addresses these technical issues. In our approach, a feature model and feature-binding information are used as primary input to production plan development. A product line production plan created using our approach could be customized easily to a product-specific production plan, because when we developed the approach, we considered units of product configurations as well as their integration techniques.

1 Introduction

With the product line engineering paradigm, a common set of core assets is developed and used to develop the products of a product line. The core assets include requirements specifications, architecture models, software components, and adopted commercial off-the-shelf (COTS) components [1]. A production plan, which describes how the core assets are used to develop products, has an important role in product line engineering as a communications medium between core asset developers and product developers. That is, the production plan provides product developers with the way core assets are customized and integrated into products.

Recently, there have been efforts to address issues related to production planning [2, 3]. Chastek and McGregor propose guidelines for developing a production plan and production plan evaluation criteria [2], and Chastek, Donohoe, and McGregor describe case studies [3]. Most of these efforts, however, focus on the process and business/management aspects of production planning; not much emphasis is given to

R.L. Nord (Ed.): SPLC 2004, LNCS 3154, pp. 183–196, 2004.

technical issues such as deciding which features will be implemented as core assets and how big each core asset will be.

In this paper, we introduce a feature-based approach to product line production planning and illustrate how our approach addresses these technical issues. In our approach, a feature model (which captures the commonality and variability information of a product line) and feature-binding information [4] about which features are included in products and delivered to customers, and when, are used as primary input to production plan development. In product line engineering, a feature model plays a central role in the management and configuration of multiple products. Therefore, core assets should be identified based on features. Also, feature-binding analysis provides asset developers with information on the granularity of and binding techniques for the core assets.

The final work product of our approach is a product line production plan document for which we follow the structure of a production plan described by Chastek and McGregor [2]. (Note that, of the chapters and sections in Chastek and McGregor's work [2], we describe only the sections relevant to our approach.) Also, a Home Integration System (HIS) product line, which controls and manages a collection of devices to maintain the security and safety of a building or house, is used to demonstrate the concept (See Table 1 for the product features.). An HIS generally includes the features in the table below. More advanced products may include features that optimize living conditions such as climate control and lighting.

Table 1. Product features of an HIS product line

Product Feature	Explanation
fire detection & control	Fire events are detected by monitoring smoke detectors and heat sensors installed in the house. When a fire event is detected, the HIS turns the alarm and all sprinklers on and unlocks all HIS-controlled doors. The HIS also sends a prerecorded voice message to the fire station and the owner over the telephone line to inform them of the incident. Once the fire is under control, the alarm and all sprinklers will be turned off, but doors will remain unlocked for the duration of time preset by the owner.
intrusion detection & control	Intrusion events are detected by monitoring motion sensors. When an intrusion event is detected, the HIS turns the alarm on and locks all HIS-controlled doors. Also, the HIS sends a voice message to the police station and the owner.
flood detection & control	Flood events are detected by monitoring moisture sensors. When a flood event is detected, the HIS shuts off the water main of the house. When moisture is detected on the basement floor, the sump pump will be activated.
security	The entrance and exit of all personnel are verified and recorded with identification information (e.g., name, time, ID number, and so on). There are various devices for the verification such as fingerprint recognition, voice recognition, and so forth. Also, the access to every room inside a building can be controlled by each person's job function.

Section 2 gives an overview of the activities of our approach, and the feature-binding analysis and product-line-asset identification activities are described in Sections 3 and 4, respectively. The development activity for product line core assets is described in Section 5, and the documentation for product line production plans is illustrated with an example of an HIS product line production plan in Section 6. Section 7 summarizes and concludes this paper.

2   Product Line Production-Planning Activities

Product line engineering consists of two major engineering processes: product-line-asset engineering and product engineering, each consisting of various activities [1, 5]. Of the many activities of the product-line-asset engineering process, we identified the activities related to product line production planning. (See Figure 1 for these activities and their relationships.) These activities are iterative, and the arrows in Figure 1 show data flows (i.e., the use of work products at each activity). Each activity is described briefly below.

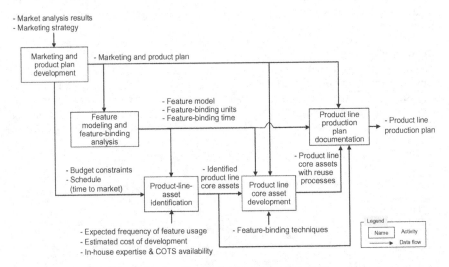

Fig. 1. Product line production-planning activities

Developing a Marketing and Product Plan (MPP) for a product line initiates product line production planning. The MPP, which includes a marketing plan and a product plan, sets a specific context for product line analysis and reuse exploration for the product line. The marketing plan in the MPP provides, for each market segment, information of an assessment of needs, the time to market, the price range, and a marketing strategy for realizing business opportunities in the market. In the product plan of the MPP, product features are identified.

In feature modeling, product features from the MPP are organized into an initial feature model that is extended with design features such as the operating environments, domain technologies, and implementation techniques to be used. Feature-binding analysis then identifies feature-binding units from the feature model and determines the binding time between binding units. The results of this activity are a feature model, feature-binding units, and the feature-binding time information.

The product-line-asset identification activity takes the feature model and the feature-binding analysis results as primary input. For each feature-binding unit, its asset type (i.e., core asset, product-specific asset, or COTS) is determined with consideration of budget constraints, the time to market, and other business/technical items including the availability of in-house expertise.

The primary input to the development of product line core assets includes a feature model and feature-binding units and their binding time. In this activity, variation points are identified, and feature-binding techniques are explored to support the required feature-binding time.

The documentation activity for product line production plans integrates the work products provided by the other activities, as shown in Figure 1. After the marketing and business analyses information from the MPP is incorporated into the production plan, it is refined with binding units and identified product line core assets. Then, feature-binding units, which are annotated with the binding information and reuse processes, are documented.

Of the production-planning activities, details on marketing and product plan development can be found in the work of Kang, Lee, and Donohoe [5] and Kang and associates [6]. The rest of the production-planning activities are described in the following sections. We adapted and used the MPP example provided by Kang, Lee, and Donohoe [5] to illustrate our approach (See Table 2.).

Table 2. An MPP example for an HIS product line

Marketing and Product Plan for an HIS product line			
Market segments		Office building (high-end product)	Household (low-end product)
Marketing plan	Need assessment	The customer's choices of features for high-end products are in the wide range of variability. Moreover, the *Security* feature has customer-specific requirements.	The customers are budget conscious, and they only require features that are essential for HIS products.
	Time to market	Less than six months	Less than three months
	Price range	To be a competitive product, the price should be less than $20,000.	Less than $1,000
	Marketing strategy (product delivery methods)	Develop and deliver a product for each customer.	Prepackaged
Product plan	Product features	Fire, Intrusion, Flood, Security, and other customer-specific features	Fire, Intrusion
	Quality attributes	Safety, Reliability, Scalability	Safety, Reliability, Usability

3   Feature Modeling and Feature-Binding Analysis

A feature model captures the commonalities and variabilities of a product line in terms of product features. Figure 2 shows the feature model of an HIS product line. The capability features of an HIS consist of service features (e.g., *Fire, Intrusion, Flood,* and so on) and operational features (e.g., *Alarm, Pumping,* and so on). The operating environment features of an HIS include *Moisture Sensor* and *Sump Pump,* and domain technology features include technical features (e.g., *Monitoring & Detecting*) for implementing service and operational features. Compared with domain technology features, implementation technique features are more generic and might be applicable to other product lines. For example, the *TCP* and *UDP* features are used to provide an Internet connection in the HIS product line, but they can also be used in other product lines. Details of feature analysis and modeling guidelines are provided by Lee, Kang, and Lee [7].

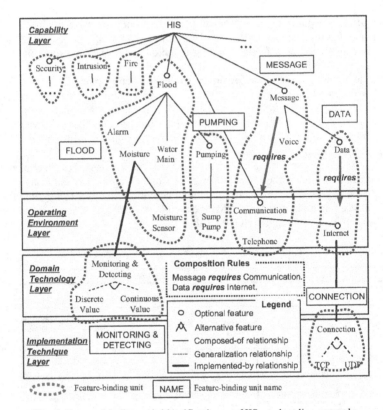

Fig. 2. Feature-binding unit identification: an HIS product line example

After feature modeling, feature-binding analysis is performed using the feature model and the MPP. Feature binding is examined from three perspectives: (1) which features are bound together (feature-binding units), (2) when features are bound into products (feature-binding time), and (3) how features are bound (feature-binding techniques). Feature-binding unit and feature-binding time analyses are discussed in this section. The feature-binding techniques are explored briefly in Section 5.2.

3.1   Feature-Binding Unit Analysis

We define a feature-binding unit as a set of features that are related to each other via composed-of, generalization/specialization, or implemented-by relationships and the composition rules (i.e., require and mutually exclude) of a feature model. Features that belong to a binding unit work for a common service. Therefore, they have to exist together for correct operation of the service.

Feature-binding-unit identification starts with the identification of independently configurable service features. (For short, we will call these features *service features* in the remainder of this paper.) A service feature represents a major functionality of a system and may be added or removed as a service unit. In an HIS, *Flood, Fire,* and *Intrusion* features are examples of service features.

A service feature uses other features (e.g., operational, environmental, and implementation features) to function properly, and the constituents of a binding unit can be found by traversing the feature model along the feature relationships and composition rules. For example, as we start from the *Flood* service feature, *Alarm, Moisture, Water Main, Pumping, Moisture Sensor, Sump Pump,* and *Monitoring & Detecting* features can be identified. All these features are needed to provide the flood service.

Within a feature-binding unit, optional or alternative features may exist that should be selected based on customers' needs. These features impose variations on the component design, so they have to be identified as separate feature-binding units. For example, only one of the subfeatures of *Monitoring & Detecting* can be selected based on the device type that a customer may choose. (See the *Monitoring & Detecting* feature at the domain technology layer in Figure 2.)

Note that the *Communication* feature is included in the *MESSAGE* feature-binding unit, although the feature is optional. This is because the *Message* feature requires the *Communication* feature according to the composition rule, and they have to be together to provide the message service properly. (See the arrows for the 'require' composition rule in Figure 2.) After all feature-binding units are identified, a name is assigned to each feature-binding unit. The feature name that represents a binding unit was given to the corresponding feature-binding unit, but the name was written in upper case letters to distinguish it from the name of the feature. (See the dotted circles and the names of binding units in Figure 2.) Once features are grouped into feature-binding units, a binding time analysis is performed for the feature-binding units.

3.2 Feature-Binding Time Analysis

Generally, feature-binding time has been looked at from the software development life-cycle viewpoint ('product-life-cycle view') [8, 9] in which the focus has been the life-cycle phase incorporating a feature into a product. In product line engineering, however, another dimension exists that is based on the *binding state* of a feature-binding unit. That is, some feature-binding units may be developed and included in product line core assets at core asset development time, but their availability can be determined at installation time by enabling or disabling the feature-binding units. Furthermore, activation of the available feature-binding units may be controlled to avoid a feature interaction problem.[1] Thus, feature-binding time analysis with an additional view on the *feature-binding state* (which includes *inclusion* and *availability* states and *activation rules*) provides a more precise framework for feature-binding analysis.

The 'product-life-cycle view' consists of four phases: (1) core asset development, (2) product development, (3) preoperation, and (4) operation. After product line core assets are developed, a product is developed with product-specific features and the core assets. Then, the product is delivered, installed, and configured for a customer during the preoperation phase.

---

[1] The problem of unexpected side effects when a feature is added to a set of features is generally known as the feature interaction problem.

Each phase of the product life cycle shows the binding states of feature-binding units. For example, if the inclusion and availability states of a feature-binding unit are determined during the development of product line core assets, the feature-binding unit is allocated to both the inclusion and availability columns of the core asset development phase. (See the *FIRE* and *INTRUSION* feature-binding units in the bottom row in Figure 3.) If the inclusion state of a feature-binding unit is determined during product development and the availability state of the feature-binding unit is determined during installation, the feature-binding unit is allocated to both the inclusion column of the product development phase and the availability column of the preoperation phase. (*FLOOD* and *MESSAGE* are examples of such feature-binding units.)

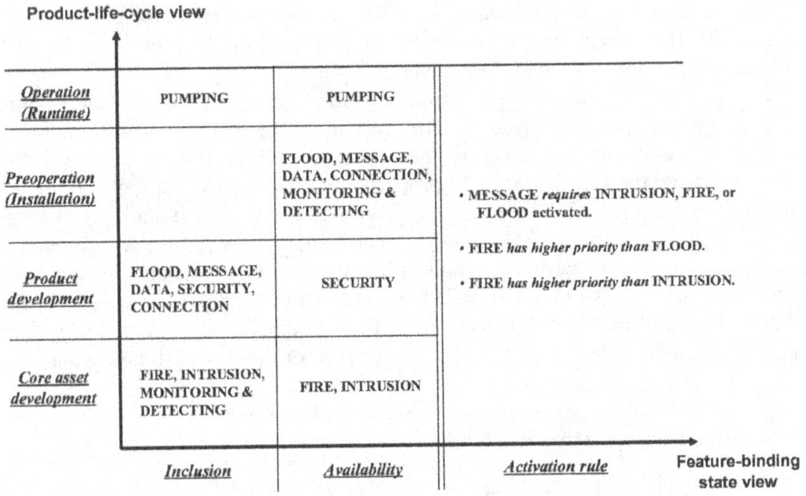

Product-life-cycle view

Operation (Runtime)	PUMPING	PUMPING	
Preoperation (Installation)		FLOOD, MESSAGE, DATA, CONNECTION, MONITORING & DETECTING	• MESSAGE *requires* INTRUSION, FIRE, or FLOOD activated.
Product development	FLOOD, MESSAGE, DATA, SECURITY, CONNECTION	SECURITY	• FIRE *has higher priority than* FLOOD. • FIRE *has higher priority than* INTRUSION.
Core asset development	FIRE, INTRUSION, MONITORING & DETECTING	FIRE, INTRUSION	
	Inclusion	*Availability*	*Activation rule*

Feature-binding state view

Fig. 3. Feature-binding time analysis

In the 'feature-binding state view,' the inclusion feature-binding state indicates when, in the product-life-cycle phases, a feature-binding unit is physically included in a product, and the availability binding state indicates when, in the product-life-cycle phases, those included feature-binding units become available to users (i.e., the feature-binding unit is ready for use with all its bound implementation techniques). Once the feature-binding unit becomes available, it is ready to be activated, as long as it abides by the activation rules among feature-binding units. (See the horizontal axis in Figure 3.)

The activation rules provide information on the concurrency of feature-binding unit activation and are defined in terms of mutual exclusion, dependency, and priority schemes. As an intuitive example, the temperature of a room can be kept stable by turning on both an air conditioner and a heater at the same time, but that is not a desirable situation. Their activation rule should be 'mutual exclusion' to avoid such situations.

The results of this activity are feature-binding units and their binding time, and it is important to note that the basic units for configuring a product in our approach are the feature-binding units. Hence, the 'Detailed production process' section of the production plan is described in terms of feature-binding units and other binding attributes such as binding time and binding techniques. In the next section, product-line-asset identification based on the feature model and feature-binding units is explained.

4 Product-Line-Asset Identification

Before developing product line core assets, we must determine which features will be made as core assets or product-specific assets, or purchased as COTS components. Therefore, for each feature, its asset type (i.e., core asset, product-specific asset, or COTS) should be determined with consideration of the budget and time-to-market constraints and other business/technical considerations such as the expected frequency of feature usage, estimated cost of development, and availability of in-house expertise. (Table 3 shows some of the identified product line assets of the HIS product line.)

Table 3. Identified product line assets

Feature-binding unit	Constituent features	Frequency of feature usage	COTS availability / COTS price (which is compared to the estimated in-house development cost)	Asset type
FIRE	Fire, Smoke, Smoke sensor, Sprinkler, ...	High	No / -	Core asset
FLOOD	Flood, Moisture, Moisture sensor, Alarm, ...	Medium	No / -	Core asset
MESSAGE	Message, Voice	Medium	Yes / Higher	Core asset
	Communication, Telephone	Medium	Yes / Lower	COTS
SECURITY	Security, Access-control, ...	Low	No / -	Product-specific asset
	Biometric	Low	Yes / Lower	COTS

For example, in the HIS product line, the *Fire* feature has a high frequency of usage (i.e., all products in the product line include it), and the estimated cost of development is low; this feature is identified as a core asset. The *Security* feature, however, has a low frequency of usage and customer-specific requirements; this feature is identified as a product-specific asset (i.e., it will be developed as an asset when it is needed). For another example, the *Biometric* feature, which is used to authenticate users, must be developed in a short period of time. However, because in-house expertise for the biometric technique is not available; COTS components will be purchased to implement this feature.

We have illustrated the product line analysis activities. In the next section, we discuss how the analysis results are used to develop product line core assets.

5 Product Line Core Asset Development

In product line engineering, core assets include requirements specifications, architecture models, software components, and adopted COTS components [1]. Of these core assets, we discuss how asset software components are developed.

The primary input to product line component development includes a feature model, feature-binding units and their binding time, architecture models, and a design object model.[2] Design objects are the embodiment of functionalities required for the product line. Once a design object model is defined, these objects in the model are allocated to components for implementation. In this section, the identification of variation points in the design object model, the exploration of binding techniques, and the specification of product line components are illustrated with examples.

5.1 Variation Point Identification

For feature binding to be feasible, variation points for optional and alternative binding units should be identified in the design object model. Since features of a binding unit should exist together, their binding to a product should be identified explicitly in the design object model. We also need to be sure that all objects that implement the features of a binding unit are bound together with the appropriate implementation techniques. For example, when the *FLOOD* binding unit is incorporated into a product and becomes available, the objects that implement each of its constituent features (i.e., *Moisture, Moisture Sensor*, and *Alarm*) should also be bound in the product for the correct operation of *FLOOD*.

To manage the variation points of a binding unit consistently, explicit mappings between binding units and variation points must be established. If there is difficulty establishing this relationship, the related objects should be examined for further decomposition, refinement, or restructuring. If a binding unit is optional and its parent binding unit is also optional, its binding requires that the parent-binding unit be bound beforehand, and this dependency should also be preserved among the variation points in the object model. For example, *FLOOD* should be bound before the binding of *PUMPING*. This dependency is preserved in the object model, as the variation point of the *FloodResponder* object is located at a lower level than the variation point of the *EventResponder* object in the aggregation hierarchy. (See Figure 4.)

In Figure 4, each bubble represents an optional or alternative binding unit, and arrows show the corresponding variation points (denoted by ■) identified in the object model. For example, the variation point for *FLOOD* is identified at the end of the line connecting *EventResponder* and *FloodResponder* objects for an aggregation relationship. That is, if *FLOOD* is determined not to be available in a product at preoperation time (see Figure 3), the aggregation relation between the two objects is removed, and the objects that implement the *FLOOD* binding unit are not accessible by users. After the variation points are identified, implementation techniques for feature binding should be explored.

---

[2] A feature-based approach to object-oriented development is provided by Lee and associates [10].

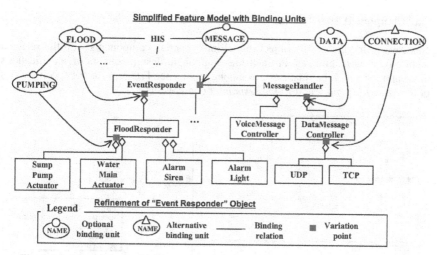

Fig. 4. Mappings between binding units and variation points in the design object model

5.2   Feature-Binding Technique Exploration

The selection of binding techniques depends both on the binding time and quality attributes (e.g., flexibility) required for products. Delaying binding time to a later phase of the life cycle may provide more flexibility, but applicable implementation techniques are limited and usually require more performance overhead. Therefore, guidelines for the selection of feature-binding techniques are required to help asset developers make decisions properly.

For that purpose, we propose a classification of feature-binding techniques based on the feature-binding states: binding techniques for the feature 'inclusion' and those for the feature 'availability.' Techniques belonging to the former class should be able to control feature inclusion by including or excluding code segments or components from products. Code generation, preprocessing, macroprocessing [11], ICD (Internet Component Download) [12] are some examples of this class. These techniques allow products to include multiple features physically, but their availability can be determined at a later phase. (See the two left columns in Figure 3.)

The second class of techniques provides mechanisms for enabling or disabling accesses to features. Load tables and authentication-based access control [13] are techniques that belong to this class. In the HIS product line, for instance, the load table technique is used to determine the availability of *FLOOD*, *DATA*, and so on at the preoperation phase. When the system starts to execute, it refers to the load table to determine which features should be made available to the user.

In addition to those techniques belonging to the two classes, we should also explore techniques for the dynamic or static binding of features. While some features may be bound statically, other features may require dynamic binding for flexibility or memory space efficiency. The dynamic binding of objects, menus, and plug-ins [14] are techniques that belong to this class. For example, *PUMPING* is bound at the operation time, as its device drivers for sump pumps may vary.

In the following section, an implementation of the HIS example is illustrated.

5.3 Component Specification

Next, we refine the design object model into concrete components with the selected feature-binding techniques. Product line component design consists of specifications of components and the relationships among them. (See Figure 5 for the specifications of the *EventResponder* and *FloodResponder* components.)

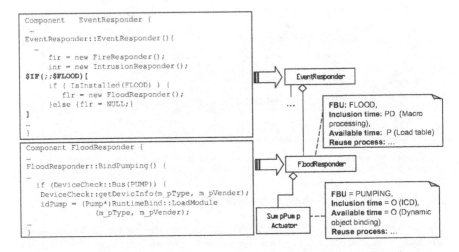

- FBU: Feature-Binding Unit - PD: Product Development time - P: Preoperation time
- O: Operation time - ICD: Internet Component Download

Fig. 5. Component specifications of *EventResponder* and *FloodResponder* with annotations of feature-binding information

For product development time inclusion of *FLOOD*, the macrolanguage—that is, IF(;;$FLOOD) [...]—is used, and for the preoperation time availability, the load table is used. The instantiation of the *FloodResponder* depends on the return value of IsInstalled(FLOOD), which confirms whether *FLOOD* is allowed to be made available. (See the upper left part of Figure 5.)

As a customer is authorized to use *PUMPING* at operation time (see the operation time row in Figure 3), the FloodResponder::BindPumping method of the *FloodResponder* is invoked. Then, it searches for an appropriate device driver for the installed sump pump and binds it to provide the pumping service. (See the lower left part of Figure 5.)

Once product line components are developed, each component is annotated with binding information such as mappings to feature-binding units, their binding time, and binding techniques, and a reuse process. (See the notes attached to *FloodResponder* and *SumpPumpActuator* in Figure 5.) For example, *FloodResponder* is mapped to the *FLOOD* binding unit, and the time when it is included in the product and the time when it becomes available for use are product development time and preoperation time, respectively. Also, binding techniques used are described in parentheses. For the product development time inclusion of *FLOOD*, the macroprocessing is used and, for the preoperation time availability, the load table is used.

In the next section, the documentation activity for product line production plans, which integrates the work products of other activities, is described.

6 Product Line Production Plan Documentation

This activity starts with documenting the information from the MPP. For instance, the target products in the product plan for each market segment are documented in the 'Products possible from available assets' section of Figure 6. Also, the product delivery methods in the marketing strategy, which describe how products will be delivered to customers, initially outline the 'Production strategy' section in the production plan. For example, products for the low-end market segment only have core features (i.e., *Fire* and *Intrusion*), and these features are prepackaged in all products; an automatic code-generation approach is used to develop the low-end products. On the other hand, products for the high-end market segment include customer-specific features (e.g., *Security*), and these products are developed for each customer. A custom-made approach in which a product is developed for each customer is used for the high-end products.

After the information from the MPP is incorporated into the production plan, the 'Overview of available core assets' section is refined with binding units and identified product line core assets. In our approach, the product-line-asset identification results (i.e., Table 3 in Section 4) are used to provide an overview, which is in the middle of Figure 6.

Now the feature-binding units are documented in the 'Detailed production process' section with information on the commonality, the asset type, associated binding units, a functional description, the binding time, binding techniques, and reuse processes. For example, *FLOOD* is an optional binding unit, and it has the *PUMPING* child-binding unit. The reuse process describes the way product developers can include *FLOOD* and make it available for use. To include *FLOOD*, product developers should select the *Flood* feature when generating code for a product. Also, product developers should release the product with the HIS-Installer package, which configures the load table, so that the availability of *FLOOD* can be controlled at installation time.

Finally, the production plan should be validated to see if the products in the MPP could be produced following the production process.

7 Conclusion

In this paper, we introduced a feature-based approach to product line production planning, and illustrated how a feature model and feature-binding information are used to identify core assets and develop a product line production plan. A product line may be targeted for more than one market segment, and each segment may require a unique set of features, a certain feature-binding time, and/or different feature-binding techniques. Therefore, product line assets must be identified with consideration of not only the commonalities and variabilities of a product line, but also its feature-binding requirements. The explicit identification of a feature-binding unit and binding time is

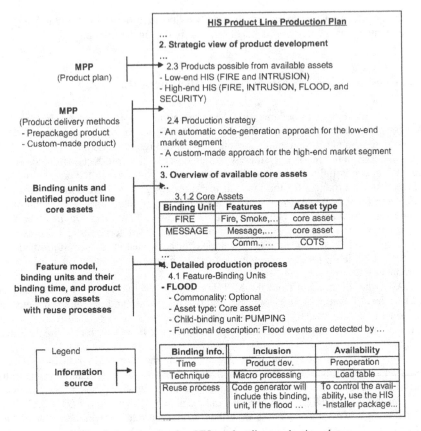

Fig. 6. An example of an HIS product line production plan

essential for identifying and managing consistency among variation points and selecting appropriate binding techniques.

We found that our approach provided asset developers with an explicit way to identify and organize core assets, and determine asset types with technical and business/management considerations. A product line production plan developed using our approach could be customized easily to a product-specific production plan, because when we developed the approach, we considered units of product configurations as well as their integration techniques (i.e., binding techniques) determined with consideration of the required binding time and organizational production strategies.

Our future work includes tool support to derive a product-specific production plan from a product line production plan. We believe that the feature orientation of our approach makes it easy to achieve this goal, and we hope that this research will lead us to develop more detailed guidelines for developing a product line production plan.

References

1. Clements, P., Northrop, L.: *Software Product Lines: Practices and Patterns*, Addison Wesley, Upper Saddle River, NJ (2002)
2. Chastek, G., McGregor, J.D.: Guidelines for Developing a Product Line Production Plan, *Technical Report CMU/SEI-2002-TR-006*, Pittsburgh, PA, Software Engineering Institute, Carnegie Mellon University (2002)
3. Chastek, G., Donohoe, P., McGregor, J.D.: Product Line Production Planning for the Home Integration System Example, *Technical Note CMU/SEI-2002-TN-029*, Pittsburgh, PA, Software Engineering Institute, Carnegie Mellon University (2002)
4. Lee, J., Kang, K.: Feature Binding Analysis for Product Line Component Development. In: van der Linden, F. (eds.): Software Product Family Engineering. Lecture Notes in Computer Science, Vol. 3014. Springer-Verlag, Berlin Heidelberg (2004) 266-276
5. Kang, K., Lee, J., Donohoe, P.: Feature-Oriented Product Line Engineering. IEEE Software, **19**(4), July/August (2002) 58-65
6. Kang, K., Donohoe, P., Koh, E., Lee, J., Lee, K.: Using a Marketing and Product Plan as a Key Driver for Product Line Asset Development. In: Chastek, G. (eds.): Software Product Lines. Lecture Notes in Computer Science, Vol. 2379. Springer-Verlag, Berlin Heidelberg (2002) 366-382
7. Lee, K., Kang, K., Lee, J.: Concepts and Guidelines of Feature Modeling for Product Line Software Engineering. In: Gacek, C. (eds.): Software Reuse: Methods, Techniques, and Tools. Lecture Notes in Computer Science, Vol. 2319. Springer-Verlag, Berlin Heidelberg (2002) 62-77
8. Czarnecki, K, Eisenecker, U.: Generative Programming: Methods, Tools, and Applications, Reading, MA: Addison Wesley Longman, Inc. (2000)
9. Bosch, J., Florijn, G., Greefhorst, D., Kuusela, J., Obbink, J. H., Pohl, K.: Variability Issues in Software Product Lines. In: van der Linden, F. (eds.): Software Product Family Engineering. Lecture Notes in Computer Science, Vol. 2290. Springer-Verlag, Berlin Heidelberg (2002) 13-21
10. Lee, K., Kang, K., Chae, W., Choi, B.: Feature-Based Approach to Object-Oriented Engineering of Applications for Reuse. Software Practice and Experience, **30**(9), (2000) 1025-1046
11. Basset, P. G.: Framing Software Reuse: Lessons From The Real World. Prentice Hall, Yourdon Press (1997)
12. Microsoft Developers Network (MSDN): Introduction to Internet Component Download (ICD), http://msdn.microsoft.com/workshop/delivery/download/overview/entry.asp
13. Sun Microsystems, Inc.: Java Authentication and Authorization Service (JAAS), http://java.sun.com/security/jaas/doc/api.html
14. Gamma, E., Helm, R., Johnson, R., Vlissides, J.: Design Patterns: Elements of Reusable Object-Oriented Software. MA: Addison Wesley Longman, Inc. (1995)

COVAMOF: A Framework for Modeling Variability in Software Product Families

Marco Sinnema, Sybren Deelstra, Jos Nijhuis, and Jan Bosch

Department of Mathematics and Computing Science, University of Groningen,
PO Box 800, 9700 AV Groningen, The Netherlands,
{m.sinnema,s.deelstra,j.a.g.nijhuis,j.bosch}@cs.rug.nl,
http://segroup.cs.rug.nl

Abstract. A key aspect of variability management in software product families is the explicit representation of the variability. Experiences at several industrial software development companies have shown that a software variability model should do four things: (1) uniformly represent variation points as first-class entities in all abstraction layers (ranging from features to code), (2) allow for hierarchical organization of the variability, (3) allow for the first-class representation of simple (i.e., one-to-one) and complex (i.e., n-to-m) dependencies, and (4) allow for modeling the relations between dependencies. Existing variability modeling approaches support the first two requirements, but lack support for the latter two. The contribution of this paper is a framework for variability modeling—COVAMOF—that provides support for all four requirements.

1 Introduction

Software product families are recognized as a successful approach to reuse in software development [6, 9, 17, 22]. The philosophy behind software product families is to economically exploit the commonalities between software products, but at the same time preserve the ability to vary the functionality between these products. Managing these differences between products, referred to as variability, is a key success factor in product families [7]. Research in the context of software product families is shifting from focusing on exploiting the commonalities towards managing the variability, referred to as variability management (e.g., [1, 2, 4, 8, 13]).

A key aspect of variability management is the explicit representation of the variability. Recent research [3, 5, 7, 8, 11, 21] agrees that this variability should be modeled uniformly over the life cycle and in terms of dependencies and first-class represented variation points.

Industrial case studies we performed at organizations that employ medium- and large-scale software product families have shown that, in addition to providing the required functionality, the main focus during product derivation is on satisfying complex dependencies (i.e., dependencies that affect the binding of a large number of variation points such as quality attributes). A key aspect of resolving these dependencies is having an overview on these complex dependencies and how they mutually relate. An example of a complex dependency is a restriction on the memory usage of a software system. An example of a relation to other dependencies is how this restriction *interacts* with a requirement on the performance. These case studies therefore

R.L. Nord (Ed.): SPLC 2004, LNCS 3154, pp. 197–213, 2004.

indicate the need for the first-class representation of dependencies, including complex dependencies, in variability models and the need for a means of modeling the relations between these dependencies.

In the past few years, several approaches have been developed for modeling the variability in software product families [3, 5, 8, 12, 18, 21]. Most of these approaches treat variation points as first-class citizens and provide means to model simple (one-to-one) dependencies, and some of the approaches model the variability uniformly over the life cycle. None of the approaches, however, supports the modeling of complex dependencies.

In this paper, we present COVAMOF—a variability modeling approach that uniformly models the variability in all abstraction layers of the software product family. It treats variation points and dependencies as first-class citizens and provides a means of modeling the relations between simple and complex dependencies. We illustrate this approach with an industrial case study.

The structure of this paper is as follows: in the next section, we present an industrial case study that serves as a guiding example throughout this paper. In Section 3, we present the problem statement. Section 4 presents our approach to variability modeling, COVAMOF, and Section 5 discusses this approach and concludes the paper.

2   Case Description

To get a better insight into families, we performed three industrial case studies at organizations that employ medium- and large-scale software product families in the context of software-intensive technical systems (i.e., Robert Bosch GmbH, Thales Naval Netherlands B.V., and Dacolian B.V.). All three cases served as the basis for this paper. In [11], we describe the first two case studies in detail. In this section, we introduce the case study we performed at Dacolian B.V. This case is used to exemplify the issues and our COVAMOF framework.

2.1   Dacolian B.V.

Dacolian B.V. is an independent SME in the Netherlands that develops mainly intellectual property (IP) software modules for intelligent traffic systems (ITS). Dacolian does not sell its products directly to end users. Its customers are internationally operating companies that are market leaders within a part of the ITS market. Products of Dacolian's Intrada® product family are often essential parts in the end product of these companies.

In our case study, we focused on the Intrada® product family whose members use outdoor video or still images as the most important sensor input. Intrada products deliver, based on these real-time input images, abstract information on the actual contents of the images. Examples are the detection of moving traffic, vehicle type classification, license plate reading, video-based tolling and parking.

Dacolian maintains a product family architecture and in-house-developed reusable components that are used for product construction. Many of these components are frameworks; for example, one provides a common interface to a number of different frame grabbers (real and virtual) (see Figure 1: Image intake), and another provides

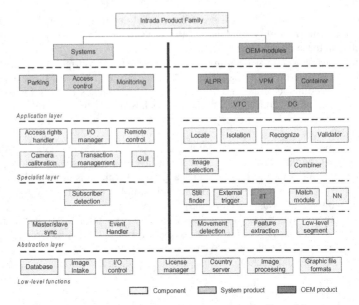

Fig. 1. The Logical view on the Intrada product family architecture

license specialization and enforcement (See Figure 1: License Manager). The infrastructure also contains special designed tooling for Model Driven Architecture (MDA) based code generation, software for module calibration, dedicated scripts and tooling for product, feature and component testing, and large data repositories. These assets capture functionality common to either all Intrada products or a subset of them.

Figure 1 presents the logical view of the Intrada product family's architecture. This view contains a number of components, the responsibilities of which are denoted by the layers in the view. Each component incorporates variability and uses some of the components in a lower abstraction level. The thick solid vertical line gives the separation between the two branches within the Intrada product family. The low-level-functions layer provides basic functionality, hides hardware detail, and gives platform independence. The abstraction layer adds semantic information to the raw image data. The specialist layer contains core components of Dacolian's Intrada product family. The blocks in this layer perform the complex calculations. The top layer defines the various products. The grey shaded blocks indicate products that are sold by Dacolian B.V. The OEM-modules (dark grey) have no interaction with hardware components, whereas the system products (light grey)—such as parking, access control, and monitoring—include components that communicate directly with the real world.

For products at the upper layer, binding is typically by configuration and license files at start-up time. Lower layers use binding mechanisms that bind before deployment. Typical examples are MDA code generation, precompiler directives, and Make dependencies. Binding at link time is almost not practiced in the Intrada product family, and Make dependencies only specify variation at compile time.

3 Problem Statement

In Section 1, we indicated the explicit representation of the variability of software product families as a key aspect of variability management. In this section, we discuss variability in terms of variation points and variability dependencies, and present requirements on variability modeling techniques. We, furthermore, verify to which extent existing approaches address these requirements.

3.1 Variation Points

Variation points are places in a design or implementation that identify the locations at which variation occurs [15]. These identifiers have been recognized as elements that facilitate the systematic documentation and traceability of variability, development for and with reuse [8], assessment, and evolution. As such, variation points are not by-products of the design and implementation of variability, but are identified as central elements in managing variability. Figure 2 shows that the hierarchy in product families is divided into three abstraction layers: (1) features, (2) architecture, and (3) component implementations, and that the hierarchy throughout these layers is defined by levels of abstraction. As variation in software product families can occur in all three abstraction layers, variation points can also be identified in all those layers. Variation points in one abstraction layer can *realize* the variability in a higher abstraction level (e.g., an optional architectural component that realizes the choice between two features in the feature tree).

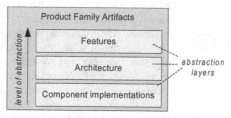

Fig. 2. Hierarchy in product families. The product family is divided into three abstraction layers: (1) features, (2) architecture, and (3) component implementations, and the hierarchy throughout these layers is defined by levels of abstraction

Each variation point is associated with zero or more variants and can be categorized as one of five basic types:

- An *optional* variation point is the choice of selecting zero or one from the one or more associated variants.
- An *alternative* variation point is the choice between one of the one or more associated variants.
- An *optional variant* variation point is the selection (zero or more) from the one or more associated variants.
- A *variant* variation point is the selection (one or more) from the one or more associated variants.
- A *value* variation point is a value chosen from a predefined range.

A variation point can be in two different *states:* open or closed. An open variation point is one to which new variants can be added. A closed variation point is one to which new variants cannot be added. The state of a variation point may change from one development phase to the next.

All variability in software product families is realized by variation points in a lower layer of abstraction or implemented by a *realization technique* in the product family artifacts. Over the past few years, several of these variability realization techniques have been identified for all three abstraction layers. Examples of these mechanisms include architectural design patterns, aggregation, inheritance, parameterization, overloading, macros, conditional compilation, and dynamically linked libraries (e.g., see the following work [15, 1]. Svahnberg, Gurp, and Bosch present a characterization of realization techniques [20]. Such techniques in the artifacts impose a *binding time* on the associated variation point, that is, the development phase at which the variation point should be bound. For example, the binding time of a variation point that is implemented by condition compilation is the compilation phase.

3.2 Variability Dependencies

Dependencies in the context of variability are restrictions on the variant selection of one or more variation points, and are indicated as a primary concern in software product families [16]. These dependencies originate from, among other things, the application domain (e.g., customer requirements), target platform, implementation details, or restrictions on quality attributes.

In product families, there are several types of dependencies. Simple dependencies specify the restriction on the binding of one or two variation points. These dependencies are often specified in terms of *requires* and *excludes* relations and expressed along the lines of "the binding of variant A1 to variation point A excludes the binding of variant B1 to variation point B." Experience in industrial product families showed that, in general, dependencies are more complex and typically affect a large number of variation points. Dependencies, in many cases, can not be stated formally, but have a more informal character (e.g., "these combinations of parameter settings will have a negative effect on the performance of the overall software system").

In some cases, the validity of dependencies can be calculated from the selection of variants of the associated variation points, and the influence of a reselection of an associated variation point on the validity can be predicted. We refer to these dependencies as *statically analyzable* dependencies. Examples of these dependencies are the mutual exclusion of two component implementations and a limitation on the memory usage of the whole system (the total memory usage can be computed from the variant selections).

In other cases, dependencies cannot be written down in such a formal way. The validity of the dependency, therefore, cannot be calculated from the variant selections, and the verification of the dependency's validity may require a test of the whole software system. Therefore, we refer to these dependencies as *dynamically analyzable* dependencies. In most cases, software engineers can predict whether a reselection of variants will positively or negatively affect the validity of the dependency. However, in some cases, software engineers cannot predict the influence of a reselection of variants at all. We found examples of these dependencies at both Thales Naval Netherlands and Dacolian B.V., where software engineers indicate that a requirement on the overall performance can be validated only by testing the whole software product.

Dependencies are not isolated entities. The process of resolving one dependency may affect the validity of others. We refer to this as *dependency interaction*. Dependencies that mutually interact have to be considered simultaneously, and resolving both dependencies often requires an iterative approach. As the verification of dependencies may require testing the whole configuration, solving dependencies that mutually interact is one of the main concerns for software engineers and hampers the product derivation process.

3.3 Requirements

Making the variability in software product families explicit has been identified as an important aspect of variability management [8, 11]. Below, we present four requirements that we recognize as important for a variability modeling technique. These requirements originate from related research, the case studies, and our experience in software product families.

R1. Uniform and first-class representation of variation points in all abstraction levels. The uniform and first-class representation of variation points facilitates the assessment of the impact of selections during product derivation and changes during evolution [7].

R2. Hierarchical organization of variability representation. Deelstra, Sinnema, and Bosch report on the impact of large numbers (hundreds of thousands) of variation points and variants on the product derivation process in industrial product families [11]. Explicitly organizing these variation points reduces the cognitive complexity these large numbers impose on engineers who deal with those variation points.

R3. Dependencies, including complex dependencies, should be treated as first-class citizens in the modeling approach. Industrial experience indicates that most of the effort during product derivation is on satisfying complex dependencies (e.g., quality attributes). As the first-class representation of dependencies can provide a good overview on all dependencies in the software product family, the efficiency of product derivation increases.

R4. The interactions between dependencies should be represented explicitly. For efficient product derivation, software engineers require an overview of the interactions between dependencies to decide which strategy to follow when solving the dependencies. Therefore, these interactions should be modeled explicitly.

3.4 Related Work

As we briefly mentioned in the introduction, several approaches to variability modeling exist. Below, we briefly present these approaches and verify to what extent each approach satisfies the aforementioned requirements.

A Meta-model for Representing Variability in Product Family Development.
Bachman and associates present a meta-model for representing the variability in
product families that consists of variation points in multiple views [3]. These views
correspond to the layers of the product family we introduced in Section 3. As the
meta-model consists of variation points that are refined during development, it is clear
how choices map between layers of abstraction. This model does not provide a hierarchical organization of variation points, and dependencies are not treated as first-class
citizens. It does provide a means of modeling 1-to-n dependencies between variation
points.

Mapping Variabilities onto Product Family Assets. Becker presents an approach in
which the representation of the variability of the product family is separated into two
levels: specification and realization [5]. The variability is defined in terms of
variabilities on the specification level and in terms of variation points on the
realization level. Variabilities specify the required variability, and variation points
indicate the places in the asset base that implement the required variability. This
model contains two types of these variation points: static (pre-deployment) and
dynamic (post-deployment). Dependencies can be specified in a one-to-one manner
and are not represented as first-class citizens.

**Generic Modeling Using Unified Modeling Language (UML) Extensions for
Variability.** Clauss presents an approach to modeling the variability of product
families by extending UML models [8]. Both the feature models and the design
models can be extended with variability. Variation points in these models are marked
with the stereotype <<variationPoint>> on features and components and are not
treated as first-class citizens. Dependencies are modeled as constraints between two
variants, can, therefore, be associated to one or two variation points, and are not
represented as first-class citizens.

Multiple-View Meta-Modeling of Software Product Lines. Gomaa and Shin present an extension to UML models to capture the variability of the product family on
the feature and design level [12]. Variation points are not treated as first-class citizens
but rather are defined implicitly by marking features or classes as optional or variant.
Dependencies are modeled as first-class citizens by dependency meta-classes and
restrict the selection of two variants.

A Composable Software Architecture for Consumer Electronics Products. Van
Ommering [18] presents how Koala [19] can be used in the context of software product families. Koala is an approach to realize the late binding of components. Components are specified recursively in terms of the first-class provided and required interfaces. The variability in the design is specified in terms of the selection of components, parameters on components, and the runtime routing of function calls. Dependencies are specified by the interfaces of components and define, among other things,
whether two components are compatible.

Systematic Integration of Variability into Product Line Architecture Design. In their paper on architectural variability, Thiel and Hein [21] propose an extension to the IEEE P1471 recommended practice for architectural description [14]. This extension includes using variation points to model variability in the architecture description. Variation points in the variability model include aspects such as binding time, one or more dependencies to other variation points, and resolution rules that capture, for example, which architectural variants should be selected with which options.

3.5 Summary

Table 1 presents a summary of the existing variability approaches and their adherence to the requirements. Some of the approaches support up to two requirements, but none of them supports all four. In the next section, we present COVAMOF, an approach to variability modeling that addresses all four requirements.

Table 1. The adherence of approaches to variability modeling to the requirements in Section 3.3

	R1	R2	R3	R4
Bachman and associates [3]	+ +	+ +	-	- -
Becker [5]	+	+ +	-	- -
Clauss [8]	-	+	- -	- -
Gomaa and Shin [12]	-	+/-	+/-	- -
van Ommering [18]	-	+	- -	- -
Thiel and Hein [21]	-	+/-	-	- -

4 ConIPF Variability Modeling Framework (COVAMOF)

During the Configuration in Industrial Product Families (ConIPF) project [10], we developed the ConIPF Variability Modeling Framework (COVAMOF). COVAMOF consists of the COVAMOF Variability View (CVV) that provides a view on the variability provided by the product family artifacts. The CVV can be derived from the product family artifacts manually or automatically, and we are currently working on tool support for the automatic derivation of this view. The CVV encompasses the variability of artifacts on all the abstraction layers of the product family (from features down to code), as shown in Figure 3. This figure also shows that the COVAMOF defines two views on the CVV: the Variation Point View and the Dependency View. In the following section, we describe the structure of the CVV. In Section 4.2, we show how the two views of the CVV are used during product derivation.

4.1 COVAMOF Variability View (CVV)

The CVV captures the variability in the product family in terms of variation points and dependencies. The graphical notations of the main entities in the CVV are shown in Figure 4. We describe the entities and relations between them in more detail below.

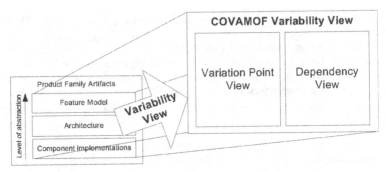

Fig. 3. COVAMOF provides the COVAMOF Variability View (CVV) on the provided variability of the product family artifacts on all layers of abstraction. In addition, COVAMOF defines two views on the CVV: the Variation Point View and the Dependency View

Fig. 4. Graphical notations of variation points, variants, and dependencies in the CVV

Variation Points. Variation points in the CVV are a view on the variation points in the product family. Each variation point in the CVV is associated with an artifact in the product family (e.g., a feature tree, a feature, the architecture, or a C header file). In correspondence to Section 3.1, there are five types of variation points in the CVV: (1) optional, (2) alternative, (3) optional variant, (4) variant, and (5) value. Figure 5 presents the graphical representation of these types.

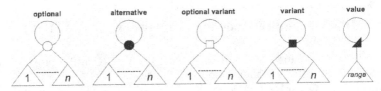

Fig. 5. The graphical notation of the five types of variation points in the CVV

The variation points in the CVV specify, for each variant or value, the actions that should be taken to realize the choice, for that variant or value, in the product family artifacts (e.g., the selection of a feature in the feature tree, the adaptation of a configuration file, or the specification of a compilation parameter). These actions can be specified formally (e.g., to allow for automatic component configuration by a tool) or in natural language (e.g., a guideline for manual steps that should be taken by the software engineers).

A variation point in the CVV furthermore contains a *description* and information about its *state* (open or closed), the *rationale* behind the binding, and the *realization mechanism* and its associated *binding time* (where applicable). The *rationale* behind the binding defines on what basis the software engineer should make his or her choice between the variants when the information from the associated realization relations (see below) does not suffice.

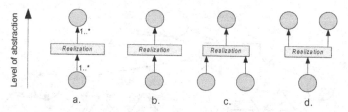

Fig. 6. The possible number of variation points associated with a realization relation (a.), a variation point realizing one other variation point on a higher level of abstraction (b.), two variation points realizing one variation point (c.), and one variation point realizing two variation points (d.)

Realization Relations. Variation points that have no associated realization mechanism in the product family artifacts are realized by variation points on a lower level of abstraction. These realizations are represented by *realization relations* between variation points in the CVV. (See Figure 6a.) The realization relation in the CVV contains rules that describe how a selection of variation points depends directly on the selection of the variation points in a higher abstraction level in the product family. Figure 6 also presents three typical examples of realization relations between variation points. In practice, any combination of these realization relations exists in software product families. Realization relations between variation points imply that the binding time of the variation points being realized depend on their realization at a lower level of abstraction. These realization relations define not only the realization between the levels of abstraction within one abstraction layer, but also how variation points in one abstraction layer (e.g., in the architecture) realize variation points in a higher abstraction layer (e.g., in the features).

We present three examples from the case studies that illustrate the usage of variation points and realization in the CVV.

Example: Figure 7 presents an example of one variation point realizing another. A feature of the Intrada product family is the image source. The offered alternatives are digital/analog video input, files stored on a hard disk, or pointers to chunks of memory that contain the image data. VP1 shows the available variants from which one should be selected as the image source. This variation point is realized by variation point VP2, which offers two variants that accommodate the alternatives of VP1.

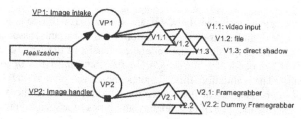

Fig. 7. Realization example – one variation point realizing another at a higher level of abstraction

Example: Figure 8 presents an example of multiple variation points realizing one variation point. Many Intrada products can be configured to recognize license plates

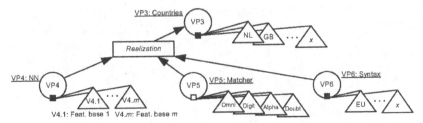

Fig. 8. Example of multiple variation points realizing one variation point

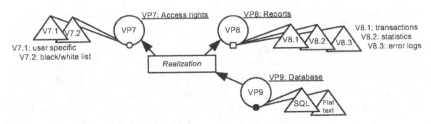

Fig. 9. Example of one variation point realizing two variation points at a higher level

from one or more countries simultaneously. This feature is expressed by the variant variation point VP3, where each variant represents one country. At a lower level, VP3 is realized by three variation points: VP4, VP5, and VP6. Which variants of VP4, VP5, and VP6 are included in the derived products depends on the logical "requires"-dependencies between VP3 and the aforementioned variation points. VP5 is an optional variant variation point, and its variants are used only when there is no speed limitation to improve the performance.

Example: Figure 9 presents an example of one variation point realizing two others. The parking, access control, and monitoring products allow access rights differentiation. For the three Intrada products, this is respectively subscriber specific, group specific, or no differentiation. Within the product family, this is represented by a variation point (VP7). Also, various methods of transaction logging, statistics, and error reporting can be selected (VP8). Both VP7 and VP8 are realized by VP9 which provides database and search facilities.

Dependencies. Dependencies in the CVV are associated with one or more variation points in the CVV and restrict the selection of the variants associated to these variation points. The properties of dependencies consist of the *type* of dependency, a *description* of the dependency, the *validation time*, and *the types of associations* to variation points. The validation time denotes the development stage at which the validity of the dependency can be determined with respect to the variation point binding. We describe the type of dependency and types of association in detail below.

Types of associations. On the level of dependencies, the CVV distinguishes between three types of associated variation points. The type of the association of a variation point depends on the available knowledge about the influence of the variant selection on the validity of the dependency. (See also Figure 10).

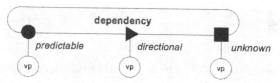

Fig. 10. The three types of knowledge about the influence of the associated variation points on the dependency

Predictable associations represent variation points whose influence of the variant selection on the validity of the dependency is fully known. The impact of variant selection on the validity of the dependency can be determined before the actual binding of the selected variant(s).

Directional associations represent variation points whose influence of the variant selection on the validity of the dependency is not fully known. Instead, the dependency only specifies whether a (re)selection of variants will positively or negatively affect the validity of the dependency.

Unknown associations represent variation points of which it is known that the variant selection influences the validity of the dependency. However, the dependency does not specify *how* a (re)selection of the variants influences the validity.

In Section 3.2, we introduced the distinction between statically analyzable and dynamically analyzable dependencies. Note that statically analyzable dependencies correspond to dependencies in the CVV that only have predictable associations. Dynamically analyzable dependencies correspond to dependencies in the CVV that have at least one directional or unknown association.

Types of dependencies. The CVV distinguishes between three types of dependencies: (1) logical, (2) numerical, and (3) nominal. Figure 11 shows the graphical notation of each type of dependency.

Logical dependencies specify a function *valid* that yields the validity of the dependency for each selection of variants of the associated variation points. This can, for example, be the mutual exclusion of two component implementations. As the influence of each associated variation point is defined by the *valid* function, variation points are predictably associated only to logical dependencies. Therefore, logical dependencies can always be analyzed statically.

Numerical dependencies define a numerical value N. The value of N depends on the variants selection of the associated variation points. The validity of the dependency is expressed by the specification of a valid range on the numerical value N. An example of a numerical dependency is the restriction of the total memory consumption of a software system to 64 megabytes. These dependencies can have all three types of associated variation points. The new value of N after a (re)selection of a predictable associated variation point can be calculated. The dependency specifies whether the (re)selection of a directional associated variant will increase or decrease the value of N. It does not specify the influence of unknown dependencies.

Nominal dependencies specify a set of categories. The binding of all variation points associated to the dependency map to one of the categories. The validity of the dependency is expressed by the specification of the valid categories. Only unknown associated variation points are associated to nominal dependencies.

logical   numerical   nominal

Fig. 11. The graphical notation of the three types of dependencies and three types of associations to variation points

To exemplify the usage of dependencies in the CVV, we provide two examples from the case studies.

Example: Figure 12a presents the representation of the logical dependency "countries." This dependency captures the complex logical relations that exist between the variants of the involved variation points VP3, VP4, VP5, and VP6. Rules that are represented by this dependency include, among other things, "variant V3.NL requires variant V4.1 and V6.EU, variant V4.3 excludes variant V4.4." (See Figure 8 for more details on the involved variation points.)

Example: Figure 12b presents the representation of a numerical dependency "error rate." The possible values for the "error rate" that can be obtained by the Intrada product family depend on the selected feature bases (VP4), the included matchers (VP5), and the settings of the various range parameters associated with the Isolate variation point (VP10). Whether a variant will improve or worsen the "error rate" score is known only for variants of the matcher variation point. The actual influence of the two other variation points is unknown and can only be determined by test procedures.

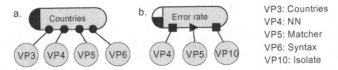

VP3: Countries
VP4: NN
VP5: Matcher
VP6: Syntax
VP10: Isolate

Fig. 12. An example from the case study of the representation of a logical dependency (a.) and a numerical dependency (b.)

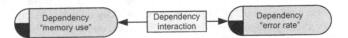

Fig. 13. An example of a dependency interaction from the case study

Dependency interactions. *Dependency interactions* in the CVV specify how two or more dependencies mutually interact. The interaction provides a description of the origin of the interaction and specifies how to cope with the interaction during product derivation.

Example: To illustrate the dependency interactions in the CVV, we present an example from the case study in Figure 13. There is a mutual interaction between the two numerical dependencies "memory use" and "error rate." Both dependencies include the variation point "matcher" (see Figure 8). Including additional matcher variants will improve the "error rate" dependency but downgrade the "memory use" dependency. Individual scores on each dependency and the costs of the associated quality attributes will determine the order in which the dependencies should be handled.

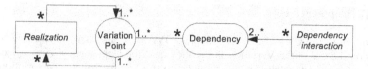

Fig. 14. The main entities in the CVV meta-model

Notation. The main entities in the CVV meta-model are presented in Figure 14. It summarizes the CVV: variation points in the CVV realize other variation points in an n-to-m manner and are associated with zero or more dependencies. Dependencies are associated with one or more variation points, and dependency interactions define relations between two or more dependencies.

We use the CVVL (CVV Language), a language based on the Extensible Markup Language (XML), to represent the CVV in text. Variation points and dependencies are represented as first-class entities, and its notation is illustrated in Figures 15 and 16.

```
<variationpoint id="[id]">
  <artefact>[artefact identifier]</artefact>
  <abstractionlayer>[abstraction layer]</abstractionlayer>
  <description>[description]</description>
  <type>optional/alternative/optional variant/variant/value<type>
  <variants> <!-- if not type=value -->
    <variant id="[id]">
    . . .
    <variant id="[id]">
  </variants>
  <range>[range specification]</range> <!-- if type=value -->
  <state>open/closed</state>
  <mechanism>[mechanism]</mechanism>
  <bindingtime>[bindingtime]</bindingtime>
  <rationale>[rationale]</rationale>
</variationpoint>
```

Fig. 15. The notation of variation points in the CVVL

```
<dependency id="[id]">
  <description>[description]</description>
  <type>logical/numerical/nominal</type>
  <validationtime>[validation time]</validationtime>
  <associations>
    <association type="predictable/directional/unknown">
      <variationpoint id="[id]">
    </association>
    . . .
    <association type="predictable/directional/unknown">
      <variationpoint id="[id]">
    </association>
  </associations>
  <logical> <!-- if type=logical -->
    <valid>[valid function]</valid>
  </logical>
  <numerical> <!-- if type=numerical -->
    <N>[description and origin of N]</N>
    <range>[valid range of N]</range>
  </numerical>
  <nominal> <!-- if type=nominal -->
    <categories>
      <category valid="yes/no">[category]</category>
      . . .
      <category valid="yes/no">[category]</category>
    </categories>
  </nominal>
</dependency>
```

Fig. 16. The notation of dependencies in the CVVL

4.2 Development Views

In addition to the CVV described above, COVAMOF also defines two development views on the CVV: the Variation Point View and the Dependency View. (See Figure 17.) These views enable software engineers to shift the focus between variation points and dependencies in order to develop a strategy to derive products.

Variation Point View. The Variation Point View in the CVV provides the software engineers with an overview of the variation in all abstraction levels of a product family in terms of variation points. The realization relations provide the structure on the set of variation points, and the dependencies in this view are attributes of the variation points.

Dependency View. The main entities in the Dependency View are the dependencies and the dependency interactions that provide the structure on the set of dependencies. Variation points in this view are attributes of the dependencies. The Dependency View provides software engineers with an overview of the most critical dependencies (e.g., based on their type, number of associated variation points, or number of dependency interactions) that can be used to develop a strategy to resolve the dependencies during product derivation.

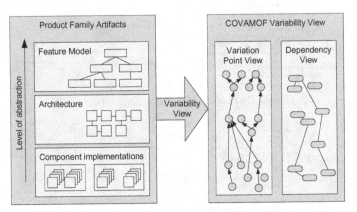

Fig. 17. COVAMOF provides two development views on the artifacts: the Variation Point View and the Dependency View

5 Conclusion and Future Work

In this paper, we presented four requirements that we deem important for modeling variability in the context of software product families. We showed that none of the related approaches addresses all the requirements. In response to the observed limitations, we have developed COVAMOF, a framework for modeling variability in software product families. Below, we show how COVAMOF addresses these requirements.

R1. Uniform and first-class representation of variation points in all abstraction levels. COVAMOV provides a view, the CVV, in which the variability of features, architecture, and component implementations are all modeled and uniformly represented by variation points as first-class citizens. COVAMOF, therefore, fully satisfies requirement R1.

R2. Hierarchical organization of variability representation. In the CVV, the realization relation defines how variation points realize variation points at higher levels of abstraction. As these realization relations provide a hierarchical organization of the variability, COVAMOF fully satisfies requirement R2.

R3. Dependencies, including complex dependencies should be treated as first-class citizens in the modeling approach. COVAMOV provides a view, the CVV, in which dependencies are modeled as first-class citizens. These dependencies restrict the selection of one or more variation points. COVAMOF, therefore, fully satisfies requirement R3.

R4. The interactions between dependencies should be represented explicitly. The dependency relation defines which dependencies should be considered simultaneously and whether one dependency should be solved before another. COVAMOF, therefore, fully satisfies requirement R4.

A well-known problem with modeling is the issue of how to keep the model consistent with the artifacts. As we mentioned in Section 4, the COVAMOF Variability View can be derived from the product family artifacts manually or automatically. We are currently working on the *intrinsic modeling* of the variability in the artifacts and the required tooling support for the automatic derivation of the model. *Intrinsic modeling* means that the product family artifacts themselves capture their own variability model (in terms of variation points and dependencies) and that each variability realization technique in the artifacts provides the variability modeling elements. With respect to COVAMOF, these variability modeling elements in intrinsically modeled product families *are* the CVV, and changes to the product family artifacts *are* changes to the CVV. Note that this addresses the problem of keeping the model consistent with the artifacts.

Acknowledgements. This research has been sponsored by Configuration in Industrial Product Families (ConIPF) project [10], under contract no. IST-2001-34438. The ConIPF project aims to define and validate methodologies for product derivation that are practicable in industrial applications. We thank the industrial partners—in particular Dacolian B.V.—for their valuable input.

References

1.   M. Anastasopoulos, C. Gacek: Implementing product line variabilities. In: Symposium on Software Reusability (SSR'01), Toronto, Canada, Software Engineering Notes 26 (3) 109–117, 2001.
2.   F. Bachmann, L. Bass: Managing variability in software architecture. In: Proceedings of the ACM SIGSOFT Symposium on Software Reusability (SSR'01), pp. 126–132, 2001.

3. F. Bachman, M. Goedicke, J. Leite, R. Nord, K. Pohl, B. Ramesh, A. Vilbig: Managing Variability in Product Family Development, accepted for the 5th Workshop on Product Family Engineering (PFE-5), November 2003, to be published in Springer Verlag Lecture Notes on Computer Science, 2004.
4. D. Batory, S. O'Malley: The Design and Implementation of Hierarchical Software Systems with Reusable Components, ACM Transactions on Software Engineering and Methodology, 1(4): pp. 355-398, October 1992.
5. M. Becker: Mapping Variability's onto Product Family Assets, Proceedings of the International Colloquium of the Sonderforschungsbereich 501, University of Kaiserslautern, Germany, March 2003.
6. J. Bosch: Design & Use of So ftware Architectures, Adopting and Evolving a product-line approach, Addison-Wesley, ISBN 0-201-67494-7, 2000.
7. J. Bosch, G. Florijn, D. Greefhorst, J. Kuusela, H. Obbink, K. Pohl: Variability Issues in Software Product Lines, Proceedings of the Fourth International Workshop on Product Family Engineering (PFE-4), pp. 11–19, 2001.
8. M. Clauss: Modeling variability with UML, GCSE 2001 - Young Researchers Workshop, September 2001.
9. P. Clements, L. Northrop: Software Product Lines: Practices and Patterns, SEI Series in Software Engineering, Addison-Wesley, ISBN: 0-201-70332-7, 2001.
10. The ConIPF project (Configuration of Industrial Product Families), http://www.rug.nl/conipf.
11. S. Deelstra, M. Sinnema, J. Bosch: Product Derivation in Software Product Families; A Case Study, accepted for the Journal of Systems and Software, 2003.
12. H. Gomaa, M.E. Shin: Multiple-View Meta-Modeling of Software Product Lines, 8th International Conference on Engineering of Complex Computer Systems (ICECCS 2002), IEEE Computer Society 2002, ISBN 0-7695-1757-9, pp. 238-246, 2002.
13. L. Griss, J. Favaro, M. d'Alessandro: Integrating feature modeling with the RSEB, Proceedings of the Fifth International Conference on Software Reuse (Cat. No. 98TB100203), IEEE Computing Society, xiii+388, pp.76-85, 1998.
14. IEEE Recommended Proactice for Architectural Description of Software-Intensive Systems (IEEE Standard P1471), IEEE Architecture Working Group (AWG), 2000.
15. I. Jacobson, M. Griss, P. Jonsson: Software Reuse. Architecture, Process and Organization for Business Success. Addison-Wesley, ISBN: 0-201-92476-5, 1997.
16. M. Jaring and J. Bosch: Variability Dependencies in Product Family Engineering, accepted for the 5th Workshop on Product Family Engineering (PFE-5), November 2003, to be published in Springer Verlag Lecture Notes on Computer Science, 2004.
17. M. Jazayeri, A. Ran, F. van der Linden: Software Architecture for Product Families: Principles and Practice, Addison-Wesley, 2000.
18. R. van Ommering: A Composable Software Architecture for Consumer Electronics Products, XOOTIC Magazine, March 2000, Volume 7 number 3, 2000.
19. R. van Ommering, F. van der Linden, J. Kramer, J. Magee: The Koala Component Model for Consumer Electronics Software, IEEE Computer, p78-85, March 2000.
20. M. Svahnberg, J. Gurp, J. Bosch: A Taxonomy of Variability Realization Techniques, technical paper ISSN: 1103-1581, Blekinge Institute of Technology, Sweden, 2002.
21. S. Thiel, A. Hein: Systematic integration of Variability into Product Line Architecture Design, Proceedings of the 2nd International Conference on Software Product Lines (SPLC-2), August 2002.
22. D.M. Weiss and C.T.R. Lai: Software Product-Line Engineering: A Family Based Software Development Process, Addison-Wesley, ISBN 0-201-694387, 1999.

Observations from the Recovery of a Software Product Family

Patricia Lago and Hans van Vliet

Vrije Universiteit, Amsterdam, The Netherlands,
{patricia,hans}@cs.vu.nl

Abstract. The problem of managing the evolution of complex and large software systems is well known. Evolution implies the reuse and modification of existing software artifacts, and this means that the related knowledge must be documented and maintained.

This paper focuses on the evolution of software product families, although the same principles apply in other software development environments as well. We describe our experience gained in a case study recovering a family of six software products. We give an overview of the case study, and provide lessons learned, implicit assumptions reconstructed during the case study, and some rules we think are generally applicable. Our experience indicates that organizing architectural knowledge is a difficult task. To properly serve the various uses of this knowledge, it needs to be organized along different dimensions and tools are required. Our experience also indicates that, next to variability explicitly designed into the product family, a "variation creep" is caused by different, and evolving, technical and organizational environments of the products. We propose explicitly modeling invariabilities, next to variabilities, in software product lines to get a better grip on this variation creep.

1 Introduction

This paper reports a list of observations we made about a case study recovering a software product family (PF) from a set of existing software products in the telecommunication domain. A reactive approach has been used [6].

These observations include some lessons learned and a list of assumptions. Lessons learned define experience we gained in applying software engineering techniques to real cases; assumptions formalize example requirements and constraints that quite often exist in our mind and are implicitly applied to production, but that we rationally ignore. If, later on, we reuse existing software artifacts to derive new products, ignoring these assumptions can lead to conflicts or defects. This happens easily if they are not made explicit and formalized in the architecture description. By modeling the invariability of the assumptions next to variability, we may achieve an even better support for software product line evolution.

Even though our observations are derived from a software PF, we think they can be applied in other software production environments as well. Accordingly, we report two general rules that we elaborated from our observations.

R.L. Nord (Ed.): SPLC 2004, LNCS 3154, pp. 214–227, 2004.

The remainder of this introduction gives a flavor of the problems we had with our initial set of products, the chosen solutions, and the actions we took to realize these solutions.

Across a period of about seven years, our research group participated in a series of research projects and contracts in collaboration with industrial partners that involved the development of software-intensive systems in the next generation networks application domain. The software systems had to support a variety of customer-oriented communication services, integrating always newer technologies. The services were adding new requirements, and the service features were increasing in number and complexity.

After the first five years, when the number of products started to grow, we realized we could no longer keep track of all the knowledge necessary to manage all existing products and their associated documentation.

The next developments could potentially reuse existing assets (e.g., software-configuring network resources, components implementing some selected service features) and modify them to derive new products. Unfortunately, the effort required to reconstruct the knowledge about certain reusable assets was so high that it would have been more cost-effective to build them from scratch.

As we were also willing to reconstruct the family of software products in our university laboratory to make it accessible to and usable by students and researchers, we decided to make an inventory of our maintenance and reuse problems. We identified the following problems and their possible solutions:

Manage evolution: The PF became unmanageable: it was too complex in terms of cross dependencies among architectural entities and with the underlying technology. For instance, we could not reconstruct which components developed in past projects where using which version of the Java Virtual Machine, or how to properly configure the platform resources (like router or voice gateway) to deploy a certain service. We identified this as a knowledge management problem.

To solve this problem, we needed two things: (1) traceability support from architecture descriptions to implementation, so we could associate design elements to things such as source code, configuration files, and documentation, and (2) a classification of the reusable assets, so we could represent services at a high level, in terms of service features, and then reuse existing design and implementation assets by using the classification.

Plan reuse: There was no planned reuse schema: theoretically, features could be freely selected and combined to build new products. In practice, the implications of these combinations where too difficult to reconstruct (e.g., to verify feature compatibility and completeness), hence making reuse more expensive than building from scratch. To provide better support for reuse, we needed a domain model that (1) offered a formalized feature organization, and (2) mapped domain features to implemented ones.

Support communication: The features part of the different products could not be communicated to stakeholders with different skills and background in a straightforward way. The stakeholders involved in our developments included
  – developers with general software implementation skills, but no experience in the telecommunication domain. Further, as they usually were not involved in previous developments, they had to learn everything about the existing software.

- managers working for our industrial partners, with poor or no technical skills
- university colleagues, to whom we had to explain the various research issues (e.g., the extension of general-purpose modeling notations to represent domain-specific properties)

To better support the communication of service features toward and among these stakeholders, we needed three things: (1) visualization/abstraction mechanisms generating views tailored to the type of stakeholder they address, (2) traceability from features to architectural and implementation assets, so that knowledge could be navigated easily, and (3) tool automation aiding the generation of views reflecting selectable stakeholders' criteria.

These problems motivated us in studying and applying techniques devised for software product lines (or families[1]) and trying to enhance them to fulfill our requirements. We defined a notation and developed associated tool support [16] fulfilling the requirements in the following way:

Classification of features: We characterized the application domain by defining the types of service features that describe it. We articulated them via a mechanism merging the feature graph used in software product line engineering to define design decisions and their relationships [4, 13], and the utility tree used (e.g., to define software quality requirements [2]).

Next, we defined features on two abstraction levels: (1) at the PF Level, where features reflect generic functionality not necessarily mapped to concrete solutions currently implemented, and (2) at the Product Level, where features are concrete assets implemented by one or multiple products, each providing its own design and implementation solution.

Concrete features at the Product Level are linked to the generic features (at the PF Level) for which they provide a product-specific solution. The types of features and relationships between them, as well as visualization conventions are inspired by existing notations [20]. Further details are given by Lago, Niemelä, and van Vliet [15].

Traceability: We defined the whole chain of links between the representation of features in the PF and family members, their architectural solution, and the associated documentation and implementation artifacts. Generic features (at the PF Level) keep the traces to the concrete features (at the Product Level) implementing them. Further, at the Product Level, the structure of each software system is modeled by a component diagram showing which structural elements (objects, interfaces, components) realize which concrete feature(s). Next, structural elements are linked to implementation files and documentation, realizing traceability down to code. This link chain supports traceability in a smooth way, a requirement put forth by Weiler [24]. In the literature, no other comprehensive method covers the representation of the complete life cycle of a product family. Instead, the common approach is to focus on a single [21, 9], or a few development phases [23, 1, 10].

View generation and tool support: As described by Lago, Niemelä, and van Vliet [16], we developed tool support for representing the knowledge about a software PF and

---

[1] In the context of this paper, we use the terms *product family* and *product line* as synonyms.

supporting traceability from features to code. Further, we implemented an initial solution to view generation: to aid the stakeholder in defining his/her personalized views on the feature representations, we implemented filtering mechanisms that allow to select the feature- and association types to be visualized.

After defining the notation and associated tool support, we carried out a case study (summarized in Section 2) that covered the whole series of projects and had a twofold objective: (1) to put our PF under control for future evolution, and (2) to assess whether our method was really meeting our needs. In doing this, we drew our list of observations.

The remainder of this paper is structured as follows. Section 2 reports the starting point of the case study and summarizes the process we followed. Section 3 contains the core of the paper, describing the observations we made after the case study was done. It includes some lessons learned and the assumptions that were implicitly made about our software systems. Section 4 draws some general rules derived from our observations that we think are widely applicable. Section 5 concludes the paper.

2   The Communication PF

2.1   Starting Point

Our case study had the following starting conditions:

– The case study had to recover six existing products developed for different projects/contracts with industrial partners. These products belonged to the same application domain–software services running on an integrated Telephony-Internet network [18].
– These products were made of different components (i.e., they were varying in space [5]), and, in some cases, they were also including the same components but in different versions. This was introducing a second dimension to the variability management problem–variability in time [5].
– Each product was made of about 20,000 SLOC (only application code, excluding middleware such as java libraries, basic distributed communication components, and the like). As compared to the many experience papers published in the literature (e.g., [7,19,3,12]), one could claim that our PF is rather small in size. Still, we believe it is representative as some type of "boundary example": in spite of its relative small scale, its evolution became unmanageable.
– The application domain (advanced communication services on converged Internet-Telephony networks) is naturally extensible (e.g., by adding new features) and combinable (by composing features in different ways to build new services).
– To manage its increasing complexity, we first tried to reorganize the software architecture of the existing products according to a common architectural style (three-tiers with peer components). This helped to better organize the implementation files. More specifically
    • Others successfully adopted a similar approach; for example, by defining an ADL tailored for multi-tier architectures [22] or by organizing software product lines in *federated architectures* made of multiple generality layers [8]).

- Our case is similar to the case study described by Faust and Verhoef [8], in that they also identify at least three layers. In our case, we defined the application layer for client-side interactive components, the middleware layer including the components implementing general-purpose service features, and the platform layer for proprietary network technologies [14].
- At the implementation level, the three tiers help differentiate the general-purpose components from the service-specific ones. This is a first step to defining commonality and variability.

A three-tier architecture by itself however is not sufficient for achieving effective reuse.

- We decided to reverse engineer our six products, define the related feature and component models and traceability across them, and validate the support obtained by deriving a new product. To do this, we had to start with a domain engineering step: define a classification of the features in the domain to characterize the problem space.

2.2   Description of the Case Study

Our case study started with the reconstruction of the characteristics of our PF, and its evolution, summarized in Figure 1. The graph on the top side of the figure shows the precedence order in which the products were developed. In particular, products 4 and 5 were developed in parallel, starting from the same baseline (product 3). Product 7 was developed as part of our case study, to test the usefulness of our approach.

The table in Figure 1 shows the main aspects of the evolution of these products. Besides project duration and project objective (the latter expressed in terms of type of product and type of development), the table gives an idea of the evolution of the various components. The three central columns characterize the components of the three architectural tiers, whereas the last column shows the technology used to support distributed communication (i.e., the middleware platform). All components are represented by a keyword (e.g., "A" stands for authentication and "Tel-Adpt" stands for "Telephony Adapter"). The columns represent all the components that make up the product. When a component is missing, it means that it has been replaced by some other, new or modified component. When a component is in boldface, it means that some modifications have been applied to it. If a component is repeated as is, it means that it is part of that product with no modification at all.

For example, in project 2, components A and FS are reused as they are, components UP and CC are modified (renamed UP' and CC' respectively), and all platform service components have been replaced by three new components.

From this gross picture, we can sense how difficult it is to formally trace the evolution details. For example, project 2 eliminated many middleware service components (DS, PC, and IH). What happened to the functionality provided by these components? Is it completely deleted? Is it included in some other modified components?

There is no way to keep track of such information, unless we explicitly document it. Indeed, the new component CC' merged the functionality of CC together with the generic profile control (PC) functions, invocation handling (IH) became obsolete because

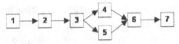

Pro ject	Duration (months)	Main development scope, goal	Application components	Middleware service components	Platform service components	Communication Technology
1	24	Infrastructure , integration	R | P | C | UP | UPadm	A | UP | DS | FS | PC | IH | CC	Tel-Adpt | Int-Adpt | Int-I	CORBA (IIOP)
2	12	Infrastructure , porting	Idem	A | **UP'** | FS | **CC'**	Tel-S | T2I | I-S	CORBA (IIOP)
3	12	Infrastructure , porting	Idem	A | UP² | FS | CC'	**I-S'**	CORBA (IIOP)
4	08	Service, development	R | P | C | UP | SU | L | SM	A | UP³ᵃ | **FS'** | CC² | **S | L**		**CORBA' (IIOP),** EJB and Servlets (RMI/HTTP)
5	08	Service, development	R | P | C | UP | UPadm | GM | GTM	A | UP³ᵇ | FS² | CC³ | GP		CORBA (IIOP)
6	12	Service, integration	R | P | C | **UP'** | **SU'** | **L'** | **SM'** | **GM'** | **GTM'**	A | UP³ᵃ⁺ᵇ | FS³ | CC⁴ | S | L | GP		CORBA' (IIOP), EJB and Servlets (RMI/HTTP)

Fig. 1. Overview of the PF development projects

of new communication technologies, and component UP' covered the service-dependent PC functions.

Another important issue concerns parallel development: as we developed products 4 and 5 in parallel, starting from product 3, their components are alternatives. This is syntactically represented by the component name (e.g., component UP2 is modified into components UP3a and UP3b): the semantics behind these versions must be described elsewhere.

As a last example, the last column shows that the same CORBA platform was used for the first three projects, and that project 4 modified it. But why? The reason behind this change is that project 4 decided to develop its new components on RMI over HTTP by using an EJB container. Next, some tests revealed that the old CORBA platform was not compatible at the protocol level (i.e., the IIOP - RMI mapping was not working), and we had to move to another compatible CORBA platform. Hence, in this case, the change was not due to direct functional or quality requirements, but to technology immaturity instead.

After the reconstruction of the characteristics and the evolution of our PF, our case study was organized in two main phases shown in Figure 2. The *first phase* focused on the recovery of the PF for the existing products (products 1-6), that is, for each product, it iteratively studied the code, design, and documentation to reconstruct the PF Feature Map, its mapping on the Product Feature Map, and all traceability information down to code. The *second phase* started from the produced Feature Maps and traceability information to derive a seventh product. This second phase produced a feedback to the first phase, updating the Feature Maps to include the new product in the PF. The details of the two phases are given in Figure 3, which presents the steps concerning the PF recovery in white and those deriving product 7 in gray.

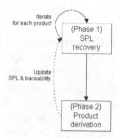

Fig. 2. Process overview: SPL recovery and product derivation process

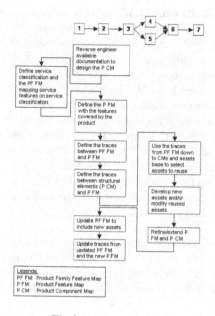

Fig. 3. Process overview

A detailed description of these recovery steps and the differences between the family products are provided by Lago [14].

3   Post-mortem Observations

When our case study was concluded, we were able to describe some observations in terms of lessons learned and assumptions that were made implicitly about the invariability of the software products but not documented anywhere. By making these invariabilities explicit (as "stability points") next to variabilities (as "variation points"), we can get a better grip on the *variation creep* due to the different dimensions in the evolution of a software product line.

3.1 Lessons Learned

Traceability for knowledge communication. Traceability is usually considered a necessary mechanism supporting software development and maintenance [24]. Traceability can also be used as a fundamental means of communication, for transferring the knowledge about an existing system to "outsiders." Traceability allows one to dynamically choose which aspects are more interesting than others, and hence examine them more deeply. In other words, thanks to traceability information, one can tailor the knowledge he/she wants to look at on the fly, and this implicitly creates personalized views. Of course, tool support for traceability is a fundamental factor in successful knowledge communication.

Abstraction for complexity control. We used two different abstraction mechanisms to control the complexity of a PF and its members. The *separation between PF Level and Product Level* draws a fundamental line between the model of our application domain and the population of existing products. The first belongs to the problem space and reflects the core business of the company; the second belongs to the solution space and makes up our reusable assets base. This separation into two levels helps the stakeholder reason, for example, about the market share that the company wants to target, or about the product-specific knowledge acquired (in terms of reusable assets).

The second abstraction mechanism we used is *filtering and view generation*: when we want to examine some specific aspects about one or multiple products, we need support to select these aspects among all the information gathered. Filtering supports the stakeholder in stating the aspects he/she wants to look at, and view generation based on the selected aspects provides visualization focused on these aspects only. If the filter is well defined, the generated view can even be used as the starting point to derive a new product.

A difficult problem to solve concerns the management of consistency among all PF views, especially if generated views must be stored and kept up to date. Let us consider two examples. If we want to create and keep a view showing only those features related to security, we want this view to dynamically reflect all the components implementing security control in all products. If new products are engineered that add new components supporting new security mechanisms, we want to be able to find back these new components in our "security-focused" view. As a second example, if we want to derive a new product and generate a view representing its initial Product Feature Map and linked Component Map, we will probably add/delete some elements and/or modify some others. Here, we need to carefully identify which elements are shared between different products and which instead are created as modified versions of elements. Of course, all these modifications must be traceable at both the PF and Product Levels. This problem can be partially solved in an automated way (see the next item), but it needs further investigation.

Automation for product derivation. As introduced before, when we want to derive a new product by reusing existing assets, we need automated support at the Product Level for the initial composition of this new product: once its required features are chosen, we look for the components implementing them and add/remove/modify them at needed. This all means that we create a new Product Feature Map for the selected features and a new Component Map for its solution. Both need automation to discover inconsistencies and support careful reuse. Also, their traceability from the PF Level must be kept, and tool support can at least provide a tentative solution; for example, to include a new feature in the PF Feature Map or to add a new component as a new solution for an existing feature. Further investigation is needed in this respect, too.

Integration of architectural information. In our case study, we used an approach that is mainly feature oriented. Architectural information is partially captured at the Product Level by Component Maps, but the overall architecture is only represented by documentation decorating the PF Feature Map. For example, architectural styles and patterns, or reference architectures, play a secondary role in development by providing descriptive documentation that can potentially be inconsistent with design and implementation.

We think that a structural viewpoint similar to the Product Feature Map should be part of the PF Level as well and that the dependencies between architectural and feature-oriented information need to be made explicit as traceability information.

3.2 Assumptions

The post-mortem assessment carried out after the recovery of our PF identified a set of assumptions that were made implicitly during development and made explicit afterwards. The following presents the main assumptions we reconstructed. They are classified in three types: (1) technical, (2) organizational, and (3) management [17]. *Technical* assumptions concern the technical environment in which a system is going to run: programming languages, database systems, operating systems, and middleware software are examples. *Organizational* assumptions reflect the company as a whole and its social settings and principles. These assumptions concern the organizational aspects in the company brought implicitly into software development. Examples include the workflow, the organizational structure reflected in development teams and departments, and the technology adopted as a company standard. Organizational assumptions can refer to the organization developing the software product or the one using it. Lastly, *management* assumptions reflect the decisions taken to achieve business objectives. These assumptions concern the solutions and the operational tasks to achieve organization-level objectives. Examples include management strategies and plans, experience brought into projects, and expansions toward new/different market segments.

Earlier work investigating the relation between assumptions and software architecture concerns technical assumptions at the component level [11]. This resulted in the notion of architectural mismatch. We look into assumptions from a broader perspective: we consider both nontechnical assumptions and assumptions that result in crosscutting issues.

Technical Assumptions

Tracing base technology versions. A product typically relies on a certain configuration of the software environment in which it can execute. This software configuration includes both special-purpose technology (e.g., a certain software platform for distributed communication) and general-purpose technology (e.g., a certain version of the JVM). We usually keep track of the first technology type, while we implicitly assume that the second type of technology is in place. This, of course, leads to inconsistencies and conflicts when we reuse components originally based on different technologies and hence when we need to reconstruct their original execution environment.

Heterogeneity in base technology. Special- and general-purpose technologies are different for different components within the same product. We usually assume that the execution environment is an atomic unit and that, once in place, it automatically supports all the components. In general, this is true if we consider the product as a whole. When we split up the product to reuse some of its components, we have a problem, because we do not know anymore exactly which technologies are needed for the components we are reusing. This leads to unexpected conflicts if we assume that two components that are functionally compatible will also rely on the same technology type. For example, two CORBA components are compatible provided that they are developed for the same CORBA platform or for two platforms that implement the same standard interfaces and associated behavior.

Information management. Similar to underlying technology, we need to make explicit the assumptions about the data exchanged or shared between different components. Compatibility of the data formats used for information exchange is a known problem, and it is usually described in the specification of component interfaces. Often, components share information stored using a certain external data storage system (e.g., a database), or they manipulate or use information that is partially overlapping or complementary. This implies that we need to make the assumptions about the storage system explicit, as well as those about the overall logical information schema. Otherwise, we might reuse components by selecting versions that do not use the same database or that rely on inconsistent logical information schemes.

Security. The first family product we developed in 1998 implemented secure communication by using SSL and encryption implemented by a US package that we acquired for academic use only. In 2001, we developed the fourth family product. One requirement was to support user authentication as provided by an authentication service implemented in application servers. At that time, the Orion application server became available as free software. It was providing integration with the CORBA/IIOP protocol and a security API supporting both SSL and various encryption algorithms. Unfortunately, the CORBA platform we were using revealed many incompatibilities, and we had to change the CORBA platform too. This had an impact on all the components and required extensive module and integration testing. During the design of this fourth product, we realized that we *implicitly* assumed that all the components where going to be based on CORBA, and we had not foreseen the integration with different middleware platforms as a possible future requirement.

Organizational Assumptions

Modularization versus company expertise. In the design of our first family product, the overall software architecture was organized in components partially reflecting the business role played by the different industrial partners. As partners were geographically dispersed and (most importantly) played well-established business roles in the market, it was politically important to clearly separate service-specific features from service-common ones. Service-specific features provide functionality that is specific to a particular type of application (e.g., video on demand); they are commercialized by service providers. Service-common features provide basic functionality reusable across different applications; they are commercialized by vendors and network providers.

In a similar way, service-specific behavior and communication management are separated. To ensure this separation, additional components were needed to mediate the interaction between the two levels. In both cases, the distribution of functionality on components reflects the business model of the application domain. This can lead to lower quality (e.g., decreased performance) in the final product. It is therefore important to make explicit in the documentation which modularization decisions are driven by the business model.

Management Assumptions

Company participation in standardization bodies. The second family product was developed for an industrial customer collaborating with third-party industries. In this collaboration, components developed by different companies had to be integrated to test their compatibility. As our customer was acting in the telecommunication sector, integration was crucial for future interoperability, as stated by international regulatory bodies. During integration, we found out that some of these companies had the mandate to be compliant to certain telecommunication interface standards. All the components handling communication were impacted by this decision, and all the interfaces had to be changed to reflect this standard, even if, in some cases, this implied lower performance and tricky solutions.

End-user communication as a service. At the PF feature level communication has been modeled as a feature belonging to the platform level only, that is, it was implicitly assumed that all users were having their own communication application deployed in the terminal. Moreover, it was somehow "obvious" that the PF was about offering communication service features to customers. Therefore, under the "End User Functionality" feature category you cannot find any end-user service feature supporting communication.

4   General Rules

From the observations and assumptions described in the previous sections, we are able to draw the following generally applicable rules.

Documentation rule. Documentation about the external environment should be provided for each reusable asset individually. For example, in a component-based system (like ours), each component should be decorated with all the information describing its external environment. Instead, current practice usually provides this documentation at the system level, once for the complete system. This finer-grained form of documentation helps to reason about the technological assumptions that we sometimes left implicit and that play a significant role (e.g., when reusing existing software elements).

To apply the documentation rule, we devised the following component template:

```
ID Component
    % Component properties
    Developer IDs'
    Component tier [A|M|P]
    Component assumptions
    Interface ID % for each interface
            Interface assumptions


    % Environment configuration
    % Distributed communication platform
    Middleware ID
            Middleware protocol type
            Middleware protocol standard ID


    % Environment configuration
    % General purpose platform
    Programming language
            Compiler/Interpreter version
    Data storage type/ID/version
    ...


    % Specific platform technologies
    ...
```

Analysis of the organizational/management impact. Once the software architecture of a system is defined, we should always assess it against the structure of the organization and its management issues. This helps make organizational and management assumptions explicit, so their embodiment in the software architecture is analyzed and verified explicitly whenever the system evolves. For example, we observed in the previous section that participation in standardization bodies and business roles played by industrial partners have an impact on the architecture and its quality. This impact should definitely be a deliberate choice coming from careful evaluation of the advantages and drawbacks.

5   Conclusions

This paper describes experience gained in a case study recovering a software PF. It reports a list of lessons learned, a list of implicit assumptions reconstructed after the case study, and some rules that we think are generally applicable, together with a template for the documentation of reusable software components.

The general objective of our case study was twofold: (1) to put our PF under control for future evolution and (2) to assess our method. We verified the achievement of our objective by successfully deriving a seventh product. This derivation phase was carried out by a person not previously involved in any development of the existing products. Hence, as he did not have particular problems, we think that our method can effectively contribute to knowledge management and reuse.

From this case study, we observe that organizing architectural knowledge is a complex issue. It can be done along different dimensions: feature oriented, structure oriented, stakeholder oriented, and so on. Each of these dimensions is relevant for answering certain questions. Flexible tool support, which allowed for the filtering of information and the generation of appropriate views, was found to be of great help.

We also observe that, next to the explicit variability designed into the products, there is kind of a "variation creep." Because of assumptions made regarding the environment in which the products function, assumptions which later turn out to be no longer appropriate, an extra and possibly unwanted type of variation in the PF is introduced. We conjecture that, for PFs, it is helpful to model not only the variation points, but the "stability points" as well. These stability points concern the assumptions we make–things we assume to remain constant over time and space. By modeling invariability next to variability, we may achieve an even better support for software product line evolution.

Acknowledgments. We would like to thank research support from Eurescom (the European Institute for Research and Strategic Studies in Telecommunications), the Cisco Program for Directed Research, the TINA Fellowship Programme, and Telecom Italia Lab. Thanks to their support, we could initiate the industrial collaborations that made our case study possible.

References

1. F. Bachmann and L. Bass. Managing variability in software architectures. In *Proceedings of the Symposium on Software Reusability*, pages 126–132, Toronto, Ontario, Canada, 2001.
2. L. Bass, P. Clements, and R. Kazman. *Software Architecture in Practice*. SEI Series in Software Engineering. Addison-Wesley, second edition, 2003.
3. G. Böckle, J. Muñoz, P. Knauber, C. Krueger, J. Sampaio do Prado Leite, F. van der Linden, L. Northrop, M. Stark, and D. Weiss. Adopting and institutionalizing a product line culture. In S. Verlag, editor, *Proceedings of the Software Product Lines Conference*, volume 2379 of *Lecture Notes in Computer Science*, pages 49–59, San Diego, CA, USA, Aug. 2002.
4. J. Bosch. *Design and Use of Software Architectures – Adopting and evolving a product-line approach*. Addison-Wesley (Pearson Education), 2000.
5. J. Bosch, G. Florijn, D. Greefhorst, J. Kuusela, J. Obbink, and K. Pohl. Variability issues in software product lines. In *Proc. of the fourth Software Product-Family Engineering Workshop (PFE)*, number 2290 in Lecture Notes in Computer Science, pages 13–21, Oct. 2001.
6. P. Clements and C. Krueger. Being Proactive Pays Off/Eliminating the Adoption Barrier. *IEEE Software*, 19(4):28–31, Aug. 2002.
7. P. Clements and L. Northrop. Salion, Inc.: A software product line case study. Technical Report CMU/SEI-2002-TR-038, Software Engineering Institute, CMU, Nov. 2002.
8. D. Faust and C. Verhoef. Software product line migration and deployment. *Software Practice and Experience, John Wiley & Sons, Ltd.*, 33(10):933–955, Aug. 2003.
9. C. Gacek and M. Anastasopoules. Implementing product line variabilities. In *Proceedings of the Symposium on Software Reusability*, pages 109–117. ACM Press, 2001.
10. A. Garg, M. Critchlow, P. Chen, C. Van der Westhuizen, and A. van der Hoek. An environment for managing evolving product line architectures. In *International Conference on Software Maintenance*, pages 358–367, Sept. 2003.

11. D. Garlan, R. Allen, and J. Ockerbloom. Architectural mismatch: Why reuse is so hard. *IEEE Software*, 12(6):17–26, Nov. 1995.
12. M. Jaring and J. Bosch. Representing variability in software product lines: A case study. In S. Verlag, editor, *Proceedings of the Software Product Lines Conference*, volume 2379 of *Lecture Notes in Computer Science*, pages 15–36, San Diego, CA, USA, Aug. 2002.
13. K. Kang, S. Cohen, J. Hess, W. Novak, and A. Peterson. Feature-oriented domain analysis (FODA) feasibility study. Technical Report CMU/SEI-90-TR-21, Software Engineering Institute, CMU, Nov. 1990.
14. P. Lago. The UNIK project: from product family to product line. Technical Report PDT-DAI-PI-P-001-B0, Politecnico di Torino, Italy, Aug. 2002.
15. P. Lago, E. Niemelä, and H. van Vliet. Integrating features and structural aspects in engineering software product families. Submitted, 2003.
16. P. Lago, E. Niemelä, and H. van Vliet. Tool support for traceable product evolution. In *Proceedings of the European Conference on Software Maintenance and Reengineering*, pages 261–269, Tampere, Finland, Mar. 2004. IEEE Computer Society Press.
17. K. Laudon and J. Laudon. *Management Information Systems – Managing the Digital Firm*. Prentice Hall, eight edition, 2004.
18. A. Modarressi and S. Mohan. Control and management in next-generation networks: challenges and opportunities. *IEEE Communications Magazine*, 38(10):94–102, Oct. 2000.
19. C. Riva and C. del Rosso. Experiences with software product family evolution. In *Proceedings of the International Workshop on Principles of Software Evolution*, pages 161–169, Sept. 2003.
20. S. Robak. Feature modeling notations for system families. In *International Workshop on Software Variability Management*, pages 58–62, 2003.
21. K. Schmid and I. John. A practical approach to full-life cycle variability management. In *International Workshop on Software Variability Management*, pages 41–47, 2003.
22. R. Taylor, N. Medvidovic, K. Anderson, E. Whitehead, J. Robbins, K. Nies, P. Oreizy, and D. Dubrow. A component- and message-based architectural style for GUI software. *IEEE Trans. Software Eng.*, 22(6):390–406, June 1996.
23. D. Webber and H. Gomaa. Modeling variability with the variation point model. In C. Gacek, editor, *Proceedings of the International Conference on Software Reuse*, volume 2319 of *Lecture Notes in Computer Science*, pages 109–122. Springer Verlag, Apr. 2002.
24. T. Weiler. Modeling Architectural Variability for Software Product Lines. In J. van Gurp and J. Bosch, editors, *Proceedings of the Workshop on Software Variability Management*, pages 55–63, Feb. 2003.

Product Line Potential Analysis

Claudia Fritsch and Ralf Hahn

Robert Bosch GmbH
Corporate Research and Development
P.O. Box 94 03 50, D-60461 Frankfurt, Germany
{Claudia.Fritsch|Ralf.Hahn}@de.bosch.com

Abstract. A *Product Line Potential Analysis* enables us to make a quick decision as to whether the product line approach (PLA) is suitable for a given set of products and target market. The PLA framework offers no support for this as yet.

A Product Line Potential Analysis is executed in a half-day workshop. A structured interview based on a questionnaire examines products, software, markets, and customers. The answers are compared to a set of criteria for the applicability of the PLA. The analysis results primarily in one of these decisions: "yes" (the PLA is suitable for these products and markets), "no", or "investigation required". Up to now, our team has performed four Product Line Potential Analyses.

We present the list of criteria, a part of our questionnaire, and the workshop format. We discuss Product Line Potential Analysis in the light of related work and its limits and lessons learned, and we look at future work.

1 Introduction

1.1 PLA Introduction at Bosch

Robert Bosch manufactures and sells automotive products and industrial products, as well as consumer goods and building products worldwide. Many products are software-intensive systems with embedded software. Most of the software products form a product line.

Bosch started a product line approach (PLA) initiative in 1999 to increase software quality and development efficiency. The PLA should be introduced in those business units or product units where it makes sense.

Bosch business units are facing the question of whether to use the PLA. Before spending time and resources on a PLA, the business units must be certain that it is suitable for their products. To make this decision, the business unit needs to understand its *product line potential,* that is, the business opportunity of building software product lines in a systematic way.

The purpose of the Product Line Potential Analysis is to provide confidence in whether product line potential exists.

R.L. Nord (Ed.): SPLC 2004, LNCS 3154, pp. 228–237, 2004.

1.2   Product Line Potential

Product line potential exists if a set of software-intensive systems sharing a common set of features that satisfy the specific needs of a particular market segment or mission can be developed from a common set of core assets.

This definition is derived from the definition of a software product line in Clements' and Northrop's book [2]: A software product line is a set of software-intensive systems sharing a common set of features that satisfy the specific needs of a particular market segment or mission and that are developed from a common set of core assets in a prescribed way.

The difference is that product line potential only requires that systems *can* be developed from a common set of core assets. When considering that *potential,* the current practices are irrelevant. Instead, the question is if systematic product line development would be helpful.

Bosch's business units have developed embedded software for decades and have been following established processes and techniques. Over the years, the software has grown in complexity and size. Some business units now develop a variety of software products. How can a business unit find out if the PLA would be appropriate?

A Product Line Potential Analysis examines a business unit's product line potential through discussions with business unit managers who know their organization's business goals, products, and market requirements. This has to be done as quickly as possible: business unit managers have a tight schedule.

2   Approach

2.1   Overview

A Product Line Potential Analysis answers the following question: Would the PLA be suitable for a given set of products and target market? This question is too hard to answer as a whole, so we broke it down into a set of *criteria* relevant to the applicability of the PLA.

Figure 1 shows the development and application of the Product Line Potential Analysis (PLPA) method. Based on the definition of product line potential, product line suitability criteria are derived. The criteria, in turn, provide the basis for the questionnaire contents. In a Product Line Potential Analysis workshop, the answers are compared to the criteria. This comparison yields one of three decisions: "yes" (the PLA is suitable for these products and markets), "no", or "investigation required." In the written report, the answers are mapped to the definition of product line potential, providing the rationale.

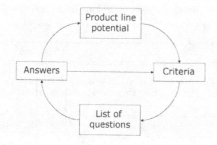

Fig. 1. PLPA cycle

2.2   Criteria

The following criteria are relevant to product line potential:

- **Main criteria** are essential for product line development and have to be fulfilled:
  - The business unit develops more than one product.
  - Products have common features.
  - Products have common qualities.
- **Inclusion criteria** indicate that product lines already exist:
  - The same part of software is used in more than one product.
- **Supporting criteria** apply if a business unit has problems that the PLA addresses:
  - The business unit has quality problems.
  - The business unit has complexity problems.
  - The business unit expects increasingly differentiated products.
- **Exclusion criteria** rule out an economically advantageous product line:
  - There is an immature, instable market for the products.
  - There is technological change.
  - The software is small; optimization will not be profitable.
  - The software development effort is negligible. It would be better to focus on other improvements.
  - New product development is too seldom.
  - The business unit develops specific, commissioned custom products.
- **Additional information** is useful data that cannot be assigned to one of the preceding criteria:
  - the competitive situation

Some criteria may appear to be trivial; for example, more than one product. But experience shows that this criterion should be checked.

Note: One fulfilled exclusion criteria does not imply that the PLA can not make sense. It only indicates that the PLA *may* not make sense.

From these criteria, questions that help to check the criteria have been derived. Table 1 shows a part of the questionnaire with 11 questions and their

Table 1. A part of our questionnaire: questions and their correlation to criteria. Criteria and their qualifiers are given in short form for a better overview

No.	Question		Criterion
Products			
P_1	Which products do you manufacture or sell at the moment?	main	More than one product
P_2	Which products do you develop at the moment? When do they go into production?	excl	Immature, instable market
		excl	Technological change
P_3	How many products did you deliver during the last 12 months?	excl	New product development is too seldom.
P_4	Which features do your products for one market segment have in common?	main	Common features
...	...	...	...
Hardware and software			
S_1	How big is your software (lines of code, RAM-/ROM usage, number of developers)?	excl	Software is small.
S_2	What is the proportionate cost of the software in a product?	excl	Software development effort negligible
S_3	Do you use the same software parts in more than one product?	incl	Same software in more than one product
S_4	Which differences between the products do you implement in software?	incl	Same software in more than one product
...	...	...	...
Market			
M_1	What is your market forecast for your products?	excl	Immature, instable market
		supp	Increasingly differentiated products
M_2	Which market segments do you address? In what way are they different?	excl	New product development is too seldom.
		main	Common qualities
...	...	...	...
Customers			
C_1	Do your customers commission you to develop products and demand for software reuse?	incl	Same software in more than one product
...	...	...	...

correlation to the criteria. Questions P_i help to understand what kind of products the business unit builds. Questions S_i look at the hardware and software. Questions M_i about the market and C_i about the customers' habits close the questionnaire.

The correlation between questions and criteria is not always evident. For example, question P_2 ("Which products do you develop at the moment?") finds out whether there is an *immature, instable market*. If the products currently developed are different from those currently sold (question P_1), this exclusion criterion is fulfilled.

2.3   Questions

While the criteria were derived from the definition of product line potential, the questions arose from experience. The questions were iterated several times, reconsidering successful product line development efforts, as well as attempts that failed.

Some questions ask what a business unit *has* done, such as P_1, P_3, and P_4. In principle, products that a business unit *plans* to develop are more interesting – the PLA can have no influence on products already on sale. Nevertheless, questions about things that a business unit *has* done are especially attractive because they are facts – as opposed to plans, intentions, or forecasts.

Redundant questions ensure a consistent picture of products and markets. Usually, a product manager talks about the products in a different way than the head of development does. The criteria are therefore assessed from different perspectives. For example, two questions address the criterion *same software in more than one product*: S_3 "Do you use the same software parts in more than one product?" and C_1 "Do your customers [...] demand for software reuse?" Only two matching answers ensure that a criterion is covered.

The small set of keywords used in the questions helps to interpret information consistently. Ambiguous terms, such as "platform" or "component," have been avoided. Instead, more neutral terms are used, such as "products," "software," and "software parts."

The phrasing of the questions meets the principles of human communication: be open, positive, non-suggestive, and simple. The questions aim at informative answers: instead of "How many products do you manufacture or sell ...?" the better question is P_1 *"Which* products do you manufacture or sell ...?" Some questions are rather indirect, because direct questions might force someone onto the defensive. For example, "Will you supply an immature and instable market?" would probably not yield a satisfying answer. Instead, the reply to question M_1 "What is your market forecast for your products?" will allow the appropriate conclusions. Although some questions seem to miss the point, they have proven to serve their purpose very well.

Table 2. Structure of a Product Line Potential Analysis workshop

1. Presentation of PLA and Product Line Potential Analysis method
2. Presentation of product portfolio and market
Break
3. Structured interview using the questionnaire
4. Review criteria and articulate the result

2.4   Workshop Format

The goal of the workshop is to

- inform the business unit personnel about potential benefits of the PLA
- inform the business unit personnel about what the PLA means in the context of the business unit's products
- learn about the business unit's goals, products, software, markets, and customers
- analyze products, software, markets, and customers to decide whether the PLA is suitable

The Product Line Potential Analysis addresses managers in business units or product units who have heard about the PLA but do not exactly know what it is. These managers call for information and want to know if the PLA is suitable for them. They are willing to spend some hours of their precious time, so they make an appointment for a Product Line Potential Analysis.

Preparation. Before the workshop, the client is asked to prepare presentations of his product portfolio and market. Usually, appropriate slides are already available.

The client gets the list of questions and is asked to bring one or two people who can answer them in the workshop. Usually, two or three business unit employees participate: a product manager, the head of the development department, and sometimes an architect.

Three of us team up for such a workshop: one is the lead who presents the PLA and Product Line Potential Analysis and asks the questions, one takes notes, and one acts as the observer and timekeeper.

Execution. The structure of a Product Line Potential Analysis workshop is shown in Table 2. During the presentation of the PLA and the Product Line Potential Analysis, the workshop lead informs the client about the PLA and sets the expectations for the Product Line Potential Analysis. After that, the product manager and the head of development present their markets and products.

After the presentations the team uses the break to cross out questions in the list that have already been answered. Questions whose discussion can be shortened are marked.

Then, the structured interview starts, guided by the questionnaire. The business unit personnel answer the questions while the lead explains them and links their answers to the PLA. In this way, the business unit employees learn about the PLA in relation to their products and software. While the lead asks the questions, he or she ticks off the fulfilled criteria.

After the interview, the lead reviews the criteria and clarifies with the workshop participants which of them are fulfilled. Depending on the portion of the criteria that has been fulfilled, he or she articulates the result: "yes," "no," or "investigation required."

Reporting. After the workshop, the team prepares a written report containing the result, the rationale, and a recommendation.

The rationale maps the personnel's core responses to the product line potential definition; for example, the information provided on the number of products plus the amount and cost of their software is used to justify the assertion that there is a set of software-intensive systems.

Typical recommendations are

- to perform a Product Line Technical Probe[SM] (PLTP[SM])[1]
- to do an Architecture Tradeoff Analysis Method (ATAM[SM]) evaluation
- to perform a Scoping workshop

The PLTP[SM] as described by Clements and Northrop [2] is a method for examining an organization's readiness to adopt the PLA. A PLTP[SM] can be recommended if the Product Line Potential Analysis result is "yes."

An ATAM[SM] [3] examines the risks contained in a particular software architecture. An ATAM[SM] can be recommended if the Product Line Potential Analysis reveals that a software architecture already exists and should be used for product line development.

Scoping defines which products should be part of a product line or which product lines a business unit should develop. A Scoping workshop can be recommended if the Product Line Potential Analysis reveals that it is not clear which products are to be developed in the product line.

3   Discussion

3.1   Example

So far, our team has performed four Product Line Potential Analyses, the results being four "yes" decisions plus one "investigation required." Before we started performing Product Line Potential Analyses, we had expected to exit each workshop with a single result. But in one Product Line Potential Analysis, we experienced something different.

---

[1] PLTP, Product Line Technical Probe, ATAM, and Architecture Tradeoff Analysis Method are service marks of Carnegie Mellon University.

A business unit had asked for a Product Line Potential Analysis for its new generation of systems. The unit planned to manufacture two kinds of large systems: A and B. From type A, about 40 small, specific systems should be derived, $A_1 - A_{40}$.

The result of the analysis was twofold:

1. The PLA makes sense for a product line including systems A and $A_1 - A_{40}$.
2. Investigation is required to decide whether B belongs to this product line, too.

Systems A and B are just two products, even though they are highly configurable systems. To decide whether the PLA makes sense anyway, we would need a closer look. Therefore, we recommended a Scoping workshop.

3.2   Related Work

If a business unit is considering launching a product line, some analysis methods would provide a good start, notably

(a) Domain Potential Analysis ([1])
(b) Product Line Analysis ([5])
(c) Product Line Benefit and Risk Assessment ([6])
(d) PuLSE™-Intro ([4])
(e) Product Line Technical Probe[SM] ([2])

The fundamental difference between these methods and the Product Line Potential Analysis is the effort involved. The Product Line Potential Analysis is designed to take a quick look. It doesn't analyzes reuse benefits and risks (as (a) – (d) do) or assess expertise (e).

These activities require thorough analysis and are therefore time-consuming – for the consultants as well as for the clients. Experience shows that business units are not willing to spend time and resources on extensive analysis before they *know* that a product line approach fits their product palette. Product Line Potential Analysis gives them confidence within a few hours.

The above mentioned method (c) is an assessment, (d) is called a probe. A Product Line Potential Analysis is neither. It is a survey done in partnership. Both sides give and take information. In particular, the result emerges during the workshop as opposed to assessments where the team works out the result on its own *after* the interviews.

3.3   Limits

The guaranteed result of the Product Line Potential Analysis is a "yes," "no," or "investigation required" decision. In our Product Line Potential Analysis presentation, we explain carefully to the business unit personnel that this and nothing more can be expected. The time is needed to understand the products, markets, and some essential properties of the software. There is no time to analyze possible product lines, domains, or architectures. However, after each workshop we've done so far, we were able to give one or two recommendations. But we cannot promise to give one; it is an add-on.

Product Line Potential Analyses bear the risk of missing possible product lines, because the scope of a Product Line Potential Analysis corresponds to the scope our interviewees have. Organizations and products reflect traditional divisions. In a Product Line Potential Analysis, we talk to personnel of one business unit. Thus, we can see product line potential inside one division. We can't see a possible product line that would include products of two divisions. A Product Line Potential Analysis has to comply with these limitations.

The Product Line Potential Analysis was designed in the context of Bosch, including automotive products and building products. We think that the method would transfer to other organizations, because it analyzes the products, not their development. If limitations in transfer exist, they probably lie on the market and customer side. So far, we have analyzed known markets and products: the contracting customers of automotive products are the car manufacturers. Perhaps some questions would need to be changed or added if the markets or customers were not that well known.

4   Conclusions

4.1   Summary

A Product Line Potential Analysis decides in a half-day workshop whether the PLA is suitable for a given set of products and their market using a structured interview based on a questionnaire. The result is basically "yes," "no," or "investigation required." We have presented

- the criteria relevant to PLA applicability
- a part of our questionnaire
- how Product Line Potential Analysis workshops are executed
- a discussion of the method

4.2   Lessons Learned

- Each criterion is relevant. It is important to play it safe. Even if some of them may seem trivial; for example, the requirement that there be *more than one product:* A product unit showed interest in applying the PLA. They fulfilled all main and inclusion criteria, except one. They *sold* different products, but they *developed* only one – a configurable software.
- We have learned to conduct the interview in such a way that business unit employees feel good. They want to understand the purpose of our questions. We explain it. We explain immediately how their answers relate to the PLA, too. This gives them confidence and motivation.

– We regard a Product Line Technical Probe^{SM} as the most effective and efficient initiation of a PLA. However, executives hesitate to order it. A PLTP^{SM} is an investment that ties up resources of about two person-months. Holding a positive Product Line Potential Analysis result in the hand reduces the inhibition threshold: the executive knows that the effort of performing a PLTP^{SM} is well invested. On the flip side, the information we get during the Product Line Potential Analysis shortens the preparation of a PLTP^{SM}.

– Performing a Product Line Potential Analysis is a very effective and efficient way to understand the business, the products, and the market of a business unit. And we make contact with the executive manager of a business unit or product unit. This provides valuable information for a Scoping workshop and helps to find the right stakeholders.

4.3   Future Work

So far, only PLA experts can lead a Product Line Potential Analysis, because our criteria are soft. When we ask "How big is your software?" (LOC, RAM/ROM usage, or number of developers), we do not know how big would be just big enough. In case we run into a conflict, we either recommend further investigation or recognize that this factor will not change the result. Doubtlessly, we would prefer to have hard data to decide such issues.

Having this hard data would make our questionnaire much more precise. We could refine it so that a Product Line Potential Analysis could be led by other corporate units or maybe by the business units themselves.

References

1. S. Bandinelli, G. Sagardui Mendieta *Domain Potential Analysis: Calling the Attention on Business Issues of Product-Lines* in *Proceedings of Software Architectures for Product Families, International Workshop IW-SAPF-3, Las Palmas de Gran Canaria, Spain, March 15-17 2000*, Lecture Notes in Computer Science 1951 Springer 2000, ISBN 3-540-41480-0
2. P. Clements, L. Northrop *Software Product Lines*, Addison-Wesley 2002
3. P. Clements, R. Kazman, M. Klein *Evaluating Software Architectures*, Addison-Wesley 2002
4. Fraunhofer Institute for Experimental Software Engineering (IESE) *PuLSE^{TM}-Intro – Identifying the potential for effective development of software product variants*, www.iese.fgh.de
5. G. Sagarduy, S. Bandinelli, R. Lerchundi *Product-line Analysis: Do we go ahead?* in *Proceedings of Software Product Lines: Economics, Architectures, and Implications, Workshop #15 at 22nd International Conference on Software Engineering (ICSE), Limerick, Ireland, June 10th 2000*
6. K. Schmid, I. John *Developing, Validating and Evolving an Approach to Product Line Benefit and Risk Assessment*, in *Proceedings of 28th Euromicro Conference (EUROMICRO'02), September 04-06, 2002, Dortmund, Germany*, IEEE 2002

Generalized Release Planning for Product Line Architectures

Louis J.M. Taborda

Macquarie Graduate School of Management,
Macquarie University, NSW 2109, Australia
ltaborda@procentric.com

Abstract. This paper elaborates on the coordination and management of evolving software product lines, where development teams work around a shared and reusable domain infrastructure. The trend away from monolithic applications and towards component-based, product line architectures has enabled the development of complex software to be undertaken by autonomous and often, geographically separated teams. Delivering a complete product or product line requires significant coordination to bring the separate development streams together, at agreed-upon points in the schedule, for integration and test. In such complex development scenarios, a Release Matrix has been proposed as a generalization of release planning and tracking, addressing multiple products, components, and their interdependencies at an enterprise or marketplace level. Here, we describe the results of the practical trials of the Release Matrix that provide pragmatic guidelines for its use and indicate areas for future research. Relationships to established processes, including requirements engineering and configuration management, are clarified, and the methodology-neutral technique is shown to complement work in areas, including Agile Methods and component contracts.

1 Introduction

Component-based development (CBD) [1] and product line architectures (PLAs) [2] are becoming increasingly popular because of the economic, quality, and time-to-market benefits that result from the systematic reuse they enshrine. These architectures have influenced the organizational structures adopted for software-intensive programs, offering new, flexible alternatives to managing the complexity and distribution of development activities [3, 4].

Increasingly, the development of software is undertaken by autonomous, and often, geographically separated software teams. Each of the teams can work on one or more separate, large-grained components, or subsystems, that provide part of the product capabilities. They may use different technologies and development processes and can have their own internal release schedules, as long as the components can be integrated into the end product at some point in the schedule. At one extreme, system components may be commercial off-the-shelf (COTS), in which case they behave as black boxes in both the management and technical sense. At the other end of the scale, components can be developed in-house and be subject to changes as a result of evolving business needs.

R.L. Nord (Ed.): SPLC 2004, LNCS 3154, pp. 238–254, 2004.
© Springer-Verlag Berlin Heidelberg 2004

Irrespective of their nature, delivering the completed product or product line requires the confluence of these different development streams at agreed-upon points in the schedule to enable integration and testing. This entails higher order processes than traditional software development and includes the identification, selection, integration, test, and release activities necessary to get the products to the market [5, 6]. While the technical aspects of integrating such component-based products are familiar, the complex set of coordinated steps that have to be performed just to get the correct versions of the appropriate components together in a suitable environment and assemble them into the end product, remains an open challenge.

Many of these essential logistical or management aspects of development fall into the realm of configuration management, and this discipline and its associated tools are seen as essential to managing the complexity of such environments [2, 7, 8]. But while these are everyday concerns for many software organizations, the traditional approaches to managing standalone development projects are proving to be inadequate [9, 10, 11] in the face of increasing complexity.

The Release Matrix has been proposed [12] as a mechanism for facilitating the planning, communications, and coordination of incremental releases by consolidating the traditional requirements engineering and configuration management principles. While these principles provide valuable guidance in any development scenario, they are based on the premise of single-product development. The Release Matrix is a generic, methodology-neutral technique that is, and has been shown to be, a generalization of traditional release planning for situations in which there are multiple products and components [13]. It offers a simple template that explicitly records the enterprise or marketplace configuration that is the entire PLA and can capture different stakeholder viewpoints of the development artifacts across the life cycle.

This paper reports on preliminary trials in a complex software development project that set out to create a new product based on several pre-existing subsystems. The trial-project team conducted a review of the Release Matrix technique using interviews to validate the fundamental assumptions that underpin the technique. The technique was then applied to key feature sets, in parallel with the mainstream development activity, to demonstrate its applicability and validity.

The remainder of this paper is organized as follows. Section 2 discusses the challenges that increasing software complexity creates for development and the calls for new management paradigms to address them. Section 3 briefly reviews the fundamental concepts behind the Release Matrix, and Section 4 recounts the experiences of preliminary trials of the technique, placing it in the context of related work. Finally, the paper concludes by summarizing the key characteristics and benefits of the Release matrix, indicating areas of future research.

2   The Challenge to Current Best Practices

The rising tide of complexity is increasingly taxing current best practices, and PLAs represent one of the most significant management challenges of our times. Planning for a product line requires tremendous management and technical effort that can then be too easily wasted when changes have to be made. Such frustrations are not unique to PLAs. Rather, they are representative of the increasing dissatisfaction with and questioning of traditional best practices that are taking place today.

2.1 Growing Disenchantment with Best Practices

The tremendous interest in standards and methodologies in the 1990s has been replaced by a growing disenchantment with these planned approaches to development. Fitzgerald reviews the pressure for increased formalism and the literature bias in favor of methodologies [14]. He describes the pressures for new approaches to systems development that include the changing nature of business and development, as well as the need for rapid application development. In a subsequent study that traced the origins of the then current development methodologies [15], he argues that most were founded on concepts that emerged in the period from about 1967 to 1977. While this study predates the emergence of component-based development and PLAs, they can be seen as evolutionary outgrowths of object-oriented concepts that can themselves be traced back to earlier times. The conclusion that is drawn from this work is that "new methodological canons more appropriate to the needs of current development" need to be derived.

A more recent call for new development paradigms was made by the Agile Manifesto [16] authored by a group of methodologists and industry experts who banded together to express their disenchantment with the state of current best practices as expressed in standards and industry practices advocated by, for example, the Software Engineering Institute in its Capability Maturity Models. Instead, the authors called for simpler, more flexible approaches to software development that value individuals and interactions over processes and tools; working software over documentation; customer collaboration over contract negotiation; and responding to change over following a plan.

A number of the proponents of Agile Methods, such as Highsmith [17], have adopted biological metaphors for software development and propose a more adaptive and iterative approach to development that corresponds to the self-organizing principles of complex systems in nature. The word methodology, therefore, has to be used cautiously in an Agile context, and Highsmith instead proposes the term "ecosystem" as the preferred description of the flexible, collaborative, and responsive environment that is necessary for modern software development.

The debate on the relative merits of Agile and traditional, planned development methods continues, and the purpose of this discussion is not to advocate one of these development philosophies. Rather, it is presented to support the argument that traditional approaches to managing development are increasingly under strain. The deficiencies in best practices noted above are exacerbated only when the complexity of product lines is considered. The fundamental debate appears to be between the merits of the tacit knowledge advocated by the "few good people" needed for Agile Methods versus the codified knowledge of standards and other best practices.

The underlying question that motivates the current research (and which when answered could ease the concerns of both Agile and more traditional methodologists alike) is whether current best practices, with their focus on single products, single customers, and single suppliers, are addressing the real-world situations that modern developers face. Perhaps a more appropriate representation of the current complexity would allow the tacit knowledge that is held by an experienced software expert to be better codified.

2.2 Management Patterns for Growing Complexity

System decomposition, and thus the principles that underlie CBD, are a result of standard reductionism applied to system complexity. But while component architectures that localize and insulate changes and enable large-scale reuse provide significant benefits, a tradeoff has to be made in terms of the increased management burden they impose.

The growing success of component-based technologies is resulting in the separation of software teams into producers of specialized, reusable components (or services) and consumers of these components who then combine them into marketable applications, systems, or products. The presence of these two views of development—labeled the *Marketplace Pattern* [13]—is recognizable within enterprises where teams work with a common domain architecture, or identifiable in industry alliances that use or produce a shared software infrastructure.

The orthogonality of products, domain assets, and components is a recognizable pattern [12, 18] that is also evident in environments in which there is a shared infrastructure—including information systems in which common systems or services (e.g., those provided by an external agency) behave in the same manner as reused software components. Software product lines provide the perfect example of the Marketplace Pattern, since their development requires the cooperation of multiple product teams that use common domain components. Clearly defined product (and market/customer) responsibilities and the recognition that the architecture is the key to the product line combine to make the dependencies between component producers and consumers more pronounced (and recognized).

2.3 Holistic Management

The complexity of product lines and other componentized software architectures has a significant influence on how the development organization is structured. While a component-based architecture and the variations in change volatility can result in components having different release cycles, it is the organization—the teams that actually do the development—that ensures separate responsibilities for each release and gives rise to the complex coordination necessary to effect a product delivery.

In product line development, the software teams that participate in the development process can behave as decentralized, independent agents that interact to achieve the product releases. The multiplicity of components, interrelationships, and mutual dependencies evident in product lines deserves the designation of a complex software ecosystem, in acknowledgement of the Agile methodologists. Such environments are recognized as a management challenge beyond the standard software development [2]. In particular, the configuration management (CM) problem in such environments is significantly increased, and common CM techniques are often inadequate or have to be "stretched" to tackle the different levels at which the problem manifests itself [2, 19].

While traditional methods focus on the development activities needed to create and release a component, processes are also needed to assemble the wider configuration of products. Planning and coordination need to take place in both dimensions simultaneously, and it has been shown previously that to plan each release in isolation is suboptimal [12].

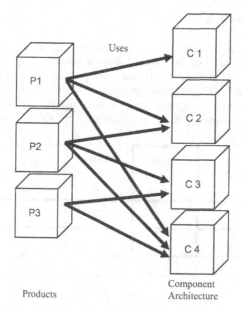

Fig. 1. Marketplace Pattern for multiple products and components

With more than one product to manage in a product line, this research argues that the appropriate generalization is to consider the entire product line as a single configuration where all products and components are managed together with their relationships. This superconfiguration has to be treated holistically (much as systems engineering attempts to do) to take an integrated viewpoint of a complex, decomposed system configuration. The difference between product line architectures and an "ordinary" complex system, however, is the reuse relationships that reduce the control of any single product [13] and make it necessary to plan and coordinate all releases in the ecosystem holistically and collaboratively.

3   Reprise of the Matrix Model

The Marketplace Pattern, simplistically illustrated in Figure 1, captures development ecosystems, such as PLAs, where concurrent product development is based on a reusable, component-based framework. There are two distinct, orthogonal management views that can be taken of such development environments [12]: the first based on the products and the second based on the components. The pattern can be shown to be sufficient to derive a matrix representation [13] that is more suited to the management of such complex software developments.

3.1 The Release Matrix

A matrix representation offers the ability to record relevant, life-cycle information in each individual cell, while capturing the dependencies between members of the eco-system. In particular, a Release Matrix has been proposed as a means of planning and tracking the evolution of the system architecture over time. As shown in Figure 2, the Release Matrix records the components (x-axis) and the products (y-axis) that use these components, integrating them into the market offering.

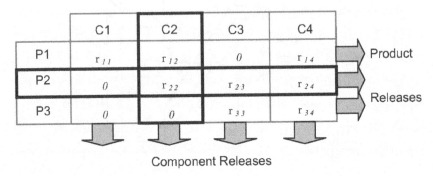

Fig. 2. A Release Matrix consolidates the product and component perspectives

The matrix can be seen to correspond to the relationships shown in Figure 1 where the existence of a relationship between a product (P_i) and component (C_j) results in an entry in the intersecting cell (r_{ij}). When no relationship exists between a product and component, there is a zero or null entry in the corresponding cell. The content of the cells of a Release Matrix can be regarded simply as the scheduled dates of the set of dependent releases; however, a family of similar matrices can be employed to record different life-cycle data depending on the usage of the matrix. For example, to derive and coordinate the release schedules for all products and components, a separate matrix can be used to record the product requirements that have been allocated to the different components. With reference to the release-planning scenario previously described, the P2 row could represent the bill-print project where C2, C3, and C4 would be the display, storage, and print-management components.

The multiplicity of releases that are a feature of CBD environments can benefit from the clarification offered by the Release Matrix. It provides a succinct and ex-plicit means of recording the dependencies between products and components, while supporting the "separation of concerns" principle by extricating the two perspectives. Each row of the Release Matrix represents a product's release plan that is derived from, and must be compatible with, the component releases on which the product is reliant. Similarly, each column represents a component's release plan, based on the total set of product requirements that are to be implemented in the release. As a whole, the Release Matrix represents a master release plan that consolidates and syn-chronizes the individual release plans of both the products and the components.

By way of example, the highlighted column in Figure 2 represents the perspective of the team responsible for component C3 that needs to balance the demands of prod-ucts P2 and P3. The highlighted row corresponds to the reliance that project P2 has on three components—C2, C3, and C4—that may need to have coordinated releases to effect a business change. The intersection of these two perspectives indicates the specific plan or contract between the P2 and C3 teams. Similar plans must be negotiated for all non-null cells as they point to a dependency between the stakeholders that requires coordinated attention to achieve an agreed-upon and consistent set of releases.

In general, Figure 2 shows that each product group must attempt to align the components it relies on across the row, while each component producer must weigh and prioritize the requirements of its customers shown in that column. These orthogonal perspectives represent the different tensions that have to be balanced in a complex component-based environment.

4 Application in the Real World

The Release Matrix is a relatively simple concept that is the result of capturing and elevating a widely recognized pattern in complex component-based systems to become the central tenet of its management paradigm. Its usefulness however can be truly gauged only by application in a real-world industry setting.

Trials of the Release Matrix were therefore conducted in a large software development organization that was undertaking a challenging new program. This required the reuse and minor modification of pre-existing, large-grained components that were then integrated and packaged for a new market segment—even as each of these existing components continued to be marketed separately. As such, the scenario represented an example of the Marketplace Pattern with a number of separate products competing to have their features developed by the separate component teams that themselves had to balance these and other demands.

The following provides an overview of the pilot study where the organization's architecture and activities were mapped into the Release Matrix's axes to determine the applicability of the technique and the benefits it could offer. Each aspect of the trial is described first in terms of the theoretical or ideal approach that would be advocated, and then by the pragmatic approach that had to be taken in practice.

4.1 Requirements Management

Each of the new product's features placed new requirements on the reused components and had to be completed in the next release cycle. These requirements spanned a number of the components, and each had to be implemented before the new features could be integrated and tested. The new features were not the only requirements placed on the components however, and other groups made similar demands on the development teams. While the customer release date was common to all products, internal releases that enabled product integration and testing had to be negotiated separately.

Requirements in Theory. The Release Matrix is most applicable when an incremental release strategy is adopted in an already existing PLA. New product requirements can necessitate the modification of existing components, with significant new features having the potential to force the development of entirely new components that extend the architecture. Further, component teams can have their own technical, nonproduct requirements that also have to compete for development time and resources [10].

In the Release Matrix, each product release is represented by a row with each cell capturing the set of requirements that the product places on the component represented in that column. These sets are the accumulation of the product features to be included in the release, each of which can, in general, have allocated requirements that impact more than one component. This situation is illustrated in Figure 3 and can be seen to represent the requirements allocation and traceability that is at the core of requirements engineering.

Features	Priority	Comp. 1	Comp. 2	Comp. 3	Comp. 4
P 1 Product 1 feature set	2	r_{11}	r_{12}		r_{14}
P 2 Product 2 feature set	1		r_{22}	r_{23}	r_{24}
P 3 Product 3 feature set	1			r_{33}	r_{34}

Fig. 3. Requirements allocation and traceability in the Release Matrix

Where each product row is expanded to describe each feature and its allocated requirements explicitly, the Release Matrix can be seen to be no more than a list of individual requirements. The requirements in each cell are related to the "contract" between the user (consumer) and supplier (producer) of the component. In a product line ecosystem, however, there are multiple, potentially competing contracts between a component supplier and its different users that have to be negotiated and consolidated so as to be consistent - in an analogous fashion to the merging of different versions of a source file that has been subjected to parallel changes. While it currently lacks the formalism of research into reuse [20] and requirements [21] contracts, the matrix representation does provide the means to array the multiple, related contracts necessary for the development of product lines. The representation can also be made compatible with the separate management techniques for product line requirements proposed in the literature [22, 23] by explicitly identifying the common and variant requirements.

Requirements in Practice. Two product feature sets were studied in detail and the specific requirements allocated to the components affected. The original specification documentation was dissected and reorganized so that the common requirements that impacted all components were separated from those that had unique demands of some of the components. Even relatively simple product features were found to impact different components and required all to be implemented before the feature's benefit could be realized. While the focus of the trial project was on these new requirements, the component teams had additional requirements they had to address in the same release cycle. A simple spreadsheet was used to implement the Release Matrix, and the expanded rows containing the individual features were listed in colored product bands to identify their source. While space was limited, it was possible to summarize the key points in each cell and use hyperlinks to point to related information as required.

	Features	Priority	Comp. 1	Comp. 2	Comp. 3	Comp. 4
P 1	Product 1 feature set	2	r_{11}	r_{12}		r_{14}
P 2	Product 2 feature set	1		r_{22}	r_{23}	r_{24}
P 3	Product 3 feature set	1			r_{33}	r_{34}

Fig. 4. Cross-product release planning conducted by each component team

The Release Matrix was shown to provide clarity to the different requirements previously embedded in a number of specifications documents. This showed its potential as a communications device, especially during periods of intense negotiation when a definitive and agreed-upon set of releases was being planned. It was also observed that the Release Matrix provided value as a notation even where there was no reuse—and hence no need to negotiate the features across products. The simple grid layout (also used in Sutherland's work [22]) allowed for improved planning at the more granular level where different features within one product had to be assigned to a scheduled incremental release. The only real difference between this more detailed scenario and that of the product line release planning is the number of organizational stakeholders involved. There are still stakeholders to be satisfied in the traditional, incremental release-planning scenarios [24], but they are less visible at the enterprise level.

4.2 Release Planning

Concurrent demands placed by the separate products on the limited development resources of the component teams represent a major planning challenge in product lines. While this situation is not unusual in software projects that have to juggle and prioritize requirements from different users that have competing needs, product boundaries and priorities have to be negotiated in product lines (Figure 4). Each product can act under the illusion that its evolution can be planned separately when in fact the different demands all impact the core, reusable components and result in virtual dependencies between the product schedules. This is shown in the simple product line planning scenario described by Taborda [12].

Planning in Theory. The Release Matrix has been described not as a single matrix but as a template that allows the capture of diverse development information in what is more accurately a family of related matrices [12]. It can be considered as comprising of layers, each holding different life-cycle information appropriate to the stage of

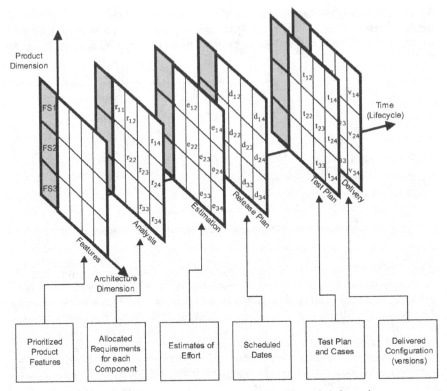

Product
Dimension

FS1

FS2

FS3

Time
(Lifecycle)

Features

Architecture
Dimension

Analysis

Estimation

Release Plan

Test Plan

Delivery

Prioritized Product Features	Allocated Requirements for each Component	Estimates of Effort	Scheduled Dates	Test Plan and Cases	Delivered Configuration (versions)

Fig. 5. Layers of the Release Matrix containing life-cycle information

the development (Figure 5). When scoping a release, the cells can capture the separate estimates made by the affected component teams for each product's prioritized feature, ultimately followed by a record of the agreed-upon schedule dates or build cycles.

As detailed planning commences, each product team should have a prioritized list of features proposed for the release. In product lines, this prioritization is not just within one product as in traditional development projects [25]; rather, the common domain architecture necessitates that prioritization be done across all products. Cross-product requirement dependencies must be added to those evident in single-product development [10], complicating the planning activities. Release planning therefore takes place in both dimensions of the Release Matrix, with products prioritizing their features and components having to estimate and plan the implementation effort needed for the allocated requirements.

Complications arise because product features often require a number of component modifications to be completed to achieve the desired capability, and partial implementation is not practicable. Whether the organization works to a fixed release cycle or derives its schedule based on the agreed-upon features in a release determines whether the feature's availability is pushed out to the latest component team's implementation date or, potentially, dropped from the release. In either case, separate rounds of planning and negotiation may have to take place before all component teams can agree to the contents of the release.

A set of commitments eventually results from the product line's stakeholders and can be captured in the Release Matrix. For each feature, the negotiated commitment is represented by a "tick-in-the-box" for each affected component team, so each feature row in the expanded matrix has the relevant component team's committed schedule. Thus, the Release Matrix can be seen to provide a consolidated view of the multiple, individual component contracts [20, 21] that have to be negotiated in a product line environment.

Planning in Practice. If planning a release for a single product is hard, the effort and communication necessary to achieve an agreed-upon schedule for a PLA introduce another dimension of complexity. While the multiplicity of stakeholder views is traditionally funneled through an "analyst," in the case of the trial project's cross-product setting, each product's feature set had to be negotiated directly with the product representatives.

While the trial was separate from the mainstream planning process undertaken by the organization, it was evident that the number of stakeholders directly involved in the planning was significant, and the communications necessary to reach an agreed-upon plan were considerable. The organization worked to fixed date releases and had already aligned the release of each component and product team to allow a single, synchronized release for the entire product line. Planning was required not simply for the final release but also for a number of interim releases necessary to integrate and test specific feature sets before final delivery.

Since the release planning was across multiple products, the adopted strategy was to review the prioritized feature lists and whittle them down to meet its published ship-date. Therefore, the negotiations between the different stakeholders were intense with each component team effectively having a "right of veto" in deciding on the feasibility of a product feature. Unless a feature can be implemented separately in each component (and so be released incrementally over multiple release cycles, which introduces further planning complexity even where technically feasible), a component team being unable to commit to implementing its allocated requirement in the release cycle ran the risk of the feature being dropped. Given that such a scenario was not the product manager's desired outcome and so was unpalatable, hard decisions regarding the elimination of features were difficult to make. There was some evidence that it was easier to appear to agree to include features, letting them be either de-scoped or dropped by attrition later in the release cycle. What was evident and frustrating to the product team was that a definite schedule for the availability of component capabilities was difficult to pin down, making integration and testing of the product problematic.

In interviews, it was evident that the need for a prerelease product review milestone drove the need for some certainty, and thus led to the usage of a table that resembles the Release Matrix. In this table, each capability to be demonstrated was represented in a row, and the development managers responsible for each component had to supply the date by which their (allocated) requirement would be met. When all component teams implementing part of the capability had committed to a date, that feature was then tracked from delivery to integration, test, and finally demonstration.

The result of the preliminary trials of the Release Matrix has shown its potential to be used as a holistic planning tool that allows better visualization of the planning process and the completeness and stability of the product line's release commitments and schedules. It offers a means to improve team communications and support decision making in the early planning stages and in the maintenance and tracking of the plan, as was used to manage the product review milestone.

4.3 Shared Architecture

As previously stated, the components recorded in the columns of the Release Matrix were a part of a pre-existing architecture. Similar to the product dimension, these can be broken down from a subsystem into the lower level components impacted by the different features. Thus, the Release Matrix presents the enterprise or marketplace architecture comprising the entire inventory of software (and potentially other) assets that comprise the product line.

Architecture in Theory. The columns of the Release Matrix represent the high-level, architectural "clumps" that relate directly to the configuration items of classical, systems configuration management. It should be noted that this represents the architectural view from a management perspective that traditionally breaks down a system (or product) into lower level components. While object-oriented (OO) thinking has overtaken structured, top-down, functional methods in design and development, the need to divide a program's scope into manageable "clumps" remains valid in a management context. Therefore, even where the architecture may be achieved through different means, it is argued that from a management and organizational context, it can be viewed as decomposable, at least at the higher levels of abstraction.

When the Release Matrix was first introduced [12], there was a brief discussion of the composition of the columns. A PLA comprises of both product-specific components and shared domain components. While the use-reuse relationships gave rise to the Marketplace Pattern that resulted in the Release Matrix, configuration management considerations led to the inclusion of both shared and product-specific components in the columns of the matrix. This also had the benefit of avoiding semantic discussions about what constituted domain components and avoided the separate treatment of reused components that are not part of the domain.

Discussion of the Release Matrix as applied to product lines is not complete without a clarification of its relationship to variation management. Kruger clearly articulates the configuration management challenges faced in product line development [26] and introduces variation management as a new dimension to traditional CM. The role of the Release Matrix in managing variation points has not currently been explored with the discussions and trials to date treating product variability as a design challenge, rather than a management one. The influence of CM thinking is evident in the management focus taken here at the expense of design variability. CM has traditionally viewed its role as independent from the details of the configuration itself [27] that supports the view that variability be considered a design problem rather than a CM problem [28].

Architecture in Practice. The first realization in applying the Release Matrix was that real-world architectures are not the idealized structures of textbooks and that their evolution over time can lead to component structures that are highly intertwined. The organization conducting the trials had an emerging product line that meant that many reuse opportunities were still to be realized, and component relationships were complex and still evolving.

In applying the Release Matrix, identifying the columns at the subsystem level was not difficult but proved insufficient to actually describe the feature impacts. Drilling deeper meant descending into an increasingly complex architecture where the dependencies between products and components far exceeded the idealized, many-to-many relationship of the Marketplace Pattern. There were ambiguities over what a component was and what a product was, since some relatively low-level components were marketed separately. Subsystems, when decomposed into their components, were shown to have lower level components in common. There were familiar pathological dependencies identified in the detail [10] where a component would bundle lower level modules, yet the products that used the component also directly used the capabilities of some of the modules. Therefore, the idealized image of a decomposable architecture captured by the columns of the Release Matrix, while potentially a useful goal, did not exist in reality. Indeed, the marketplace pattern was evident at different levels in the architecture, as reuse was evident at different levels of granularity.

Therefore, the trials took on a more pragmatic approach that attempted to apply the Release Matrix to the components that were actually "in play" when considering different feature sets. Allocated requirements were often more appropriately discussed at a lower level of detail; thus, the low-grained components were replaced with only those lower level components that were affected This proved to be valuable in that it eliminated components that were not impacted by the features from the view and focused discussion at a level at which the participants were comfortable.

Using a spreadsheet to capture the Release Matrix necessitated the creation of separate spreadsheets dependent on the feature set and the affected components—a limitation that could be overcome easily with a more sophisticated tool that supported the Release Matrix concept. The ultimate goal in such a tool would be to undertake the analysis at the detailed level, which the tool could then consolidate with other requirements placed on the components.[1] In this manner, the complete scope demanded of each architectural component could be viewed and assessed in the planning stage.

4.4 Organizational Considerations and Impacts

The manner in which the development organization is structured influences the packaging and delivery of the software capabilities. Different organizational structures—whether a small in-house team, a remote or off-shore development group, or a third-party contractor or vendor—result in the bundling of the capabilities within their scope into releases. The organization of the development should follow the architectural boundaries, but this may not necessarily be the case. The organizational struc-

---

[1] Technology support for the matrices described in this paper is the subject of a patent application to protect the commercialization of these concepts.

ture, therefore, serves to increase the number of separate deliverables that have to be integrated together to provide the end product.

Organizations in Theory. The headings in the twin dimensions of the Release Matrix identify the significant stakeholders involved in the product line. The row headings identify the products that aim to satisfy the market segment that their product services. The column headings have been identified above as the configuration items that relate to the high-level PLA. While each item is an architectural component or subsystem, its selection is rooted deeply in the organization structure to be used. The only requirement to use the Release Matrix, however, is that each of these components is developed and released separately [10].

The selection of the configuration items has long been a contentious and vague process in CM. Today, where incremental and iterative development methods are the reigning paradigm, the decision to manage (or control in a CM sense) a component separately entails effort to bundle, build, test, and deliver capabilities in a series of evolutionary releases. If the Release Matrix technique were to assume the full weight of CM best practices, it too would become enmeshed in the debate of what was the perfect organizational structure to manage a particular program or architecture—a topic that warrants further research in its own right.

To be effective in different environments, the Release Matrix technique is, therefore, positioned as a capture of organizational decisions already made and in practice. If its application throws some new light on the effectiveness of these decisions, its purpose has been served. Any improvements that result from a review of the development organization or release strategy can then be captured in a subsequent release (matrix).

Organizations in Practice. The trial program involved a multisite organization with geographically separated development groups based around the key subsystem components. Product managers represented each product group, while each component team had a development lead. When project and test managers are included along with domain experts and developers, the organization that formed around any initiative grew quite large. Therefore, when cross-product domain components were affected, the number of affected stakeholders involved in relatively simple product line enhancements could quickly become difficult to manage. Getting a firm commitment from these cross-product, cross-functional groups was not easy, and, as previously described, communications consumed a lot of time.

While the alignment between organizational structure and architecture was shown to be good at the higher level, the correspondence grew murky in the detail. It was clear that the organizational units largely influenced the determination and scope of release packages. Irrespective of the architecture demarcations, it was the team that had to overcome any problematic design dependencies through careful implementation and management attention.

The Release Matrix can naturally be related to the matrix organizational structure, and, by considering just the stakeholders who represented products and components, a virtual matrix organization was clear and echoed the decision-making forums that had emerged. What also became clear during the trial was the relative instability of the ecosystem that the Release Matrix represented. The only force binding the Release Matrix together and preventing its breakup into independent development streams was the decision by top executives to deliver on the new product. At lower levels in the organization, there were numerous tensions arising from competing priorities and incentive mismatch [29], which, if left unchecked, could present a risk to the program. Failure to balance the different needs of the stakeholders would result in a reversion to the individual product strategy and loss of the benefits of systematic reuse.

5 Conclusion

This paper has elaborated on the application of the Release Matrix that has been proposed as a technique for the planning and tracking of software product lines. Trials of the technique in a new development program that added a new product variant to an existing product line are discussed.

The marketplace pattern was found to be clearly evident at multiple levels within the architecture, and a Release Matrix was created for the two key feature sets that were studied. The concurrent requirements placed on the different component teams were represented in a concise and clear format so that their work scope could be more easily estimated and negotiated. Although the Release Matrix was not used for the actual planning of the trial program, a similar construct was independently used to drive the commitment for, and track the delivery of, a product review milestone. The complex and interdependent architecture was shown to require the "micro-application" of the technique, which, with the assistance of suitable tools, still offers the opportunity to establish the scope of work and roll up the results into a consolidated Release Matrix.

The results of the trial showed the potential of the Release Matrix as a catalyst for focusing attention on organizational and architectural anomalies. The experience gained, therefore, has resulted in both an opportunity to refine the technique to suit the imperfections of real-world product line development and to show the trial-project team opportunities for process improvement. In particular, the concepts embodied in the Release Matrix are being used to focus the multisite, cross-functional, and cross-product communications and provide improved support for decision making.

The trial helped to flesh out the initial descriptions of the technique, which were high level and lacking detail. In particular, the role of the Release Matrix as a template to be used to populate different life-cycle information was clarified. Arguably, the singular "matrix" is confusing as there are multiple facets to a release. In the incremental release strategies popular today, a release is not simply an event, but encompasses the life cycle of an iteration including the gathering of requirements, estimation of effort, negotiating and planning, and finally capturing and tracking the agreed-upon schedule. Therefore, the Release Matrix attempts to consolidate this critical development information and presents it as different views of the release's status.

Further research is being undertaken on both the application and refinement of the Release Matrix technique. Case studies and trials are proposed in organizations working with component-based or product lines that exemplify software reuse. The marketplace pattern that motivates the Release Matrix is evident in many other environments, and its wider application in IS and other complex environments remains to be explored. As a context and methodology-neutral technique, the Release Matrix should be further investigated as a generic management method that is appropriate in any environment characterized by concurrent demands being placed on limited, shared resources.

References

1. Szyperski, C.: Component Software, Beyond Object-Oriented Programming, Addison-Wesley. ISBN 0201178885 (1997)
2. A Framework for Software Product Line Practice, Version 4.1, Software Engineering Institute, A Framework for Software Product Line Practice, Version 4.1, Software Engineering Institute, http://www.sei.cmu.edu/plp/framework.html
3. Toft, P., Coleman, D., Ohta, J.: A Cooperative Model for Cross-Divisional Product Development for a Software Product-line. Proceedings of the 1st Software Product Line Conference (2000)
4. Bosch, J.: Software Product-Lines: Organizational Alternatives. Proceedings of the 23rd International Conference on Software Engineering (2001)
5. William D. Burg, et. al. Exploring a Comprehensive CBD Method: Use of CBD/e in Practice, Proceedings of the 3rd International Workshop on Component-Based Software Engineering: Reflection on Practice.
6. Bayer, J., Flege, O., Knauber, P. et. al.: PuLSE: A Methodology to Develop Software Product-lines. Proceedings of the Symposium on Software Reusability (1999)
7. Technology Dimensions of Product-line Implementation Approaches, Fraunhofer Institute, IESE-Report No. 051.02/E, September (2002)
8. van Ommering, R.: Configuration Management in Component-Based Product Populations. Proceedings of the 10th International Workshop on Software Configuration Management (SCM-10), Toronto, Canada (2001)
9. Bosch, J.: Product-Line Architectures in Industry: A Case Study. Proceeding of the Twenty-first International Conference on Software Engineering (1999)
10. Crnkovic, I. and Larsson, M.: Challenges of Component-Based Development. Journal of Systems and Software, Vol. 61, No. 3 (2002)
11. Crnkovic, I. and Larsson, M.: A Case Study: Demands on Component-Based Development. Proceeding of the International Conference on Software Engineering, ICSE (2000)
12. Taborda, L. J.: Planning and Managing Product Line Evolution. Proceedings of Fifth Product Family Engineering (PFE-5), LNCS. Siena, Italy (2003)
13. Taborda, L. J.: The Release Matrix for Component-Based Software Architectures, Macquarie Graduate School of Management Working Paper 2004-3 (2004)
14. Fitzgerald, B.: Formalised Systems Development Methodologies: A Critical Perspective, The Information Systems Journal, Vol. 6, No. 1, pp. 3-23 (1996)
15. Fitzgerald, B.: Systems Development Methodologies: The Problem of Tenses, Information Technology & People, Vol. 13, No. 3, pp. 13-22 (2000)
16. Agile Manifesto: http://www.agilemanifesto.org (2001)
17. Highsmith, J.: Agile Software Development Ecosystems, Addison-Wesley. ISBN 0201760436 (2002)
18. van Ommering, R.: Roadmapping a Product Population Architecture. Proceedings of Fourth Product Family Engineering (PFE-4), LNCS. Bilboa, Spain (2001)
19. Sowrirajan, S. and van der Hoek, A.: Managing the Evolution of Distributed and Interrelated Components. Proceedings of the Eleventh International Workshop on Software Configuration Management, Portland, Oregon (2003)
20. Steyaert, P., Lucas, C., Mens, L.: Reuse Contracts: Making Systematic Reuse a Standard Practice. Proceedings of the Object-Oriented Programming Systems, Languages and Applications (1996)

21. Andreas Rausch, Software Evolution in Componentware using Requirements/Assurances Contracts. International Conference on Software Engineering (2000)
22. Sutherland, M.: Product Line Requirements Management, Proceedings of the Twelfth Annual International Symposium of the International Council on Systems Engineering (2002)
23. Faulk, S.R.: Product-Line Requirements Specification (PRS): An Approach and Case Study. Fifth IEEE International Symposium on Requirements Engineering (2001)
24. Pär Carlshamre, Björn Regnell, Requirements Lifecycle Management and Release Planning in Market-Driven Requirements Engineering Processes,
25. Karlsson J, Software Requirements Prioritizing, Proc. 2nd International Conference on Requirements Engineering, IEEE CS Press, April 1996.
26. Krueger, C.: Variation Management for Software Production Lines. Proceedings of the 2nd International Software Product-Line Conference (2002)
27. Estublier, J. (2000). Software Configuration Management: A Roadmap. International Conference of Software Engineering.
28. Zeller, A., Fruhaul, K.: Software Configuration Management: State of the Art, State of the Practice. Dagstuhl Seminar (1999)
29. Fichman, R.G., Kemerer, C. F.: Incentive Compatibility and Systematic Software Reuse. Journal of Systems and Software, Vol. 57, No. 1 (2001)

A Methodology for the Derivation and Verification of Use Cases for Product Lines

A. Fantechi[1], S. Gnesi[2], G. Lami[2], and E. Nesti[1]

[1] Dipartimento di Sistemi e Informatica, Università di Firenze - (Italy)
[2] Istituto di Scienze e Tecnologie dell'Informazione "A.Faedo", C.N.R. – Pisa (Italy)

Abstract. In this paper, we present a methodology to express, in a formal way, the requirements of products belonging to a product line. We relied on a formalism allowing the representation of variabilities at the family level and the instantiation of them in order to move to the requirements of a single product. The proposed methodology also allows the formalization of the family constraints to be taken into account for the construction of the products belonging to it, along with the verification of the compliance to those constraints of a single product requirements document. This approach is promising due to its simplicity and effectiveness for being supported by automatic tools.

1 Introduction

Product lines and use cases are two important and well-established paradigms of modern industrial development [2, 8, 10]. In this introduction, we briefly describe them, underlining the reasons why they are becoming so popular.

The need for quality, easy reuse, and the minimization of development costs and times of new products leads to the adoption of the product line (also known as product family) approach. A product line can be seen as a set of products with common characteristics that link them together. While developing a product line, it is possible to move from the family level (which represents those common features) to the product level (which represents the single product, with all its particular characteristics) by an instantiation process and conversely from the product level to the family level by an abstraction process. Figure 1 shows the Process Reference Model (PRM) defined in the CAFE project [10], which well represents the classical product line development approach.

One of the main reasons to use a product line approach is reuse, which extends far beyond mere code reuse. Each single product can be developed following the analysis, design, coding, planning, and testing efforts already done for previous products of the same product line. However, the advantages of reuse come at some cost:

- The architecture of the product line provides a template for every single product of the family that will be developed. This means that investing a good amount of energy designing a solid yet flexible architecture will lead to a simpler and less error-prone development of the company's products. However, this also means that the architecture needs to be open to deal with issues such as variabilities [7] which determine additional constraints, costs, and efforts.

R.L. Nord (Ed.): SPLC 2004, LNCS 3154, pp. 255–265, 2004.

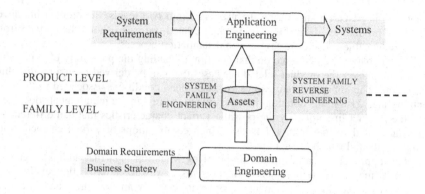

Fig. 1. The CAFÉ-PRM reference framework

- Tools and processes are needed to help manage variation and make changes to the products. Such tools and processes must be more solid than those used for single products; thus, they are more expensive and complex. However, the tools can be used for every product of the family, and the initial complexity later favours an easy development and reuse.
- Common software components can and must be developed with a higher level of quality, because they are used in every single product. This implies a reduction in the development costs and time for many products, but it also means that common components must be robust and applicable across a wide range of product contexts, thus raising their complexity and development costs.
- Workers play a role in many products at a time instead of just one. This enhances personnel mobility among different projects and raises productivity. However, to reach these advantages, training is needed, which implies initial additional costs.

Due to the initial costs of adopting a product line approach, some companies have been reluctant to do so. However, it was widely documented how the advantages of using product lines largely overcome the disadvantages and the initial effort needed to change the organization of the work inside a company. Also, a reactive, more relaxed product line approach can be used for those companies that cannot afford the risks and costs of a more proactive approach.

Use cases [3] are an easy, natural way to express the functional requirements of a system. The popularity of use cases derives from the simplicity of their approach: a well-structured, easy-to-understand document written in controlled natural language.

Use cases are widely used in modern industrial development, so it seems natural to try to find an effective way to combine them with the product line paradigm. While use cases are already used in this context, the real challenge is to be able to semi-automatize them to instantiate single product use cases from more general ones.

In previous works, we proposed the notation of product line use cases (PLUCs) [1, 6], a version of the notation of Cockburn's use cases [4] aimed at express requirements of product lines. Cockburn's use cases allow the functional requirements of a system to be described by imposing a specific structure on requirements documents. That structure separates the various cases in which the system can be used by external actors and, for each case, defines scenarios of correct and incorrect usage. The PLUC notation is based on structuring the use cases into two levels: the product line level and the product level. In this way, product-related use cases should be derived from the product-line-related use cases by an instantiation process.

In this paper, we elaborate on that notation by adding the possibility of expressing constraints over the product-related use cases that can be derived from a product line use case. The constraints are expressed as Boolean conditions associated to the variability tags. Using this notation, it is possible to express in the requirements document of the product line not only the possible variant characteristics that can differentiate products of the same family, but also which combinations of variant characteristics are "legal" and which are not.

Our approach is based on the proposal by Mannion [11] that addresses general product line model requirements. He presents a way to describe the relationships between product line requirements in order to formally analyze them and to extract information about the internal consistency of the requirements (i.e., they provide a valid template for at least one single product) and of the single products derived from the product line model (i.e., they satisfy all the constraints of the product line requirements).

We adopt a similar approach and apply it to the PLUCs by transforming the described relationships between product line requirements into relationships between PLUC tags and between different PLUCs. In addition, we extend the set of basic relationships with some composed new ones.

The information we add to the PLUCs provides on one hand the ability of automatically checking whether a product-related use case is conformant to the family requirements; on the other hand, the adoption of constraint-solving techniques may even allow for automatic generation of product-specific use cases from the family-level use cases document.

2   PLUC Notation

Use cases are a way to express the functional requirements of a system. A use case defines a goal-oriented set of interactions between external actors and the system under consideration. Actors are parties outside the system that interact with the system. An actor may be a class of users, roles users can play, or other systems. There are two kinds of actors: primary and secondary:

- A primary actor is one having a goal requiring the assistance of the system.
- A secondary actor is one from which the system needs assistance.

A use case is initiated by a primary actor to achieve a goal and completes successfully when that goal is satisfied. It describes the sequence of interactions between actors and the system necessary to accomplish the task that will lead to the goal. It also includes possible alternative sequences that can arise due to errors, alternative paths, and so forth. The system is often treated as a black box.

In [1] we extended the classical use case definition given by Cockburn [4] to product lines, adding variability to this formalism. The results are PLUCs, which are essentially use cases that allow variability through the use of special *tags* to derive single product use cases (PUCs).

In PLUCs, variations are implicitly enclosed into the components of the use cases. The variations are then represented by tags that indicate those parts of the product line requirements that need to be instantiated for a specific product in a product-related document.

Product line requirements can be considered, in general, as composed of a constant part and a variable part [1, 9]. The constant part includes all those requirements dealing with features or functions common to all the products in the product line and, for this reason, do not need to be modified. The variable part represents those aspects that can be changed to differentiate one product from another. A possible extension of use cases to express variability during the requirements engineering of product lines is based on structuring the use cases into two levels: the product line level and the product level. In this way, use cases for a specific product are derived from the generic use cases by an instantiation process.

For the generic use cases, the variations are represented by tags that indicate those parts of the product line requirements that need to be instantiated for a specific product in a product-specific document. Tags for doing that are included in the use case scenarios (both main scenario and extensions) to identify and specify variations. There are three types of tags:

1. alternative: Alternative tags express the possibility to instantiate the requirement by selecting an instance from a predefined set of possible choices, each of them depending on the occurrence of a condition.
2. parametric: The instantiation of parametric tags is connected to the actual value of a parameter in the requirements for the specific product.
3. optional: The instantiation of optional tags can be done by selecting indifferently from a set of values that are optional features for a derived product.

The instantiation of these types of variabilities will lead to a set of different product-related use cases.

This extension of the use cases representation is called PLUC, and two examples of it are provided in Figure 2 and Figure 3.The example in Figure 2 describes how the function of answering an incoming call is carried out at the family level, while the example in Figure 3 describes the behaviour of the phones belonging to the family when a game is played by the user. In both examples, the variation points are represented by means of tags according to the PLUC formalism.

A PLUC describes the general behaviour that all family members (PUCs) should have during the accomplishment of a specific task. The PLUC acts like a template from which it is possible to derive single PUCs by the instantiation process of its tags. There are many types of tags, as we will detail in Section 3.

3 PUC Derivation from a PLUC

In this section, we describe our approach to formalizing variabilities for specifying the PLUC and a way to effectively verify the compliance of a PUC to the family constraints.

USE CASE: CallAnswer
Goal: Answer an incoming call on a **[V0]** Mobile Phone
Scope: The **[V0]** Mobile Phone
Precondition: Signal is available;Mobile Phone is switched on
Trigger: Incoming call
Primary actor : The user
Secondary actors: The { **[V0]** Mobile Phone} (the system)
                                        The Mobile Phone Company

Main success scenario
1. The user accepts the call by pressing the Accept button
2. The system establishes the connection by following the {
    [V1] appropriate } procedure.
Extensions
1a. The call is not accepted:
    1a.1. the user presses the Reject button
    1a.2. scenario terminates

PL Variability Features
V0: Alternative:
        0. Model 0
        1. Model 1
        2. Model 2

V1: Parametric:
case (V0) of
0: Procedure A:
    2.1 Connect Caller and callee
1 or 2: if **V5**= a then Procedure B:
            2.1 Interrupt the game
            2.2 Connect Caller and callee
else if **V5**= b then Procedure C:
            2.1 Save current game status
            2.2 Interrupt the game
            2.3 Connect Caller and callee

    V5 Alternative:
        a. games available, but if interrupted status is not
           saved
        b. games available, and if interrupted status is saved

---

Fig. 2. An example of a PLUC

3.1 Specification of the PLUC

The specification of the tags into the PLUC is a critical step for making the PLUC approach effective in practice. The definition of a method to formalize the three kinds of tags described in Section 2 (alternative, optional, and parametric) is a necessary preliminary step for the verification of the compliance of a PUC to the family constraints. In fact, the constraints that characterize the products belonging to a family

USE CASE: Play a Game
Goal: Play a game on a **[V0]** Mobile Phone and record score
Scope: The **[V0]** Mobile Phone
Precondition: the function GAME has been selected from the
main menu
Primary actor : The user, the **[V0]** Mobile Phone (the system)
Secondary actors: The { **[V0]** Mobile Phone}
Main success scenario
1. The system displays the list of the available games:
   Snakell, Space Impact, Bantumi, Pairs II and {**[V1]** additional
2.   The user selects a game
3.   The system displays the logo of the selected game
4.   The user selects the difficulty level by following the
   {**[V3]** appropriate} procedure and press YES
5.   The system starts the game and plys it until it goes over
6.   The user records the score achieved and {**[V4]** possibly}
   sends the score to Game Club via WAP
7.   The system displays the list of the {**[V2]** available}
   games
8.   The user presses NO

PL Variability Features
V0: Alternative:
        0. Model 0
        1. Model 1
        2. Model 2 ·

V1: Parametric:
case (V0) of
0: Procedure A:
   2.1 Connect Caller and callee
1 or 2: if V5= a then Procedure B:
              2.1 Interrupt the game
              2.2 Connect Caller and callee
else if V5= b then Procedure C:
              2.1 Save current game status
              2.2 Interrupt the game
              2.3 Connect Caller and callee

V2 - Optional:
      if (V0 == 1) then 'Bumper'

V3 - Parametric:
      if (V0 == 1 || V0 == 0) then Procedure D:
              4.1 press Select
              4.2 scroll to Settings and press YES
              4.3 scroll to Difficulty Level and press YES
              4.4 select the desired difficulty level, press YES

```
if (V0 == 2) then Procedure E:
            4.1 press Select
            4.2 scroll to Level and press YES
            4.3 select the desired difficulty level, press YES

V4 - Parametric:
       if (V0 == 0 || V0 == 1) then 'function available'
       else if ( v0 == 2) then 'function not available'

V5 - Alternative:
       c. games available, but if interrupted status is not
          saved
       b. games available, and if interrupted status is saved
```

Fig. 3. Another example of a PLUC

can be expressed in terms of the relations among the different tags indicating the variation points in a PLUC.

To express the variability tags of the PLUCs in a formal way, we have to take into account all the possible situations that can arise during the writing of a PLUC, paying particular attention to the variable tags of the PLUC itself.

First of all, we have to define the formalism to be used for expressing those relationships. Propositional calculus is a simple and effective way to describe them at high level, so we will use propositional connectives between PLUC components. According to this formalism, the basic symbols used in the following formulas are '||' (the logical OR operator), '&&' (the logical AND operator), '==' (the 'equal to' logical operator), and '~' (the logical NOT operator). The operands of the expressions representing the different tags included in a PLUC are the variabilities to be instantiated when moving to a PUC.

A formalism to describe the essential set of tags is described below. For each type of tag, a logical expression able to capture its meaning is described:

- The *alternative tag* indicates mutual exclusion, which means that, during the instantiation process, one and only one value from a set of values can be assigned to the tag. This type of relationship can be expressed with a logical **Exclusive or**.

- The *optional tag* represents a subset of a PLUC steps that can or cannot be present in an instantiated PUC, depending on the value of some other instantiated tag. (That is, if a mobile phone type contains game C, the PUC called "starting a game" will have a step "print GAME C on screen." Otherwise, this step will not be present in the PUC). The correct propositional connective to be used for this type of relationship is **Bi-conditional:**

  ```
  a bi-cond b iff
  [(a==true)&&(b==true)] || [(a==false)&& (b==false)].
  ```

- The *parametric tag* indicates that some subsets of PLUC steps can be chosen in such a way that at least one of them will be chosen to be inserted in a specific PUC. However, more than one can be chosen (i.e., there can be more than one way to start a game in a mobile phone interface, and at least one must be present). This relationship is modelled with a logical **or**.

The two examples of PLUCs shown in Figure 2 and Figure 3 can be used to show the process to be followed to represent the tags indicating variability in a formal way using the formalism described above. For each variability tag in the two PLUCs, we derive a logical expression:

```
V0_tag (alternative): (V0 == 1 XOR V0 == 2 XOR V0 == 0);
V1_tag (parametric): (V0 == 0 && V1 == "procedure A") ||
((V0 == 1 || V0 == 2) && V5 == a && V1 == "procedure B") ||
((V0 == 1 || V0 == 2) && V5 == b && V1 == "procedure A");
V2_tag (optional): (V2 == bumper && V0 == 2) || (~(V2 ==
bumper) && (V0 == 1 || V0 == 0));
V3_tag (parametric): (V0 == 2 && V3= == "procedure E") ||
((V0 == 0 || V0 == 1) && V3 == "procedure D");
V4_tag (parametric): (V0 == 2 && V4 == "function not avail-
able") || ((V0 == 0 || V0 == 1) && V3 == "function avail-
able"));
V5_tag (alternative): (V5 == a XOR V5 == b)
```

It is possible to define some more complex and structured relationships that can be used to more easily describe some common situations we can find when we read through a PLUC.

As we can have tagged steps that have to be present if another tag has a particular value, we can also have tagged steps that don't have to be present if another tag assumes a particular value. This is simply the opposite of the logical **Bi-conditional**, which we call logical **Excludes**. It is a meant to include logical **not** into our set of logical predicates: given two tagged steps a and b, we can establish the following relationship:

```
a excludes b iff not[a and b] or [(not a) and (not b)]
```

Sometimes, we can choose zero or more steps from a subset of PLUC steps. This situation is modelled by the use of logical **Bi-conditional** and logical **or** at the same time: given a tagged step a and a set of tagged steps $(b\_1, \ldots, b\_n)$, we can establish the following relationship:

```
a excludes (b_1, ... , b_n) iff
[a and b_1] or [(not a) and (not b_1)] or ... or  [a and b_n]
or [(not a) and (not b_n)].
```

It is possible to define other new logical relationships by simply using the basic ones we presented.

The constraints that define the borders and the characteristics of a family and that must drive the specification of a PUC are expressed by means of the formalization of the tags as seen above. These tags may be considered as the way to represent the conditions to be satisfied in order to make a variability solution not contradictory with the family characteristics.

3.2 Derivation and Verification of a PUC

In this section, we discuss the instantiation of the PLUC tags to derive a PUC and the method to be used for the verification of the compliance of the PUC to the family constraints set up in the tag description.

The process of instantiating tags consists of assigning an actual value to each variable appearing in the tag expressions of PLUCs in which we are interested. The instantiation of the tags expressing the variabilities of the family corresponds to the definition of the compulsory characteristics of the PUC we are deriving. In other words, the instantiation of the tags defines the requirements of a particular product belonging to the family.

A possible instantiation of the tags in the two PLUCs in Figures 2 and 3 is

```
V0 = 1
V1 = "procedure A"
V2 = none
V3 = "procedure D"
V4 = "function not available"
V5 = b
```

A PLUC consists in a series of steps in which we can find tags indicating variation points from which we can instantiate different PUCs; the most common relationship is the relation between subsequent steps, such as those which form the main success scenario. Logical **and** can be used to represent this kind of relationship, because every single step must be evaluated true to allow the entire PLUC to be evaluated to `true`.

A PUC is compliant to the family if, evaluating the tag expressions with the instantiation of variables given for that PLUC, all the tags are evaluated to true. The logical operator **and** is sufficient for doing that. Otherwise, the PUC cannot be accepted as belonging to the family: an inconsistent PUC has been identified.

```
if (V0_tag && V1_tag && ... && Vn_tag)
    then 'PUC is compliant'
    else 'PUC is not compliant'
```

From the simple final logical expressions to be used to verify the compliance of a PUC to the family constraints, those components having the value false can be identified, and they are the single points determining the noncompliance. Then, it is simple to identify those instantiations to be modified to achieve the compliance to the family constraints.

In the example, the value of relations expressing the variabilities of the PLUC with the actual values of the variables above are

```
V0_tag: true
V1_tag: true
V2_tag: true
V3_tag: true
V4_tag: false
V5_tag: true
```

The logical expression that we obtain stating from the above values is

```
V0_tag && V1_tag && V2_tag && V3_tag && V4_tag && V5_tag &&
V6_tag
```

It is easy to see that this expression evaluates to false: this means that a PUC with the variabilities solved with the above values does not describe any valid product of the family.

The structure of the tags allows those variability instantiations that determined the noncompliance of the derived PUC with respect to the PLUC to be easily identified. In this case, the lack of compliance is due to the erroneous instantiation of V4.

4 Conclusions and Future Work

In this paper, we presented a methodology to express, in a formal way, the requirements of products belonging to a product line. We relied on a formalism previously defined allowing the representation of variabilities at the family level and the instantiation of them to move to a single product. The instantiation of the tags (that can assume different values from a predefined range) in a PLUC-based requirements document determines the identification of the use-case-based requirements of a particular product (PUCs) belonging to the family with a configuration of the tag values.

Not all the possible instantiations of tags actually represent valid PUC-based requirements, because they do not satisfy given family constraints. The proposed method allows the formalization of these family constraints and the verification of the compliance to those constraints of a PUC-based requirements document.

One of the principal merits of the methodology we described in this paper is the ease of inserting changes in family requirements expressed by means of PLUCs. In fact, if a tag is modified, because of the parametric nature of the approach, the effects of the modification affect only its definition and not its individual occurrences over the PLUCs. Moreover, if some new tags have to be added, the effort of doing so is concentrated mainly on the corresponding formal definition. Once the new tag formula has been defined, the updating of the family requirements simply consists of the inclusion of the tag at the appropriate place in the affected PLUCs.

It is interesting to note how the described methodology can be used for supporting the impact analysis of possible new variabilities on the existing (or planned) products belonging to the family. When a new variable feature is to be added in the product line, it is of interest to evaluate its impact on the whole set of the family products. In particular, for evaluating if the new variability will determine incompatibility with some of the existing or planned products of the family, a preliminary verification can be made adopting the verification procedure shown in Section 3.2.

This approach is promising due to its simplicity and effectiveness for being implemented in an automatic way. In fact, it gives the advantage of an explicit identification of the variability points in a product line requirements document by means of the tags.

This characteristic may strongly facilitate the application of our approach in the industry, because it allows the use of automatic tools for the identification of variabilities. In fact, suitable languages for expressing the different types of tags and products for making the verification automatic exist, and they can be put together for building an environment where the proposed methodology can be implemented. That will be the object of the next steps of our research activity. Indeed, we plan to extend the QuARS tool [5] with the aim of making it able to also cover the analysis of use cases and the automatic guided derivation of PUC belonging to the family.

References

1. A. Bertolino, A. Fantechi, S. Gnesi, G. Lami, A. Maccari, Use Case Description of Requirements for Product Lines, REPL'02, Essen, Germany, September 2002.
2. P. C. Clements and L. Northrop. Software Product Lines: Practices and Patterns. SEI Series in Software Engineering. Addison-Wesley, August 2001.
3. A. Cockburn, Structuring Use Cases with goals, Journal of Object-Oriented Programming, Sep-Oct 1997 (part I) and Nov-Dec 1997 (part II),
4. A. Cockburn. Writing Effective Use Cases. Addison Wesley, 2001.
5. A.Fantechi, S.Gnesi, G.Lami, A.Maccari. Linguistic Techniques for Use Cases Analysis. Proceedings of the IEEE Joint International Requirements Engineering Conference - RE02. Essen, Germany, September 9 -13 2002.
6. A. Fantechi, S. Gnesi, I. John, G. Lami, J.Dörr Elicitation of Use Cases for Product Lines, Fifth International Workshop on Product Family Engineering, PFE-5, Siena 4-6 November, 2003, to appear on LNCS Springer Verlag, 2004.
7. G. Halmans, K. Pohl Communicating the Variability of a Software-Product Family to Customers Journal of Software and Systems Modeling, Springer, 2003
8. M. Jazayeri, A. Ran, F. van der Linden. Software Architecture for Product Families: Principles and Practice, Publishers: Addison-Wesley, Reading, Mass. and London, 1998.
9. I. John, D. Muthig, Tailoring Use Cases for Product Line Modeling, REPL'02, Essen, Germany, September 2002.
10. F. van der Linden Software Product Families in Europe: The ESAPS & Café Projects, IEEE Software July/August 2002.
11. M. Mannion, J. Camara, Theorem Proving for Product Line Model Verification, Fifth International Workshop on Product Family Engineering, PFE-5, Siena 4-6 November, 2003, to appear on LNCS Springer Verlag, 2004.

Staged Configuration Using Feature Models

Krzysztof Czarnecki[1], Simon Helsen[1], and Ulrich Eisenecker[2]

[1] University of Waterloo, Canada
[2] University of Applied Sciences Kaiserslautern, Zweibrücken, Germany

Abstract. Feature modeling is an important approach to capturing commonalities and variabilities in system families and product lines. In this paper, we propose a cardinality-based notation for feature modeling, which integrates a number of existing extensions of previous approaches. We then introduce and motivate the novel concept of staged configuration. Staged configuration can be achieved by the stepwise specialization of feature models. This is important because in a realistic development process, different groups and different people eliminate product variability in different stages. We also indicate how cardinality-based feature models and their specialization can be given a precise formal semantics.

1 Introduction

Feature modeling is a key approach to capturing and managing the common and variable features of systems in a system family or a product line. In the early stages of software family development, feature models provide the basis for scoping the system family by recording and assessing information such as which features are important to enter a new market or remain in an existing market, which features incur a technological risk, what is the projected development cost of each feature, and so forth [1]. Later, feature models play a central role in the development of a system family architecture, which has to realize the variation points specified in the feature models [2,3]. In application engineering, feature models can drive requirements elicitation and analysis. Knowing which features are available in the software family may help customers decide which features their system should support. Knowing which desired features are provided by the system family and which have to be custom-developed helps to better estimate the time and cost needed for developing the system. A software pricing model could also be based on the additional information recorded in a feature model.

Feature models also play a key role in generative software development [4,2,5, 6,7]. Generative software development aims at automating application engineering based on system families: a system is generated from a specification written in one or more textual or graphical domain-specific languages (DSLs). In this context, feature models are used to scope and develop DSLs [2,8], which may range from simple parameter lists or feature hierarchies to more sophisticated DSLs with graph-like structures.

Feature modeling was proposed as part of the Feature-Oriented Domain Analysis (FODA) method [9], and since then, it has been applied in a number of domains including telecom systems [10,11], template libraries [2], network

R.L. Nord (Ed.): SPLC 2004, LNCS 3154, pp. 266–283, 2004.
© Springer-Verlag Berlin Heidelberg 2004

protocols [12], and embedded systems [13]. Based on this growing experience, a number of extensions and variants of the original FODA notation have been proposed [10, 14, 15, 16, 11, 17, 13].

1.1 Contributions and Overview

In this paper, we make the following contributions: we present a cardinality-based notation for feature models, which integrates and adapts four existing extensions to the FODA notation–namely feature cardinalities, group cardinalities, feature diagram references, and attributes. We also propose the novel concept of staged configuration based on specializing feature models and illustrate how specialization can be achieved in a sound way. Finally, we briefly indicate how a cardinality-based feature model can be formalized. The details of this formalization are elaborated elsewhere [18].

The remainder of the paper is organized as follows. Section 2 reviews background concepts and related work on feature modeling. Our cardinality-based notation for feature modeling is presented in Section 3. Staged configuration is described in Section 4. Section 5 gives a glimpse of an approach to formalize feature models. Appendix A gives a comparison of three different notations for feature modeling.

2 Background and Related Work

2.1 Features, Feature Diagrams, and Feature Models

A *feature* is a system property that is relevant to some stakeholder and is used to capture commonalities or discriminate between systems. Features are organized in *feature diagrams*. A feature diagram is a tree with the root representing a concept (e.g., a software system), and its descendent nodes are features. In the FODA feature diagram notation (see the leftmost column of Table 1 in Appendix A), features can be *mandatory, optional,* or *alternative. Feature models* are feature diagrams plus *additional information* such as feature descriptions, binding times, priorities, stakeholders, and so forth.

Feature diagrams offer a simple and intuitive notation to represent variation points in a way that is independent of implementation mechanisms such as inheritance or aggregation. It is important not to confuse feature diagrams with part-of hierarchies or decompositions of software modules. Features may or may not correspond to concrete software modules. In general, we distinguish the following four cases:

- *Concrete* features such as data storage or sorting may be realized as individual components.
- *Aspectual* features such as synchronization or logging may affect a number of components and can be modularized using aspect technologies.
- *Abstract* features such as performance requirements usually map to some configuration of components and/or aspects.

- *Grouping* features may represent a variation point and map to a common interface of plug-compatible components, or they may have a purely organizational purpose with no requirements implied.

2.2 Summary of Existing Extensions

Since its initial introduction in the technical report by Kang and associates [9], several extensions and variants of the original FODA notation have been proposed. In the following summary, we abstract from variations in concrete syntax and focus on the conceptual extensions.

- *feature cardinalities.* Features can be annotated with cardinalities, such as [1..*] or [3..3]. Mandatory and optional features can be considered special cases of features with the cardinalities [1..1] and [0..1], respectively. Feature cardinalities were motivated by a practical application [13] (after they were initially rejected [2]).
- *groups and group cardinalities.* Alternative features in the FODA notation can be viewed as a grouping mechanism. Two further kinds of groups were proposed in Czarnecki's thesis [14]: the inclusive-or group and the inclusive-or group with optional subfeatures (see the middle column of Table 1 in Appendix A).[1] The concept of groups was further generalized in [17] as a set of features annotated with a cardinality specifying an interval of how many features can be selected from that set. The previous kinds of groups become special cases of groups with cardinalities (see the rightmost column of Table 1 in Appendix A).
- *attributes.* Attributes were introduced by Czarnecki and associates [13] as a way to represent a choice of a value from a large or infinite domain such as integers or strings. An elegant way to model attributes proposed by Bednasch [19] is to allow a feature to be associated with a type (such as integer or string). A collection of attributes can be modeled as a number of subfeatures, where each is associated with a desired type.
- *relationships.* Several authors [10, 16, 11] proposed to extend feature models with different kinds of relationships such as *consists-of* or *is-generalization-of*.
- *feature categories and annotations.* FODA distinguishes among context, representation, and operational features. FeatuRSEB [10] proposes functional, architectural, or implementation feature categories. Section 2.1 gives yet another categorization. Additional information on features suggested in FODA include descriptions, constraints, binding time, and rationale. Other examples are priorities, stakeholders, default selections, and exemplar systems [14, 2].

---

[1] Inclusive-or features were introduced independently by Czarnecki [14] and Griss and associates [10]. However, inclusive-or features in Griss and associates' work [10] imply reuse-time binding, whereas inclusive-or features in Czarnecki's work [14] are independent of binding time.

– *modularization*. A feature diagram may contain one or more special leaf
nodes, each standing for a separate feature diagram [19]. This mechanism
allows the breaking up of large diagrams into smaller ones and the reuse of
common parts in several places. This is an important mechanism because,
in practice, feature diagrams can become too large to be considered in their
entirety.

3   Cardinality-Based Feature Modeling

This section proposes a *cardinality-based notation for feature modeling*, which
is based on modest changes to the previously introduced concepts of feature
cardinalities, group cardinalities, and diagram modularization (see Section 2.2).

In particular, a feature cardinality specification may consist of a sequence of
intervals. Furthermore, our notation does not allow features that are members of
a feature group to be qualified with feature cardinalities. This is because a feature
cardinality is a property of the relationship between a single subfeature and its
parent. Similarly, a group cardinality is a property of the relationship between
a parent and a set of subfeatures. Next to cardinalities, we have the notion of
feature diagram references, which allow us to reuse or modularize feature models
in a similar fashion as described by Bednasch [19]. In contrast to Bednasch's
work [19], feature diagram references allow *recursion*, which may be either direct
or indirect. Direct recursion occurs when a feature diagram reference refers to
the feature diagram in which it resides, while indirect recursion involves more
than one diagram.

The chosen set of conceptual extensions and their adaptations are motivated
both by practical applications and the urge to achieve a balance between simplicity and conceptual completeness. Feature cardinalities and attributes are
common in modeling both embedded software [13] and enterprise software (see
our example in Section 3.1). The primary motivation for including group cardinalities is elegance and completeness. Although our experience so far shows that
the vast majority of groups are either exclusive-or or inclusive-or, other group
cardinality values may still be useful in more exotic situations (e.g., [17] and
the example in Section 3.1). Compared to the more profound semantic implications of feature cardinalities, the addition of group cardinalities is semantically
relatively straightforward.

In our notation, we do not consider relationships between features such as
consists-of or *is-generalization-of* because we think that they are better modeled
using other notations such as entity-relationship or class diagrams. In general,
we believe that a feature modeling notation should focus purely on capturing
commonality and variability. However, if necessary, a tool with an extensible
metamodel [19, 20] may allow the user to introduce additional kinds of relationships. Finally, feature categories and other additional information are domain
dependent, and as previously argued by Czarnecki and associates [13], we think
that they are better handled as user-defined, structured annotations. Such annotations are also supported through an extensible metamodel [19].

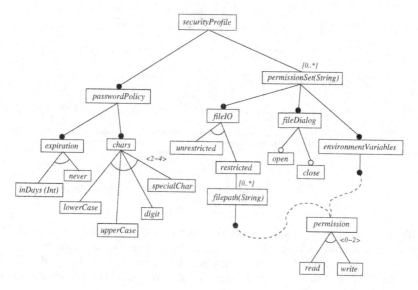

Fig. 1. Security profile example

3.1   A Security Profiling Example

As a practical example to demonstrate the expressiveness of our feature modeling language, consider a feature model of an operating system security profile in Fig. 1.

The password policy of the security profile has an expiration time and possible requirements on the kind of characters to be used. Passwords can be set to never expire, or to expire only after a given number of days. The number of days a password remains valid can be set in the integer attribute of the `inDays` feature. Generally, whenever a feature has an attribute, we indicate its type within parentheses after the feature name; for example, `myFeature (Int)`. It is also possible to specify a value of the associated type immediately with the type; for example, `myFeature (5 : Int)`. The constraints on the kind of characters required in a password are specified by a feature group with cardinality ⟨2–4⟩. This means that any actual password policy must specify between two and four (different) requirements on the kind of characters.

In our example, since no cardinality was specified for the group of `expiration` policies, the cardinality ⟨1–1⟩ is assumed (i.e., the `expiration` policies form an *exclusive-or* group).

The security profile also has zero or more permission sets. This is indicated with the feature cardinality [0..*]. If a feature cardinality is [1..1], we draw a little filled circle above the feature. Observe that features belonging to a group do not have a feature cardinality.

A permission set determines various permissions for executing code. In our simple model, a permission set has a string attribute to specify its name, and

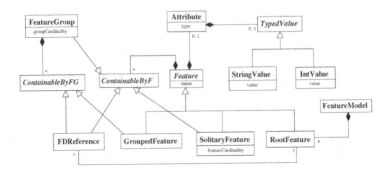

Fig. 2. UML metamodel for cardinality-based feature models

allows us to specify permissions with respect to file IO, file dialogs, and environment variables. (Other examples would be permissions to access a database, invoke reflection, access a Web address, etc.) According to our model, file IO can be restricted to a list of file paths, or it is unrestricted. For each file path, we can specify its name and associated read/write permissions.

Notice that we use a feature diagram reference for the permission model because we want to reuse it for environment variables. In this paper, we use a dashed line to represent a feature diagram reference, but it should be noted that, in practice, a different representation may be necessary to avoid a convoluted diagram. This is especially important if the purpose of the feature diagram reference is to modularize a large feature model over different diagrams.

Finally, the permission to open a file dialog and to close it can be selected independently. The empty circle above the features open and closed indicates that those features are optional (i.e., they have the feature cardinality [0..1]).

3.2   A Metamodel

Now that we have seen an example of a cardinality-based feature model, we explain the available concepts more accurately by means of an abstract syntax model, where we will refer to the example in Fig. 1 for clarification.

Consider the Unified Modeling Language (UML) metamodel for cardinality-based feature models in Fig. 2. A feature model consists of any number of *root features*, which form the root of the different feature diagrams in the model. In the security profile example, both the features securityProfile and permission are root features.

A root feature is only one of three different kind of features. The other two are the *grouped feature* and the *solitary feature*. The former is a feature which can only occur in a *feature group*. For example, the feature never is a grouped feature in a feature group, which is contained by the feature expiration. A solitary feature is a feature which is, by definition, not grouped in a feature group. Many features in a typical feature model are solitary; for example, the feature passwordPolicy and permissionSet.

Features can have an optional attribute of a certain type, and those attributes can have an optional value. In this simplified model, we only have integer and string attributes.

Fig. 2 also has a class named *FDReference* that stands for a feature diagram reference. It can refer to only one root feature, but a root feature can be referred to by several references. In the example, the feature **permission** is referred to by two references.

The abstract classes *ContainableByFG* and *ContainableByF* stand for those kind of objects that can be contained by a feature group and a feature, respectively. A feature group can contain only grouped features or feature diagram references, whereas a feature can contain only solitary features, feature groups, and references.

A solitary subfeature of a feature f is qualified by a *feature cardinality*.[2] It specifies how often the solitary subfeature (and any possible subtree) can be duplicated as a child of f. A feature cardinality I is a sequence of intervals of the form $[n_1..n'_1]\ldots[n_l..n'_l]$, where we assume the following invariants:

$$\forall i \in \{1, \ldots, l-1\} : n_i, n'_i \in \mathbb{N} \quad n_l \in \mathbb{N} \quad n'_l \in \mathbb{N} \cup \{*\}$$
$$\forall n \in \mathbb{N} : n < * \quad 0 \leq n_1$$
$$\forall i \in \{1, \ldots, l\} : n_i \leq n'_i \quad \forall i \in \{1, \ldots, l-1\} : n'_i < n_{i+1}$$

An empty sequence of intervals is denoted by ε.

An example of a valid specification of a feature cardinality is $[0..2][6..6]$, which says that we can take a feature 0, 1, 2, or 6 times. Note that we allow the last interval in a feature cardinality to have as an upper bound the Kleene star $*$. Such an upper bound denotes the possibility of taking a feature an unbounded number of times. For example, the feature cardinality $[1..2][5..*]$ requires that the associated feature is taken 1, 2, 5, or any number greater than 5 times. Semantically, the feature cardinality ε is equivalent to $[0..0]$ and implies that the subfeature can never be chosen in a configuration.

A feature group expresses a choice over the grouped features in the group. This choice is restricted by the *group cardinality* $\langle n-n' \rangle$, which specifies that one has to select at least n and at most n' distinct grouped features in the group. Given that $k > 0$ is the number of grouped features, we assume that the following invariant on group cardinalities holds: $0 \leq n \leq n' \leq k$.

At this point, we ought to mention that, theoretically, we could generalize the notion of group cardinality to be a sequence of intervals as we did for feature cardinalities. However, we have found no practical applications of this usage, and it would only clutter the presentation.

Grouped features do not have feature cardinalities because they are not in the solitary subfeature relationship. This avoids redundant representations for groups and the need for group normalization that was necessary for the notation in Czarnecki's work [14]. For example, in that notation, an inclusive-or group

---

[2] More precisely, a feature cardinality is attached to the solitary subfeature *relationship*. This relationship is implicit in the metamodel.

with both optional and mandatory subfeatures (corresponding to feature cardinalities [0..1] and [1..1] respectively), would be equivalent to an inclusive-or group in which all the subfeatures were optional. Keeping feature cardinalities out of groups also avoids problems during specialization (see Section 4.3). For example, the duplication of a subfeature with a feature cardinality $[n..n']$, where $n' > 1$, within a group could potentially increase its size beyond the upper bound of the group cardinality.

Even without the redundant representations for groups, there is still more than one way to express the same situation in our notation. For example, the following two different diagrams are identical in their semantics.

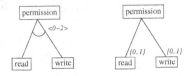

Conceptually, we keep these two diagrams distinct and leave it up to a tool implementer to decide how to deal with them. For instance, it might be useful to provide a conversion function for such diagrams. Alternatively, one could decide on one type of *preferred form* which is shown by default.

In Appendix A, we discuss a comparison of the new cardinality-based notation with the FODA notation and the notation introduced in [2, 17]. For the sake of readability, we will keep using the latter notation whenever an appropriate equivalent exists. However, because the cardinality-based notation has no feature cardinality in groups, we will not use the filled circle on top of grouped features.

4   Staged Configuration

4.1   Motivation

A feature model describes the configuration space of a system family. An application engineer may specify a member of a system family by selecting the desired features from the feature model within the variability constraints defined by the model (e.g., the choice of exactly one feature from a group of alternative features).

The process of specifying a family member may also be performed in stages, where each stage eliminates some configuration choices. We refer to this process as *staged configuration*. Each stage takes a feature model and yields a specialized feature model, where the set of systems described by the specialized model is a *proper* subset of the systems described by the feature model to be specialized.

The need for staged configuration arises in the context of *software supply chains* [7]. Let us take a look at an example based on a real scenario involving the configuration and generation of basic services for electronic control units (ECUs) embedded in an automobile. Basic services such as tasking support, network drivers, network management, flash support, diagnosis, and so forth, are implemented as components by different software vendors. A software vendor may deliver different configurations of its component to different car manufacturers to reflect the differing requirements of the individual manufacturers (such as different terminologies or provided interfaces). Doing so constitutes the first configuration stage. In a second stage, each car manufacturer has to further configure the components for each different ECU in a car, depending on the needs of the control functions (such as break control or engine management) to be installed on the given ECU. The second configuration stage may be even more complex, as some global settings and available options may be determined by the manufacturer, while other settings may be provided by the suppliers of the control functions. Finally, given a concrete configuration, the code implementing the basic services is generated. Based on the outlined requirements, it should be possible to perform configuration in stages and to compose (possibly specialized) feature models.

In general, supply chains require staged configuration of platforms, components, and services. However, staged configuration may be required even within one organization. For example, security policies could be configured in stages for an entire enterprise, its divisions, and the individual computers. The enterprise-level configuration would determine the choices available to the divisions, and the divisions would determine the choices available to the individual computers.

4.2 Configuration Versus Specialization

A *configuration* consists of the features that were selected according to the variability constraints defined by the feature diagram. The relationship between a feature diagram and a configuration is comparable to the one between a class and its instance in object-oriented programming. The process of deriving a configuration from a feature diagram is also referred to as *configuration*. *Specialization* is a transformation process that takes a feature diagram and yields another feature diagram, such that the set of the configurations denoted by the latter diagram is a true subset of the configurations denoted by the former diagram. We also say that the latter diagram is a *specialization* of the former one. A *fully specialized* feature diagram denotes only one configuration. Finally, *staged configuration* is a form of configuration achieved by successive specialization followed by deriving a configuration from the most specialized feature diagram in the specialization sequence.

In general, we can have the following two extremes when performing configuration: a) deriving a configuration from a feature diagram *directly* and b) specializing a feature diagram down to a full specialization and then deriving the configuration (which is trivial). Please note that sometimes we might not be interested in arriving at one specific configuration. For example, a feature diagram that still contains unresolved variability could be used as an input to a generator. This could be useful when generating a specialized version of a framework (which still contains variability) or when generating an application that should support the remaining variability at runtime.

4.3   Specialization Steps

In Section 4.1, we described the process of staged configuration as the removal of possible configuration choices. In this section, we discuss in more detail what kind of configuration choices can be eliminated. We will call the removal of a certain configuration choice a *specialization step*.

There are six categories of specialization steps: a) refining a feature cardinality, b) refining a group cardinality, c) removing a grouped feature from a feature group, d) assigning a value to an attribute which only has been given a type, e) *cloning* a solitary subfeature, and f) unfolding a feature reference. We discuss each of these possibilities in more detail below.

Refining feature cardinalities. A feature cardinality is a sequence of intervals representing a (possibly infinite) set of distinct natural numbers. Each natural number in the cardinality stands for an accepted number of occurrences for the solitary subfeature. Refining a feature cardinality means to eliminate elements from the subset of natural numbers denoted by the cardinality. This can be achieved as follows:

1. remove an interval from the sequence; or
2. if an interval is of the form $[n_i..n_i']$ where $n_i < n_i'$,
   a) reduce the interval by increasing n_i to n_i'' or decrease the n_i' to n_i''' as long as $n_i'' \leq n_i'''$. If $n_i' = *$, then it is possible to replace $*$ with a number m such that $n_i \leq m$; or
   b) split the interval in such a way that the new sequence still obeys the feature cardinality invariant and then reduce the split intervals.

A special case of refining a feature cardinality is to refine it to $[0..0]$ or ε. In either case, it means we have removed the entire subfeature and its descendents. We leave it up to a tool to decide whether to visually remove features with feature cardinality $[0..0]$ or ε.

Refining group cardinalities. A group cardinality $\langle n_1 - n_2 \rangle$ is an interval indicating a minimum and maximum number of distinct grouped features to be chosen from the feature group. Its form is a simplification of a feature cardinality and can only be refined by reducing the interval (i.e., by increasing n_1 to n_1' and decreasing n_2 to n_2' as long as $n_1' \leq n_2'$). Currently, we do not allow *splitting* an interval because we have no representation for such a cardinality. Of course, such an operation should be incorporated whenever we allow sequences of intervals for group cardinalities.

Removing a grouped feature from a feature group. A feature group of size k with group cardinality $\langle n_1 - n_2 \rangle$ combines a set of k grouped subfeatures and indicates a choice of at least n_1 and at most n_2 distinct grouped features. A specialization step can alter a feature group by removing one of the grouped subfeatures with all its descendents, provided that $n_1 < k$. The new feature group will have size $k - 1$, and its new group cardinality will be $\langle n_1 - \mathrm{min}(n_2, k - 1)\rangle$, where $\mathrm{min}(n, n')$ takes the minimum of the two natural numbers n and n'. The following is an example specialization sequence where each step removes one grouped subfeature from the group:

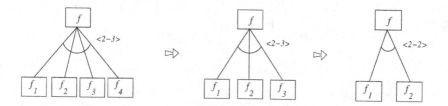

It is not possible to remove grouped subfeatures from a feature group once $n_1 = k$. In that case, all subfeatures *have* to be taken, and all variability is eliminated.

Assigning an attribute value. An obvious specialization step is to assign a value to an uninitialized attribute. The value has to be of the type of the attribute.

Cloning a solitary subfeature. This operation makes it possible to *clone* a solitary subfeature and its entire subtree, provided the feature cardinality allows it. Moreover, the cloned feature may be given an arbitrary, but fixed, feature cardinality by the user, as long as it is allowed by the original feature cardinality of the solitary subfeature.

Unlike the other specialization operations, cloning may *change* the diagram without removing variabilities. However, the new diagram will generally be more amenable to specialization, so we consider it a specialization step nonetheless.

We explain this process with an example:

The feature cardinality $[2..2][4..*]$ of the original subfeature f_0 indicates that f_0 must occur at least two times or more than three times in a configuration. In the specialized diagram above, we have cloned f_0 (to the left) and assigned it a new feature cardinality $[3..3]$. The *original* feature f_0 (to the right) has a new cardinality that guarantees the new diagram does not allow configurations previously forbidden. In the example, because we have chosen to give the left f_0 the fixed feature cardinality [3..3], the feature cardinality of the rightmost f_0 has to be [1..*]. Specialization has occurred since the new diagram does not allow a user to select only f_0 two times.

Consider another example:

In this case, no actual specialization took place. The cloned feature f_1 to the left has been given the fixed cardinality [2..2]. However, because the original feature cardinality was [2..*], the rightmost f_1 now has cardinality [0..*].

More generally, suppose $I = [n_1..n_1'] \ldots [n_l..n_l']$ and $0 < m$. Provided we have $(n_l' = *) \vee (m \leq n_l' < *)$, it is possible to clone the solitary subfeature f' of f with feature cardinality I as follows:

Given that we always have $* - n = *$ for any $n \in \mathbb{N}$, we can define the function $L(m, I)$ as follows:

$$L(m, \varepsilon) = \varepsilon$$

$$L(m, [n..n']I) = \begin{cases} if\ (m \leq n) & : & [(n - m)..(n' - m)]L(m, I) \\ if\ (n < m) \wedge (m \leq n') & : & [0..(n' - m)]L(m, I) \\ if\ n' < m & : & L(m, I) \end{cases}$$

The reader may wonder why we only allow the cloned feature to be given a *fixed* feature cardinality. This is because, in general, it is impossible to construct a correct feature diagram by cloning a feature and giving it an arbitrary interval or sequence of intervals without some more expressive form of additional constraints. However, there are a few useful special cases for this situation that we do not consider in this paper and leave for future work.

Unfolding a feature diagram reference. Finally, we have a specialization step that allows the user to *unfold* a feature diagram reference. This basically means that we substitute the reference for the entire feature diagram it refers to by means of its root feature. Although this operation never removes variability, we consider it a specialization step for the same reasons as mentioned above for

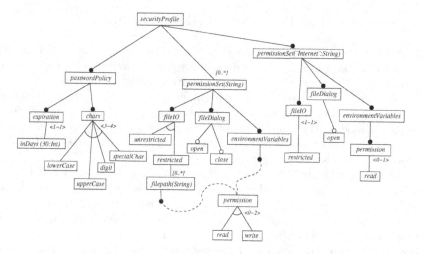

Fig. 3. Sample specialization of the security profile

the cloning of a solitary feature: it makes the new feature model potentially more amenable for specialization because each unfolded feature diagram can now be specialized differently.

4.4   Security Profiling Example Revisited

Let us now apply the notion of staged configuration to the security profile example from Section 3.1. Assume, for instance, that the IT infrastructure of a company supports the security profile from Fig. 1. The company then decides to specialize this profile to define a standard enterprise-level security profile as depicted in Fig. 3.

The specialization is achieved by a combination of steps from Section 4.3. In the feature `passwordPolicy`, we have eliminated the ability to have a non-expiring password and set the expiry time at 30 days. On top of that, the company requires at least three different kind of characters to be used instead of two.

Moreover, we clone the feature `permissionSet` and assign it the name "Internet" because we want to specify a specific permission set for programs running from the Internet. In particular, we want file IO to be restricted and allow no access to local file paths. Moreover, file dialogs may be allowed only to be opened, but Internet programs may be given the permission to read environment variables. Observe that we unfolded the `permission` feature diagram reference under the `environmentVariables` feature. If desired, the enterprise-level security profile could be further specialized by individual departments and then for individual computers within the departments.

5   Feature Models as Context-Free Grammars

The semantics of a feature model can be defined by the set of *all possible configurations*. A configuration itself is denoted by a structured set of features chosen according to the informal rules of interpretation of feature diagrams.

Although this description is sufficient in practice, it is helpful to provide a formal semantics to improve the understanding of some of the intricacies of feature modeling. For example, a formal semantics allows us to define exactly what it means when two apparently different feature models are *equivalent* (i.e., denote the same set of configurations).

More interestingly, if feature model specialization maps to the semantic interpretation of a feature model, it would be possible to formally establish that feature model specialization reduces the set of possible configurations.

Our approach to obtaining such a semantics is to cast feature models back into a well-known formalism: context-free grammars. The semantic interpretation of a feature diagram then coincides with a natural interpretation of the sentences recognized by the grammar. It is beyond the scope of this paper to provide a detailed account of exactly how a feature model can be translated into a context-free grammar, but the interested reader is invited to examine the details in an accompanying technical report [18].

We have to mention that feature diagrams, as they are presented in this paper, can actually be modeled as *regular grammars*[3] and do not require the additional expressiveness of context-free grammars. The main reason to use context-free grammars instead is purely for convenience.

It is not only possible to specify cardinality-based feature models as a context-free grammar. Feature model specialization can be mapped onto a set of operations on the context-free grammar. Those operations are such that it is possible to determine that the set of all configurations of a specialized feature model is never greater than the set of configurations of the original feature model.

6   Conclusion and Future Work

Cardinality-based feature modeling provides an expressive way to describe feature models. Staged configuration of such cardinality-based feature models is a useful and important mechanism for software supply chains based on product lines.

AmiEddi [21,22] was the first editor supporting the feature modeling notation from [2]. As a successor of the first prototype, CaptainFeature [19,20] implements a cardinality-based notation that is similar to the one described in this paper. In future work, we plan to extend our model with external constraints and reference attributes [13]. Meanwhile, commercial tools supporting variant configuration for product lines are starting to emerge (e.g., GEARS [23] and Pure::Consul [24, 25]). Pure::Consul is even directly based on FODA-like feature modeling. More

---

[3] Regular grammars require that the right-hand side of a production can only have one terminal possibly followed by a nonterminal.

advanced capabilities such as staged configuration and cardinality-based feature modeling still need to be addressed by these tools.

The study of specialization at the grammar level [18]) has helped to better understand possible specialization steps at the diagram level. In fact, such an analysis has revealed specialization steps other than those described in Section 4.3. Some of them can be quite involved, and some cannot even be translated back into the concrete syntax of the proposed feature diagram notation. The current specialization steps in this paper (Section 4.3) are an attempt to balance simplicity and practical relevance.

We think that specialization and direct configuration should be two distinct procedures. Although any desired configuration can be achieved through specialization, specialization offers finer grained steps that would be unnecessarily tedious for direct configuration. We already have experience with tool support for configuration based on existing tool prototypes: ConfigEditor [13] and CaptainFeature [19, 20]. Both support configuration in a strictly top-down manner. This contrasts with our approach where staged configuration of a feature model can be achieved in an arbitrary order.

Adequate tool support for the newly introduced cardinality-based feature notation as well as its specialization is under way.

Acknowledgements. We would like to thank Michal Ankiewicz for fruitful discussions about the metamodel presented in this paper. We also would like to thank Thomas Bednasch for his work on CaptainFeature, which helped us to advance our understanding of feature modeling.

References

1. DeBaud, J.M., Schmid, K.: A systematic approach to derive the scope of software product lines. In: Proceedings of the 21st International Conference on Software Engineering (ICSE), IEEE Computer Society Press (1999) 34–43
2. Czarnecki, K., Eisenecker, U.W.: Generative Programming: Methods, Tools, and Applications, Addison-Wesley (2000)
3. Bosch, J.: Design and Use of Software Architecture: Adopting and evolving a product-line approach, Addison-Wesley (2000)
4. David M. Weiss, D.M., Lai, C.T.R.: Software Product-Line Engineering: A Family-Based Software Development Process, Addison-Wesley (1999)
5. Cleaveland, C.: Program Generators with XML and Java, Prentice-Hall (2001)
6. Batory, D., Johnson, C., MacDonald, B., von Heeder, D.: Achieving extensibility through product-lines and domain-specific languages: A case study, ACM Transactions on Software Engineering and Methodology (TOSEM) 11 (2002) 191–214
7. Greenfield, J., Short, K.: Software Factories: Assembling Applications with Patterns, Models, Frameworks, and Tools, Wiley (2004) To be published
8. van Deursen, A., Klint, P.: Domain-specific language design requires feature descriptions, Journal of Computing and Information Technology 10 (2002) 1–17
9. Kang, K., Cohen, S., Hess, J., Nowak, W., Peterson, S.: Feature-oriented domain analysis (FODA) feasibility study. Technical Report CMU/SEI-90TR-21, Software Engineering Institute, Carnegie Mellon University, Pittsburgh, PA (1990)

10. Griss, M., Favaro, J., d' Alessandro, M.: Integrating feature modeling with the RSEB. In: Proceedings of the Fifth International Conference on Software Reuse (ICSR), IEEE Computer Society Press (1998) 76–85
11. Lee, K., Kang, K.C., Lee, J.: Concepts and guidelines of feature modeling for product line software engineering. In: Gacek, C. (ed.): Software Reuse: Methods, Techniques, and Tools: Proceedings of the Seventh Reuse Conference (ICSR7), Austin, USA, Apr.15–19, 2002. LNCS 2319, Springer-Verlag (2002) 62–77
12. Barbeau, M., Bordeleau, F.: A protocol stack development tool using generative programming. In: Batory, D., Consel, C., Taha, W. (eds.): Proceedings of the ACM SIGPLAN/SIGSOFT Conference on Generative Programming and Component Engineering (GPCE'02), Pittsburgh, October 6–8, 2002, LNCS 2487, Springer-Verlag (2002) 93–109
13. Czarnecki, K., Bednasch, T., Unger, P., Eisenecker, U.W.: Generative programming for embedded software: An industrial experience report. In: Batory, D., Consel, C., Taha, W. (eds.): Proceedings of the ACM SIGPLAN/SIGSOFT Conference on Generative Programming and Component Engineering (GPCE'02), Pittsburgh, October 6–8, 2002, LNCS 2487, Springer-Verlag (2002) 156–172
14. Czarnecki, K.: Generative Programming: Principles and Techniques of Software Engineering Based on Automated Configuration and Fragment-Based Component Models, PhThesis, Technical University of Ilmenau, Ilmanau, Germany (1998). Available from http://www.prakinf.tu-ilmenau.de/~czarn/diss
15. Hein, A., Schlick, M., Vinga-Martins, R.: Applying feature models in industrial settings. In: Donohoe, P. (ed.): Proceedings of the Software Product Line Conference (SPLC1), Kluwer Academic Publishers (2000) 47–70
16. Svahnberg, M., van Gurp, J., Bosch, J.: On the notion of variability in software product lines. In: Proceedings of The Working IEEE/IFIP Conference on Software Architecture (WICSA). (2001) 45–55
17. Riebisch, M., Böllert, K., Streitferdt, D., Philippow, I.: Extending feature diagrams with UML multiplicities. In: 6th Conference on Integrated Design & Process Technology (IDPT 2002), Pasadena, California, USA (2002)
18. Czarnecki, K., Helsen, S., Eisenecker, U.: Formalizing cardinality-based feature models and their staged configuration. Technical Report 04-11, Departement of Electrical and Computer Engineering, University of Waterloo, Canada (2004) http://www.ece.uwaterloo.ca/~kczarnec/TR04-11.pdf
19. Bednasch, T.: Konzept und Implementierung eines konfigurierbaren Metamodells für die Merkmalmodellierung, Diplomarbeit, Fachbereich Informatik, Fachhochschule Kaiserslautern,Standort Zweibrücken, Germany, (2002) Available from http://www.informatik.fh-kl.de/~eisenecker/studentwork/dt_bednasch.pdf (in German)
20. Bednasch, T., Endler, C., Lang, M.: CaptainFeature (2002–2004). Tool available on SourceForge at https://sourceforge.net/projects/captainfeature/
21. Selbig, M.: A feature diagram editor — Analysis, design, and implementation of its core functionality, Diplomarbeit, Fachbereich Informatik, Fachhochschule Kaiserslautern, Standort Zweibrücken, Germany (2000)
22. Selbig, M.: AmiEddi (2000–2004). Tool available at http://www.generative-programming.org
23. Krueger, C.W.: Software mass customization. White paper (2001). Available from http://www.biglever.com/papers/BigLeverMassCustomization.pdf
24. pure-systems GmbH: Variant management with pure::consul. Technical White Paper. Available from http://web.pure-systems.com (2003)

25. Beuche, D.: Composition and Construction of Embedded Software Families, PhD thesis, Otto-von-Guericke-Universität Magdeburg, Germany. Available from http://www-ivs.cs.uni-magdeburg.de/~danilo (2003)

A   Overview of Feature Modeling Notations

The cardinality-based feature modeling notation of this paper is a continuation of existing modeling notations [2, 17]. Table 1 compares the current proposal with the extended notation from [2, 17] and the FODA notation.

Table 1 compares three different notations for feature diagrams. The leftmost column shows the FODA notation [9] which has mandatory (f_1), optional (f_2), and alternative subfeatures ($f_k \ldots f_1$). In the extended notation [14, 2], depicted in the middle column, alternative groups come in two flavors: inclusive-or

Table 1. Comparison of feature modeling notations

FODA notation in [9]	Extended notation in [14, 2]	Cardinality-based notation
mandatory and optional subfeatures	*mandatory and optional subfeatures*	*mandatory and optional subfeatures*
f ... ... f_1 f_2	f ... ... f_1 f_2	f .... [1..1] [0..1] f_1 f_2
alternative subfeatures	*exclusive-or group*	*group with cardinality* $\langle 1{-}1 \rangle$
f ... ... f_k .... f_1	f ... ... f_k .... f_1	f .... $\langle 1{-}1\rangle$ f_k .... f_1
n/a	*inclusive-or group*	*group with cardinality* $\langle 1{-}k \rangle$
	f ... ... f_k ... f_1	f .... $\langle 1{-}k\rangle$ f_k .... f_1
n/a	*exclusive-or group with optional subfeatures*	*group with cardinality* $\langle 0{-}1 \rangle$
	f ... ... f_k .... f_1	f .... $\langle 0{-}1\rangle$ f_k .... f_1

and exclusive-or groups. Moreover, an exclusive-or group can also have optional subfeatures. The right column shows some possibilities of the cardinality-based notation that have an equivalent diagram in the extended notation. Of course, the cardinality-based notation allows for many additional features and feature groups that cannot be expressed in either the FODA notation or the extended notation.

However, to improve readability, we suggest using the extended notation of the middle column whenever possible, except for the use of filled circles above grouped features that belong to a feature group. A feature modeling tool may provide the appropriate *syntactic sugar* for those cases.

Scenario-Based Decision Making for Architectural Variability in Product Families

Pierre America[1], Dieter Hammer[2], Mugurel T. Ionita[2],
Henk Obbink[1], and Eelco Rommes[1]

[1]Philips Research, Prof. Holstlaan 4, 5656 AA Eindhoven, The Netherlands
{Pierre.America,Henk.Obbink,Eelco.Rommes}@philips.com
[2]Technical University Eindhoven, P.O. Box 513, 5600 MB Eindhoven, The Netherlands
{D.K.Hammer,M.T.Ionita}@tue.nl

Abstract. In this paper, we present a systematic approach towards decision making for variability in product families in the context of uncertainty. Our approach consists of the following ingredients: a suitable set of architectural views that bridge the gap between customer needs and available technology, a multi-view variation modeling technique, the selection of several scenarios of different kinds, and a quantitative analysis of quality aspects for these scenarios.

1 Introduction

When developing an architecture for a software-intensive product family, we should take into account that during its lifetime this architecture will have to accommodate new requirements from the market, but might also profit from new technological developments. To achieve this, the architects and other members of the development team will have to make a large number of choices, not only at the start of the development but also later as the product family and its architecture evolve. These choices ultimately determine how well the products in the family serve their various purposes, now and in the future. Typically, architectural choices determine in the first place the quality aspects of the products [4]. Therefore, the architects need good insight into the relationship between the architectural choices and the resulting quality aspects of the product family members, and all of this in the context of an uncertain future.

In this paper, we describe our approach to dealing with variability at a system architecture level for product families. We started from a few existing approaches [5,22] and combined their ingredients with our own ongoing research on system architecture for product families [2,19]. In a couple of case studies conducted together with Philips Medical Systems, we investigated new ways to deal with variability of the architectures early in the design of a product (see Section 2 for an introduction to the case study that we use as a running example in this paper). From these studies, a method, called Scenario-Based Architecting (SBA), emerged for identifying and quantifying the potential benefits of the different architectural variability options. The method takes into consideration the functional and quality properties of a system, and can serve as an initial basis in decision making for variability choices at an architectural level.

R.L. Nord (Ed.): SPLC 2004, LNCS 3154, pp. 284–303, 2004.
© Springer-Verlag Berlin Heidelberg 2004

Our approach can be sketched as follows. It all starts with a suitable set of views for structuring the architecture description. Here, we adopted the CAFCR views [17,19], which are summarized in Section 3. The next step is to get an overview of all relevant choices. For this purpose, we developed the multi-view variation modeling approach [3] described briefly in Section 287. Since the number of possible variants allowed by these variation models is huge, we cannot analyze them all individually. Therefore, we choose a small number of representative scenarios. Section 5 discusses the various kinds of scenarios that we consider. Finally, the relevant quality aspects of these scenarios are evaluated, and the results are presented in a form that facilitates architectural decision making. This process is described in Section 6. The paper then ends with some conclusions.

2   The Cathlab Case Study

The Catheterization Laboratory, in short *cathlab*, is a specialized area in a hospital or clinic where patients who suffer from a narrowing of their heart blood vessels (called *stenosis*) are diagnosed and treated (see Figure 1). For diagnostic purposes, the cardiologist operating in the cathlab can use studies of the heart blood vessels employing imaging techniques (called *modalities*) like magnetic resonance (MR) or X-ray. Images acquired with MR can be used for diagnostic purposes. In case the patient needs intervention, the best modality is X-ray because it can offer high-resolution pictures of the vessels in real time. In a typical catheterization procedure, the cardiologist is locating the stenosis by inserting a catheter in a major blood vessel and navigating it towards the heart, looking at the catheter using live X-ray images. For visualizing the blood vessels, the cardiologist releases from time to time small amounts of special contrast fluid that scatters the X-rays better. The contrast fluid and X-rays are harmful for the human body if administered in large quantities or for more than a few seconds; therefore, the catheterization procedure has to be fast and use as little X-ray dose and contrast fluid as possible.

The cathlab consists of two main rooms: the intervention room (IR) where the actual catheterization takes place, and the control room (CR) from which a technician assists the cardiologist during the procedure.

The product family we consider comprises cardiovascular X-ray systems. The main source of variation is the application of these systems: vascular, cardiac, neurological, and electrophysiology procedures each pose specific demands on the X-ray system used. For example, the size of the X-ray detector, the kind of stand that holds it, and many aspects of the controlling software vary with the purpose of the system.

In our case study, we also examined the possibilities for integration among the various systems in the cathlab. In particular we considered three-dimensional (3D) rotational angiography (3DRA), a technique to construct a 3D model of the arteries from a large number of X-ray images taken from different angles [1]. Such a model can help the cardiologist diagnose and treat heart problems.

Other systems that one typically finds in a cathlab, besides the X-ray system, are the following:

- contrast fluid injector
- hemodynamics system, monitoring sensors such as ECG and blood pressure

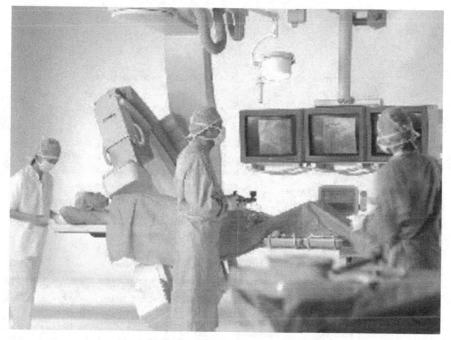

Fig. 1. Cathlab – The intervention room

- terminal for a Picture Archiving and Communication System (PACS), which stores medical images (e.g., made during previous examinations)
- terminal for a Cardiology Information System (CIS), which stores other medical data

3   The CAFCR Views

To describe an architecture that can bridge the gap between the needs and wishes of the customer and their realization in technology, we use five architectural views: Customer, Application, Functional, Conceptual, and Realization (CAFCR). This framework has been developed within Philips and is taught in architecture courses inside and outside Philips [17,18,19]. Figure 2 shows all five views, each with a short explanation.

The views are filled with artifacts (a generic term for documents, models, code, etc., used among others in the Unified Process [13]). Table 1 describes the way we propose to do that. The rows on functionality, qualities, and supporting artifacts have been adapted largely from various existing architecting approaches, such as Brede-meyer [8], Siemens [10], RUP [14], and COPA [19]. The approach to variation, how-ever, is a new contribution from our SBA approach, which we will discuss in Sections 4 and 5. For more information about the other artifacts, see an earlier paper [3].

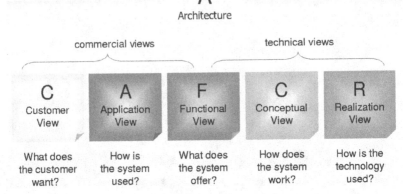

Fig. 2. The CAFCR architectural views

Table 1. Artifacts in the CAFCR views

	Customer	Application	Functional	Conceptual	Realization
Variation	Variation model, Scenarios	Variation model, Scenarios	Variation model, Scenarios	Variation model, Scenarios	Variation model, Scenarios
Functionality	Value proposition	User scenarios	Feature dictionary	System decomposition	Technology mapping
Qualities	Customer drivers	Quality requirements	Quality properties	Principles, Mechanisms	Mechanisms, Conventions
Supporting artifacts	Context diagram, Trend analysis, PESTLE analysis, Competitor-complementer analysis	System context, Workflow context, Domain model	Feature-value matrix	Collaborations, Information models	Collaboration estimations, Supplier roadmaps

4   Variation Modeling

When considering various possible architectures, it is important to get an overview of the commonalities and differences among them. Here, the construction of variation models can help in several ways:

1. to structurally explore the variation space in the various views and the relationships between them
2. to guide and document the choices that were made, as well as the options that were disregarded
3. to enhance communication and raise awareness about these choices among the architecture's stakeholders

We will now look at ways to model variation in and across the CAFCR views. The models presented here were simplified for the purpose of this publication. For more details about our cross-view variation modeling approach, see the paper titled "Multi-View Variation Modeling for Scenario Analysis" [3].

We start with the functional variation model because it is closely related to the various existing approaches to feature modeling for product families (see, for example, the work of Ferber and associates, which served as our starting point [9]). The functional variation model gives an overview of the features relevant for our product family. We use a tree model (generalized to a directed acyclic graph) giving the main structure of the feature variation. Figure 3 gives an explanation of the notation for the tree model.

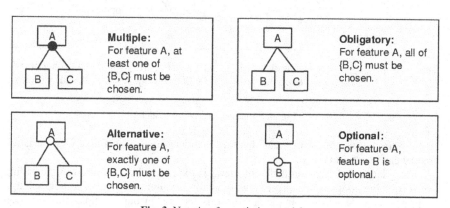

Fig. 3. Notation for variation models

An example variation model for the functional view is shown in Figure 4. It shows the possible features of the 3D cathlab and how we can choose among them.

The 3D cathlab should support generating 3D images, viewing them, or both. Generating 3D images is done through 3DRA support. Optionally, the cathlab could have an "auto 3DRA reconstruction" feature, which is a workflow enhancement. The 3DRA functionality can be offered by a separate workstation (remote 3DRA), or it can be built into the X-ray equipment (local 3DRA). If a separate 3DRA workstation is used, the viewing of 3DRA images can be performed on this workstation. If 3DRA is available locally, the cathlab must have 3D viewing support.

3D viewing support is also obligatory if there is no support for 3DRA. Multimodality support means that the cathlab can handle 3D images from modalities other than X-ray (e.g., MR). It is optional, and without it only 3DRA images are supported, possibly generated by other 3D cathlabs. Either the "NGUI support" or "GUI support for 3D viewing" feature must be implemented. If desired, both can be. NGUI support means that the cathlab has some sort of non-graphical user interface (NGUI) to support 3D viewing.

For the conceptual view, the same notation can be used, but the concept of "feature" must be interpreted more broadly. The conceptual variation model consists largely of "internal features." Such an internal feature is a property of the system that cannot be observed from the system's behavior alone, but refers to the way the system is designed. Typically, such an internal feature concerns the incorporation of a design

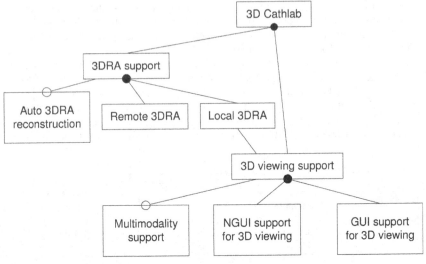

Fig. 4. Functional variation model

concept in the system. Some "real" features that occur in the functional view variation model can also turn up here.

The relationship between different views is expressed by a feature in a preceding view showing up in a subsequent view, typically becoming the root of a subgraph that explores possible ways of implementing this feature. In our example, the variation model for the conceptual view, shown in Figure 5, indicates how the features from the functional view could be implemented by architectural concepts. Such "functional features" are marked with the letter "F."

To implement the feature "local 3DRA," we need both a 3DRA reconstructor and 3D viewing support. The latter relationship is also part of the functional variation model. A reconstructor has the task of using many parts of two-dimensional X-ray data to calculate a 3D model. This can be done by a real-time reconstructor specialized for this type of X-ray equipment, or by a slower, but portable reconstructor. This indicates a tradeoff between performance and reusability.

The "3D viewing support" feature is taken from the functional variation model. It can be implemented in two ways: by a native 3D viewer or by a hosted 3D PACS client. A native viewer is dedicated to the cathlab environment. It needs a 3D renderer to visualize the 3D images, as well as some sort of 3D navigation controls to enable the user to manipulate the models. In turn, these controls could be implemented as software (GUI controls for 3D navigation) or in hardware (NGUI controls for 3D navigation). These controls are conceptual implementations of the GUI and NGUI support for 3D viewing from the functional view, which we have omitted in Figure 5 for simplicity.

A Picture Archiving and Communication System (PACS) supports the long term storage and viewing of medical images. Typically, such a system has client software for viewing all kinds of medical data, including 3D models. The 3D viewing feature could be implemented by hosting such a PACS client on the X-ray equipment. As such, a client would have its own GUI controls, providing a NGUI is optional.

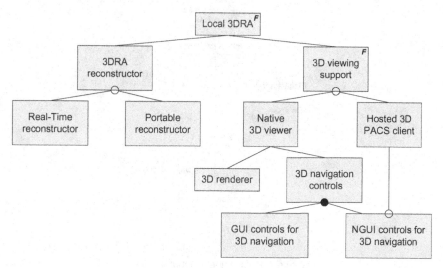

Fig. 5. Conceptual variation model

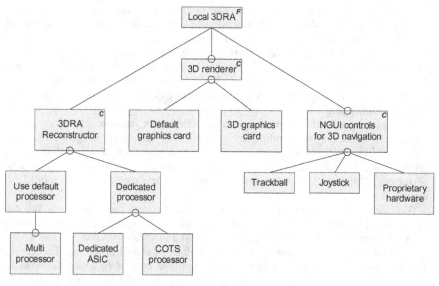

Fig. 6. Realization variation model

The realization variation model again contains "internal features," where a realization feature is a possible choice in the realization view. The same notation as above can be used for the realization view. The letter "C" or even "F" indicates a feature at the conceptual or functional level. In our example (Figure 6), we see different ways to map the architectural concepts from the conceptual view onto available technology. We will not further elaborate on these here.

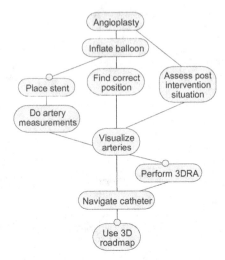

Fig. 7. Application variation model

Building an application variation model is difficult. A single moderately complex, but well-engineered system can typically be used in a large number of different ways. If we also want to model the variation allowed by a number of architectural variants of such a system, the resulting variation is extremely large.

Capturing all these variations in a single model is impossible in most cases. Therefore, it can be a good idea to build smaller models around the issues that are most difficult to address. Often, it is useful to build mixed models, where variation points in the application view are related to variation points in the other views (usually customer and functional view).

The application variation model contains actions, not features. Therefore, we use rounded rectangles, corresponding to the Unified Modeling Language (UML) notation for activities [6]. Note that this model is not a workflow model: it does not express the order of activities, but rather only whether a particular activity is or is not performed. This way, our variation model can be somewhat simpler than a full UML activity diagram.

The variety of procedures performed in a cathlab is very large. Even our full case study model does not cover all possible variations. In Figure 7, we show a small model with the possible subactivities of a particular medical procedure.

Angioplasty is a procedure where a tiny balloon is placed at the tip of a catheter. The balloon is navigated to a blocked artery and then inflated to widen the blockage and restore local blood flow. To prevent the artery from closing again, a wire mesh tube called a stent may be left behind in the artery. It is necessary to perform some measurements on the blockage to determine the correct width and length of the stent.

To find the correct position of such a balloon or stent, it is necessary to visualize the surrounding arteries and assess their situation. This is done using X-ray equipment and a catheter, as described in Section 2. Navigation of the catheter can be done optionally using a 3D roadmap. Such a roadmap could result from an earlier diagnostic procedure or be constructed during this procedure using 3DRA. Note that, to perform

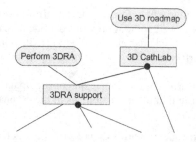

Fig. 8. Adding application elements (actions) to the functional variation model

3DRA, it is also necessary to navigate the catheter. In addition to the ballooning, the new situation is assessed by visualizing the arteries again.

Having explained application view variation modeling, we can make the relationship with the functional variation model explicit. Figure 8 shows a small part of that model, together with the activities that especially concern the 3D support in the cathlab. The use of a 3D roadmap is supported by the 3D cathlab. To be able to perform 3DRA, the cathlab must have support for it. Letters are not needed to distinguish activities from features because of the different forms of the nodes.

Because the variation model in the customer view must deal with different kinds of variation, we use a different notation for it that's based on UML. The details are outside the scope of this article, but they are explained by America and associates [3]. For our present purpose, it is sufficient to say that the customer variation model will contain UML action symbols that return in the application variation model to express the relationship between the models (for example, "angioplasty" in Figure 7).

5   Scenarios

5.1   Strategic Scenarios

One of the goals of the scenario-based architecting method is to make architectures more resilient against future changes. It is important to remember that changing the architecture itself is not difficult, but effecting these changes in the implementation typically requires a major effort. Therefore, we want to choose the architecture changes carefully.

Of course, the changes to the requirements that will occur in the future are very uncertain. Therefore, we consider a number of scenarios that describe the possible developments of the world in the future, along the lines of Schwartz's book [21]. Of course, these scenarios concentrate on the aspect of the world that is relevant for our field of business. In our case study, this would be the area of healthcare for cardiac patients. (Another set of scenarios might describe possible technological advancements relevant for cathlab systems.) Such scenarios form a good basis for business decisions, so we call them strategic scenarios. As examples for the purpose of this paper, we use the following highly simplified set of strategic scenarios:

1. severe economic downturn, only few people can afford cathlab treatment
2. cathlab treatment performed without previous cardiac diagnostic imaging
3. cathlab treatment performed after cardiac diagnostic imaging using ultrasound
4. cathlab treatment performed after cardiac diagnostic imaging using computed tomography
5. cathlab treatment performed after cardiac diagnostic imaging using MR
6. New and effective drug treatment for stenosis in the coronary artery makes cathlab treatment obsolete.

Unfortunately, these strategic scenarios do not provide much direct support for architecting (real strategic scenarios are even worse than our examples above). Therefore, we have to translate them into architectural responses, which we will call *architectural scenarios*. Not all of the strategic scenarios are architecturally relevant. In our case study, scenarios 1 and 6 call for a business response; there is no suitable cathlab architecture that deals with them (aside from their low probability). We can therefore safely reduce the set by eliminating these strategic scenarios. For each of the other strategic scenarios, we write one or more architectural scenarios that are consistent with it. From these scenarios, we develop an architecture that implements the features described in the architectural scenarios. This architecture is shown diagrammatically in Figure 9.

Existing approaches to making architecting decisions using scenarios are called *sensitivity analysis* [15,16], or *maintainability impact analysis* [7]. In these methods, scenarios are developed describing possible changes in requirements to the architecture; the consequences of which are then analyzed. However, there is no clear approach for choosing these change scenarios. Since they do not take strategic scenarios into account, there is no assurance that the chosen scenarios are representative of the future changes.

5.2   Architectural Scenarios

Figure 9 gives a simplified view of architecture. An architecture description does not consist only of boxes connected by lines. Rather, a good architecture is described by a number of different views, where each view answers a different and important question. We prefer to use the CAFCR views.

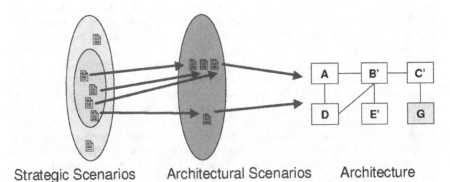

Strategic Scenarios   Architectural Scenarios   Architecture

Fig. 9. From strategic scenarios via architectural scenarios to architecture (simplified)

Moreover, we do not want a different architecture for each scenario, or a single, static architecture that tries to cover them all. Rather, we want a description that gives us a range of choices for our architecture, or in other words, a certain degree of variation. This variation should be expressed explicitly, so we have a good overview of the various choices. Such an overview makes it easier to identify common parts in scenarios, and to make and document our decisions. To this end, we use the mechanisms described in the previous section to model the variation space in each CAFCR view.

However, the variation models themselves are not enough for evaluating architectural choices. Typically, we cannot assess the consequences of a single choice in a variation model because these consequences also depend on other choices. On the other hand, the number of possible sets of choices is likely to be astronomical, so we certainly cannot assess them all. Therefore, we need to restrict ourselves to a limited number of architectural scenarios.

On the basis of the ingredients described above, we propose that each architectural scenario should describe the architecture from a single view. More precisely, such an architectural scenario should consist of a single set of choices in that view's variation model, where of course the set of choices is consistent with the semantics of that variation model.

For example, starting with the functional variation model of Figure 4, we can make such a consistent set of choices as indicated by thick lines and dark shading in Figure 10, and we can take that set as a scenario in the functional view. For the other views, we can proceed in a similar way.

When we relate the scenarios to the variation models, we see that the models describe the variation space, whereas the scenarios define a few individual points in this space, which will be considered for further analysis. In view of this, it is most useful if the scenarios, besides being consistent with the variation models, satisfy a few other criteria:

- The scenarios should be reasonable, in the sense that the set of choices as a whole should show a certain balance. For example, it would not be reasonable to omit a basic feature from a high-end system, although technically this would be possible.

- The total set of scenarios should be interesting, in the sense that they are sufficiently different from each other and thus span a sufficiently large part of the variation space.

- The set of scenarios should be quite small, around five per view, so that their analysis will not take too much effort.

In choosing the architectural scenarios, we take the strategic scenarios into account. For example, the 3D cathlab scenario of Figure 10 supports 3D image data during cathlab procedures. This is in line with strategic scenarios 3 to 5, which describe how diagnostic images are acquired in a pre-interventional diagnostic procedure on non-X-ray modalities. Each modality considered will yield 3D image data.

Strategic scenarios pertaining to the application domain will typically guide the architectural scenarios in the application and functional views, whereas strategic scenarios about technology may give direction to the realization view.

While, in general, it is a good idea to first chart the possible choices in variation models and then choose suitable architectural scenarios, during the construction of the scenarios, we might find out that the choices offered by the variation models are not enough; for example, to establish a proper architectural scenario as a response to a

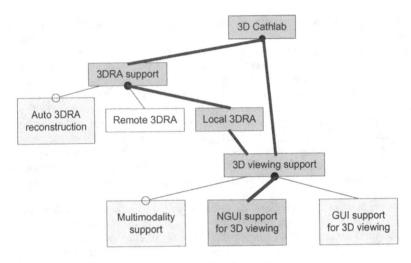

Fig. 10. A functional scenario

particular strategic scenario. In such a case, we have to go back to the variation models and adapt them accordingly.

For scenarios in different views, we say that the scenarios correspond to each other when they describe choices that are consistent across the views, according to the cross-view relationship of the variation models. To continue our example from Figure 10, we recall that our conceptual variation model, depicted by Figure 5, is related to the functional variation model in Figure 4 by showing a number of functional features. Now we can define a set of choices (see Figure 11) in the conceptual variation model that is not only consistent with the semantics of the conceptual model, but also contains exactly those functional features that are also chosen in Figure 10. In this way, we obtain a conceptual scenario that corresponds to the functional scenario of Figure 10.

In our case study, we started from a set of functional scenarios that were distinguished according to the degree of integration among the various cathlab products:

- **Minimal integration** means a situation in which only standardized mechanisms for integration (e.g., DICOM) are used for integrating the cathlab systems.
- **Data integration** focuses on the sharing of data. If data is produced by one system, a second system can read, understand, and change that data whenever applicable.
- **Presentation and control integration** are two sides of the same coin. Presentation integration is accomplished when two or more systems can present their results in a similar way. Control integration on the other hand, means that two or more systems can be controlled in similar ways. In practice, these types of integration are rarely separated: rather, they are joined to create a common look and feel.
- **Workflow integration** means that systems work together to support the workflow of their users. It is important that this behavior is flexible and can be adjusted to meet specific workflow needs and habits.

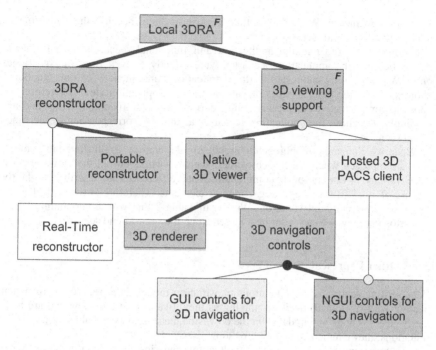

Fig. 11. A conceptual scenario

- **Full integration** represents a fully integrated cathlab system. Besides the above-mentioned integration levels, new features that are enabled by this high level of integration are described.

From those scenarios, we could work forward and backward through the architectural views to arrive at the set of architectural scenarios described in Table 2. Here, scenarios in different views that occupy adjacent table cells correspond to each other. (In a situation with a more complicated correspondence relationship, arrows instead of adjacency in the table could indicate this.)

This table also illustrates a few other things about scenarios and their cross-view relationships. First, note that it is not necessary to fill up horizontal rows completely. In our example, the minimal function scenario has no corresponding conceptual or

Table 2. Architectural scenarios and cross-view relationships

Customer	Application	Functional	Conceptual	Realization
Academic	Minimal	Minimal	-	-
	Data	Data	DM Integration	Multihost
	Presentation & Control	Presentation & Control	HW Switch	
Production			Alt-Tab	Cohost
	Workflow	Workflow	Coordinator	
	Full	Full	Luxury	Flat Screen

realization scenarios. We didn't bother to develop them because the scenario was unattractive to potential customers.

Furthermore, note that the application and functional scenarios have the same names because the application scenarios were directly derived from the functional ones. We were only interested in the application consequences of our functional choices, not in the other sources of variation in the application view. Therefore, we chose to limit ourselves to the variability derived from the functional view, and accordingly, we chose the application scenarios as directly corresponding to the functional scenarios.

When we compare our approach to architectural scenarios, as illustrated in Table 2, with an approach where each architectural scenario works out all the views, we see the advantage of our approach: commonalities and differences are described explicitly instead of implicitly by repeating common elements. Therefore, we can deal more easily with the essential variation. We see in Table 2 that with a maximum of five scenarios per view we can describe a larger number of end-to-end scenarios.

5.3   Other Representations of Scenarios

Representing scenarios as annotations of variation models is especially useful when dealing with (technical) decision making as they give a good overview and are relatively easy to create and update. On the downside, because they remain abstract representations, they can be less suitable for some uses.

We have found it useful to create application scenarios in the form of stories, written in natural language using the jargon of the application domain. These so-called user scenarios describe in the form of a narrative text the interaction between the system and its users. These scenarios are especially useful when created by a team of multidisciplinary stakeholders early in the architecting process. The scenarios can then serve as a tool to come to a shared vision of the product line and to outline its scope. For this purpose, it is best, though not absolutely necessary, to have a one-to-one correspondence between application scenarios and user scenarios. Early in our case study, we created user scenarios for each of the five application scenarios. More details on this can be found in Rommes' work [20].

Other representations of scenarios we have used at times are customer profiles for customer scenarios, animated slides for application scenarios, use cases for functional scenarios, collaboration diagrams for conceptual scenarios, and simple simulation models for realization scenarios.

6   Analyzing the Scenarios

The architectural scenarios based on the variation models are of little use without being able to evaluate their relative benefits and consequences. By this we mean a quantitative and systematic manner of differentiating between the possible quality aspects triggered by the different scenarios. Our approach for scenario-based quality analysis was introduced in the paper titled "Quantitative Architecture Usability Assessment with Scenarios" [11] where we presented such an analysis for usability. An essential part of this approach is the translation of qualitative, fuzzy, descriptions of quality requirements into precise, preferably quantitative definitions. In a few cases, this may be straightforward, but in general this is a difficult task. In our usability example, we have translated the criteria of effectiveness, efficiency, and satisfaction [12] into the following quantitative factors affecting each task to be performed:

- the number of times the cardiologist must leave the intervention room (e.g., to go to the control room)
- the number of staff members needed (split up according to different skills)
- the number of atomic actions the users have to perform on the system (e.g., pressing a key, moving the cursor, navigating a menu)
- the number of times the cardiologist has to resterilize his hands due to interaction with nonsterile items
- the number of training hours the medical personnel has to spend learning how to operate the system

Note that we tried to find usability factors that have objective definitions, rather than judgments like "low, medium, or high." This has the following advantages:

- There is little misunderstanding or disagreement among the stakeholders on what is meant by a certain factor.
- The estimates obtained before or during system development can be calibrated by experiments, either later when the system is finished, or even now using an existing predecessor system.

The largest risk involved in this step of the method is that the quantitative factors do not cover the intuition of the quality aspect completely and precisely, but nevertheless become goals by themselves. This may lead to unbalanced choices later in the process.

Once we have quantitative definitions of the various factors contributing to the quality aspect under consideration, we can also fix the acceptance criteria in a quantitative way.

Before we can properly analyze the scenarios with respect to the quality factors, we must determine the relevant architectural views. Typically, we must distinguish two views, which may or may not be the same:

- the *determining view:* This is the view where the architectural decisions are made that determine the quality of the system.
- the *assessment view:* This is the view where the resulting system qualities can be assessed.

In the usability example described in the paper titled "Quantitative Architecture Usability Assessment with Scenarios" [11], the determining view is the functional view, since the features chosen in it ultimately determine the system's usability. However, the assessment view is the application view, since the usability of the system can be assessed only by considering how the system is used. For different architectural qualities, these views are different, as shown in Table 3 with a few example qualities. Typically, qualities that can be observed from the system itself have the application view as their assessment view, while qualities that affect mainly system development have the conceptual or realization view. Qualities related to the market are best assessed in the customer view (if the market segment is the main factor) or the functional view (if the product itself is dominant).

Table 3. Determining and assessment views for a few quality aspects

Quality Aspect	Determining View	Assessment View
Usability	Functional	Application
Performance	Conceptual, Realization	Application
Sellability	Functional	Functional, Customer
Development cost	Conceptual, Realization	Conceptual, Realization
Usage hazards	Conceptual, Realization	Application
Development Risk	Conceptual	Conceptual

Whenever we analyze scenarios for a particular quality aspect, we start from the scenarios in the determining view, because we want to evaluate the consequences of architectural decisions made in that view. If the assessment view is different from the determining view, we must find the corresponding scenario (or scenarios) in the assessment view; for example, by using a table such as Table 2. Then, we use those scenarios for the evaluation.

Typically, we use a structuring principle specific for the assessment view to perform this evaluation. In our usability example, we use the fact that the scenarios in the assessment view (in this case, the application view) can also be represented by the user scenarios, which are subdivided into scenes. Therefore, we can evaluate the quality factors per scene and then accumulate the results.

For the evaluation itself, any suitable method can be used. For each quality aspect, the professional literature provides a number of methods. Unfortunately, most of these methods are much too labor-intensive for scenario-based architecting, since the evaluation must be done for each scenario. Also, many relevant details of the system are typically still unknown at the time of evaluation. Therefore, we often use expert judgment to evaluate the quality factors. Although this approach may not be as accurate as other approaches, its accuracy is often good enough, and it is certainly quicker.

After all the important quality factors have been evaluated for all scenarios, we can present the end results in the form of a profile for each scenario. Here, we start, of course, from the scenarios in the determining view. Typically, it is useful to compare multiple quality aspects together. If their determining views are different, it is nevertheless often possible to relate them by considering the cross-view correspondence relationships among the scenarios. This is illustrated by Table 4, which lists a number of quality factors belonging to different quality aspects. Note the slightly different subdivision of the row on "3D model reconstruction," which is a performance aspect where the conceptual view is the determining one.

Although architectural decisions could be made on the basis of the quality profiles resulting from the previous step, this would be premature in most cases. Instead, it is better to see first whether problematic areas for certain scenarios can be improved

Table 4. Overview of the scenarios' quality profiles

	Min	Data	PC	WF	Full
Nr of walks	4	3	0	0	0
Personnel involved	3	3	2	2	2
Learning duration	6	6	10	10	15
Time for 3D reconstruction		300s	300s 30s	30s	30s
High impact on the architecture	Low	Low	Med	Med	Med
Single point of failure	Low	Low	Med	High	High
Fail to meet the qualities	Low	Low	Low	High	High
Too late on the market	Low	Low	Low	Med	High
Inaccurate stent deployment	Med	Med	Low	Low	Low
Cathlab cost % increase	0%	5%	10%	15%	20%
Reduction of disposable cost	0%	0%	5%	10%	10%
Reduction of personnel cost	0%	0%	20%	20%	20%
Maintenance costs	0%	5%	10%	10%	10%

without touching the essentials of the scenarios. In our example, the larger values for "number of walks" and "personnel involved" in the minimum and data integration scenarios are essential consequences of the low degrees of integration among the systems. However the 3D model reconstruction times can definitely be improved, even for a multihost realization scenario.

After such improvements, the analysis and presentation steps must be adapted according to the changes in architectural decisions. Such an iterative improvement strategy is very common in widely used architecting approaches [7].

After making the most urgent improvements to the scenarios, the real architectural decisions can be made on the basis of the quality profiles of the individual scenarios. This is rarely a matter of simply selecting the best scenario, since, typically, each scenario has advantages and disadvantages when compared to others. Moreover, the whole point of scenario-based architecting was to make architectures more future-proof, which means they can respond gracefully to new, as yet unknown requirements. Therefore, the best way to proceed is to choose a suitable architectural scenario for the short term, based on the currently available information. It is also a good idea to identify for each strategic scenario at least one architectural scenario that is a reasonable response. However, the latter decisions are not meant to be final. Instead, the whole set of steps should be repeated at regular intervals (e.g., each year) to see where the analysis must be changed on the basis of new information and where decisions must be revised. Fortunately, such a revision typically requires much less effort than the original analysis.

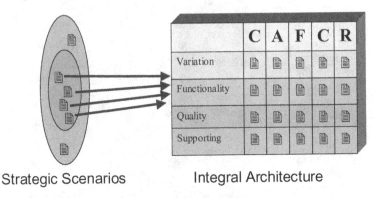

Fig. 12. From strategic scenarios to architecture

7   Conclusions

The main ingredients of our approach towards future-proof architectures are the following:

- the CAFCR views, which enable architects to bridge the gap between customer needs and wishes on the one hand and technological realizations on the other hand. We also propose number of artifacts that can be used in these views.
- cross-view variation modeling, which provides an overview of the most relevant architectural choices in each view, together with the relationships between these choices within and across views
- architectural scenarios, which group together consistent, reasonable, and interesting sets of choices within a single architectural view and represent possible responses to external events summarized in strategic scenarios. Here, architectural scenarios per view with a correspondence relationship across views are more powerful and flexible than overall architectural scenarios.
- quantitative analysis, which assesses the different architectural scenarios with respect to the most important quality aspects, eventually leading to an overview on which decisions for the short and the long term can be based

Together, these ingredients allow an architect to assess and improve the ability of the architecture to deal with new, currently unknown requirements. Our overall architecture has become dynamic, flexible, and responsive, and therefore, we can summarize our approach as in Figure 12.

Although we have tried to limit the effort required for this approach as much as possible, performing the complete analysis for the first time is definitely a major endeavor for an architect. However, doing this architectural work up front is much cheaper in total for an organization than later implementing architectural changes that could have been avoided.

Acknowledgements. We are grateful to our colleagues Hans Jonkers, Ron Koymans, André Postma, Marc Stroucken, and Jan Gerben Wijnstra, and many people from Philips Medical Systems for their assistance and feedback. This research was funded by Stichting Technische Wetenschappen (STW) in the AIMES Project EWI.4877 and by the Eureka Σ! 2023 Program in the ITEA project ip02009 Families.

References

1. Save Time and Lives with a Faster, Smarter 3D-RA. *WWW*, Philips Medical Systems, November 2002. http://www.medical.philips.com/main/news/theme/3dra/3dra.pdf
2. Pierre America, Henk Obbink, Rob van Ommering, and Frank van der Linden: CoPAM: A Component-Oriented Platform Architecting Method Family for Product Family Engineering. In: Patrick Donohoe, ed.: *Software Product Lines: Experience and Research Directions, Proceedings of the First Software Product Lines Conference (SPLC1)*, Denver, Colorado, August 28-31, 2000, Kluwer, p. 167-180.
3. Pierre America, Eelco Rommes, and Henk Obbink: Multi-View Variation Modeling for Scenario Analysis. In: Frank van der Linden, ed.: *PFE-5: Fifth International Workshop on Product Family Engineering*, Siena, Italy, November 4-6, 2003, Springer, LNCS.
4. Len Bass, Paul Clements, and Rick Kazman: *Software Architecture in Practice*. Addison-Wesley, 1998.
5. Len Bass, Mark Klein, and Felix Bachmann: Quality Attribute Design Primitives and the Attribute Driven Design Method. In: *4th International Workshop on Product Family Engineering*, Bilbao, Spain, October 3-5, 2003.
6. Grady Booch, James Rumbaugh, and Ivar Jacobson: *The Unified Modeling Language User Guide*. Addison-Wesley, 1998.
7. Jan Bosch: *Design and Use of Software Architectures: Adopting and evolving a product-line approach*. Addison-Wesley, 2000.
8. Dana Bredemeyer: Software Architecture Workshop. 2002. www.bredemeyer.com
9. Stefan Ferber, Jürgen Haag, and Juha Savolainen: Feature Interaction and Dependencies: Modeling Features for Reengineering a Legacy Product Line. In: Gary J. Chastek, ed.: *Software Product Lines: Second International Conference (SPLC2)*, San Diego, California, August 19-22, 2002, Springer, LNCS Vol. 2379, p. 235-256.
10. Christine Hofmeister, Robert Nord, and Dilip Soni: *Applied Software Architecture*. Addison-Wesley, 1999.
11. Mugurel T. Ionita, Pierre America, Henk Obbink, and Dieter. Hammer: Quantitative Architecture Usability Assessment with Scenarios. In: Morten Borup Harning, ed.: *Closing the Gaps:Software Engineering and Human-Computer Interaction, Workshop at Interact 2003*, Zürich, Switzerland, September 1-2, 2003.
12. ISO TC 159/SC4: Ergonomic requirements for office work with visual display terminals (VDTs) -- Part 11: Guidance on usability. Standard 9241-11, ISO, 1998.
13. Ivar Jacobson, Grady Booch, and James Rumbaugh: *The Unified Software Development Process*. Addison-Wesley, 1998.
14. Philippe Kruchten: *The Rational Unified Process, an Introduction*. Addison-Wesley, 1999.

15. Chung-Horng Lung, Sonia Bot, Kalai Kalaichelvan, and Rick Kazman: An Approach to Software Architecture Analysis for Evolution and Reusability. In: J. Howard Johnson, ed.: *CASCON '97*, Toronto, Ontario, Canada, November 10-13, 1997.

16. Chung-Horng Lung and Kalai Kalaichelvan: An Approach to Quantitative Software Architecture Sensitivity Analysis. *International Journal of Software Engineering and Knowledge Engineering*, Vol. 10, No. 1, p. 97-114, 2000.

17. Gerrit Muller: Gaudí System Architecting Homepage. *WWW*, 2003. http://www.extra.research.philips.com/natlab/sysarch/

18. Henk Obbink and Pierre America: Towards Evergreen Architectures: On the usage of scenarios in system architecting. In: *International Conference on Software Maintenance ICSM 2003*, Amsterdam, The Netherlands, September 22-26, 2003, IEEE, p. 298-303.

19. Henk Obbink, Jürgen K. Müller, Pierre America, Rob van Ommering, Gerrit Muller, William van der Sterren, and Jan Gerben Wijnstra: COPA: A Component-Oriented Platform Architecting Method for Families of Software-Intensive Electronic Products. Tutorial for SPLC1, the First Software Product Line Conference, Denver, Colorado, August 2000. http://www.extra.research.philips.com/SAE/COPA/COPA_Tutorial.pdf

20. Eelco Rommes: A People Oriented Approach to Product Line Scoping. In: Klaus Schmid and Birgit Geppert, eds.: *PLEES'03: International Workshop on Product Line Engineering: The Early Steps: Planning, Modeling and Managing*, Kaiserslautern, Germany, September 2003, Fraunhofer IESE, p. 23-27.

21. Peter Schwartz: *The Art of the Long View*. Doubleday, 1996.

22. Mikael Svahnberg, Claes Wohlin, Lars Lundberg, and Michael Mattson: A Quality-driven Decision Support Method for Identifying Software Architecture Candidates. *International Journal of Software Engineering and Knowledge Engineering*, Vol. 13, No. 5, 2003.

Software Factories: Assembling Applications with Patterns, Models, Frameworks, and Tools

Jack Greenfield

Visual Studio Enterprise Frameworks & Tools
Microsoft Corporation
One Microsoft Way
Redmond, WA 98053, USA
jackgr@microsoft.com

Increasingly complex and rapidly changing requirements and technologies are pushing the limits of the current approach to application development. Because of these trends, stakeholders are increasingly turning to software product line practices to reduce risk, cost, and time to market while improving product quality through systematic reuse. Adopting organizations are starting to demand the kind of tool support available in Rapid Application Development (RAD) environments for software product lines. This talk describes a methodology developed at Microsoft called Software Factories. The goal of the methodology is to enable automation of life-cycle tasks in software product line contexts by integrating innovations in model-driven development (MDD), component-based development (CBD), and agile development methods. Software Factories is based on a four-part pattern for building patterns, models, frameworks, and tools for specific domains, such as user interface construction or database design. The key to the methodology is reducing the cost of implementing the pattern, making it cost-effective for narrower and more specialized domains, such as B2C application development and business process automation. The central concept is the software schema—a network of viewpoints describing the artifacts that constitute the members of a family of software products and identifying the patterns, languages, frameworks, tools, processes, and other assets used to build those artifacts. Mappings between viewpoints support artifact transformation and provide constraints on the development process that enable a scalable approach to agile development. By automating many aspects of the product development process, the Software Factories methodology provides a basis for industrializing software development and promotes the formation of software supply chains, paving the way for software mass customization.

R.L. Nord (Ed.): SPLC 2004, LNCS 3154, p. 304, 2004.
© Springer-Verlag Berlin Heidelberg 2004

Product Line Binding Times: What You Don't Know Can Hurt You

Charles W. Krueger – Panels Chair and Panel Moderator

BigLever Software, 10500 Laurel Hill Cove, Austin, TX 78730, USA
ckrueger@biglever.com

Abstract. Choosing the right variation binding time – the point in the software engineering process at which decisions for variation instantiation are made – is often one of the most critical, most contentious, and least well understood issues for software product line organizations. This panel explores some of the fundamental binding time issues and insights based on the research, best practices, and real world experiences of the panelists.

Overview

One of the most critical, most contentious, and least well understood issues in a software product line approach can be the selection of the optimal binding time(s) and associated binding mechanism(s). There are often different agendas for the different stakeholders, plus preconceived and possibly inaccurate ideas about software product line engineering that can lead to strong differences of opinions about how to go about implementing a software product line. The goal of this panel is to expose the fundamental issues, myths, and hidden agendas surrounding binding time selection.

The essential distinction between software product line engineering and conventional software engineering is the presence of variation in some of the software assets. In the early stages of the engineering process in a software product line approach, software assets contain *variation points* that represent unbound options about how the software will behave. At some point during the production process, the decision model is used to select among the options for the variation points, after which the behavior of the variation point in the final product is fully specified.

The time at which the decisions for a variation point are bound is referred to as the *binding time,* and the means by which the decisions are used to instantiate the variation points is referred to as the *binding mechanism.* Examples of binding times include source reuse, development, source instantiation, build, package, install, start-up, and execution time. Examples of different binding mechanisms include language *templates*, manual production, preprocessors, off-the-shelf product line tools, build scripts, CM *views*, installers, *config files*, and language conditionals.

Some of the questions and issues addressed by the panel include
1. What makes binding time selection a critical decision?
2. What are the criteria for selecting among different binding times? How do you identify the optimal choice?
3. When is it appropriate to use multiple binding times?
4. What are the different stakeholder agendas, and which ones can be detrimental?

R.L. Nord (Ed.): SPLC 2004, LNCS 3154, pp. 305–306, 2004.

Panelists

☐ Dale Churchett, Salion, USA, dale.churchett@salion.com
☐ Jan Bosch, University of Groningen, The Netherlands, Jan.Bosch@cs.rug.nl
☐ Jim Snyder, Coremetrics, USA, JSnyder@coremetrics.com
☐ Rob van Ommering, Philips, The Netherlands, rob.van.ommering@philips.com
☐ Others pending

Avoiding, Surviving, and Prevailing over Pitfalls in Product Line Engineering

Charles W. Krueger – Panels Chair and Panel Moderator

BigLever Software, 10500 Laurel Hill Cove, Austin, TX 78730, USA
ckrueger@biglever.com

Abstract. In this panel, pioneers from some of the software product line field's best-known success stories share their experiences on how to detect potential pitfalls, how to avoid looming pitfalls, how to survive pitfalls that are unwittingly encountered, and how to turn the negative aspects of pitfalls into positive advantages.

Overview

It is inevitable that with every software product line success story, *a little rain must fall*. In retrospect, stories about the trials and tribulations that arise along the way to a software product line's success can provide insight, guidance, education, portent, inspiration, and even entertainment.

This panel is comprised of key leaders from well-known software product line success stories, sharing how they

- avoided the pitfalls that they were insightful enough – or lucky enough – to perceive before it was too late
- survived the pitfalls that surprised them along the way and how, in hindsight, they might have detected and avoided them
- prevailed over unavoidable pitfalls, turning negatives that could have doomed their efforts into positives that worked in their favor

The audience is encouraged to ask the panel for insight about specific pitfalls they have encountered.

Panelists

- Ross Buhrdorf, BetweenMarkets, Salion, USA, rbuhrdorf@betweenmarkets.com
- Jim Dager, Cummins, USA, Jim.C.Dager@Cummins.com
- Ulf Olsson [Ulf finding us a substitute], Ericsson, Celsius Tech (now Saab Tech), ulf.i.olsson@ericsson.com
- Andres Heie [tentative], Nokia, USA, anders.heie@nokia.com
- Martin Verlage [tentative], MARKET MAKER, Germany, m.verlage@market-maker.de

R.L. Nord (Ed.): SPLC 2004, LNCS 3154, p. 307, 2004.
© Springer-Verlag Berlin Heidelberg 2004

How Can Testing Keep Pace with Accelerated Development in Software Product Line Engineering?

Charles W. Krueger[1] (Panels Chair) and Birgit Geppert[2] (Panel Moderator)

[1] BigLever Software, 10500 Laurel Hill Cove, Austin, TX 78730, USA
ckrueger@biglever.com
[2] Avaya Labs Research, 233 Mt. Airy Road, Basking Ridge, NJ 07920, USA
bgeppert@research.avayalabs.com

Abstract. This panel explores the topic of software product line testing. Techniques for accelerated product development are widely published, but what are the implications to product testing in a software product line organization?

Overview

Although many organizations have reported ways in which software products can be created at a greatly accelerated pace using software product line techniques, little has been reported about the testing of those products. How do the test groups within these organizations keep pace with the accelerated product development?

This critical question is asked frequently by organizations considering the move to software product line engineering, particularly as they do their return-on-investment analysis. Without a convincing argument that testing can achieve similar accelerators, testing looms as the limiting bottleneck, making it appear that the test group must scale its expensive resources to support brute-force testing of all the new products rather than scaling the efficiency of its existing resources.

This panel brings together software product line test practitioners and researchers to shed light on this important topic and to address the following questions and more.

1. Is brute-force scaling of testing resources sufficient for software product line testing? Is it necessary?
2. The two guiding principles in software product line development are (a) capitalize on commonality and (b) formally manage variation among the products. Do the same principles guide software product line testing?
3. Conversely, are there other and possibly more important guiding principles that are unique to product line testing?
4. Is the variation space for development and testing the same? Can we leverage results from earlier development phases (such as decision modeling) for testing?
5. Are there additional problems that come up when dealing with variabilities that might even hinder/slow down testing?
6. *Domain engineering* of core assets is the prominent activity in software product line development, with significantly less effort dedicated to *application engineering* of the individual products. Intuitively, it seems that testing requires the oppo-

R.L. Nord (Ed.): SPLC 2004, LNCS 3154, pp. 308–309, 2004.

site balance: more effort on integration and system testing rather than unit testing. Is this true? How do you find the appropriate balance?

7. How much does improved product quality reduce the testing burden?

Panelists

- Carl Shaulis, Salion, USA, Carl.Shaulis@salion.com
- Henry Muccini, University of L'Aquila, Italy, muccini@di.univaq.it
- Tim Trew, Philips Research Laboratories, UK, tim.trew@philips.com
- Claudia Fritsch, Bosch, Germany, Claudia.Fritsch@de.bosch.com
- Others pending

Product Line Analysis

Gary Chastek and Patrick Donohoe

Software Engineering Institute, Carnegie Mellon University,
Pittsburgh, Pennsylvania 15213
{gjc, pd}@sei.cmu.edu

Product line analysis (PLA) is early requirements engineering for a product line of software-intensive systems. It encompasses the rapid elicitation, analysis, specification, and verification of the requirements for a product line. The premise of product line analysis is that a sound initial understanding of the problem to be solved is essential before an organization embarks on a software product line as a solution.

This tutorial provides practitioners with a practical introduction to product line requirements modeling. It describes the semantics, properties, and interrelationships of the PLA work products that constitute a model of the product line requirements and provides guidance on their construction and use. A running example, based on home automation systems, illustrates PLA concepts.

The goal of the tutorial is to provide attendees with an understanding of how to capture and represent product line requirements in a systematic, repeatable way, and in a form that can be easily communicated to product line architects and product builders. The intended audience is practitioners (i.e., the product line requirements engineers), product line architects, and technology developers interested in creating supporting tools. Attendees are assumed to have some familiarity with software product lines and software analysis. Familiarity with object technology, including object modeling and use cases, is also assumed.

This is a half-day introduction to product line analysis. It provides a quick overview rather than a detailed description. By completing this tutorial, attendees should be able to

- define product line analysis
- explain its purpose and benefits
- apply the concepts to their own software product lines
- understand the importance of tailoring requirements for the product line architect

R.L. Nord (Ed.): SPLC 2004, LNCS 3154, p. 310, 2004.
© Springer-Verlag Berlin Heidelberg 2004

Industrial-Strength Software Product Line Engineering

John Klein, Deborah Hill, and David Weiss

Avaya Labs
{kleinjr,deborahhill,weiss}@avaya.com

Software product line engineering is one of the few approaches to software engineering that shows promise of improving software productivity by factors of 5 to 10. But, there are still relatively few examples of its successful application on a large-scale project, due in part to the complexity of the problem of initiating a product line engineering project and to the many factors that must be addressed for such a project to be successful. Practitioners and researchers alike are confronted with issues such as the following:

- What approaches have been tried? What is successful?
- How do I construct a convincing business case for product line engineering?
- What are the key activities needed to start a product line engineering project and to have it be successful? Can an incremental approach be used?
- How do I measure the effectiveness of product line engineering in my organization?
- How do I maintain momentum during the transition to product line engineering?

Tutorial Objectives

This tutorial draws on experience in introducing and sustaining product line engineering in Lucent Technologies and Avaya to answer such questions. Participants will take away an understanding of what drives a large software development organization to use product line engineering, the obstacles that can be encountered in putting product line engineering theory into practice, and practical approaches to overcoming such obstacles in a systematic way. Participants will learn both technical and organizational aspects of the problem. For example, the tutorial discusses areas that are critical to success in product line engineering but typically not covered by theory, such as who must be convinced to use product line engineering and what arguments to use. Finally, participants should leave the tutorial with ideas on how to transition a large organization to product line engineering while it is in the midst of developing and delivering products.

Participants will receive an inside look at an organization that is transitioning into product line engineering on a large scale. Success in such a project depends on both technical issues in creating and evolving a product line, and organizational issues in transforming an organization to be compatible with the product line engineering process.

R.L. Nord (Ed.): SPLC 2004, LNCS 3154, p. 311, 2004.

Quality Assurance for Software Product Lines

Ronny Kolb and Dirk Muthig

Fraunhofer Institute for Experimental Software Engineering (IESE)
Sauerwiesen 6, D-67661 Kaiserslautern, Germany
{kolb,muthig}@iese.fraunhofer.de

The product line approach to software development is based on the systematic, large-scale reuse of development artifacts such as architecture, design, and components between a set of functional similar products. It promises, among other things, to shorten the development time of software systems and to significantly reduce development and maintenance costs. To achieve the promised improvements, however, the components and artifacts intended for reuse must be of high quality. Therefore, more than for traditional software development, quality assurance becomes a very crucial part of every product line effort.

Even though quality assurance has become not only more critical for software product lines, but also more complex due to the special properties of product lines such as genericity of software components, research in the field of software product lines to date has focused primarily on analysis, design, and implementation. In particular, the quality assurance challenges that arise in a product line context have been addressed insufficiently so far, and there is little guidance for product line organizations on how to systematically assure the quality of their product lines and reusable artifacts.

The overall goal of the tutorial is to provide an understanding of the problem of quality assurance in the context of software product lines and its importance for successful product line development. In particular, the tutorial aims at providing attendees with a detailed understanding of how the quality assurance process for product lines and generic software components needs to be different from traditional software systems and how quality assurance can be performed in the context of software product lines. To this end, the tutorial provides a discussion of the difficulties and challenges of quality assurance for software product lines and investigates the implications of product lines and reusable components on quality assurance. Finally, the tutorial aims to provide an understanding of existing quality assurance techniques and methods and how they can be applied in a product line context.

The tutorial addresses industrial practitioners, as well as applied researchers, working in the area of quality assurance or software product lines. In particular, the tutorial provides researchers with a concise overview of the current state of the art of quality assurance in the context of software product lines. In addition, the tutorial presents relevant issues and approaches in the area of quality assurance for software product lines, while providing industrial practitioners with a profound understanding of best practices they can apply.

R.L. Nord (Ed.): SPLC 2004, LNCS 3154, p. 312, 2004.
© Springer-Verlag Berlin Heidelberg 2004

Product Line Architectures
for Global Software Development

Daniel J. Paulish, Roman Pichler, and Wolfgang Kuhn

Siemens Corporate Research, Inc.
755 College Road East
Princeton, NJ 08540 USA
daniel.paulish@siemens.com

This half-day tutorial discusses how product line practices can be applied to software projects with development teams distributed around the world. Software products are growing in complexity, and the development organizations that implement new features are growing in staff size. Business managers are seeking new approaches, such as offshoring and outsourcing, to get new software products to market quicker, while reducing their overall development investments. Siemens has been performing research to decompose large-scale requirements into a well-structured set of software components that can be developed in parallel among globally distributed development teams. This tutorial describes an approach using product line architecture methods for multi-site development projects in which software components are commissioned by a central product management and engineering organization for development at distributed sites.

As a participant in this tutorial, you will learn product line approaches based on best practices for developing your software products using globally distributed development organizations.

Our approach for global development consists of improved practices in three key areas:

1. requirements engineering: Model the functionality using current best practices and drive all aspects of the product line solution development from the model.
2. software architecture: Drive the product line towards standard common data models and a component framework that will help enable integration.
3. global development: Optimize the organization of product solution development using small, agile distributed component development teams synchronized by a central organization.

A central product management and engineering team controls the requirements model and high-level product architecture. The requirements model and architecture are designed such that component sizes are defined to be relatively small with a maximum specified size in terms of lines of code (LOC), function points, development time, and development effort. The distributed development teams are constrained with respect to functionality, delivery schedule, effort, and schedule for developing their commissioned components. However, they are free to use any local agile processes as long as they meet the constraints. Central product management and engineering synchronize the concurrent development of the planned components and their functionality and are responsible for component acceptance testing and integration.

R.L. Nord (Ed.): SPLC 2004, LNCS 3154, p. 313, 2004.
© Springer-Verlag Berlin Heidelberg 2004

Architecture-Centric Software Engineering

Jan Bosch

University of Groningen,
Department of Computing Science,
The Netherlands.
Jan.Bosch@cs.rug.nl

Many software organizations are in the process of moving from project- and product-centric software engineering to architecture-centric software engineering. Typically, this move is made for two reasons: (1) the architecture allows for a clear breakdown in parts, whereas a project-centric approach easily leads to a monolithic system and (2) the organization is interested in exploiting the commonalities between its products or systems.

This tutorial addresses this development by providing an overview and in-depth treatment of the issues around architecture-centric software engineering [1]. The first topic is concerned with the design of software architectures in the presence of existing components and infrastructure (e.g., designing the architecture in a top-down or bottom-up fashion). Two issues discussed in the context of architecture design are the notion of architecture design decisions and software variability management. Architecture design decisions lack first-class representation in the architecture descriptions. We are developing solutions to address this. Software variability management is concerned with explicitly managing the points of variation in software artifacts and in the software architecture in particular.

The second topic is the evaluation and assessment of software architectures. As architectural changes late in a development project or during evolution are often prohibitively expensive, verifying that the architecture has the right quality properties is of great importance. The aim is to, preferably quantitatively, predict the qualities of a software system based on its software architecture.

The final topic of the tutorial is concerned with the use of the software architecture, especially in the context of software product families and highly configurable products. In this part, not only the technical aspects, but also the process and organizational viewpoints are discussed, and the relation between the different dimensions is presented. In addition, evaluation models and adoption approaches are discussed. The topics are illustrated extensively by examples and experiences from many industrial cases.

References

1. Jan Bosch, Design and Use of Software Architectures: Adopting and Evolving a Product Line Approach, Pearson Education (Addison-Wesley & ACM Press), ISBN 0-201-67494-7, May 2000.

R.L. Nord (Ed.): SPLC 2004, LNCS 3154, p. 314, 2004.

Software Variability Management

Jan Bosch

University of Groningen,
Department of Computing Science,
The Netherlands.
Jan.Bosch@cs.rug.nl

In a variety of approaches to software development, software artefacts are used in multiple contexts or for various purposes. The differences lead to so-called variation points in the software artefact. During recent years, the amount of variability supported by a software artefact is growing considerably, and its management is developing as a main challenge in the development, usage, and evolution of software artefacts. Areas where the management of variability is evolving as a challenge include software product families [1], component-based software development, object-oriented frameworks, and configurable software products such as planning systems for enterprise resources. For example, in a typical software product family, the number of variation points may easily range in the thousands.

Software variability is the ability of a software system or artefact to be changed, customized, or configured for use in a particular context [2]. A high degree of variability allows the use of software in a broader range of contexts (i.e., the software is more reusable). Variability can be viewed as consisting of two dimensions: space and time. The space dimension is concerned with the use of software in multiple contexts (e.g., multiple products in a software product family). The time dimension is concerned with the ability of software to support evolution and changing requirements in the software's various contexts.

Successful management of variability in software artefacts leads to better customizable software products that are, in turn, likely to result in higher market success. In the information systems domain, the products are more easily adaptable to the needs of different user groups; in the embedded systems domain, the software can be more easily configured to work with different hardware and environmental constraints.

The tutorial first establishes the importance of software variability management, among other things through industrial examples consisting of thousands of variation points and dependencies. Second, the tutorial defines the concept of variability and discusses notational and visualization aspects, including the COVAMOF model. Third, we discuss the assessment of software artefacts for variability (i.e., COSVAM) and the design of architectures and components for variability. Fourth, the use of variation points is presented (e.g., while configuring instantiated software artefacts). Finally, some advanced issues including variation versus composition are discussed.

R.L. Nord (Ed.): SPLC 2004, LNCS 3154, pp. 315–316, 2004.

References

1. Jan Bosch, Design and Use of Software Architectures: Adopting and Evolving a Product Line Approach, Pearson Education (Addison-Wesley & ACM Press), ISBN 0-201-67494-7, May 2000.
2. Jilles van Gurp, Jan Bosch, Mikael Svahnberg, On the Notion of Variability in Software Product Lines, Proceedings of The Working IEEE/IFIP Conference on Software Architecture (WICSA 2001), pp. 45-55, August 2001.

Designing Software Product Lines
with the Unified Modeling Language (UML)

Hassan Gomaa

Department of Information and Software Engineering
George Mason University
Fairfax, Virginia 22030
hgomaa@gmu.edu

This tutorial addresses how to develop object-oriented requirements, analysis, and design models of software product lines using the Unified Modeling Language (UML) 2.0 notation. During requirements modeling, the tutorial covers how to develop kernel, optional, and alternative use cases for defining the software functional requirements of the system. The tutorial also describes the feature model for capturing product line requirements and how it relates to the use case model. During analysis, the tutorial covers how to develop static models for defining kernel, optional, and variant classes and their relationships. It also describes how to create dynamic models in which interaction models describe the dynamic interaction between the objects that participate in each kernel, optional, and alternative use case, and in which statecharts define the state-dependent aspects of the product line. The tutorial then covers how to develop component-based software architecture for the product line using the new UML 2.0 notation for structured classes and composite structure diagrams. That notation allows components, ports, and connectors, as well as provided and required interfaces, to be depicted. The tutorial gives an overview of the architectural structure patterns and architectural communication patterns that can be used in designing component-based product lines. The tutorial is illustrated by several examples and based on the book by Hassan Gomaa titled *Designing Software Product Lines with UML* to be published by Addison-Wesley in July 2004.

R.L. Nord (Ed.): SPLC 2004, LNCS 3154, p. 317, 2004.
© Springer-Verlag Berlin Heidelberg 2004

Developing a Measurement Program for Software Product Lines

Sholom Cohen, Dave Zubrow, and Gary Chastek

Software Engineering Institute, Carnegie Mellon University,
Pittsburgh, Pennsylvania 15213
{sgc,dz,gjc}@sei.cmu.edu

Product line management should use measurement to anticipate the future rather than to simply record the past. The benefit and value of software measurement for product lines comes from the decisions and actions taken to support the product line in response to analysis of the data, not from the collection of the data. Addressing this management need is the primary goal of this tutorial.

Implementing measures for a software product line requires coordination across multiple projects. They must establish common goals and develop measures to track results on individual projects. We have developed this tutorial to help product line managers, software product development managers, software core asset development managers, and Software Engineering Process Group (SEPG) members support that activity. The tutorial will help the audience set measurable goals and determine if the software product line is producing the expected results. To benefit from the tutorial, attendees need no prior experience in measurement.

While the half-day format does not provide hands-on interaction, it will describe three sets of activities to develop a measurement program for software product lines:

1. Identifying Goals – explains transitioning from high-level product line goal statements to actionable measurement goals
2. Defining Indicators – describes the charts, tables, or measures that will address the software product line manager's goals
3. Creating an Action Plan – shows a plan for implementing the defined indicators

By following this approach, the risk of having data gathered, but not used, is minimized.

The tutorial also describes a range of measurements relevant to software product lines. The measures suggested here range from relatively mature to those whose general utility has yet to be validated. Therefore, a product line organization needs to assess its ability to generate the measures and the value those measures are likely to return to the organization. In most cases, an organization may wish to start with a subset of the product line measures described.

A case study in establishing a software product line measurement program illustrates the approach and use of software product line measurements. The organization covered in the case study established a Software Measurement Team to develop and monitor a measurement program. That measurement team includes representatives from programs using a core asset base. Four projects currently contribute to the measurement program.

R.L. Nord (Ed.): SPLC 2004, LNCS 3154, p. 318, 2004.
© Springer-Verlag Berlin Heidelberg 2004

Starting Product Lines (I) —
Systematic Product Line Planning and Adoption

Klaus Schmid and Isabel John

Fraunhofer IESE, Sauerwiesen 6, 67661 Kaiserslautern, Germany
{Klaus.Schmid,Isabel.John}@iese.fraunhofer.de

1 Description

To successfully and effectively adopt a software product line approach, the transition must be well aligned to the specific product line situation. As more and more organizations aim at a product line transition, this becomes increasingly an issue. To successfully and effectively adopt a software product line approach, a thorough analysis of the economic implications of the adoption must be performed, and the product line introduction needs to be adequately planned. This requires a precise picture of the product line through product analysis and modeling. A thorough analysis of the economic implications of the adoption must be performed, and the introduction of the product line needs to be correspondingly planned. Of course, such a transition has serious ramifications for the component structure of the software. We will discuss these consequences and show how the economic analysis itself can be used as a basis for deriving an adequate structure for the software. Thus, this tutorial provides a concise overview of the current state of the art of product line planning and adoption that is aimed at both researchers and practitioners of product line development.

2 Structure

The tutorial covers the following topics:
- introduction to product line development
- product line economics as a basis of software product line adoption and planning
- product line planning: aligning the product line plan with the business strategies of the organization
- overview on product line scoping: This includes an overview of existing scoping technologies and their advantages and disadvantages. We will also discuss the three levels of scoping: (1) product portfolio scoping, (2) domain scoping, and (3) asset scoping.
- product line adoption and transition to product line development
- product line management
- product line evolution covers analyzing the impact of new products, introducing the knowledge about the existing asset base, and steering the ongoing development from an economic point of view.

R.L. Nord (Ed.): SPLC 2004, LNCS 3154, p. 319, 2004.

Starting Product Lines (II) —
Product Line Analysis and Modeling

Isabel John and Klaus Schmid

Fraunhofer IESE, Sauerwiesen 6, 67661 Kaiserslautern, Germany
{Isabel.John,Klaus.Schmid}@iese.fraunhofer.de

1 Description

Product line engineering is recognized as a viable approach to large-scale software reuse. This tutorial provides a concise overview of the current state of the art of product line analysis and modeling and aims at giving an understanding of how to identify, analyze, and model commonalities and variabilities. It also provides an overview of the vast range of existing techniques for product line analysis and modeling. In particular, this tutorial provides researchers with a better understanding of the breadth of relevant issues and approaches, while providing industrial practitioners with a profound understanding of best practices they can apply. As the systematic identification and description of commonalities and variabilities are key in product line development to achieving successful reuse, the adequate selection or extension of modeling techniques can be regarded as a key to the overall goal of the SPLC. The modeling tutorial is a half-day tutorial, however, it can be combined with the tutorial titled "Starting Software Product Lines (I) — Systematic Product Line Planning and Adoption" to yield a full-day tutorial covering the early phases of product line development.

2 Structure

The tutorial covers the following topics:
- the importance of product line analysis and modeling as a key factor for successful product line engineering
- key principles of product line analysis and modeling (e.g., commonality and variability, decision modeling, domain analysis, application analysis, and traceability to all interrelated phases)
- overview of product line analysis and modeling techniques. We will also show how existing system modeling techniques (e.g., UML use cases) can be adapted for modeling product line requirements.
- application analysis and derivation of product-specific models
- the PuLSE-CDA approach to product line modeling and analysis as an example modeling approach
- the interaction of analysis and modeling with other product line engineering phases (scoping and architecture and application modeling)

R.L. Nord (Ed.): SPLC 2004, LNCS 3154, p. 320, 2004.
© Springer-Verlag Berlin Heidelberg 2004

Generative Software Development

Krzysztof Czarnecki

University of Waterloo, Canada

System family engineering seeks to exploit the commonalities among systems from a given problem domain while managing the variabilities among them in a systematic way. In system family engineering, new system variants can be created rapidly based on a set of reusable assets (such as a common architecture, components, models, etc.) [1]. Generative software development aims at modeling and implementing system families in such a way that a given system can be automatically generated from a specification written in one or more textual or graphical domain-specific languages [2–8]. In this tutorial, participants will learn how to perform domain analysis (i.e., capturing the commonalities and variabilities within a system family in a software schema using feature modeling), domain design (i.e., developing a common architecture for a system family), and implementing software generators using multiple technologies, such as template-based code generation and model transformations. The relationship to model-driven development will be also discussed. The presented concepts and methods will be demonstrated using a case study.

References

1. Clements, P., Northrop, L.M.: Software Product Lines: Practices and Patterns. Addison-Wesley (2001)
2. Neighbors, J.M.: Software Construction using Components. PhD thesis, Department of Information and Computer Science, University of California, Irvine (1980) Technical Report UCI-ICS-TR160; available at http://www.bayfronttechnologies.com/ thesis.htm.
3. Cleaveland, J.C.: Building application generators. IEEE Software 5 (1988) 25–33
4. Weiss, D.M., Lai, C.T.R.: Software Product-Line Engineering: A Family-Based Software Development Process. Addison-Wesley (1999)
5. Czarnecki, K., Eisenecker, U.W.: Generative Programming: Methods, Tools, and Applications. Addison-Wesley (2000)
6. Cleaveland, C.: Program Generators with XML and Java. Prentice-Hall (2001)
7. Batory, D., Johnson, C., MacDonald, B., von Heeder, D.: Achieving extensibility through product-lines and domain-specific languages: A case study". ACM Transactions on Software Engineering and Methodology (TOSEM) 11 (2002) 191–214
8. Greenfield, J., Short, K.: Software Factories: Assembling Applications with Patterns, Models, Frameworks, and Tools. Wiley (2004) To be published.

R.L. Nord (Ed.): SPLC 2004, LNCS 3154, p. 321, 2004.
© Springer-Verlag Berlin Heidelberg 2004

An Introduction to Software Product Lines

Linda M. Northrop and Paul C. Clements

Software Engineering Institute, Carnegie Mellon University
Pittsburgh, Pennsylvania 15213
{lmn,clements}@sei.cmu.edu

Software product lines have emerged as a new software development paradigm of great importance. A software product line is a set of software-intensive systems sharing a common, managed set of features, and that are developed in a disciplined fashion using a common set of core assets. Organizations developing their family of products as a software product line are experiencing order-of-magnitude improvements in cost, time to market, staff productivity, and quality of the deployed products.

This tutorial provides an overview of software product lines. It covers the basic concepts of software product lines, the essential software engineering and management practices, and a sampling of product line practice patterns that help organizations apply the practices in a way best suited to their individual needs. The concepts are illustrated with a detailed case study of an actual organization's experiences with the software product line approach. This tutorial is based on the book *Software Product Lines: Practices and Patterns* by Paul Clements and Linda Northrop.

This tutorial is appropriate for managers and practitioners. Participants should have experience in designing and developing software-intensive systems and some familiarity with modern software engineering concepts and management practices. The goal of the tutorial is for participants to understand the essential activities and practices involved in a software product line approach and to appreciate software product lines as an effective reuse strategy.

R.L. Nord (Ed.): SPLC 2004, LNCS 3154, p. 322, 2004.
© Springer-Verlag Berlin Heidelberg 2004

Adopting Software Product Lines

Linda M. Northrop and Lawrence Jones

Software Engineering Institute, Carnegie Mellon University
Pittsburgh, Pennsylvania 15213
{lmn,lgj}@sei.cmu.edu

The tremendous benefits of taking a software product line approach are well documented. Organizations have achieved significant reductions in cost and time to market and, at the same time, increased the quality of families of their software systems. However, to date, there are considerable barriers to organizational adoption of product line practices. Phased adoption is attractive as a risk reduction and fiscally viable proposition.

This tutorial describes a phased, pattern-based approach to software product line adoption. It begins with a discussion of software product line adoption issues and then presents the *Adoption Factory*, a variant of the *Factory* pattern. The *Factory* pattern describes the entire product line organization. The *Adoption Factory* pattern provides a roadmap for phased, product line adoption. The tutorial covers the *Adoption Factory* in detail, including focus areas, phases, subpatterns, related practice areas, outputs, and roles. Examples of product line adoption plans following the pattern are used to illustrate its utility. The tutorial also describes strategies for creating synergy within an organization between product line adoption and ongoing CMMI or other process improvement initiatives.

The objective of the tutorial is to acquaint participants with product line adoption barriers and two ways to overcome them:

1. a phased, pattern-based adoption approach
2. explicit linkage with other improvement efforts

Participants should have experience in designing and developing software-intensive systems and familiarity with software product line concepts.

R.L. Nord (Ed.): SPLC 2004, LNCS 3154, p. 323, 2004.
© Springer-Verlag Berlin Heidelberg 2004

Using Domain-Specific Languages, Patterns, Frameworks, and Tools to Assemble Applications

Jack Greenfield

Visual Studio Enterprise Frameworks & Tools
Microsoft Corporation
One Microsoft Way
Redmond, WA 98053, USA
jackgr@microsoft.com

Increasingly complex and rapidly changing requirements and technologies are making application development increasingly difficult. This tutorial explores this phenomenon, and presents the Software Factory pattern for building languages, patterns, frameworks and tools for specific domains, such as user interface construction or database design. We then explore innovations, such as adaptive assembly, software product lines and model driven development, which reduce the cost of implementing the pattern, making it cost effective for narrower and more specialized domains, such as B2C application development and business process automation. We introduce the concept of the software schema, a network of viewpoints describing artifacts comprising the members of a family of software products, and we show how mappings between these viewpoints can be used to provide constraints supporting model transformation and self organizing processes. Finally, we discuss the formation of software supply chains and show how the Software Factory pattern distributes across organizational boundaries.

R.L. Nord (Ed.): SPLC 2004, LNCS 3154, p. 324, 2004.
© Springer-Verlag Berlin Heidelberg 2004

SPLiT – Workshop on Software Product Line Testing

Birgit Geppert[1], Charles Krueger[2], and J. Jenny Li[1]

[1] Avaya Labs, Basking Ridge, NJ, USA
{bgeppert,jjli}@avaya.com
[2] BigLever Software, Austin, TX, USA
ckrueger@biglever.com

Product line engineering (PLE) has become a major topic in industrial software development, and many organizations have started to consider PLE as state of the practice. One topic that needs greater emphasis is testing of product lines. Product line testing is crucial to the successful establishment of PLE technology in an organization. The workshop aims at addressing some of the open fundamental challenges of testing in a PLE setting. How can we manage the complexity of the test space? Can we leverage our established testing tools and procedures? A particularly hard challenge for test groups in a PLE setting is keeping pace with development productivity gains. If software developers can create unique product instances 10 times faster using PLE techniques, how does the test organization keep pace without having to hire 10 times as many test engineers? Are there PLE techniques that can provide efficiency gains for testing similar to those for development? These are questions that we have to face when transitioning to PLE, and, without adequate answers, testing becomes the bottleneck in PLE.

In this workshop, we aim at bringing together both researchers and practitioners from testing and PLE on all aspects of product line testing, from designing test cases with variation points over test coverage to testing tools. We are especially interested in exchanging industrial experience in product line testing and comparing different approaches to enable an integration of different ideas. Our goal is to provide a context for such an information exchange and to provide an opportunity to discuss innovative ideas, set a research agenda, and start collaborations on this topic. To achieve this, we invited experts not only from PLE, but also from testing, to participate in organizing the workshop and to help bring together both worlds and make this effort a success. Our program committee consists of the following members:

For PLE:
- Guenter Boeckle, Siemens AG, Germany
- Jan Bosch, Univ. of Groningen, The Netherlands
- Krzysztof Czarnecki, Univ. of Waterloo, Canada
- John McGregor, Clemson University, USA
- Dirk Muthig, Fraunhofer IESE, Germany
- Frank Roessler, Avaya Labs, USA

For Testing:
- Hira Agrawal, Telcordia, USA
- John Linn, Texas Instruments, USA
- Henry Muccini, University of L'Aquila, Italy
- Mladen A. Vouk, North Carolina State University, USA
- Eric Wong, University of Texas, USA

R.L. Nord (Ed.): SPLC 2004, LNCS 3154, pp. 325–326, 2004.
© Springer-Verlag Berlin Heidelberg 2004

The results of the workshop will be published as part of the Avaya Labs report series and will be available online at http://www.research.avayalabs.com/techreportY.html. More information about the workshop is provided on the workshop's homepage http://www.biglever.com/split2004/.

SPLYR – The First Software Product Lines Young Researchers Workshop

Birgit Geppert[1], Isabel John[2], and Giuseppe Lami[3]

[1] Avaya Labs, Basking Ridge, NJ 07920, USA
bgeppert@avaya.com
[2] Fraunhofer IESE, Sauerwiesen 6, 67661 Kaiserslautern, Germany
john@iese.fraunhofer.de
[3] ISTI CNR, via Moruzzi, 1; 56124 Pisa, Italy
giuseppe.lami@isti.cnr.it

Description

The Software Product Lines Young Researchers (SPLYR) workshop addresses research activities in the field of software product lines (SPLs). Topics of interest include all aspects of developing, managing, evaluating, reusing, and maintaining SPLs. The peculiarity of this workshop is that it is specifically addressed to young researchers having original ideas and initiatives in the SPL field. We address mainly PhD work in progress but also encourage the submission of other work in progress such as master's or diploma theses. Another characteristic of this workshop is that it will not involve blind reviews. Instead, each young researcher will be assigned one panelist/reviewer whose name will be disclosed as part of the review report. This provides a unique opportunity for the participating young researchers to get in contact with their reviewers and to receive valuable input for their work and presentations before the actual workshop takes place.

The workshop itself aims at providing a platform for young researchers to present their work to an international audience and to discuss it with their peers and experts in the field. The panelists will comment on the presentations and give feedback for further developing the work. This represents a unique opportunity for the presenting young researchers to receive invaluable feedback from the panelists, to get in contact with other researchers in the field, to present their work professionally, and to become familiar with other approaches and future research topics.

Panelists

–   Len Bass, Software Engineering Institute, USA
–   Jan Bosch, University of Groningen, Netherlands
–   André van der Hoek, University of California, Irvine, USA
–   Dirk Muthig, Fraunhofer IESE, Germany

R.L. Nord (Ed.): SPLC 2004, LNCS 3154, pp. 327–328, 2004.
© Springer-Verlag Berlin Heidelberg 2004

References

1. 1 Proceedings of SPLYR - The 1st Software Product Lines Young Researchers Workshop, IESE Report, Fraunhofer IESE, Germany, to appear 2004

Workshop on Modeling Business Issues of Software Product Lines

Sholom Cohen

Software Engineering Institute, Carnegie Mellon University
Pittsburgh, Pennsylvania 15213
sgc@sei.cmu.edu

Many organizations require financial justification before proceeding with a product line approach. The approach may appear very attractive in an intuitive sense, and it offers the obvious benefits of a faster time to market and higher quality. But, without the cost figures, the decision makers won't budget funds or personnel resources to carry out the up-front asset construction tasks. In addition, not all organizations are ready to commit up front to a full asset set—one that covers most if not all product line features. They favor a more incremental approach that tackles the areas of highest and most readily available commonality first.

Business modeling is a fundamental practice that provides input into a number of decisions that are made by organizations using or considering using the product line strategy. The purpose of this workshop is to present and discuss models that support the estimation of the costs and benefits in a product line development organization. The models should support decisions such as whether to use a product line strategy in a specific situation and the appropriateness of acquiring or building specific assets. Participants will illustrate the scope of their models by presenting scenarios where the models apply and by integrating the model into product line development patterns.

Models should address all or some of the following topics:

- Product lines introduce extra complexity in software development but offer high returns: What are the tradeoffs and when should software firms decide to go for a product line approach?
- What are the success and failure factors for introducing software product lines in organizations?
- Is it possible to predict when product line investment pays in a specific domain and environment?
- How can the benefits of a product line's success be quantified, taking into account nonfinancial factors?
- What are the effects of sustainment on the long-term benefits offered by the product line approach?

R.L. Nord (Ed.): SPLC 2004, LNCS 3154, p. 329, 2004.
© Springer-Verlag Berlin Heidelberg 2004

Workshop on Quality Assurance in Reuse Contexts

Ronny Kolb[1], John D. McGregor[2], and Dirk Muthig[1]

[1] Fraunhofer Institute for Experimental Software Engineering (IESE)
Sauerwiesen 6, D-67661 Kaiserslautern, Germany
{kolb,muthig}@iese.fraunhofer.de
[2] Dept. of Computer Science, Clemson University
Clemson, SC 29634
johnmc@cs.clemson.edu

The systematic, large-scale reuse of software development artifacts over multiple products is a promising approach to address today's software development problems and to make the development process more efficient. Recently, reuse-based software development paradigms such as component-based development and software product lines have increasingly received attention as they promise—and have shown—to shorten the development time of software systems and to reduce development and maintenance costs. To achieve the promised improvements, however, high-quality artifacts intended for reuse are required. Thus, more than for traditional software development, quality assurance becomes a crucial part of every reuse-based development effort. However, a number of specifics caused by software reuse (such as the variable usage of components or genericity of artifacts) must be faced during quality assurance. To enable an organization to fully experience the expected efficiency gain through reuse, therefore, a quality assurance approach is required that enables the validation of products built from reusable artifacts as effective and as efficient in a non-reuse context.

Despite the criticality of quality assurance and the special problems caused by reuse-based software development, research in the field of software product lines and component-based development has focused primarily on analysis, design, and implementation to date. Only very few results address the quality assurance problems and challenges that arise in a reuse context. Therefore, with the growing acceptance of reuse-based development paradigms such as software product lines, effective and efficient methods and techniques for ensuring the quality of reusable artifacts and products built by reusing existing artifacts are required.

The aim of the workshop is to establish a forum for the successful exchange of experience and ideas among practitioners and researchers to improve the state of the art and state of the practice in quality assurance for product lines and other reuse-based development approaches. The workshop will provide an opportunity to exchange views, experiences, and lessons learned, to advance ideas, and to discuss recent work and work in progress on topics dealing with quality assurance for software artifacts intended for reuse and products built using reusable artifacts. It intends to bring together researchers and practitioners from both academia and industry to share ideas on the foundations, techniques, methods, strategies, and tools of quality assurance for reuse-based software development paradigms.

R.L. Nord (Ed.): SPLC 2004, LNCS 3154, p. 330, 2004.

Workshop on Software Variability Management for Product Derivation — Towards Tool Support

Tomi Männistö[1] and Jan Bosch[2]

[1] Helsinki University of Technology, Software Business and Engineering Institute
P.O. Box 9210, FI-02015 HUT, Finland
`Tomi.Mannisto@hut.fi`
[2] University of Groningen, Department of Computing Science
P.O. Box 800, NL-9700 AV Groningen, The Netherlands
`Jan.Bosch@cs.rug.nl`

Workshop Topic and Goal

Software product lines aim at providing the means for achieving large software variability in an effective manner. However, systematic methods and tools are needed for describing and managing the variability so that large variability can be supported and an effective means for deriving product instances can be achieved.

Earlier workshops (at SPLC2 02, Groningen 03, ICSE03) on variability management have provided an initial understanding of the area and formed a basis for managing the variability of software product lines. Relevant results and lessons learned can also be found from traditional products (mechanical and electronic). In particular, the field of product configuration, which is an area using techniques of artificial intelligence, has recently started dealing with configuring software products that exhibit very large variability. The topic of software product configuration has been addressed in various workshops on configuration (e.g., in connection to the ECAI00, IJCAI01, ECAI02, IJCAI03 conferences).

Furthermore, initial computer-based tools or prototypes for managing variability in software product lines have already been demonstrated, and some projects addressing tool support exist in both industry and academia. Software variability management is thus moving towards tool support, although many theoretical and practical challenges remain to be resolved.

The workshop intends to bring together industrial developers and researchers who are building tools or working towards enabling tool support for software variability management. The theoretical underpinnings of variability modeling tools, such as modeling languages and requirements, are also within the interest of the workshop.

The workshop aims at moving from the current status of variability management towards tool support that would enable increasing the variability and customization possibilities of software product families in a feasible manner. In addition, the workshop promotes the transfer of knowledge between research and practice of traditional product families and software product families.

R.L. Nord (Ed.): SPLC 2004, LNCS 3154, p. 331, 2004.
© Springer-Verlag Berlin Heidelberg 2004

International Workshop on Solutions for Automotive Software Architectures: Open Standards, References, and Product Line Architectures

Stefan Ferber[1], Andreas Krüger[2], Stefan Voget[3], and Matthias Weber[4]

[1] Robert Bosch GmbH, Corporate Systems Engineering Process Group,
Robert Bosch Str. 2, 71701 Schwieberdingen, Germany
Stefan.Ferber@de.bosch.com
[2] Audi AG, I/EE-93, 85049 Ingolstadt, Germany
Andreas.Krueger@audi.de
[3] Robert Bosch GmbH, Research and Development department software-technology,
Eschborner Landstrasse 130-132, 60489 Frankfurt, Germany
Stefan.Voget@de.bosch.com
[4] DaimlerChrysler AG, Research and Technology, 069/U119-RIC/SM,
Alt-Moabit 96A, 10559 Berlin, Germany
Matthias.n.Weber@daimlerchrysler.com

1 Goals

- Get an overview about existing and future software architectures for networked engine control units (ECUs) in automobiles.

- Give an overview about the international initiatives working on this topic.

- Get to know the key players.

2 Motivation

More and more product lines spread in the automotive industry. This is true for vehicle manufacturers as well as for suppliers. If both sides – customer and supplier – use the product line technology, the interfaces between both stakeholders become more important. The answer of the automotive industry to this challenge is the development of open standard architectures [3]. Several initiatives currently follow this path; for example, the ITEA/EAST-EEA [1] and AUTOSAR [2] Web sites.

During the workshop, we want to exchange experiences from the international activities and start an informal network. Such an information exchange should improve the product line technology for the automotive industry.

R.L. Nord (Ed.): SPLC 2004, LNCS 3154, pp. 332–333, 2004.
© Springer-Verlag Berlin Heidelberg 2004

3 Organization of Workshop

The workshop splits into two parts.

1. a presentation that includes an overview of
   - activities on software architectures in Europe, Asia, and North America—at least one presentation from each region
   - company-specific "standard" architectures—at least one presentation from an original equipment manufacturer (OEM) and one from a supplier

2. working groups. This part of the workshop incorporates a platform for group work for the participants' disposal. The number of groups will depend on the number of participants. At a minimum, the following topics will be prepared. Each one could be worked out by several groups:
   - commonalities and variants in the presented architectures. These groups should prepare a list that summarizes the given presentations on an harmonized and comparable level.
   - requirements on a global informal network for the exchange of information. These groups should collect reasons for such a network, organizational alternatives, alternatives for the kind of cooperation in such a network, and other items around this topic.

4 Expected Workshop Outputs

- a set of comparable "standard" architectures. This should increase the understandings between the architects and lead the discussion in the community to a harmonized level.

- list of points to be discussed and worked on in the informal network. Workshop participants should determine who should participate in such networks in the future. The experiences of the organizers in the last few years have shown that such a network is not unrealistic in the automotive community.

References

1. AUTOSAR: www.autosar.org
2. ITEA/EAST-EEA: www.east-eea.net
3. Schäuffele, J; Zurawka, T.: Automotive Software Engineering. Vieweg, 2003.

Author Index

Lecture Notes in Computer Science

For information about Vols. 1–3065

please contact your bookseller or Springer